Evidence
for the
Historical
Jesus

Evidence *for the* Historical Jesus

Josh McDowell
Bill Wilson

HARVEST HOUSE PUBLISHERS

EUGENE, OREGON

Cover by Koechel Peterson & Associates, Inc., Minneapolis, Minnesota

EVIDENCE FOR THE HISTORICAL JESUS
Copyright © 1988, 1993 by Josh McDowell Ministry and Bill Wilson
Published by Harvest House Publishers
Eugene, Oregon 97402
www.harvesthousepublishers.com

Library of Congress Cataloging-in-Publication Data
McDowell, Josh.
[He walked among us]
Evidence for the historical Jesus / Josh McDowell and Bill Wilson.
   p. cm.
Originally published: He walked among us. San Bernardino, CA : Here's Life Publishers, ©1988.
ISBN 978-0-7369-2871-7 (pbk.)
1. Jesus Christ—Historicity. I. Wilson, Bill, 1948- II. Title.
BT303.2.M42 2011
232.9'08—dc22
2010021676

Printed in the United States of America

11 12 13 14 15 16 17 18 19 / LB-SK / 10 9 8 7 6 5 4 3 2 1

CONTENTS

Explanation of the Reference Codes 9

Introduction 11
*What's the Real Issue? • Why Is the Historicity of Jesus Important? • Historical Search for
the Historical Jesus • Recent Portrayals of Jesus • An Overview*

PART I: EXTRABIBLICAL EVIDENCE FOR JESUS

1. The Unusual Nature of Extrabiblical References to Jesus 21
*What About Reports from Pilate? • Just How Much Survived? • How Big a Stir Did
Jesus Make? • What News Was Hot? • False Expectations Concerning References to Jesus
• Is Absence of Evidence Evidence of Absence? • Why Are Many Extrabiblical References
to Jesus Negative in Tone?*

2. References to Jesus by Ancient Secular Writers 33
*Thallus and Phlegon • Josephus • Pliny the Younger • Cornelius Tacitus •
Hadrian • Suetonius • Lucian of Samosata • Mara Bar-Serapion*

3. References from the Rabbis 53
*Writings of the Rabbis • Unreliable References to Jesus • Reliable Historical
References to Jesus*

4. Martyrs, Confessors and Early Church Leaders 69
*Weaknesses of Post-Apostolic Writers • Strengths of Post-Apostolic Writers •
Lives and Teachings of Post-Apostolic Writers • Evaluating the Evidence*

5. Agrapha, Apocrypha and Pseudepigrapha 87
*Definitions • Value • Material Confirming the Gospel Accounts • Possibly Reliable
Agrapha • Unreliable Additions to the Gospels • Conclusions*

PART II: THE HISTORICAL RELIABILITY
OF NEW TESTAMENT EVIDENCE

6. Are the Biblical Records Reliable? 105
*Bibliographical Test • Internal Evidence Test • External Evidence Test •
Who Would Die for a Lie? • What Good Is a Dead Messiah?*

7. Higher Criticism: How "Assured" Are the Results? 121
*What Is Higher Criticism? • Redaction Criticism • Scholarly Conclusions to
Higher Criticism*

8. The Gospel Before the Gospels 145
   *Trapped in a Literary Culture • The Formative Period • How Was the Information
   Preserved? • Evidence • Conclusion*

9. History and Myth 167
   *Basic Traits of Mystery Religions: How Similar Are They to the Gospels? • Alleged
   Mythical Roots of Christian Doctrine and Practice • Fallacies of Linking Christianity
   with Mystery Religions • Uniqueness of the Gospel Portrayals of Jesus • Conclusions*

10. Evidence from Historical Geography 189
    *Historical Geography • The Question of Quirinius • Geography •
    Alleged Geographical Contradictions • Verifying the New Testament?*

11. Evidence from Archaeology 203
    People • Places • Details • Events • Dead Sea Scrolls • Scholarly Conclusions

12. The Jewish Factor 223
    *Semitic Flavor of the Gospel Accounts • Hebrew Characterizations of Jesus •
    Questions Surrounding the Jewishness of Jesus • Conclusion*

13. Jesus and Miracles 249
    Are Miracles Possible? • Evaluating Miracle Claims

14. The Reliability of the Resurrection Reports 265
    *Early Origination • Historical Nature • Contrast with Jewish Legends •
    Early Christian Belief • Conclusion*

15. Messiah and Son of God? 277
    *Messianic Expectations • Did Jesus Think He Was Messiah? • Son of Man—Who
    Is He? • Was Jesus the Messiah? • Son of God • Did Jesus Really Believe He Was God? •
    Was Jesus the God He Thought He Was?*

PART III: APPLICATIONS AND CONCLUSIONS

16. Jesus and the Popular Press 305
    *So What's Wrong With Popular? • Pitfalls of the Popularizers • False Portrayals of
    the Life of Jesus • Conclusion*

Afterword: A New Beginning 319
Notes 323
Bibliography 333
Index 347

ACKNOWLEDGMENTS

Special thanks...

> *to Jo Bristow* for typing all 719 pages of the first draft of the manuscript;

> *to Jean Bryant* for her diligent and perceptive work in editing and formatting the book;

> *to Steve Gillespie, Marcus Maranto, Jim Pourchot and Leroy Tennison* for carrying the load of research in other areas while we focused the needed amount of attention on this subject;

> *to Steve Dunn* for his insights and input on specialized areas of the project;

> *and especially to our wives, Dottie McDowell and Sharon Wilson,* for their commitment, diligence and help in passing on to our children what we have received, the good news about Jesus.

EXPLANATION OF
THE REFERENCE CODES

After many of the quotes in this book you will see a reference code in small type, such as (GreM.MA 23-24). The first capital and lower case letters are taken from the author's last name (Gre = Green), and the next letter or letters (before the period) are from the author's first name (M = Michael).

The letters after the period refer to the title (MA = *Man Alive!*), and the numbers (23-24) refer to pages of the particular work quoted. Thus, the above example would direct you to pages 23 and 24 of *Man Alive!* written by Michael Green.

Some references are followed by [AS], [RS] or [R]. These abbreviations denote the section of the bibliography where the work is found: AS = Ancient Sources; RS = Rabbinic Sources; R = Reference Works.

A complete list of the codes and the sources to which they refer will be found in the bibliography.

INTRODUCTION

How many times have you asked yourself these questions: Who was Jesus, anyway? What was he really like? Or, as British New Testament scholar R. T. France questions:

> How much of our traditional understanding of Jesus is the product not so much of the historical records as of pious imagination and sentimentality? How much of it has the effect of turning Jesus into a man of our own culture, or, still worse, of no culture at all, thus effectively cutting him off from real life?...Are we not still slightly shocked at the thought that Jesus could have had a real sense of humour, or held political views? (FrR.E 158)

Doesn't it ever bother you, the critics will ask, that there seem to be relatively few references to Jesus outside of Christian writings? The fact that almost all we know about him comes from Christian documents has led some scholars to deny that he ever existed at all. Bruno Bauer, Paul Louis Couchoud, G. Gurev, Rudolf Augstein, and most recently, G. A. Wells have argued against the existence of Jesus. Others, as Dr. James H. Charlesworth of Princeton Theological Seminary puts it, "will assuredly wish to ask the following question: Is it not obvious that one conclusion of New Testament research is that nothing can be known assuredly about the Jesus of History?" (ChJ.R 9)

WHAT'S THE REAL ISSUE?

Did Jesus ever live? Most scholars will admit that a man known as Jesus of Nazareth did live in the first century and that his life was the source of various reports which circulated about him. Only a few insist that Jesus never lived at all.

The question that is hotly debated today, however, is: "Did Jesus of Nazareth actually live the kind of life the gospel accounts say he lived?" Was he actually the kind of person the Bible portrays him to be? A stream of new books continues to present Jesus as anything but the figure described in the gospel accounts. He is portrayed as a magician, a zealot, an Essene, a guru and world traveler, as one who used hypnosis, and as the husband of Mary Magdalene with whom he procreated into existence a secret lineage and society to rule the world. He is presented as a gnostic, an astronaut from outer space, a deceiver who plotted his own resurrection and as nothing more than a code name for a sacred hallucinogenic mushroom allegedly used by the first Christians.

We desire, on the other hand, to present reliable evidence to portray as accurately as possible what the historical Jesus actually was like.

WHY IS THE HISTORICITY OF JESUS IMPORTANT?

Consider a statement by John Gribbin in his popular book, *In Search of the Double Helix: Quantum Physics and Life:*

> Ask devout Christians whether they believe that Christ died and rose again, and they will say that of course they do. Ask them for evidence, and they will be baffled by the question. It is not a matter of evidence, but of belief; asking for evidence indicates doubt, and with doubt there is no faith. (GriJ.IS 21-23)

Gribbin obviously misunderstands faith and the nature of evidence. Faith is not simply believing something in the absence of evidence—one aspect of biblical faith is believing what the Bible says based on the evidence available to us. This is why religion and philosophy professor Charles Anderson is correct in declaring:

> It cannot be stated too strongly that Christianity is an historical religion, and that it is so intimately tied to history that if the historical credibility of its sources were to be proven false, it would at once collapse as a possible claimant for our loyalty. (AnC.CQ 55)

E. M. Blaiklock, former Professor of Classics at University College, Auckland, New Zealand, adds, "Since the Christian faith is rooted in history, to disturb the history is inevitably to disturb the faith." (BlE.MM 48)

The evidence presented in this book should help answer the questions you may have about the life Jesus lived as he walked among the people of the first century.

If you do not have a personal relationship with God through Jesus, we ask that you keep an open mind. We believe God has given us enough evidence of his working in history to allow us a strong conviction based on overwhelming probability, although not so certain as to force one to believe against his own will. As French physicist and philosopher Blaise Pascal put it,

> He [God] so regulates the knowledge of Himself that He has given signs of Himself, visible to those who seek Him and not to those who seek Him not. There is enough obscurity for those who have a contrary disposition. (TrW.PP 430)

HISTORICAL SEARCH FOR THE HISTORICAL JESUS

Why are some scholars today so skeptical of the gospel accounts? What has happened in the past to bring about such skepticism? I. Howard Marshall, professor of

New Testament Exegesis at the University of Aberdeen, has conveniently surveyed the "quest for the historical Jesus" through the last two hundred years. (MaIH.IB 110-142) We will touch only on the high points here, but we highly recommend Marshall's work for further study and for references to the history of scholarship on this question.

The posthumous publication in 1778 of H. S. Reimarus' writings marked a definite beginning of critical approaches to the historicity of Jesus. Reimarus, a professor of Hebrew and Oriental Language in Hamburg, Germany, viewed Jesus as a Jewish zealot who failed to set up his messianic kingdom. His disciples, says Reimarus, stole his body and made up the stories of his resurrection. In 1835, Tübingen scholar David Friedrich Strauss, at twenty-seven, published *The Life of Jesus*. This major work, highly influenced by rationalism, expressed strong skepticism regarding the gospels as historical sources. Adolf von Harnack and other nineteenth-century liberal theologians constructed their depictions in such a way that Jesus became what has been described as the "liberal Jesus"—perfectly at home as an inoffensive nineteenth-century Sunday school teacher. William Temple, Archbishop of Canterbury, later attacked this position saying, "Why anyone should have troubled to crucify the Christ of Liberal Protestantism has always been a mystery." (TeW.RIJ 24)

In 1901, William Wrede, a German New Testament scholar, published *The Messianic Secret*. According to Wrede, Jesus could not actually have told his disciples and others to keep quiet about healings he performed and about his messiahship. Therefore, these must be false statements added by Mark in the interest of theology. The gospels, then, were little more than theological fantasies.

In 1906, Albert Schweitzer released *The Quest of the Historical Jesus*. Though Schweitzer succeeded in refuting the various popularistic "Lives of Jesus" up to his day, he left behind only a deluded Jesus, hoping for the end of history to come and dying in despair when it did not. As he put it:

> The Jesus of Nazareth who came forward publicly as the Messiah, who preached the ethic of the Kingdom of God, who founded the Kingdom of Heaven upon earth, and died to give His work its final consecration, never had any existence. He is a figure designed by rationalism, endowed with life by liberalism, and clothed by modern theology in an historical garb. (ScA.QHJ 398)

Schweitzer's contribution, however, was to recognize that the historical Jesus might have been someone different from a modern man.

At just about the same time as Wrede and Schweitzer, the *Religionsgeschichtliche Schule* sought to draw parallels between early Christianity and other religious sects of the Eastern Mediterranean. The approach did not include Jewish sects. Jesus, according to this school, had his divine powers conferred on him by the gospel writers who were under the influence of pagan legends about "divine men" with miracle-working powers.

After World War I, form criticism began to exercise a considerable and increasing influence.[1] In 1919, Karl Ludwig Schmidt maintained that almost all details of time and place in the gospels were artificially constructed by the writers and were not necessarily historical.[2] Martin Dibelius in 1919 and Rudolf Bultmann in 1921 released works which sought to analyze various single units within the gospel traditions according to their form rather than their content.[3]

Common to most form criticism was (1) the assumption that oral tradition of Jesus' words and deeds suffered from additions, deletions and changes before it was finally recorded; (2) the assumption that the "life setting" *(Sitz im Leben)* of the early church controlled the contents and the manner in which the gospel accounts were written; (3) the belief that the gospel writers borrowed features of other ancient literature to incorporate into their account; (4) the assumption (particularly with Bultmann and others who followed him) that rationalism had completely done away with the possibility of miracles; and (5) the conclusion (again particularly with Bultmann and his followers) that not much in the gospels could be considered as reliable historical narrative.

Bultmann formulated the general approach that if someone either before or after Jesus could have said something which the gospels attributed to Jesus, then Jesus probably did not say it. The few deeds and words of Jesus which remained, Bultmann published in a booklet translated into English in 1934 as *Jesus and the Word*. Ernst Lohmeyer, another German scholar, described it as "a Jesus-book without Jesus." (See KüWG.NT 375ff.) Marshall summarizes:

> If A. Schweitzer had pronounced the obituary on the quest for the historical Jesus, Bultmann could be said to have laid its tombstone in place. The general effect of his work was to claim that the quest for the historical Jesus was impossible. Bultmann took the further step of declaring that the quest was illegitimate and unnecessary. (MalH.IB 126)

In reaction to Bultmann's pessimism toward possible historical material in the gospels, a number of writers maintained a more conservative and optimistic outlook. Among them were Dibelius (only slightly more conservative), Dodd, T. W. Manson, W. Manson, and V. Taylor.[4] In varying degrees, these and other scholars sought to reclaim some gospel portions as historically reliable. Even from within the followers of Bultmann, Ernst Käsemann and Günther Bornkamm reclaimed some of the material as historically reliable, but Norman Perrin maintained Bultmann's pessimism. Others outside Bultmann's camp, including Jeremias, Goppelt and Guthrie, have argued to preserve much of the gospel material as authentic.

RECENT PORTRAYALS OF JESUS

One fascinating American thriller of our times was the epic film "Raiders of the Lost Ark." This adventure of rival archaeologists uncovering the lost ark of the Jews captivated audiences across the United States. Although "Raiders of the Lost Ark" was only fiction, in the last few decades many attempts have been made by the popular press to uncover, not a Jewish artifact, but the reality of an actual, historical Jewish person: Jesus of Nazareth. You might call it "Raiders of the Lost Jesus."

In view of the innumerable mysteries which surround the proposition that Jesus of Nazareth might possibly be (according to Christian belief) the long-awaited Messiah, it is not surprising that countless authors have written various hypotheses to explain the life of Jesus. Still, we have to agree with New Testament scholar Michael Green when he says:

> It is a matter of amazement to me that books constantly get published, and television programmes produced, which set out the most bizarre interpretations of Jesus of Nazareth on the most slender of evidence. (FrR.E 7, Editor's Preface)

Consider for example, *The Lost Years of Jesus,* a popularistic reconstruction of Jesus' life which carries the typical advertisement: "An historical breakthrough that will shake the very foundations of modern Christendom!" (PrE.LY) This recently published book, by Elizabeth Clare Prophet, fantasizes that Jesus spent the seventeen years of his life between ages thirteen and thirty in India. The author presents the testimonies of four witnesses who have seen documents (how old they are no one seems to know) which preserve this tradition in India. Scholars likely will not take the book seriously.

A slightly more well-documented presentation is "the shocking international best seller" of 1982, *Holy Blood, Holy Grail.* The book entices readers with a web of speculation regarding Mary Magdalene as the wife of Jesus and the possibility that they had as many as six children. As alluring as the book's hypothesis might be to unsuspecting readers, the hard evidence for the author's position just isn't there. In fact, the authors themselves all but admit they have read into the gospel accounts what they desired to see:

> It was not our intention to discredit the Gospels. We sought only to sift through them—to locate certain fragments of possible or probable truth and extract them from the matrix of embroidery surrounding them. We were seeking fragments, moreover, of a very precise character—fragments that might attest to a marriage between Jesus and the woman known as the Magdalene. Such attestations, needless to say, would not be explicit. In order to find them, we realized, *we would be obliged to read between lines, fill in certain gaps, account for certain caesuras and ellipses. We would have to deal with omissions, with innuendos, with references that were, at best, oblique.*
> (BaM.HB 330; emphasis ours)

The authors have given, in the emphasized portion above, almost a precise definition of what biblical scholars call *eisegesis,* the practice of reading into a text a thought which is not there!

On evidence almost as slender, Thomas Sheehan demands the recognition of Jesus as simply a man who preached that all religion should come to an end. The entire thesis of his book, *The First Coming,* is based on a bizarre interpretation of Mark 1:15 ("The time is fulfilled, and the kingdom of God is at hand; repent and believe in the gospel."), a verse that, when divorced from its biblical context, has often been used to introduce novel reinterpretations of the gospel. (ShT.TFC) Sheehan, a philosopher, has produced a work of speculative philosophy, not historical investigation.

On a different slant, Morton Smith, Professor of Ancient History at Columbia University, represents Jesus as a magician who influenced his followers through the use of illusion and hypnosis. In *Jesus the Magician,* Smith reinterprets biblical texts in light of a fragment of a letter from Clement of Alexandria which he discovered in 1958. (SmM. JTM) Smith, like others who deny the credibility of the gospel accounts, states emphatically, "The gospels repeatedly contradict each other." (SmM.JTM 3)

While this statement is certainly debatable, one often overlooked observation is the way the various popular reconstructions of Jesus' life contradict one another. For example, in *Holy Blood, Holy Grail,* the wedding at Cana is supposedly that of Jesus and Mary Magdalene. Smith, on the other hand, dismisses the whole account saying, "The Cana story is probably also a fiction; it has been shown to have been modeled on a Dionysiac myth." (SmM.JTM 25. See chapter 16, "Jesus and the Popular Press," for the answer to this assertion by Smith.) But then, Smith's bias against much of anything in the gospel accounts being credible is clearly seen through his writings.

Several of Smith's conjectures were used by Ian Wilson in his book, *Jesus: The Evidence,* and even more so in the British TV series of the same name. In the book, Wilson draws on nineteenth century liberal scholarship and twentieth century form criticism to cast doubt on the reliability of the gospel accounts as historical sources. Even then the evidence forced him to conclude that Jesus existed, but favors Smith's hypothesis that Jesus performed miracles by the use of magic. Wilson toys with the ideas of possible mass hypnosis to explain the post-resurrection appearances, and the possibility that the tomb was not empty; yet finally concludes that the resurrection itself must remain a mystery.

More than sixty years ago Frenchman Paul Louis Couchoud published his *Le Mystere de Jesus.* In it, according to François Amiot, he "cheerfully invited the faithful to free themselves from the doctrine of the incarnate Son of God and to admit that the personality of Jesus was a complete forgery, an ingenious construction made up of prophetic oracles foretelling the future Messiah."

More recently, G. A. Wells has written three books of a similar conclusion: *The Jesus of the Early Christians* (1971); *Did Jesus Exist?* (1976); and *The Historical Evidence for Jesus* (1982). By dating all the books of the New Testament to AD 90 and later, he has determined to "show that recent work from critical theologians themselves provides a basis for taking more seriously the hypothesis that Christianity did not begin with a Jesus who lived on earth." (WeG.HE 218) Wells's position, by the way, was rejected by Ian Wilson in *Jesus: The Evidence.*

John Allegro, a competent Semitic scholar, recently set forth a novel approach. In *The Sacred Mushroom and the Cross,* Jesus is not a historical person but something of a code name alluding to the use of a hallucinogenic drug made from the red-topped mushroom, *Amanita muscaria*. The writers of the New Testament were allegedly members of an ancient fertility cult who committed their secrets to writing in an elaborate cryptogram, the New Testament itself. G. A. Wells (above) flatly rejected this hypothesis. (WeG.HE 221-23)

And the list goes on. Orthodox Rabbi Harvey Falk has written *Jesus the Pharisee: A New Look at the Jewishness of Jesus*. Then there are the Jesus seminars where scholars meet semiannually to grade various segments of the gospels as to how historically reliable they are. In 1985, the secular humanist publication *Free Inquiry* helped sponsor an "International Symposium on Jesus and the Gospels" at the University of Michigan. *Free Inquiry* advertised that the "Jesus in History and Myth" conference would be a convening of "leading biblical scholars, scientists, and skeptics for the first time to debate this issue."[5] In fact, conservative Christian scholarship was not represented at all, and one of the few speakers to support anything in the gospels as historical also clearly stated his rejection of the virgin birth and bodily resurrection of Jesus.

In years to come the layman, the student, the seminarian and the pastor in the pulpit all will need to be increasingly aware of these kinds of attacks on the New Testament truth of the historical actuality of Jesus. Critical scholarship (of a destructive nature) is deeply entrenched in many colleges and seminaries. And let's face it, the media gets a lot more excitement out of a bizarre new representation of Jesus than just about anything else it puts into the religion section.

Most of the popularistic lives of Jesus have several points in common. R. T. France summarizes:

> All such reconstructions of Jesus necessarily have in common an extreme skepticism with regard to the primary evidence for Jesus, the canonical gospels, which are regarded as a deliberate distortion of the truth in order to offer a Jesus who is fit to be the object of Christian worship. Instead they search out hints of "suppressed evidence," and give a central place to incidental historical details and to later "apocryphal" traditions not unknown to mainstream biblical scholarship, but which have generally been regarded as at best peripheral, and in most cases grossly unreliable. The credulity with which this "suppressed evidence" is accepted and given a central place in reconstructing the "real" Jesus is the more remarkable when it is contrasted with the excessive skepticism shown towards the canonical gospels. (FrR.E 14)

In *The Screwtape Letters*, C. S. Lewis may have given the most accurate assessment of the continuing production of popularistic lives of Jesus. In the story line, Screwtape, an elder devil, counsels his nephew on one of many strategies of deception:

> In the last generation we promoted the construction of...a "historical Jesus" on liberal and humanitarian lines; we are now putting forward a new

"historical Jesus" on Marxian, catastrophic, and revolutionary lines. The advantages of these constructions, which we intend to change every thirty years or so, are manifold. In the first place they all tend to direct men's devotion to something which does not exist, for each "historical Jesus" is unhistorical. The documents say what they say and cannot be added to; each new "historical Jesus" therefore has to be got out of them by suppression at one point and exaggeration at another, and by that sort of guessing (brilliant is the adjective we teach humans to apply to it) on which no one would risk ten shillings in ordinary life, but which is enough to produce a crop of new Napoleons, new Shakespeares, and new Swifts, in every publisher's autumn list. (LeC.SL.117)

AN OVERVIEW

You've heard it (or asked it) yourself: "How do we know Jesus ever lived, and if he did live, what he was like?" The often dogmatic assertion is, "The only historical references to Jesus are contained in biased Christian sources."

Fact or fiction? To answer that question, we'll first look, in Part I of this book, at the historical reliability of the various references to Jesus in secular and Jewish literature. We'll also evaluate the credibility of references to Jesus in the writings of the early church fathers and in the Apocrypha, Agrapha and Pseudepigrapha.

In Part II we'll investigate the historical reliability of what the New Testament tells us about Jesus. Why do some scholars doubt the authenticity of historical references in the New Testament? Should we disqualify the gospel writers because of their alleged Christian bias? How do we know they didn't make up the story of Jesus, or that it wasn't just a legend that developed between the years Jesus lived and the time someone finally bothered to write it down? Why didn't they write it down right away? What is form criticism and are its conclusions accurate? What about all the pagan myths of gods who came into the world through virgin births and performed miracles? Could this be where the gospel writers got their story? Where did they get their material about Jesus, anyway? How does the geography of Palestine help us understand some of the things Jesus reportedly said? Is archaeology helpful? What about the Jewish background to the gospel? And can one seriously trust documents that are filled with reports of the miraculous, especially the resurrection of Jesus? Finally, can writers who declare Jesus to be both Messiah and Son of God be relied upon to report their history accurately?

In the concluding chapter, we'll apply all the evidence accumulated to various popular depictions of Jesus. In the process, we will evaluate how trustworthy these works might be.

PART I

EXTRABIBLICAL EVIDENCE *for* JESUS

THE UNUSUAL NATURE
OF EXTRABIBLICAL
REFERENCES TO JESUS

Recently we received a letter from an individual who wrote, "I'm almost a believer, but I do not wish to believe on blind faith…. Can you document for me nonbiblical historical accounts of the resurrection of Christ?"

One correspondent with Professor F. F. Bruce, former Rylands Professor of Biblical Criticism and Exegesis at the University of Manchester, posed the question a little more broadly:

> What collateral proof is there in existence of the historical fact of the life of Jesus Christ? (BrF.JCO 17)

Following this chapter, the remainder of Part I is devoted to documenting and evaluating references to the life of Jesus outside the Bible. Very definitely, nonbiblical writers did speak of Jesus. But in order for us to fully appreciate these references, we must be able to answer several critical questions. And one of the most important questions is: Should we in fact expect the secular history records of Jesus' day to have preserved *any* mention of the life of Jesus at all, and if so, what kind of references should we expect? For example…

WHAT ABOUT REPORTS FROM PILATE?

If the Bible accurately portrays the life, death and resurrection of Jesus, wouldn't Pontius Pilate, of all people, have made some report about it? The noted scholar, F. F. Bruce, answers:

> People frequently ask if any record has been preserved of the report which, it is presumed, Pontius Pilate, prefect of Judea, sent to Rome concerning the trial and execution of Jesus of Nazareth. The answer is none. But let it be added at once that no official record has been preserved of *any* report

which Pontius Pilate, *or any other Roman governor of Judea*, sent to Rome about *anything*. And only rarely has an official report from any governor of any Roman province survived. They may have sent in their reports regularly, but for the most part these reports were ephemeral documents, and in due course they disappeared. (Br.F.JCO 17; emphasis ours)

It is interesting that even though we do not have today any reports from Pilate or any other Roman governor of Judea about anything, the early Christians apparently knew about Pilate's records concerning Jesus. Justin Martyr, writing in approximately AD 150, informs emperor Antoninus Pius of the fulfillment of Psalm 22:16:

But the words, "They pierced my hands and feet," refer to the nails which were fixed in Jesus' hands and feet on the cross; and after he was crucified, his executioners cast lots for his garments, and divided them among themselves. That these things happened you may learn from the "Acts" which were recorded under Pontius Pilate.[1]

Justin also says:

That he performed these miracles you may easily satisfy yourself from the "Acts" of Pontius Pilate.[2]

Bruce continues:

Similarly both Justin and Tertullian, another Christian apologist of a generation or two later, were sure that the census which was held about the time of our Lord's birth was recorded in the official archives of the reign of Augustus, and that anyone who took the trouble to look these archives up would find the registration of Joseph and Mary there. (Br.F.JCO 20)[3]

Justin's statement is a bold one if in fact no record existed. Can you imagine a respected scholar writing the President of the United States a letter, which he knows will be carefully scrutinized, and building his case on official federal documents which do not exist? It did, however, apparently bother a fourth century Christian sympathizer that this record was not available in his day. An obviously forged "Acts of Pilate" was manufactured at that time. One indication of its falsity: It was addressed to Claudius even though Tiberius was emperor when Pilate governed Judea.

But why would someone in the fourth century want to forge a document from the first century? Aside from a warped view of what the Scriptures taught about honesty, part of the reason lies in the fact that first century documents were quite rare.

JUST HOW MUCH SURVIVED?

How much nonbiblical material on any subject actually survived from the first century? And of that material, in what parts would we expect to find references to Jesus? Again, Bruce relates:

When we are asked what "collateral proof" exists of the life of Jesus Christ, would it be unfair to begin by asking another question? In which contemporary writers—in which writers who flourished, say, during the first fifty years after the death of Christ—would you expect to find collateral evidence you are looking for? Well, perhaps it would be rather unfair, as the man in the street can hardly be expected to know who was writing in the Graeco-Roman world during those fifty years; the classical student himself has to scratch his head in an attempt to remember who they were. For it is surprising how few writings, comparatively speaking, have survived from those years of a kind which might be even remotely expected to mention Christ. (I except, for the present, the letters of Paul and several other New Testament writings.) (BrE.JCO 17)

One prolific writer and contemporary of Jesus was Philo. He was born c. 15 BC and lived in Alexandria, Egypt, until his death sometime after AD 40. His works consist primarily of philosophy and commentary on Jewish Scripture and religion as they relate to Greek culture and philosophy. His family was one of the wealthiest in Alexandria. A reading of the fifteenth edition of the Encyclopedia Britannica article on Philo will readily confirm Henri Daniel-Rops' conclusion: "It is not unduly surprising that such a person should not pay much attention to an agitator sprung from the humblest of the people, whose doctrine, if he had one, had no connection with philosophy." (AmF.SLC 17-18)

E. M. Blaiklock has catalogued the non-Christian writings of the Roman Empire (other than those of Philo) which have survived the first century and which do not mention Jesus. As you will see from our summary of Blaiklock in the following paragraphs, there is very little.

From the decade of the 30s practically nothing has survived. Velleius Paterculus, a retired army officer of Tiberius, published what was considered an amateurish history of Rome in AD 30. Only part of it has survived. Jesus was just beginning his ministry.[4] Considering the time of writing, and especially the segregation between Jewish and Roman towns in Galilee, it is unlikely that Paterculus ever even heard of Jesus. The gospel writers give no evidence that Jesus ever set foot in Tiberias or any other Roman town in Galilee. Also surviving from the 30s is an inscription of Caesarea bearing two-thirds of Pilate's name. Can you believe it? That is all we have outside of the New Testament that has survived from the decade during which Jesus' ministry took place!

All that is left from the 40s are the fables written by Phaedrus, a Macedonian freedman.

Of the 50s and 60s, Blaiklock says:

Bookends set a foot apart on this desk where I write would enclose the works from those significant years. Curiously, much of it comes from Spanish emigrants in Rome, a foretaste of what the Iberian peninsula was to give to her conqueror—senators, writers, and two important emperors,

Trajan and Hadrian. Paul had foresight when he set a visit to Spain in his program. (BIE.MM 13)

The works of this period include the philosophical treatises and letters of Roman statesman, writer and tutor of Nero, Seneca; the long poem of his nephew Lucan on the civil war between Julius Caesar and Pompey; a book on agriculture by the retired soldier Columella; and large fragments of the novel *Satyricon* by the voluptuary Gaius Petronius. Also surviving from this period are a few hundred lines of Roman satirist Persius; the Elder Pliny's *Historia Naturalis* ("a collection of odd facts about the world of nature"); some fragments of Asconius Pedianus' commentary on Cicero; and the history of Alexander the Great by the little-known Quintus Curtius. Blaiklock asks:

> Of this handful of writers would any have been likely to mention Christ? Perhaps Seneca, if in fact he met and talked with Paul. But there is a small likelihood that this pleasant medieval legend is true. Besides, in AD 64, in the summer of which year Nero took hostile note of Rome's Christians, Seneca was a distracted and tormented man. A year later he was dead, driven to suicide by the mad young tyrant whom he had sought in vain to tame. (BIE.MM 16)

Check the works of the 70s and 80s to see if they might be candidates for mentioning a Jewish religious rabble-rouser now dead for forty years: Tacitus, who would become a great historian, published a minor work on oratory in AD 81. Several hundred witty poems or epigrams written by Martial in Rome survive but do not clearly mention the Christians. After Nero's mass killing of Christians in AD 64, it is no wonder that few Christians wanted to remain in Rome. Josephus wrote during this period, and we will look at his comments about Jesus in the next chapter. Two of his works, for good reasons, do not mention Jesus: *Against Apion,* an apologetic work contrasting the Jewish faith with Greek thought, and *Wars of the Jews,* a general history of the Jewish Wars from the time of the Maccabees to AD 70. A reading of both works is enough to show that any reference to Jesus in either one would have been out of place.

In the 90s, the poet Statius published *Silvae;* Quintilian published twelve books on oratory; and Tacitus published two small books, one a monograph of his father-in-law, Agricola, and the other a monograph about what is now Germany. The subject matter of none of these would be expected to include anything about Jesus. Juvenal began his writings of satire just prior to the turn of the century. He does not mention the Christians. This again is not surprising. They were outlawed in Rome and therefore had to keep out of sight. A writer always increases his popularity by poking fun at those in the limelight rather than at those whom nobody knows.

There were, in addition, some writings from Qumran in the first century. Again, it is no big surprise—but expected—that they fail to mention Jesus. F. F. Bruce observes:

> The Qumran community withdrew as far as possible from public life and lived in its wilderness retreat; Jesus carried on his ministry in places where

people lived and worked, mixing with all sorts and conditions, and by preference (it appears) with men and women whose society pious men like those of Qumran would rather avoid. And, more important still, practically all the Qumran texts dealing with religious topics (so far as they have been published to date) are assigned on paleographical grounds to the pre-Christian decades. (BrF.JCO 66-67)

When you consider the quantity and content of first-century writings which have survived, you can understand why we do not possess more non-Christian references to Jesus. R. T. France puts it this way:

> From the point of view of Roman history of the first century, Jesus was a nobody. A man of no social standing, who achieved brief local notice in a remote and little-loved province as a preacher and miracle-worker, and who was duly executed by order of a minor provincial governor, could hardly be expected to achieve mention in the Roman headlines. (FrR.G 82)

Some first-century works which did not survive almost certainly did not contain any references to Jesus. The one work with the best opportunity of mentioning Jesus but which apparently did not was the *Chronicle* by Justus of Tiberias. He was born at about the time Jesus died. Photius, in the ninth century, comments that his silence was due to his non-Christian bias as a Jew. (AmF.SLC 18) When a writer of antiquity sought to discredit someone, he often used the common device of not mentioning him. As a result, his memory would not be preserved. In some areas of the Middle East, especially in Egypt, new rulers commonly attempted to erase all evidence of a previous ruler's existence by destroying all inscriptions and writings about him. Whether Justus consciously chose to ignore Jesus of Nazareth is impossible to tell since his work can't be analyzed. Living in Tiberias may have colored what he viewed as important. He may also have ignored Jesus along with a host of others whom he considered messianic pretenders, who were common in that day.

So one reason that it is surprising that we have any non-Christian references to Jesus in the first century at all is that not much about anything of that day has survived to the present time. What did survive indicates the writers would not have known about or been interested in the person of Jesus.

HOW BIG A STIR DID JESUS MAKE?

The gospel accounts often speak of "multitudes" following Jesus. But does this mean he had necessarily attracted much attention? Synoptic Gospels specialist Dr. Robert Lindsey, who lives and teaches in Israel, tells the story of how he found his answer to this question:

> I like to remember how a bright young Israeli student of mine gave me the clue to the meaning of the strange Greek word *ochloi* ("multitudes"). This

word appears frequently in the Gospels; yet students and scholars alike have been puzzled because the translation "multitudes" seems rarely, if ever, to fit the context.

One day I mentioned in a lecture that I did not understand the odd use of *ochloi,* nor why it should appear in the plural. "Ah," this young woman responded, "that sounds exactly like the usage of the rabbis when they talk in the ancient writings of the people of a given place. Their word is *ochlosim,* a plural form, but which, of course, simply means 'the people of a locality.'"

Almost certainly this student was correct. In the story of the deliverance of a demonized man by Jesus, both Matthew and Luke say that when the demon emerged from the man, "the *ochloi* marveled." Clearly the meaning is not "multitudes," but is, as we would say in English, "those standing by."

Even in the feeding of the five thousand, where both Matthew and Luke again combine to say that "the *ochloi*" followed him, and where indeed there was a large crowd, it seems better to translate Matthew 14:19 as "He commanded the people present to sit down," rather than "He commanded the *multitudes* to sit down." After all, it was just one multitude, not several. *Ochloi* is simply the literal Greek rendering of a Hebrew text which had *ochlosim* ("the people of the area"). (BiD.UDW, Foreword)

Bauer, Arndt and Gingrich's Greek Lexicon confirms that the Greek *ochlos* (the singular form) is a loanword in rabbinic literature. In other words, the word is originally Greek, not Hebrew, but became a part of the Hebrew vocabulary when the Greek and Hebrew worlds were thrown together in Palestine.

What qualifies as a multitude? Certainly the five thousand and the four thousand plus women and children Jesus fed on different occasions would qualify as multitudes. And it would have attracted attention if it had not been in "a desolate place" and if it was a usual occurrence. Since the writers give the numbers "5,000" and "4,000," we can be sure these were unique gatherings. Also notice that the feeding of the five thousand in Luke 9 immediately follows the preaching and healing tour of the twelve. The large crowd probably gathered as a result of those who followed each disciple back to Jesus. On many other occasions, though, a crowd of fifty to one hundred, possibly five hundred at times, would be sufficient.

But the New Testament confirms that Jesus' life did not pass in obscurity. Luke 23:8 says: "Now Herod was very glad when he saw Jesus; for he had wanted to see Him for a long time, because he had been hearing about Him and was hoping to see some sign performed by Him." Obviously, though, for Herod, Jesus was little more than a wandering magician. Despite the fact that word was getting around that Jesus was attracting a following, the Romans and their chroniclers would not have paid much attention for at least two reasons.

First, just as in our own times, the first-century secular press did not take seriously any testimony to supernatural phenomena. Those who produced the secular literature of first-century Palestine were more concerned about major political events and personalities. To them, Jesus would have been no more than an obscure itinerant preacher from an almost unknown city, Nazareth, who was crucified for causing a minor disturbance which only briefly involved the Roman governor. Likewise, the Jewish leaders and journalists probably would have viewed Jesus as one of many backwoods preachers simply trying to attract attention by claiming to be the Messiah.

The second reason Jesus would not have caused much concern among Romans is that the Romans had more pressing problems. If they were to be concerned about crowds in Galilee, it would not be over the unarmed peasants who occasionally came to see Jesus in and around Capernaum.

Approximately five miles east of Capernaum, across the northern tip of the Sea of Galilee, stood the mountain fortress town of Gamala. About five miles to the southwest, the Arbel cliffs towered above the Sea of Galilee. Both Arbel and Gamala were Zealot strongholds. The Romans would be much more concerned about the activities at these locations than they would about any religious teachers roaming the countryside. Some seventy years earlier, a number of rebels jumped to their death from the Arbel cliffs rather than submit to Herod. About thirty-five years after Jesus' crucifixion five thousand Zealot terrorists at Gamala would jump to their death rather than submit to the Romans. The first-century Jewish historian Josephus tells us that in AD 6 Judas "a Gaulonite, of a city whose name was Gamala" led an armed resistance against the Romans which was brutally crushed.[5] Josephus identifies this Judas as "the author" of a fourth sect of the Jews which he does not name, but he obviously is referring to the Zealots.[6]

Jesus would have been about ten years old, and the continuous bloody defeats of the Zealot bands must have been a vivid illustration to him of the type of movement that would eventually fail. The Romans, then, would not see a military threat in Jesus and his followers. If they had, they would have crucified Jesus' disciples along with him. Therefore, from the Roman perspective, classify the Zealots "under surveillance"; classify Jesus "harmless."

Jesus was careful not to attract attention to himself along the lines of popular messianic expectations. He consistently told Jewish people whom he healed not to tell anyone.[7] When the people wanted to make him a king he left them. He did not speak of himself to large groups as "Messiah," for the Jewish leaders believed that Messiah was to be a ruling king who would deliver his people from oppression. And the Romans knew that is what they believed! (It is in marked contrast that Jesus tells the healed demoniac to go home to his non-Jewish community and tell them what God had done for him.[8] They did not have the same messianic expectations as the Jewish people.)

When the crowds became too large, Jesus retreated with his disciples to the countryside "on the other side" of the Sea of Galilee. It seems Jesus lived his life on earth with a profound consciousness of the mustard-seed parable. During his lifetime, his kingdom would be small and relatively unnoticed. Later it would become like a tree which spreads its branches over all the other plants in the garden.

WHAT NEWS WAS HOT?

If the biblical description of Jesus' activities is accurate, wouldn't Jesus have attracted sufficient attention to be mentioned in first-century writings? Aside from what was said above, we can also agree with G. A. Wells when he states, "Today Christianity has been so important for so long that one is apt to assume that it must have appeared important to educated pagans who lived AD 50–150." (WeG.DJE/75 15)

The journalists of the first century, at least those whose works have been preserved to the present day, indicate that they were concerned about such things as the major political events of the day. Read through portions of the works of Tacitus, Suetonius, even Josephus and others of that time period, and you will notice very quickly that they concern themselves almost completely with the major political and international events of the day. When it comes to religious events, only those events which had bearing on the "more important" national and international affairs are mentioned.

A perfect example is Acts 25:19 where Festus, one of the closest political figures to the events of first-century Christianity, says, in speaking of the Jews and Paul, "They simply had some points of disagreement with him about their own religion and about a certain dead man, Jesus, whom Paul asserted to be alive." What Luke preserves here is the relatively small degree of importance which ruling officials attached to the religious events in first-century Palestine, at least those which seemed to have no political consequences. As a result, we ought to expect that the secular press of the day in Rome concerned itself more with the Roman attempts to protect its borders than with what was considered to be minor disagreements about religion. As France puts it:

> Galilee and Judaea were at the time two minor administrative areas under the large Roman province of Syria, itself on the far eastern frontier of the empire. The Jews, among whom Jesus lived and died, were a strange, remote people, little understood and little liked by most Europeans of the time, more often the butt of Roman humour than of serious interest. Major events of Jewish history find their echo in the histories of the period, but was the life of Jesus, from the Roman point of view, a major event? The death of a failed Jewish insurrectionary leader was a common enough occurrence, and religious preachers were two a penny in that part of the empire, a matter of curiosity, but hardly of real interest, to civilized Romans. (FrR.E 20)

There is another factor which pushes Christianity even further down the list of priorities in terms of "hot news items." This factor has to do with the fact that more conflicts are recorded in the gospels between Jesus and the Pharisees than between Jesus and any other group of people. And yet, an increasing number of writers have begun to discover and reveal that Jesus' teaching was closer in content to at least one of the schools of the Pharisees than to any other group in Israel at that time. Some Pharisees, to be sure, were members of the ruling Sanhedrin, but this body was primarily composed of the Sadducees in Jesus' day. It is therefore reasonable to conclude that a major confrontation between Jesus and the Pharisees probably was only a meaningless religious quibble to any first-century historian—including Josephus.

Was Christianity a hot news item in the first century? For Christians it was. But for those in government and the press, not really. As France observes:

> In the light of the political prominence which Christianity achieved in the fourth century, it is natural for us to envisage it as an imposing movement from the beginning. But sociological studies indicate first-century Christianity as a predominantly lower-class movement, with only a very limited appeal to the influential classes. And the careful reader of Paul's letters and of the Acts of the Apostles does not gain the impression of a mass movement, but rather of small, rather isolated groups of Christians banding together for mutual support in a hostile environment. Such groups are not the stuff of which news stories are made. (FrR.G 82)

FALSE EXPECTATIONS CONCERNING REFERENCES TO JESUS

As you can see, our difficulty of understanding first-century events and literature is often a result of having wrong expectations. There are several false expectations that some bring with them when they begin to study the historicity of Jesus. Here are a few which reinforce and add to what has been said above.

1. *Expecting first-century issues to be the same as modern issues.* The issue of the historicity of Jesus has arisen only in the last few hundred years. During the first several centuries after the life of Jesus, there is no indication that his historical existence was in question. The debates mainly focused upon theological issues which sought to determine what his life meant, not that it was.

2. *Expecting first-century communication to be the same as ours.* The author of the book *Future Shock*, Alvin Toffler, in a succeeding book, *The Third Wave*, speaks of three distinct periods of history, three waves of civilization: the agricultural age, the industrial age and the present and future age of information. This third wave, this age of information, uses forms of communication which are far more detailed than, for example, the means of communication available in Jesus' day. The French scholar Henri Daniel-Rops agrees:

> Our civilization is one of rapid communication, there is a regular cult of detail. Through the press, radio and television we are used to knowing all that happens in the wide world; we are told, and often shown, the incidental and the insignificant. Was it so two thousand, or even

two hundred, years ago? Before this "age of wide information," those who informed their contemporaries were practically bound to confine themselves to events which caused a great stir. (AmF.SLC 13)

3. *Expecting first-century customs to be the same as ours.* Have you ever wondered what Jesus looked like or whether anyone ever drew a sketch of him? Why is it that we have no first-century artistic representations of Jesus? You'll find the answer in Exodus 20:4: "You shall not make for yourself an idol, or any likeness of what is in heaven above or on the earth beneath or in the water under the earth." The religious Jews of Jesus' day interpreted that as meaning no portraits and no sculptures. Thus, not until the third century did Gentile Christians begin to draw or paint various conceptions of Jesus. It is doubtful that any are accurate, for they often portrayed Jesus as from their own culture rather than from the Jewish culture of the first century.

4. *Expecting other events of history to be attested by a wealth of evidence.* Professor E. M. Blaiklock observes:

> Why the unease over an historical Jesus? It cannot simply be a scholar's zeal for truth. Julius Caesar is not thus dismissed, or his rather unsuccessful reconnaissance across the English Channel relegated to legend, despite the fact that our principal informant is Julius himself (in a book designed to secure his political reputation) and that confirmatory evidence of that campaign consists merely of a shield in the river at the Chelsea crossing of the Thames, a few lines in Cicero's voluminous correspondence, and only a handful of later references. [9]

IS ABSENCE OF EVIDENCE EVIDENCE OF ABSENCE?

No one denies that the Christian church existed in the first century. Scholars recognize that even though Christianity did not attract much attention among first-century writers, it still would be impossible to deny its existence. Some scholars, therefore, are inconsistent when they argue for the lack of historicity of Jesus. As France brings out:

> Those who suspect the historicity of the Jesus of the gospels on the grounds that there are so few early non-Christian references to him, must surely, by the same argument, be even more skeptical as to whether the Christian church existed in the first century. But not even George Wells wishes to deny this! As has so often been noted, absence of evidence is not evidence of absence. (FrR.E 44)

In view of what has been discussed in this chapter, consider two questions: (1) What kind of reference to Jesus by a non-Christian would need to exist in order to incontrovertibly prove his existence? (2) Is it likely that any such reference still survives today?

An incontrovertible reference to Jesus would first of all have had to be from a firsthand witness. But outside of Christian testimony, no historical literature has survived which would even be expected to refer to him from the standpoint of a direct eyewitness. Thus the modern historian must seek non-Christian evidence for the life of Jesus by the same method he must apply to every other person of antiquity who was considered insignificant by the authorities of his day. That method is to analyze the credibility of secondhand reports.

In the case of Jesus, combine secondhand reports (both non-Christian and Christian) with the eyewitness accounts recorded in the gospels, and it becomes quite apparent that Jesus compares extremely favorably with other people in history whose historicity is not doubted. Gary Habermas, Professor of Philosophy and Religion at Liberty University, states concerning Jesus:

> We can perceive all the more how groundless the speculations are which deny his existence or which postulate only a minimal amount of facts concerning him. Much of ancient history is based on many fewer sources which are much later than the events which they record.... While some believe that we know almost nothing about Jesus from ancient, non-New Testament sources, this plainly is not the case. Not only are there many such sources, but Jesus is one of the persons of ancient history concerning whom we have a significant amount of quality data. His is one of the most-mentioned and most-substantiated lives in ancient times. (HaG.AE 169)

Blaiklock adds:

> Historians would be glad to have authentic, multiple, congruent evidence on more personalities and events of ancient history. (BIE.MM 12)

WHY ARE MANY EXTRABIBLICAL REFERENCES TO JESUS NEGATIVE IN TONE?

The individual who wrote to us also asked, "Are there firsthand accounts of Christ's life which were positive yet not put into the Bible?" He did an excellent job of answering his own question with:

> To be fair to you and to show that my mind is open to accepting what I may see as the truth, I'd like to say the following: If I were a skeptical Jew living during Christ's time and I saw Christ raise Lazarus or I saw Christ days after His crucifixion and death, then I'd be the one who talked of such evidence to everyone I came in contact with. More, I'd document such firsthand evidence and probably such documentation would end up in a Bible. What I am saying is that it's most likely that positive first-hand evidence would end up in a Bible compiled by believing Christians, and negative evidence would be created by nonbelievers. Therefore the lack of non-Bible history.

Good point! But before we look at the reliability of *biblical* references, let's consider, throughout the remaining chapters of Part I, the references to Jesus in *nonbiblical* literature.

REFERENCES TO JESUS BY ANCIENT SECULAR WRITERS

I n the last chapter we spoke of why it is unusual that there are extrabiblical references to Jesus at all. In this chapter, we focus on one of several kinds of extrabiblical references to Jesus: those by ancient secular writers. These writers were not necessarily non-religious. We use the term "secular writer" to refer to the type of literature they produced, not to their respective religious beliefs. All, however, were either non-Christians or even antagonists of Christianity.

THALLUS AND PHLEGON

Possibly one of the earliest writers to mention Jesus was Thallus. His work of historical writings did not survive to the present day, but some of the early church fathers quoted Thallus on various points, thus preserving what little we know of him. (MuC.FH 517ff. contains the extant fragments of Thallus' works.) Some scholars set the date of his writing at c. AD 52, others at the end of the first century or early in the second century. (See BrF.JCO 30 and HaC.AE 93 for the earlier date. See WeG.HE for the later date.) Julius Africanus, writing c. AD 221, states concerning the darkness at the time of the crucifixion of Jesus, "Thallus, in the third book of his histories, explains away this darkness as an eclipse of the sun— unreasonably, as it seems to me."[1] Africanus was correct in objecting to Thallus. A solar eclipse cannot take place at the time of a full moon, "and it was at the season of the Paschal full moon that Christ died."[2]

The most important observation to make about Thallus' comment, however, is that he does not seek to explain away the existence and crucifixion (with the accompanying darkness) of Jesus. Thallus presented the crucifixion as a definite historical event, though one which needed a naturalistic explanation for the darkness which covered the earth at the time of the event. Africanus also states that Thallus dates this event to the fifteenth year of the reign of Tiberius Caesar (probably AD 29). (RiHA.TS 34:113)[3] Luke 3:1, though, says that was the year John the Baptist began his ministry, which places the crucifixion approximately three to three and a half years later. It appears, then, that in looking for a naturalistic explanation for the darkness surrounding the crucifixion, Thallus was willing to look for anything within the general time period of the crucifixion.

Another work similar to that of Thallus and which has not survived to the present is the *Chronicles* by Phlegon. Phlegon wrote it c. AD 140. A small fragment of that work, which Africanus says confirms the darkness upon the earth at the crucifixion, appears just after the statement by Africanus concerning Thallus. Africanus says that Phlegon referred to the same eclipse when "he records that in the time of Tiberius Caesar at full moon, there was a full eclipse of the sun from the sixth hour to the ninth."[4]

Origen, the prolific early-third-century Christian scholar, also mentions Phlegon several times in *Against Celsus*. In 2.33, Origen writes:

> And with regard to the eclipse in the time of Tiberius Caesar, in whose reign Jesus appears to have been crucified, and the great earthquakes which then took place, Phlegon too, I think, has written in the thirteenth or fourteenth book of his Chronicles.[5]

In 2.14 he says:

> Now Phlegon, in the thirteenth or fourteenth book, I think, of his Chronicles, not only ascribed to Jesus a knowledge of future events (although falling into confusion about some things which refer to Peter, as if they referred to Jesus), but also testified that the result corresponded to His predictions. So that he also, by these very admissions regarding foreknowledge, as if against his will, expressed his opinion that the doctrines taught by the fathers of our system were not devoid of divine power.[6]

In 2.59 Origen says of the earthquake and the darkness:

> Regarding these we have in the preceding pages made our defence, according to our ability, adducing the testimony of Phlegon, who relates that these events took place at the time when our Saviour suffered.[7]

A sixth-century writer, Philopon, states: "And about this darkness...Phlegon recalls it in the *Olympiads* (the title of his history)."

We need to be careful in using Phlegon as a "proof-positive" reference to Jesus. Inaccuracies in his reports demonstrate that his sources to the life of Christ are sketchy. But Phlegon is a significant reference because of one important fact. Like Thallus, he gives no hint whatsoever that in this early period the fact of Jesus' existence (and even related details such as the darkness and the crucifixion) were ever disputed. They were taken for granted as historical facts. It was only how those facts were interpreted that was a matter of debate.

JOSEPHUS

Josephus was born just a few years after Jesus died. By his own account he was a consultant for Jerusalem rabbis at age thirteen, became an ascetic in the desert at age sixteen and obtained a Galilean military command in AD 66. He apparently saw the handwriting on the wall, deserted to the Romans and secured his future by prophesying that the invading commander, Vespasian (whom he accepted as Israel's Messiah), would one day become emperor. Vespasian did become emperor, and Flavius Josephus, as he was now known after adding his master's name to his own, was free to pursue his career as a writer. He finished *The Antiquities of the Jews* in AD 93.

Three Passages of Interest to Christians

There are three passages in *Antiquities* which are of particular interest and the order of their appearance is important. The first passage—in chronological order—is found in book 18, chapter 3, paragraph 3, commonly cited as *Antiquities* 18.3.3.[8] Scholars refer to this famous passage as the *Testimonium Flavianum* because of its testimony to Jesus, but we will discuss it later.

Passage #2—John the Baptist. The next passage in sequence is also in book 18, but two chapters later in 18.5.2 (116-19). Scholars agree that this passage is as authentic as any other passage in Josephus. The subject is John the Baptist and the account vividly confirms the portrayal of him in the gospel records as you can see here:

> (2) But to some of the Jews the destruction of Herod's army seemed to be divine vengeance, and certainly a just vengeance, for his treatment of John, surnamed the Baptist. For Herod had put him to death, though he was a good man and had exhorted the Jews to lead righteous lives, to practice justice towards their fellows and piety towards God, and so doing to join in baptism. In his view this was a necessary preliminary if baptism was to be acceptable to God. They must not employ it to gain pardon for whatever sins they committed, but as a consecration of the body implying that the soul was already thoroughly cleansed by right behaviour. When others too joined the crowds about him, because they were aroused to the highest degree by his sermons, Herod became alarmed. Eloquence that had so great an effect on mankind might lead to some form of sedition, for it looked as if they would be guided by John in everything that they did. Herod decided therefore that it would be much better to strike first and be rid of him before his work led to an uprising, than to wait for an upheaval, get involved in a difficult situation and see his mistake. Though John, because of Herod's suspicions, was brought in chains to Machaerus, the stronghold that we have previously mentioned, and there put to death, yet the verdict of the Jews was that the destruction visited upon Herod's army was a vindication of John, since God saw fit to inflict such a blow on Herod.

The only possible difference between Josephus and the gospel accounts lies in the gospel portrayal of Herod putting John to death at the request of Herodias and her daughter, and his grief over their request (Matthew 14:6-12 and Mark 6:21-29). But everything reconciles perfectly in light of two observations: (1) Matthew 14:5 and Mark 6:21 show that Herod had wanted to put John to death some time before the banquet: "And although he wanted to put him to death, he feared the multitude, because they regarded him as a prophet"; and (2) Matthew 14:6 and Mark 6:21, "When Herod's birthday came," indicate that between "brought in prison to Machaerus" and "there put to death" in Josephus' account, at least some time passes. During this time Herod appears to have softened his attitude toward John while Herodias continues to seek his execution.

Now notice the details which agree so precisely with the New Testament: John's righteousness, preaching and popularity among the people; and his baptism, which foreshadows the New Testament teaching of salvation "by grace through faith" followed by baptism as an outward expression of, not condition for, justification before God. While this passage does not speak of Jesus, it does give evidence that the gospel writers accurately portrayed the lives of those they described. If they were accurate about John the Baptist, why not about Jesus as well?

Passage #3—James and Jesus. The third passage in sequence (20.9.1) appears two books after Josephus' first reference to Jesus and primarily focuses upon one Ananus (Ananias), who was the son of a previous high priest, Ananus (Ananias). This younger Ananus "[who] took the high priesthood, was a bold man in his temper and very insolent; he was also of the sect of the Sadducees who were very rigid in judging offenders, above all the rest of the Jews." Festus had just died, and his replacement, Albinus, had not yet reached Jerusalem. Josephus continues his account by saying that Ananus

> convened the judges of the Sanhedrin and brought before them a man named James, the brother of Jesus who was called the Christ, and certain others. He accused them of having transgressed the law and delivered them up to be stoned.

Louis Feldman, Professor of Classics at Yeshiva University and translator for the Loeb edition of *Antiquities,* states concerning this passage's reliability, "Few have doubted the genuineness of this passage."[9]

Some of the reasons most scholars, especially those in classical studies, accept this passage as genuine include:

- The phrase "James the brother of Jesus who is called Christ" is too noncommittal to have been inserted by a later Christian interpolator who would have desired to assert the messiahship of Jesus more definitely as well as to deny the charges against James. For our purposes it demonstrates the historicity of Jesus, but this was not an issue until recent centuries. For early Christians, this phrase proved nothing, and would not have been inserted. Therefore it had to be original with Josephus.

- Origen refers to this passage in his *Commentary on Matthew* 10.17, giving evidence that it was in Josephus prior to his time (approximately AD 200).[10]

- The word *Christ* began to be used like a proper name very early among Gentile Christians. This can be seen even in the New Testament, but the phrase, "called the Christ," as Paul Winter (not a Christian but a noted Jewish scholar) states, "betrays awareness that 'Messiah' was not a proper name, and therefore reflects Jewish rather than Christian usage." (WiPJ 432) Josephus here simply distinguishes this Jesus from the other thirteen or more he mentions in his writings. This Jesus, according to Josephus, was "the one called Christ [that is, Messiah]."

G. A. Wells tries to change the passage by having it refer simply to a Jewish leader named James. He would strike the words "the brother of Jesus who was called the Christ." But if the passage simply said "James and certain others" were arrested, the reader would be compelled to ask, "Which James?" James was another very common name, and Josephus almost always supplied details to locate his characters in history. If Josephus simply said, "James the brother of Jesus," the reader must ask, "Which Jesus? You have already mentioned at least thirteen others named Jesus." "James, the brother of Jesus, who is called Christ" is the most precise language that is consistent with the rest of Josephus' writings, and scholars have found no real reason to doubt its authenticity. This passage is therefore a very significant early reference to Jesus.

Most scholars agree on one other point concerning Josephus' reference to Jesus in conjunction with James. Winter puts it: "If...Josephus referred to James as being 'the brother of Jesus who is called Christ,' without more ado, we have to assume that in an earlier passage he had already told his readers about Jesus himself." (WiPJ 432) [11]

Even G. A. Wells says that "it is unlikely that Josephus would have mentioned Jesus here simply—as it were—in passing, when he mentions him nowhere else." (WeG.DJE 11) Wells, of course, was trying to prove that Jesus is not mentioned at all by Josephus, but his statement demonstrates that even he recognizes that the James passage is incomplete without the Testimonium. Since few scholars doubt the authenticity of the James passage, then there is good reason to accept the authenticity of the Testimonium, at least in some form. R. T. France adds:

> What is important for our purpose is the way Josephus records this title of Jesus in passing, without comment or explanation. The term "Christos" occurs nowhere else in Josephus, except in the passage we are shortly to study. This in itself is remarkable, since we know that messianic ideas, and the term "Messiah" itself, were much canvassed in first-century Judaism. (FrR.E 26)

Josephus, writing in favor of the Jewish people, but to a Roman audience, was likely very cautious about giving the Romans reason for further repression of the Jews. If he mentioned repeated messiahs arising among the Jewish people, it would only have led the Romans to believe all the more that the Jews were a rebellious people which must constantly be suppressed. But when Josephus came to the person of Jesus, writing in AD 93, Christianity had become enough identified with Gentiles that he undoubtedly felt Jesus as "Christos" posed no threat of Roman reprisals against the Jews. In fact, he may possibly have felt that Roman persecution against the Christians (e.g., that in AD 64 under Nero) was helpful to the Jews in their resistance of Christianity. Josephus, then, says only that Jesus was "the one called Christ." And his reader is left with the feeling that Josephus has introduced this one earlier. Which brings us back to the first passage of the three in sequence mentioned above.

Passage #1—The Identity of Jesus. *Antiquities* 18.3.3 (63-4)—again, known as the Testimonium Flavianum—reads:

> About this time there lived Jesus, a wise man, if indeed one ought to call him a man. For he was one who wrought surprising feats and was a teacher of such people as accept the truth gladly. He won over many Jews and many of the Greeks. He was the Messiah. When Pilate, upon hearing him accused by men of the highest standing amongst us, had condemned him to be crucified, those who had in the first place come to love him did not give up their affection for him. On the third day he appeared to them restored to life, for the prophets of God had prophesied these and countless other marvelous things about him. And the tribe of the Christians, so called after him, has still to this day not disappeared.[12]

Arguments Favoring Authenticity of the Testimonium

> As classical literature goes, the manuscript evidence that this passage is genuinely from Josephus is strong. It exists in all of the extant (still in existence) manuscripts of Josephus, and Eusebius, known as the "Father of Church History," quotes it in his *History of the Church,* written c. AD 325, and again in his *Demonstration of the Gospel,* written somewhat earlier.[13] The vocabulary and style, according to Loeb translator Louis Feldman, are, with some exceptions, basically consistent with other parts of Josephus. (J.A/L 49)

France elaborates:

> Thus the description of Jesus as "a wise man" is not typically Christian, but is used by Josephus of e.g. Solomon and Daniel. Similarly, Christians did not refer to Jesus' miracles as "astonishing deeds" *(paradoxa erga),* but exactly the same expression is used by Josephus of the miracles of Elisha. And the description of Christians as a "tribe" *(phylon)* occurs nowhere in early Christian literature, while Josephus uses the word both for the Jewish "race" and for other national or communal groups. (FrR.E 30)

In addition, the passage lays primary blame for the crucifixion of Jesus on Pilate rather than on the Jewish authorities. This is quite different from second- and third-century Christian thought which was much more condemning of the Jews as instigators of the crucifixion. As Winter states, "The distinction between the functions of Jewish priests and Roman governor betrays some awareness of what legal proceedings in Judaea were like in the time of Jesus." (WiPJ 433) He continues:

> From the time of the writers of the Acts of the Apostles and of the Fourth Gospel onward, it was being claimed by Christian preachers, apologists and historians, that the Jews acted, not only as accusers of Jesus, but also as his judges and executioners. The array of charges against them on this count is impressive. It is hard to believe that a Christian forger, bent as he would have been on extolling the status of Jesus and lowering that of the Jews, might have been the author of the words in question. (WiPJ 433-34)

Objections to Authenticity of the Testimonium

There are some solid arguments against the authenticity of the Testimonium, at least as it is quoted above.

First, it is highly unlikely that Josephus would have written of Jesus, "This was the Messiah."

Not only would his Roman employers have suspected him of treason, but he has given no indication anywhere else that he was a Christian. Further, Origen, who wrote about a century before Eusebius, says twice that Josephus "did not believe in Jesus as the Christ."[14]

Second, the Testimonium, as given above, contains other vocabulary that would not be expected from Josephus whom critics of the passage enjoy labeling as "an orthodox Jew." We note in passing that there is some question as to how orthodox Josephus really was. He seems to have accepted the Roman lifestyle rather comfortably. Still, the phrases "if indeed one ought to call him a man," "such people as accept the truth," "one who wrought surprising feats" and "on the third day he appeared to them restored to life" all require Josephus to be sympathetic to the Christian testimony. In addition, the attributing of Old Testament prophecy to Jesus indicates that these portions were likely written by a later Christian copyist.

Third, if the passage, as we have it today, was originally in Josephus, then Justin Martyr, Clement of Alexandria, Tertullian or Origen would have quoted it, for its apologetic value is tremendous.[15] As Lardner states:

> A testimony so favourable to Jesus in the works of Josephus, who lived so soon after the time of our Saviour, who was so well acquainted with the transactions of his own country, who had received so many favours from

Vespasian and Titus, could not be overlooked or neglected by any Christian apologist. (LaN.W 487)

Even though this is an argument from silence, and even though many of the works of Origen and others have been lost in antiquity and might conceivably contain the Testimonium, still the argument remains sound for there are many passages in each of the above named authors as well as others where this passage would have been of great value in proving their point.

Finally, some argue that the passage interrupts the normal flow of Josephus' narrative in such a way that "if the passage is excised, the argument runs on in proper sequence." (WeG. DJE 10) Gordon Stein, following Nathaniel Lardner, states that "the passage comes in the middle of a collection of stories about calamities which have befallen the Jews." (StG.JH 2)

Answering the Objections

Of the four objections above, the last can be dismissed immediately. Only two of the five paragraphs in Josephus' chapter containing the Testimonium are true calamities. The content of the five paragraphs of chapter three is as follows: Paragraph one speaks of a potential calamity which was overcome by the courage of the Jews as they protested against Pilate. In fact it was a victory, not a calamity. Paragraph two does speak of the calamity of the Jews where "a great number of them" were killed and others wounded. Paragraph three is the Testimonium. Paragraph four describes the account of the seduction of a virtuous woman in the temple of Isis at Rome and has absolutely nothing at all to do with the Jews or anything else in the chapter.

Finally, paragraph five deals with the banishment of the Jews from Rome. Though paragraph four does begin with the words, "about the same time another sad calamity put the Jews into disorder," Josephus makes clear that he is referring to what he describes in paragraph five which he says he will describe after his diversion to the story of the seduction of the virtuous woman in the temple of Isis. The story of the virtuous woman, occupying over one half of the entire space of chapter three, is so out of context that one is forced to the conclusion that if anything is to be removed from this chapter it is paragraph four and not the Testimonium. However, what paragraph four and other passages like it in *Antiquities* do is testify of the occasional proneness of Josephus to include human interest stories wherever they fit into his chronology regardless of whether they fit the surrounding context. We have to agree with France when he says, "All this makes one wonder how Wells can argue that if the passage about Jesus is removed, 'the argument runs on in proper sequence.'" (FrR.E 28) Therefore, there is all the more reason to accept the Testimonium, though as we will see, in a more neutral or even negative tone.

Most scholars today opt for the third alternative.[16] Rather than "reject it as a complete forgery or accept it in total, they hold that Josephus must have said something about Jesus which was later, and unfortunately for us, "doctored up" by some Christian copyist. This position answers the three other objections to authenticity above while also agreeing with the evidences in favor of authenticity also presented above.

With the first objection that Josephus would not have called Jesus "the Christ," this position agrees. According to E. M. Blaiklock, Josephus "probably wrote 'the so-called Messiah,' as he did when, two books later, he mentioned Christ again, in conjunction with the murder of James." (BlE.MM 29)

Not only does this statement agree with what Josephus probably really believed, but, along with the rest of the information in the Testimonium, it gives the necessary introduction to this Jesus which is required in book 20 when Josephus only briefly says about him, "the one called Christ."

To the second objection that some of the vocabulary is uncharacteristic of Josephus, Bruce summarizes:

> It has been argued, in the light of the context in which the paragraph appeared, that something of this sort is what Josephus said:
>
>> Now there arose about this time *a source of further trouble* in one Jesus, a wise man who performed surprising works, a teacher of men who gladly welcome *strange things.* He led away many Jews, and also many of the Gentiles. He was the *so-called* Christ. When Pilate, acting on information supplied by the chief men among us, condemned him to the cross, those who had attached themselves to him at first did not cease *to cause trouble,* and the tribe of Christians, which has taken this name from him is not extinct even today.
>
> The flavour of this rendering probably expresses Josephus' intention more closely. It includes four emendations, which are italicized above. The first one, suggested by Robert Eisler (EiR.M 50ff.; see especially p. 45), is the addition of the phrase "a source of further trouble" in the first sentence. This links the paragraph more naturally to what has gone before, for Josephus has been narrating various troubles which arose during Pilate's governorship. The second one, suggested by Henry St. John Thackeray, is the reading "strange things" (Gk. aethe) instead of "true things" (Gk. alethe). (ThH.JTM 144ff.) To Josephus, Christianity was certainly more strange than true. The third one, suggested by G. C. Richards and R. J. H. Shutt, is the insertion of "so-called" before "Christ." (RiG.CN 31:176 and RiG.TJ 42:70-71)...Some reference to our Lord's designation "the Christ" is required at this point; otherwise Josephus' readers might not understand how in fact the "tribe of Christians" got its name from Jesus. The fourth, is not an emendation in the same sense as the others. Josephus says that Jesus's disciples "did not cease," and we have to ask, "did not cease to do what?" The answer will be in accordance with the context, and in the kind of context we envisage "did not cease to cause trouble" makes good sense. (BrF.JCO 39-40)

Bruce's reconstruction above (or others like it) also answers the second objection to authenticity: that none of the early church fathers before Eusebius quote Josephus. The primary value of the passage today is to prove the historical existence of Jesus and some basic facts about his life and death under the governorship of Pilate. Since these facts were not disputed in those early centuries, there is no reason any of the church fathers should have quoted Josephus. In addition, the passage, as given above by Bruce, gives evidence that Josephus was not a Christian and is reason enough for Origen to say that Josephus did not believe in Jesus as the Christ. Prominent Israeli scholar Shlomo Pines states:

> In fact, as far as probabilities go, no believing Christian could have produced such a neutral text; for him the only significant point about it could have been its attesting the historical evidence of Jesus. But the fact is that until modern times this particular hare was never started [this discussion was never opened]. Even the most bitter opponents of Christianity never expressed any doubt as to Jesus having really lived. (PiS.AVT 69)

Dr. James H. Charlesworth of Princeton Theological Seminary writes of further evidence confirming Josephus' account of Jesus:

> For years I yearned for the discovery of a text of Josephus' Antiquities that would contain variants in the Testimonium Flavianum. Then perhaps we could support scholarly speculations with textual evidence. In fact, precisely this dream has been our good fortune. (ChJ.R 109)

Professor Charlesworth goes on to describe a fourth-century Arabic version of the Testimonium which was preserved in Agapius' tenth-century Kitab al-'Unwan. Pines translates the passage:

> At this time there was a wise man who was called Jesus. And his conduct was good, and [he] was known to be virtuous. And many people from among the Jews and the other nations became his disciples. Pilate condemned him to be crucified and to die. And those who had become his disciples did not abandon his discipleship. They reported that he had appeared to them three days after his crucifixion and that he was alive; accordingly, he was perhaps the Messiah concerning whom the prophets have recounted wonders. (PiS.AVT 16)

An eleventh-century version of the Testimonium, to which Pines refers as Michael's text, contains the sentence: "He was thought to be the Messiah." Pines argues that this sentence may preserve something closer to Josephus' original than: "He was perhaps the Messiah" (as stated in the Arabic text).

The Arabic version, according to Charlesworth, "provides textual justification for excising the Christian passages and demonstrating that Josephus probably discussed Jesus in *Antiquities* 18." (ChJ.R 110)

To conclude our discussion about Josephus, not only is his mention of Jesus in the James passage solidly reliable, but as historian Earle E. Cairns also notes:

> Even granting some interpolation by Christians, most scholars agree that this basic information just mentioned [that Jesus was a "wise man" condemned to die on the cross by Pilate] is most likely a part of the original text. Certainly Josephus was not a friend of Christianity, and thus his mention of Christ has more historic value. (CaEE.CT 50)

PLINY THE YOUNGER

Pliny the Younger (Plinius Secundus) was the nephew and adopted son of the elder Pliny, the natural historian who died in the eruption of Mount Vesuvius. Bruce says of him, "Pliny is one of the world's great letter-writers, whose letters, unlike the ephemeral notes which most of us write, intended only for the perusal of the recipient, were written with one eye on a wider public and have attained the status of literary classics." (BrF.JCO 24)

Ten volumes of Pliny's correspondence have survived to the present. In the tenth volume there is a letter from Pliny to the emperor Trajan concerning the Christians of his province. It was written c. AD 112 while Pliny was serving as governor of Bithynia in Asia Minor. We quote Pliny at some length since his letter gives excellent information regarding early Christianity from a non-Christian viewpoint. He writes:

> It is a rule, Sir, which I invariably observe, to refer myself to you in all my doubts; for who is more capable of guiding my uncertainty or informing my ignorance? Having never been present at any trials of the Christians, I am unacquainted with the method and limits to be observed either in examining or punishing them, whether any difference is to be made on account of age, or no distinction allowed between the youngest and the adult; whether repentance admits to a pardon, or if a man has been once a Christian it avails him nothing to recant; whether the mere profession of Christianity, albeit without the commission of crimes, or only the charges associated therewith are punishable—on all these points I am in considerable perplexity.
>
> In the meantime, the method I have observed towards those who have been denounced to me as Christians is this: I interrogated them whether they were in fact Christians; if they confessed it, I repeated the question twice, adding the threat of capital punishment; if they still persevered, I ordered them to be executed. For whatever the nature of their beliefs might be, I could at least feel no doubt that determined contumacy and inflexible obstinacy deserved chastisement. There were others also possessed with the same infatuation, but being citizens of Rome, I directed them to be taken to Rome for trial.

These accusations spread (as is usually the case) from the mere fact of the matter being investigated, and several forms of the mischief came to light. A placard was put up, without any signature, accusing a large number of persons by name. Those who denied they were, or had ever been, Christians, and who repeated after me an invocation to the gods, and offered formal worship with libation and frankincense, before your statue, which I had ordered to be brought into Court for that purpose, together with those of the gods, and who finally cursed Christ—none of which acts, it is said, those who are really Christians can be forced into performing—these I thought it proper to discharge. Others who were named by the anonymous informer at first confessed themselves Christians, and then denied it; true, they said, they had been of that persuasion but they had quitted it, some three years, others many years, and a few as much as twenty-five years previously. They all worshipped your statue and the images of the gods, and cursed Christ.

They affirmed, however, that the whole of their guilt, or their error, was that they were in the habit of meeting on a certain fixed day before it was light, when they sang in alternate verses a hymn to Christ, as to a god, and bound themselves by a solemn oath, not to perform any wicked deed, never to commit any fraud, theft or adultery, never to falsify their word, nor deny a trust when they should be called upon to make it good; after which it was their custom to separate, and then reassemble to partake of food—but food of an ordinary and innocent kind. Even this practice, however, they had abandoned after the publication of my edict, by which, according to your orders, I had forbidden political associations. I therefore judged it so much the more necessary to extract the real truth, with the assistance of torture, from two female slaves, who were styled deaconesses: but I could discover nothing more than depraved and excessive superstition.

I therefore adjourned the proceedings, and betook myself at once to your counsel. For the matter seemed to me well worth referring to you—especially considering the numbers endangered. Persons of all ranks and ages, and of both sexes are, and will be, involved in the prosecution. For this contagious superstition is not confined to the cities only, but has spread through the villages and rural districts. It seems possible, however, to check and cure it. It is certain at least that the temples, which had been almost deserted, begin now to be frequented; and the sacred festivals, after a long intermission, are again revived; while there is a general demand for sacrificial meat, which for some time past had met with but few purchasers. From hence it is easy to imagine what multitudes may be reclaimed from this error, if a door be left open to repentance.[17]

In his response, Emperor Trajan agreed that being a Christian was a crime worthy of punishment:

My dear Secundus: You have acted with perfect correctness in deciding the cases of those who have been charged before you with being Christians. Indeed, no general decision can be made by which a set form of dealing with them could be established. They must not be ferreted out; if they are charged and convicted, they must be punished, provided that anyone who denies that he is a Christian and gives practical proof of that by invoking our gods is to be pardoned on the strength of this repudiation, no matter what grounds for suspicion may have existed against him in the past. Anonymous documents which are laid before you should receive no attention in any case; they form a very bad precedent and are quite unworthy of the age in which we live.[18]

These two letters confirm a number of details of early Christianity which are found or implied in the New Testament. For example: (1) Christians who were citizens of Rome were sent there to be tried, as in the case of Paul; (2) some recanted of being Christians as Jesus predicted in the Parable of the Soils; (3) they held Christ to be God; (4) they possessed exemplary moral character; (5) some women in the church held the office of deaconess; (6) a large number were being added to the church; and (7) the spread of Christianity had detrimental financial repercussions for those whose trades were related to various pagan temples and religions (e.g., the silversmiths of Acts 19).

G. A. Wells, however, contends that "Pliny's testimony has no bearing on Jesus' existence.... No one doubts that by 112 Christians worshipped Christ and that Pliny's statement reproduced Christian beliefs." (WeG.HE 16) But Wells overlooks Pliny's and Trajan's bearing witness to the fact that within the first eighty years of Christianity a large number of men and women were so convinced of the actual historical life, death, burial and resurrection of Jesus that they voiced those convictions in the face of certain execution.

CORNELIUS TACITUS

Modern historians have become used to piecing together the stories of ancient times and places in spite of the fact that those who wrote about them used poor sources, were not careful in interpreting or analyzing their material and distorted the facts of their reports because of preconceived bias. For this reason, Tacitus is "universally considered the most reliable of historians, a man in whom sensibility and imagination, though lively, could never spoil a critical sense rare in his time and a great honesty in the examination of documents." (AmF.SLC 16)

Tacitus, born between AD 52 and 55, became a senator under the reign of Vespasian, later held the office of consul and in the years 112 and 113 was proconsul, or governor, of Asia. He was a respected orator and close friend of Pliny the Younger, who was governor of the neighboring province of Bithynia just before Tacitus became governor of Asia.

Writing in his *Annals* c. AD 116, Tacitus describes the response of Emperor Nero to the great fire which swept Rome in AD 64. A persistent rumor circulated that Nero himself was behind the fire and therefore had to take action to dispel the story. Tacitus speaks of Nero's actions to cut off the rumor:

> So far, the precautions taken were suggested by human prudence: now means were sought for appeasing deity, and application was made to the Sibylline books; at the injunction of which public prayers were offered to Vulcan, Ceres, Proserpine, while Juno was propitiated by the matrons, first in the Capitol, then at the nearest point of the sea shore, where water was drawn for sprinkling the temple and image of the goddess. Ritual banquets and all night vigils were celebrated by women in the married state. But neither human help, nor imperial munificence, nor all the modes of placating Heaven, could stifle scandal or dispel the belief that the fire had taken place by order. Therefore, to scotch the rumour, Nero substituted as culprits, and punished with the utmost refinements of cruelty, a class of men, loathed for their vices, whom the crowd styled Christians. Christus, the founder of the name, had undergone the death penalty in the reign of Tiberius, by sentence of the procurator Pontius Pilatus, and the pernicious superstition was checked for a moment, only to break out once more, not merely in Judaea, the home of the disease, but in the capital itself, where all things horrible or shameful in the world collect and find a vogue. First, then, the confessed members of the sect were arrested; next, on their disclosures, vast numbers were convicted, not so much on the count of arson as for hatred of the human race. And derision accompanied their end: they were covered with wild beasts' skins and torn to death by dogs; or they were fastened on crosses, and, when daylight failed were burned to serve as lamps by night. Nero had offered his Gardens for the spectacle, and gave an exhibition in his Circus, mixing with the crowd in the habit of a charioteer, or mounted on his car. Hence, in spite of a guilt which had earned the most exemplary punishment, there arose a sentiment of pity, due to the impression that they were being sacrificed not for the welfare of the state but to the ferocity of a single man.[19]

Here again, we have explicit non-Christian testimony to the origin and spread of Christianity. Even more important, this report of Tacitus provides firm historical evidence that Christians in Rome, only thirty years after the death of Christ, were being killed for their conviction that Jesus lived, died and rose again on their behalf.

A few writers have tried to attack the genuineness of this passage, but their arguments have generally fallen on unsympathetic ears. Consult the top classics authorities who deal with this issue (e.g., Oxford classicist and noted Tacitan specialist Henry Furneaux), and the conclusion is that the evidence is just too solid that this passage comes from the hand of Tacitus. Almost everyone (including Wells) admits the style is clearly "Tacitan Latin." Further, since the passage does not speak kindly of the Christians, there is no possible motive for anyone other than Tacitus to have written it.

Wells tries to attack the passage from a different angle. He argues that Tacitus' statement about Jesus has no historical value since he is probably only repeating information which he got from the Christians themselves. Since the life of Jesus, according to Wells, was only a legend, the Christians reported to Tacitus as historical fact what was only a legend.

Wells gives three supporting lines of evidence.

1. He says Tacitus "gives Pilate a title, 'procurator,' which was current only from the second half of the first century." (WeG.HE 16) But if this information came from the Christians, why does Tacitus, in *Annate* 4.5, call Lucilius Capito "procurator" when he too was in office prior to the name change? He also calls the emperor "imperitante," which Tacitus, being a senator, would have known was not the proper title of past emperors. Tacitus was merely using current terms of his day to make clear for the readers of his day what positions the various individuals held.

2. Wells says that if Tacitus got his information from official records, he would have called Jesus by his name, not by the title "Christ." But if Tacitus had said "Jesus," he would need additional information to explain how Jesus is related to the Christians; Furneaux states that "Christus," as a name, would be "the appropriate one to use here, as explaining 'Christianus.'" (FuH.A 374) In fact, if Tacitus had received his information from Christians, they would be more likely to use "Jesus" or possibly "Christ Jesus" as a more intimate reference. Tacitus may have been further motivated to use "Christus" if it was common knowledge that the Jews had "ancient oracles that a conquering Messiah would arise." (GiE.D 1:603) The use of the term "Christus" would be more likely to kindle public displeasure with the Christians.

3. Wells states that Tacitus "was surely glad to accept from Christians their own view that Christianity was of recent origin, since the Roman authorities were prepared to tolerate only ancient cults." (WeG.HE 17) Wells is trying to argue that Tacitus just accepted from the Christians that Christ died under Pontius Pilate during the reign of Tiberius.

But there are many reasons for believing that Tacitus had information other than what he heard from Christians.

1. He makes his statement about the death of Christ as a historical fact, not as something someone else said was true.

2. As mentioned in the previous chapter, both Justin[20] and Tertullian[21] challenged their readers to go read for themselves the official secular documents substantiating certain details of Jesus' life.

3. Being a Roman senator, Tacitus certainly must have had access to the best records available in the Roman Empire at the time.

4. In *Annals* 4.10, where Tacitus refutes a particular rumor, he says that he has reported from "the most numerous and trustworthy authorities." In 4.57 he says, "I have followed the majority of historians."

5. Tacitus is careful to record conflicts in his sources. In 15.38 he speaks of conflicting versions as to the source of the great fire of Rome.

6. Tacitus does not quote his sources uncritically. In *Annals* 4.57 he questions the majority report of the historians. In 15.53 he considers Pliny's statement absurd, and in 13.20 he notes Fabius Rusticus' bias. B. Walker comments that Tacitus "was a persistent skeptic towards popular rumor, even when a rumor coincided with this own prejudices" and cites *Annals* 2.68 as an example. (WaB.AT 142)

7. Tacitus hedges his opinion when others do not.[22]

8. Tacitus distinguishes between rumor and fact by using expressions such as, "Some have put it on record"; or "As the general account goes."[23] He also uses terms such as "It is said" and "They say" when he does not want to vouch for a statement's reliability.[24] Maurice Goguel, former Professor of Theology in the University of Paris, notes that the absence of words such as "it is said" in *Annals* 15.44 (the passage about Christ) should cause us to believe that Tacitus' source was a document. He states: "One fact is certain, and that is, Tacitus knew of a document, which was neither Jewish nor Christian, which connected Christianity with the Christ crucified by Pontius Pilate." (GoM.JN 40)

9. Finally, even if Tacitus had made no independent statement at all about the person of Christ, he still records the fact that men and women living thirty years after Jesus was crucified were willing to die for their belief that Jesus had lived just thirty years earlier. Some of them, for example Peter, had even heard, seen, talked and walked with him. And, as J. N. D. Anderson, the former Professor of Oriental Laws in the University of London, has remarked:

> It is scarcely fanciful to suggest that when he adds that "a most mischievous superstition, thus checked for the moment, again broke out," he is bearing indirect and unconscious testimony to the conviction of the early church that the Christ who had been crucified had risen from the grave. (AnJ.CTW 19)

HADRIAN

In the reign of Hadrian (AD 117–138), Serenius Granianus, proconsul of Asia, wrote to the emperor asking for his advice in handling charges against the Christians. He was probably experiencing the same problems that Pliny had mentioned. Christians, in the zeal of their newfound relationship with the risen Jesus, were leading others to Christ and away from the pagan cult practices. That hit certain tradesmen such as silversmiths right where it hurt the most—the pocketbook. As a result, Christians often found themselves in court for no other reason than following a god not approved by the state. Hadrian wrote back to Granianus' successor, Minucius Fundanus. His letter, preserved by Eusebius, is another piece of evidence confirming the same things Pliny had recorded:

> I do not wish, therefore, that the matter should be passed by without examination, so that these men may neither be harassed, nor opportunity of malicious proceedings be offered to informers. If, therefore, the provincials can clearly evince their charges against the Christians, so as to answer before the tribunal, let them pursue this course only, but not by mere petitions, and mere outcries against the Christians. For it is far more proper, if any one would bring an accusation, that you should examine it.[25]

SUETONIUS

In approximately AD 50, the apostle Paul arrived in Corinth. Acts 18:2 records that he found there "a certain Jew named Aquila, a native of Pontus, having come from Italy with his wife Priscilla, because Claudius had commanded all the Jews to leave Rome." By the apparent spiritual maturity of Aquila and Priscilla, which is observable in Acts 18:26, it seems they had been Christians already while in Rome prior to AD 49. That is the date when Claudius expelled all Jews from Rome.

Suetonius, another Roman historian and annalist of the Imperial House, wrote in approximately AD 120, "As the Jews were making constant disturbances at the instigation of Chrestus, he expelled them from Rome."[26]

Who is "Chrestus"? There has been some debate over this question since Chrestus seems to have been a fairly common name, especially among slaves. But there are several clues which indicate that Chrestus was probably a misspelling of "Christ" (Greek "Christus"):

> First, Chrestus is a *Greek* name. Of course many Jews did have Greek names, whether from birth or assumed later (e.g., Jesus' Galilean disciples, Andrew and Philip, and all seven of the "deacons" appointed in Acts 6:5, only one of whom is said to be a proselyte), but Chrestus is not otherwise known as a Jewish name.[27]

> And secondly Chrestus would sound very like Christus, which, with its meaning "anointed," would be unfamiliar in the Gentile world, so that a substitution of the familiar Greek name Chrestus would be easily made. Indeed, Tertullian points out that the opponents of Christianity, by mispronouncing the name as "Chrestianus," in fact testified to its "sweetness and kindness"! (FrR.E 41)

Another clue surfaces in the remainder of Acts 18 where Aquila and Priscilla are involved with Paul in his mission of "testifying to the Jews that Jesus was the Christ." Many of the Jews reacted bitterly, and if the rest of the book of Acts is typical of those times, it is likely that Aquila and Priscilla were involved in a similar controversy back in Rome in AD 49. The Christian Jews witnessing to the other Jews probably resulted in the hostilities which led to the expulsion of all Jews from Rome. The recorder of the police report would have been told that the violence was at the instigation of "Christus." But since he had never heard of "Christus," he wrote down "Chrestus," the common name familiar to him. Seventy years later, when Suetonius consulted the record, he faithfully recorded what he found. This record, then, and Suetonius' report of it, verify that within sixteen to twenty years of the death of Jesus, Jewish Christians from Judea were telling other Jews in Rome about his life, death and resurrection.

Suetonius also confirms the report of Tacitus regarding the great fire of Rome. In his *Life of Nero* Suetonius reports that after the fire, "Punishment was inflicted on the Christians, a body of people addicted to a novel and mischievous superstition."[28] Once again, a non-Christian secular source verifies that there were men and women in Rome only thirty years after the death of Christ who were being put to death for their conviction that Jesus had lived, died and risen from the dead.

LUCIAN OF SAMOSATA

Writing c. AD 170, the Greek satirist Lucian wrote of the early Christians and of "their lawgiver." The hostile nature of his testimony makes it all the more valuable:

> The Christians, you know, worship a man to this day—the distinguished personage who introduced their novel rites, and was crucified on that account.... You see, these misguided creatures start with the general conviction that they are immortal for all time, which explains the contempt of death and voluntary self-devotion which are so common among them; and then it was impressed on them by their original lawgiver that they are all brothers, from the moment that they are converted, and deny the gods of Greece, and worship the crucified sage, and live after his laws. All this they take quite on faith, with the result that they despise all worldly goods alike, regarding them merely as common property.[29]

Lucian also mentions the Christians several times in his *Alexander the False Prophet*, sections 25 and 29.

MARA BAR-SERAPION

Sometime after AD 70, a Syrian, probably a Stoic philosopher, wrote from prison to his son. In an effort to encourage his son to pursue wisdom, he mused:

> What advantage did the Athenians gain from putting Socrates to death? Famine and plague came upon them as a judgment for their crime. What

advantage did the men of Samos gain from burning Pythagoras? In a moment their land was covered with sand. What advantage did the Jews gain from executing their wise King? It was just after that that their kingdom was abolished. God justly avenged these three wise men: The Athenians died of hunger; the Samians were overwhelmed by the sea; the Jews, ruined and driven from their land, live in complete dispersion. But Socrates did not die for good; he lived on in the teaching of Plato. Pythagoras did not die for good; he lived on in the statue of Hera. Nor did the wise King die for good; he lived on in the teaching which he had given. [30]

The value of this letter's attestation to historical facts is lessened by the fact that Mara Bar-Serapion could have gained his information from Christian tradition (which does not necessarily mean it is wrong) and by the fact that his information about Athens and Samos is inaccurate. But the letter could be as early as the first century and its writer is definitely not a Christian since he refers, at another place, to "our gods" and puts Jesus on equal ground with Socrates and Pythagoras. Also, he has Jesus living on in his teaching rather than in his resurrection. He does seem to have been influenced by Gentile Christians since he blames "the Jews" for "executing their wise king." But then even the Jewish John, Jesus' disciple, repeatedly used "the Jews" to refer to particular Jewish groups or leaders, most of whom opposed Jesus, but some also who marveled at Jesus, and others who were indifferent.

We'll not take our survey of non-Christian references beyond AD 200. In the previous chapter we saw how unlikely it is that any non-Christian writer should have referred to Jesus or his followers. The evidence of this chapter indicates that the message of Jesus' actual life, death and resurrection must have begun to spread across the Roman Empire immediately after Jesus' crucifixion, for non-Christian writers were reporting its effects within nineteen to thirty years of its commission.

3

REFERENCES FROM THE RABBIS

Rabbinics is the study of commentary by Jewish rabbis on the Old Testament Scriptures. It includes commentary on commentary of the Scriptures. As various rabbis commented on Scripture or on another rabbi's commentary, they occasionally referred to people and events of their own times. One of the individuals to whom the rabbis referred was Jesus. This chapter documents both reliable and some unreliable historical references to Jesus in the rabbinic writings.

Rabbinics can be a fascinating field to explore for students of both the Old and New Testaments. However, it is not an easy field of study. R. T. France warns:

> To search in Rabbinic literature for data on any historical subject is a daunting task. The sheer bulk of the literature, its baffling complexity and (to us) lack of logical structure, its complicated oral and literary history and the consequent uncertainty about the date of the traditions it preserves, all this makes it an uninviting area for most non-Jewish readers. Add to this the fact that history as such is not its concern, so that tidbits of "historical" information occur only as illustrations of abstruse legal and theological arguments, often without enough detail to make it clear what historical situation is in view, and the task seems hopeless. In the case of evidence for Jesus we have the further complicating factor that he was, for the Rabbis, a heretical teacher and sorcerer, whose name could scarcely be used without defilement, with the result that many scholars believe that they referred to him by pseudonyms (e.g., Ben Stada, or Balaam) or by vague expressions like "so-and-so." (FrR.E 32-33)

WRITINGS OF THE RABBIS

In order to accurately understand the implications of rabbinic references to Jesus, it is important to first get a feel for the various divisions of literature produced by the rabbis. As we walk through the following introductory material, you may wish to refer to this chart. It should help put the pieces together.

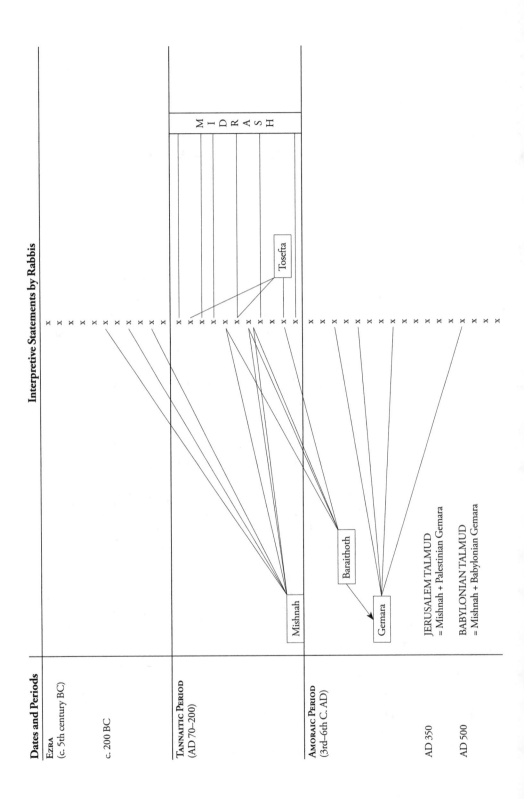

Interpretive Statements by Rabbis

Dates and Periods

Ezra
(c. 5th century BC)

c. 200 BC

Tannaitic Period
(AD 70–200)

M
I
D
R
A
S
H

Tosefta

Mishnah

Baraithoth

Gemara

Amoraic Period
(3rd–6th C. AD)

AD 350

AD 500

JERUSALEM TALMUD
= Mishnah + Palestinian Gemara

BABYLONIAN TALMUD
= Mishnah + Babylonian Gemara

From about the time of Ezra, following the rebuilding of the walls of Jerusalem, various priest-scribes and rabbis began to comment on the meaning of scriptural passages. Nehemiah 8:7,8 names various individuals who, along with the Levites and under Ezra's direction, "explained the Law to the people" and "read from the book, from the Law of God, translating to give the sense so that they understood the reading." Generation after generation, this teaching was memorized and passed on word for word in an unbroken oral tradition. And with each succeeding generation, the interpretations of their own rabbis were added to the ever-growing tradition.

By Jesus' day, the quantity of detailed prescriptions and proscriptions had become unbelievably vast, especially when you consider that it was still being conveyed not by writing, but by memory! This was the "tradition of the elders" to which the New Testament refers.[1] These interpretations of the Law were considered just as authoritative as the Law itself and would prompt Jesus to say, "You nicely set aside the commandment of God in order to keep your tradition."[2] It must have been such a time-consuming task for students of the law to memorize all the rabbinic interpretations of it, that little time was left to practice it. Perhaps this was one reason Jesus challenged the scribes saying, "You weigh men down with burdens hard to bear, while you yourselves will not even touch the burdens with one of your fingers."[3] In agreement with Jesus, Ezra's original practice had been to "set his heart to study the law of the Lord, *and to practice it*, and to teach His statutes and ordinances in Israel."[4]

When Jerusalem and the Temple fell in AD 70, Pharisees from the school of Hillel feared that Israel might lose her traditions and unity. With Roman permission, they established their headquarters in Jamnia almost directly west of Jerusalem, close to the Mediterranean coast. There they reformed the Sanhedrin, and Yohanan ben Zakkai became its new president. Their primary task was to put their oral tradition in written form. Rabbi Akiba succeeded in arranging it by subject matter but was tortured to death after the rebellion of his "Messiah," ben-Kosiba (popularly known as bar-Kokhba), was crushed by the Romans in AD 135. Akiba's pupil, Rabbi Meir, revised and continued his work. Finally, around AD 200, Rabbi Judah the Patriarch finished the compilation of what we know today as the Mishnah.

Literally, *Mishnah* means "teaching" or "repetition." The material in it is divided into six *Sedarim,* each *Seder* covering the teaching on a particular subject. The six main subjects are agriculture, feasts, women, damages, hallowed things and cleanness. Each Seder is divided into smaller sections called *tractates.*[5] Each tractate is divided into chapters containing "sections," with each section being somewhat longer than a Bible verse.

Parallel to Mishnah is *Midrash.* Its name comes from the verb *darash* meaning "to seek, explore or interpret." Midrash is more of a running commentary on Scripture, whereas Mishnah may teach certain interpretations independent of their scriptural basis. There are two kinds of Midrash: *Halakhah,* more legislative, and *Haggadah,* more inspirational in approach. These same terms are often used to describe the kind of material in the Mishnah, almost all of which would be called *halakhic.*

Another body of material, comprised of commentary from the Tannaitic period not selected for the Mishnah, is called *Tosefta*, meaning "addition" or "supplement." These teachings expand or give parallel versions of sayings presented in the Mishnah.

The period from AD 70 to 200 is designated the Tannaitic period. The name comes from the *Tanna'im* or "repeaters" of the material codified in the Mishnah and Tosefta. During the Tannaitic period, more traditions were produced which were outside of or external to the Mishnah. These traditions were known as *Baraithoth* (singular, *Baraitha*) and were preserved in the *Gemara* (commentary on the Mishnah) of the Amoraic period.

The Amoraic period consists of the third through the sixth centuries AD. The teachers of this period, called Amoraim, produced commentary on the Mishnah known as *Gemara*. The name comes from the Hebrew *gemar*, meaning "to finish." There were two independent schools of Amoraim during this period: one in Babylonia; one in Palestine. About AD 350–425, the Palestinian school compiled its Mishnah (Tannaitic Period) and Gemara (Amoraic Period) into the Palestinian or Jerusalem Talmud. The other school, existing in Babylonia, allowed its commentary on the Mishnah to continue expanding until c. AD 500. At that time, its Mishnah and Gemara were brought together to form the Babylonian Talmud, a much larger collection than the Palestinian Talmud. The literal meaning of *Talmud* is "learning."

Out of the vast body of rabbinic commentary, both Christian and Jewish scholars agree that there are several passages which unambiguously refer to Jesus. This fact is rather exceptional in view of several important observations.

First, only a small number of manuscript copies of the ancient Talmud are extant. The church must bear a good deal of responsibility for this situation. In her persecutions of the Jews, the church often confiscated Jewish manuscripts and destroyed them by fire.

Second, in light of the persecutions, the Jewish communities imposed censorship on themselves to remove references to Jesus in their writings so that they might no longer be a target of attack. Morris Goldstein, former Professor of Old and New Testament Literature at the Pacific School of Religion, relates:

> Thus, in 1631 the Jewish Assembly of Elders in Poland declared: "We enjoin you under the threat of the great ban to publish in no new edition of the Mishnah or the Gemara anything that refers to Jesus of Nazareth.... If you will not diligently heed this letter, but run counter thereto and continue to publish our books in the same manner as heretofore, you might bring over us and yourselves still greater sufferings than in previous times."

> At first, deleted portions of words in printed Talmuds were indicated by small circles or blank spaces but, in time, these too were forbidden by the censors.

As a result of the twofold censorship the usual volumes of Rabbinic literature contain only a distorted remnant of supposed allusions to Jesus. (GoMo.
JJT 4)

Third, the rabbis during the "Second Temple Period" were not prone to mentioning
events and people of this period unless they were highly relevant to a Scripture or commentary being expounded. The noted Jewish scholar Joseph Klausner, not a Christian
and writing primarily to the Jewish people, explains:

> The Talmud authorities on the whole refer rarely to the events of the period
> of the Second Temple, and do so only when the events are relevant to some
> halakhic discussion, or else they mention them quite casually in the course
> of some haggada. What, for example, should we have known of the great
> Maccabaean struggle against the kings of Syria if the apocryphal books,
> I and II Maccabees, and the Greek writings of Josephus had not survived,
> and we had been compelled to derive all our information about this great
> event in the history of Israel from the Talmud alone? We should not have
> known even the very name of Judas Maccabaeus! (KlJ.JN 19)

Since Jesus lived during the Second Temple Period, the references to him are all
the more noteworthy.

Fourth, in light of the Roman oppression of the Jewish nation, the appearance of Jesus
was relatively unimportant to the rabbis. Again from the Jewish scholar Klausner:

> The appearance of Jesus during the period of disturbance and confusion
> which befell Judaea under the Herods and the Roman Procurators, was so
> inconspicuous an event that the contemporaries of Jesus and of his first
> disciples hardly noticed it; and by the time that Christianity had become a
> great and powerful sect the "Sages of the Talmud" were already far removed
> from the time of Jesus. (KlJ.JN 19)

The factors above, along with other reasons, influence how historically reliable a
statement about Jesus in the rabbinic literature might be. Therefore, in the following
two sections, we give first some of the unreliable historical references to Jesus followed
by those considered to be reliable.

UNRELIABLE REFERENCES TO JESUS

Almost all passages referring to Jesus that originated later than the Tannaitic time
period we designate as unreliable. There are many such passages, but in the Amoraic
Period they primarily refer to Jesus in Christian doctrine, not Jesus in his historical
existence. Some late passages could preserve early testimony, but generally this cannot
be demonstrated to be true. Below are specific references usually recognized as unreliable in telling us anything about the historical Jesus. It can be said, however, that these

passages do continue to speak of Jesus as a historical person even though the details given may be far from accurate. In other words, they once again demonstrate that the existence of Jesus was never questioned in ancient times.

References to "Ben Stada"

For centuries Christians and others felt that the "Ben Stada" passages referred to Jesus. As a result they often criticized Jews for the comments which supposedly referred negatively to Jesus. It now seems clear that Ben Stada was not Jesus, but the Egyptian mentioned in Acts 21:38. There the Roman commander says to Paul, "Then you are not the Egyptian who some time ago stirred up a revolt and led the four thousand men of the assassins out into the wilderness?" Josephus says this Egyptian arose just after Felix was made procurator of Judea in AD 52:

> Moreover, there came out of Egypt about this time to Jerusalem, one that said he was a prophet, and advised the multitude of the common people to go along with him to the Mount of Olives, as it was called, which lay over against the city, and at the distance of five furlongs. He said further, that he would shew them from hence, how, at his command, the walls of Jerusalem would fall down; and he promised them that he would procure them an entrance into the city through those walls, when they were fallen down. Now when Felix was informed of these things, he ordered his soldiers to take their weapons, and came against them with a great number of horsemen and footmen, from Jerusalem, and attacked the Egyptian and the people that were with him. He also slew four hundred of them, and took two hundred alive. But the Egyptian himself escaped out of the fight, but did not appear any more.[6]

Obviously the Egyptian was not Jesus! But the following passage from the Babylonian Talmud, Shabbath 1046, confuses the two:

> "He who cuts upon his flesh." It is a Baraitha tradition: Rabbi Eliezer said to the Sages, "Did not Ben Stada bring sorcery from Egypt in a cut upon his flesh?" They answered him, "He was a madman, and we do not adduce proof from mad persons." Ben Stada? He was Ben Pandera! (Variant spellings of this name include Pantira, Pantera, Panthera, Pantiri, and Panteri.) Rab Hisda said, "The husband was Stada; the lover, Pandera." Was not the husband Pappos ben Yehudah; his mother, Stada? His mother was Miriam, a women's hairdresser. As they say in Pumbeditha, "*Stath da* (this one strayed) from her husband."

Since the Tanna'im never identify Ben Stada with Jesus or Ben Pandera, scholars have concluded that Rab Hisda and other Amoraim confused the Egyptian (or Ben Stada) with Jesus. In fact, even "Rabbenu Tarn (Shabbath 1046) declared that this was not Jesus of Nazareth." (KIJ.JN 20) Klausner shows that the unreliable nature of the

Amoraim may be seen in the above text in that (1) they confuse Pappos ben Yehudah (a contemporary of Akiba just before AD 135) with the father of Jesus; (2) they confuse Mary Magdalene with Mary, the mother of Jesus, by calling Jesus' mother a women's hairdresser (Hebrew, *m'gadd'la n'shaya*); and (3) they equate Stada with *s'tathda,* meaning "gone astray," and apply the name to Mary, the mother of Jesus. Since none of the Tannaitic passages equate Ben Stada with Jesus or Ben Pantera, and since the Amoraic passages are unreliable, then none of the Ben Stada passages can be reliable historical references to Jesus.

References to Balaam

Several passages seem to refer to Jesus by using the name Balaam. According to Klausner, the reference to Jesus as Balaam became so accepted among Jewish scholars as to no longer require proof. This is no longer true. Consider the following passages from the Mishnah:

> Three kings and four commoners have no part in the world-to-come. Three kings are: Jereboam, Ahab and Manasseh.... Four commoners are: Balaam, Doeg, Ahitophel and Gehazi. (M. Sanhedrin 10, 2) [RS]

> The disciples of Balaam the wicked shall inherit Gehenna and go down to the pit of destruction, as it is said: "Men of blood and deceit shall not live out half their days." (M. Aboth 5, 19) [RS]

There is no reason to equate Balaam with Jesus in these passages since: (1) There was no reason for the compilers of the Mishnah to conceal Jesus' identity if they were speaking of him. (2) Whenever the rabbis did wish to conceal Jesus' identity they used the term "such-an-one." (3) Balaam was not an Israelite, but Jesus was. (4) If Balaam is a cover name for someone, it could apply to many others as well. It does not specifically single out Jesus. (5) Some of the passages which equate Balaam with Jesus are late and therefore are unreliable as historical references to Jesus.

The main reason Balaam cannot be Jesus, though, is that some passages have both Jesus and Balaam within them as two separate individuals. Consider the following late Tannaitic passage:

> R. Eliezer ha-Kappar said: God gave strength to his (Balaam's) voice so that it went from one end of the world to the other, because he looked forth and beheld the nations that bow down to the sun and moon and stars, and to wood and stone, and he looked forth and saw that there was a man, born of a woman, who should rise up and seek to make himself God, and to cause the whole world to go astray. Therefore God gave power to the voice of Balaam that all the peoples of the world might hear, and thus he spake: Give heed that ye go not astray after that man, for it is written, "God is not man that he should lie." And if he says that he is God, he is a liar; and he will deceive and say that he departed and cometh again at the end. He

saith and he shall not perform. See what is written: And he took up his parable and said, "Alas, who shall live when God doeth this." Balaam said, Alas, who shall live—of what nation which heareth that man who hath made himself God.[7]

Rabbi Eliezer ha-Kappar died c. AD 260, so his statement's value in attesting historically to Jesus is restricted. But it does show that in the late Tannaitic and early Amoraic periods, when there would have been greater reason to use a pseudonym for Jesus, the name Balaam referred to someone else. In the Babylonian Talmud, a passage probably from the Amoraic Period (although Klausner puts it earlier) makes it even clearer:

> The story is told of "Onkelos son of Kalonymos, son of Titus' sister," that he wished to become a proselyte. He first called up Titus by means of spells. Titus advised him not to become a proselyte because Israel had so many commandments and commandments hard to observe; rather would he advise him to oppose them. Onkelos then called up Balaam, who said to him in his rage against Israel, "Seek not their peace nor their good." Not till then did he go and "raise up Jesus by spells and say to him: What is the most important thing in the world? He said to him, Israel. He asked, And how if I should join myself with them? He said to him, Seek their good and do not seek their harm; everyone that hurteth them is as if he hurt the apple of God's eye. He then asked, And what is the fate of that man? he said to him, Boiling filth. A Baraita has said: Everyone that scoffeth against the words of the wise is condemned to boiling filth. Come and see what there is between the transgressors in Israel and the prophets of the nations of the world."[8]

The Story of the Impudent One

> "An impudent one." R. Eliezer holds that this means a bastard, while R. Yehoshua says that it is a "son of uncleanness" [ben *niddah;* see Lev. xv. 32]; R. Akiba holds that it is both the one and the other. The elders were once sitting [at the gate]. Two children passed before them, one covered his head and the other uncovered his head. The one who uncovered his head, R. Elizer calls a "bastard," R. Eliezer, "son of uncleanness," and R. Akiba, "bastard and son of uncleanness." They asked R. Akiba, How do you dare to contradict the findings of your colleagues? He said to them, I will prove what I say. He went to the mother of the child and saw her sitting and selling peas in the market. He said to her, My daughter, if you tell me what I ask, I will bring thee to the life of the world to come. She said to him, Swear it to me. R. Akiba swore with his lips but disavowed it in his heart. He said to her, What is the nature of this thy son? She answered, When I entered the bridal chamber I was in my uncleanness and my husband remained apart from me and my groomsman came in unto me and I had this son. The child was thus both a bastard and a "son of uncleanness." Then said

they, Great was R. Akiba who put his teachers to shame. At the selfsame hour they said, Blessed be the Lord God of Israel, who revealed his secret to R. Akiba ben Yosef.[9]

This passage only occurs in two tractates which were put together at a very late period and which contain "many accretions which were then either new in substance or corrupt in form." (KIJ.JN 31) Also, since R. Akiba was put to death by the Romans in AD 135, there is no way that he would have been a respected rabbi when Jesus was just a child!

Toledoth Yeshu

"Toledoth Yeshu" means "Life of Jesus." It is a booklet which "intends to narrate the story of Jesus." (GoMoJ.JT 147) It may have been first put together as early as the fifth century AD. The story speaks of Jesus, an illegitimate and impudent child, learning "the Ineffable Name" in the temple, writing it on a slip of paper which he sews into the flesh of his thigh, by it performing many miracles, and attracting a following. The sages of Israel then got "Yehuda Iskarioto," one of their own, to learn "the Ineffable Name" and come against Jesus with signs and wonders including a battle in the sky where Yehuda flies higher than Jesus and defiles him so that he falls to the earth. There are many more wild adventures, but eventually Jesus is arrested and hanged on the eve of Passover on a cabbage stem. After his body is buried, a gardener removes it and throws it into a water channel. The disciples, finding Jesus' body missing, begin to proclaim the resurrection. But Rabbi Tanchuma (who in actual history lived four hundred years after Jesus!) finds the body and reveals the hoax. The disciples flee and take their religion all over the world. Shimeon Kepha (Peter) ends up living in a tower built for him (the church of St. Peter in Rome) where he composes hymns and songs to send all over the world. We need only quote Klausner's evaluation:

> The most superficial reading of this book serves to prove that we have here nothing beyond a piece of folklore, in which are confusedly woven early and late Talmudic and Midrashic legends and sayings concerning Jesus, together with Gospel accounts (which the author to the Tol'doth perverts in a fashion derogatory to Jesus), and other popular legends, many of which are mentioned by Celsus, and Tertullian and later Church Fathers, and which Samuel Krauss labels a "folkloristische Motive." Specially noticeable is the attitude adopted by the Tol'doth to the Gospel accounts. Scarcely ever does it deny anything: it merely changes evil to good and good to evil. (KIJ.JN 51; parentheses are Klausner's)

RELIABLE HISTORICAL REFERENCES TO JESUS

"On the Eve of Passover They Hanged Yeshu"

> It has been taught: On the eve of Passover they hanged Yeshu. And an announcer went out, in front of him, for forty days (saying): "He is going

to be stoned, because he practiced sorcery and enticed and led Israel astray. Anyone who knows anything in his favor, let him come and plead in his behalf." But, not having found anything in his favor, they hanged him on the eve of Passover.[10]

The Munich manuscript of this baraitha (from the AD 70–200 period) reads: "Yeshu the Nazarene." "Yeshu" translates through Greek to English as "Jesus." Says Morris Goldstein, "The exaction of the death penalty on the eve of Passover is strong verification that Jesus, the Christ of Christianity is meant." (GoMo.JJT 25)

The word *hanged* also referred to crucifixion. Both Luke 23:39 and Galatians 3:13 use it this way. This baraitha also agrees with John 19:14 in putting the crucifixion "on the eve of Passover." But why were Jewish authorities "hanging" Jesus rather than stoning him as their law prescribed? The best explanation is that the word *hanged* attests to the historicity of Jesus' crucifixion under the Romans.

This passage is significant because of what it does not deny. First, it does not deny Jewish involvement in Jesus' death. In fact, it does not even mention the Romans. Rather, it seeks to demonstrate that the Jewish authorities carried out the sentencing, albeit justifying the manner in which it was done. The result is a clear affirmation of the historicity of Jesus and his death. Second, this passage does not deny that Jesus performed miracles. Rather, it tries to explain them away as being accomplished through sorcery or magic. The same response to Jesus' miracles is reported in Mark 3:22 and Matthew 9:34; 12:24. Once again, there is a clear affirmation of the historicity of Jesus, and this time of his miracles as well.

This passage also affirms that Jesus gathered a following among the Jewish people saying that he "enticed and led Israel astray." The forty days may only be an apologetic device designed to deny that the trial was a speedy one. But it could possibly be related to an official announcement that Jesus was being sought by the authorities. John 8:58-59 and 10:31-33,39 indicate that the Jewish leaders were seeking to arrest him for some time before the crucifixion.

Following the baraitha, Ulla, the late third-century Amora, comments:

> Would you believe that any defence would have been so zealously sought for him? He was a deceiver, and the All-merciful says: "You shall not spare him, neither shall you conceal him." It was different with Jesus, for he was near to the kingship.

The phrase, "near to the kingship," has been taken either as a reference to Jesus' genealogical descent from David or possibly a reference to Pilate's symbolic washing of his hands before turning Jesus over to be crucified.

"Yeshu Had Five Disciples"

Also in Sanhedrin 43a, immediately after the first baraitha concerning Jesus, is another baraitha about him:

> Our rabbis taught: Yeshu had five disciples—Mattai, Nakkai, Netzer, Buni, and Todah.

Then follows a late Amoraic addition of several centuries after the baraitha. The commentary is filled with puns on the five names, and is so detached from historical reality that virtually no scholar accepts the story line as reliable. The baraitha, however, originating somewhere between AD 70 and 200 is accepted as a reliable reference to Jesus and his disciples. Except for Mattai with Matthew, it would be hard to identify the names given with the names of disciples in the gospel accounts. That Jesus only has five disciples could be explained by the fact that other teachers in the Talmud, viz. Yohanan ben Zakkai and Akiba, are also described as having five disciples or students. "In any event," says Goldstein, "we have here an early passage naming Jesus and his five disciples." (GoMo.JJT 32)

Healing in the Name of Yeshua ben Pantera

> It happened with R. Elazar ben Damah, whom a serpent bit, that Jacob, a man of Kefar Soma, came to heal him in the name of Yeshua ben Pantera; but R. Ishmael did not let him. He said, "You are not permitted, Ben Damah." He answered, "I will bring you proof that he may heal me." But he had no opportunity to bring proof, for he died. (Whereupon) R. Ishmael said, "Happy art thou, Ben Damah, for you have gone in peace and you have not broken down the fence of the Sages; since everyone who breaks down the fence of the Sages, to him punishment will ultimately come, as it is in Scripture: 'Whoso breaketh through a fence, a serpent shall bite him.'"[11]

This and other passages refer to Jesus as "ben Pantera." Scholars have debated at length how Jesus came to have this name attached to his. Strauss thought it was from the Greek word *pentheros,* meaning "son-in-law." Klausner and Bruce accept the position that *panthera* is a corruption of the Greek *parthenos* meaning "virgin." Klausner says, "The Jews constantly heard that the Christians (the majority of whom spoke Greek from the earliest times) called Jesus by the name 'Son of the Virgin,'…and so, in mockery, they called him *Ben ha-Pantera,* i.e., 'son of the leopard.'" (KlJ.JN 23)

The theory most sensational but least accepted by serious scholars was dramatized by the discovery of a first-century tombstone at Bingerbruck, Germany. The inscription read, "Tiberius Julius Abdes Pantera, an archer, native of Sidon, Phoenicia, who in 9 C.E. was transferred to service in Germany." (DeA.LAE 73-74) This discovery fueled the fire of the theory that Jesus was the illegitimate son of Mary and the soldier, Panthera. Even Origen writes that his opponent, Celsus, in c. AD 178, said that he heard from a Jew that "Miriam" had become pregnant by "Pantheras," a Roman soldier; was divorced by her husband, and bore Jesus in secret.[12]

If "Pantheras" were a unique name, the theory of Mary's pregnancy by the Roman soldier might be more attractive to scholars. But Adolf Deissmann, the early twentieth-century German New Testament scholar, verified, by first-century inscriptions, "with absolute certainty that Panthera was not an invention of Jewish scoffers, but a widespread name among the ancients." (DeA.LAE 73-74) Rabbi and Professor Morris Goldstein comments that it was as common as the names Wolf or Fox today. He comments further:

> It is noteworthy that Origen himself is credited with the tradition that Panther was the appellation of James (Jacob), the father of Joseph, the father of Jesus.... So, too, Andrew of Crete, John of Damascus, Epiphanius the Monk, and the author of *Andronicus of Constantinople's Dialogue Against the Jews,* name Panther as an ancestor of Jesus. (GoMo.JJT 38-39)

Jesus being called by his grandfather's name would also have agreed with a statement in the Talmud permitting this practice.[13] Whereas Christian tradition identified Jesus by his hometown, Jewish tradition, having a greater concern for genealogical identification, seems to have preferred this method of identifying Jesus. Goldstein presents more evidence to argue the case convincingly.

This passage indicates that teaching and healing were part of the ministry of Jesus' disciples, and therefore of Jesus' ministry as well. Notice the evidence of controversy between rabbis as to whether healing in Jesus' name might be permissible. The episode probably occurs in the early second century and indicates the widening separation of the Jewish authorities from Christian Jews. By AD 135, some Jewish Christians would come under harsh treatment for failing to support the rebellion of Israel's "Messiah," bar Kokhba.

This Tosefta passage supports the previous baraitha, which said Jesus "practiced sorcery," and it agrees with the New Testament narratives describing the Jewish response to the healing activity of Jesus and his disciples.

Jacob, Disciple of Jesus, as One of the Minim (Heretics)

> Our teachers have taught: When R. Eliezer {the Great} was arrested for *minuth* [heresy] they brought him to the tribunal for judgment. The Procurator said to him, Does an old man like you busy himself with such idle matters? He answered, I trust him that judges me. So the Procurator thought that he spoke of him, whereas he spoke of his heavenly father. The Procurator said to him, Since you trust in me you are *dimissus,* acquitted. When he returned home his disciples came in to console him, but he would not accept their consolations. R. Akiba said to him, Suffer me to tell you one thing of what you have taught me. He answered, (Say on). He said, Perhaps {a word of} *minuth* [heresy] came upon you and pleased you and therefore you were arrested. (Tosefta reads: Perhaps one of the *Minim* [heretics] had said to thee a word of *minuth* and it pleased thee?) He answered, Akiba, you have reminded me! Once I was walking along the upper market

(Tosefta reads "street") of Sepphoris and found one {of the disciples of Jesus of Nazareth} and Jacob of Kefar Sekanya (Tosefta reads "Sakkanin") was his name. He said to me, It is written in your Law, "Thou shalt not bring the hire of a harlot, etc." What was to be done with it—a latrine for the High Priest? But I answered nothing. He said to me, So {Jesus of Nazareth} taught me (Tosefta reads "Yeshu ben Pantere"): "For of the hire of a harlot hath she gathered them, and unto the hire of a harlot shall they return"; from the place of filth they come, and unto the place of filth they shall go. And the saying pleased me, and because of this I was arrested for *minuth* [heresy]. And I transgressed against what is written in the Law: "Keep thy way far from her"—that is *minuth;* "and come not nigh the door of her house"—that is the civil government.[14]

Klausner shows that Rabbi Eliezer was born by AD 40 or possibly 30. Therefore this baraitha had to originate very early in the Tannaitic Period (AD 70–200) and the disciple mentioned was one from either the first or second generation of Jesus' disciples. Below we quote Joseph Klausner. It is important to know that Klausner was not a Christian, and that as a Jewish scholar of the highest calibre, he wrote the monumental *Jesus of Nazareth* in Hebrew, and not for the pleasure of the outside world. He felt in this way he could ensure the highest objectivity. He wrote:

> In spite of M. Friedlander's various attempts to persuade us that "every Talmudist worthy of the name knows that the few Talmudic passages which speak of Jesus are a late addition," and "the Talmudic sources of the first century and the first quarter of the second afford not the least evidence of the existence of Jesus or Christianity"—in spite of this, there can be no doubt that the words, "one of the disciples of Jesus of Nazareth," and "thus Jesus of Nazareth taught me," are, in the present passage, both early in date and fundamental in their bearing on the story; and their primitive character cannot be disputed on the grounds of the slight variations in the parallel passages. (KIJ.JN 38)

Klausner accepts the conclusion that the arrest of R. Eliezer took place in AD 95 and that Eliezer was recalling his encounter with Jacob of Kefar Sekanya about AD 60. Jacob would have been around fifty or sixty years old by then if he had heard Jesus teach some thirty years previous to the meeting with Eliezer.

In the passage, R. Eliezer is taught by a disciple of Jesus (possibly James, Jesus' brother, according to Klausner), and the rabbi thought the teaching was pretty good. It "pleased" him. But in his old age he had come to regard the Christians as *minim*—false teachers, heretics or apostates. It is interesting that at one time Christians and Jews were able to enjoy conversation together despite their individual convictions about who Jesus was. As we saw earlier, Josephus also speaks of the high regard that the Jews had for James the brother of Jesus.

Also in support of the historicity of Jesus, Klausner answers a question that naturally surfaces concerning the content of this disciple's teaching:

> Certainly, at first sight, this exposition dealing with the hire of the harlot and the latrine does not accord with the character of Jesus' teachings as we know them from the Gospels: there we are accustomed to see him preach only about ethics and personal piety.... It is not only the Talmud which expounds Scripture in ways which, to our modern taste, are unseemly, but even Jesus, in the Gospels, speaks of human needs with a freeness unacceptable in these days: "Whatsoever goeth into the mouth passeth into the belly and is cast out into the draught" (Matthew 16.17); "Whatsoever entereth a man from without, cannot defile him; because it goeth not into his heart but into his belly and goeth out thence into the draught" (Mark 7:18-19). (KIJ.JN 43)

Such-an-One

> They asked R. Eliezer, "What of such-an-one as regards the world to come?" He said to them, "You have only asked me about such-an-one.... What of a bastard as touching inheritance?—What of him as touching the levirate duties? What of him as regards whitening his house?—What of him as regards whitening his grave?"—not because he evaded them by words, but because he never said a word which he had not heard from his teacher.[15]

This early Tannaitic passage, according to Klausner, does refer to Jesus since the term "such-an-one" is used for Jesus in the Amoraic Period. Some scholars think that R. Eliezer here affirms that Jesus will have a place in the world to come. The questions he asks those who first questioned him all have "Yes" answers indicating that his answer to them is, "Yes, Jesus will have a place in the world to come." Other scholars, however, think Eliezer is dodging their question.

Another passage shows once again the natural reaction of the opponents of Jesus and his disciples to their report of the virgin birth:

> R. Shimeon ben 'Azzai said: I found a genealogical roll in Jerusalem wherein was recorded, "Such-an-one is a bastard of an adulteress."[16]

If Mary was not pregnant by Joseph, then, the argument goes, she was pregnant by someone else—that is adultery—and Jesus was therefore illegitimate. Even in the New Testament, the scribes and Pharisees challenge Jesus about his birth: "We were not born of fornication..." implying that his birth was illegitimate.[17]

Perhaps Celsus (the opponent of Origen) got his information from a Jew quoting these words. The passage brings up some interesting questions. What did Joseph report on Jesus' birth record in the blank marked "father"? When did Joseph and Mary tell others of the miraculous birth?

That such-an-one refers to Jesus in this passage is commonly accepted among scholars. The passage seems pointless without a name, and such-an-one was a suitable cover for the name of Jesus when the church began to confiscate writings critical of Jesus.

The Historical Jesus According to Early Rabbis

Did the early Jewish rabbis think Jesus was a myth or a legend? Absolutely not. There is not a hint of a suggestion of this hypothesis, regardless of what some modern philosophers and theologians may conclude. According to Klausner, the earliest and most historically reliable rabbinic sources give us the following facts about who they thought Jesus was:

> that his name was Yeshu'a (Yeshu) of Nazareth; that he "practiced sorcery" (i.e., performed miracles, as was usual in those days) and beguiled and led Israel astray; that he mocked at the words of the Wise; that he expounded Scripture in the same manner as the Pharisees; that he had five disciples; that he said that he was not come to take aught away from the Law or to add to it; that he was hanged (crucified) as a false teacher and beguiler on the eve of the Passover which happened on a Sabbath; and that his disciples healed the sick in his name. (KlJ.JN 46; parentheses are Klausner's)

Klausner also concludes that the attitude of the earliest and most learned of the Tannaim toward Jesus and his teachings was not as bitter and hostile as that of the later rabbis. Though there is much in the rabbinic writings which speaks negatively of Jesus, the most revealing fact regarding these sources is that they everywhere confirm the historical existence of an extraordinary person, Jesus of Nazareth. France concludes:

> Uncomplimentary as it is, this is at least, in a distorted way, evidence for the impact Jesus' miracles and teaching made. The conclusion that it is entirely dependent on Christian claims, and that "Jews in the second century adopted uncritically the Christian assumption that he had really lived" is surely only dictated by a dogmatic skepticism. Such polemic, often using "facts" quite distinct from what Christians believed, is hardly likely to have arisen within less than a century around a non-existent figure. (FrR.E 39)

4

MARTYRS, CONFESSORS
AND EARLY CHURCH LEADERS

I n the first two centuries after Jesus' birth, things were somewhat different from today in much of the Western world. An atheist was someone who did not believe in the gods of the Roman Empire—the emperor being one of those gods. Other religions were tolerated from time to time, but inevitably they were subject to restriction and at times banishment. The Roman policy generally allowed other religions, especially in newly conquered lands, to practice their beliefs as long as they didn't cause problems for the Romans. The Christians, however, caused problems.

The Christians did not cause problems out of contempt or resistance, though. They had a different message for the world, and when Roman cultists were attracted to it, attendance at pagan temples decreased. Former cult members stopped buying statues of the pagan gods. They stopped buying and offering sacrifices to those gods. In some areas, as we saw earlier in the letter from Pliny the Younger, virtual economic crisis occurred. Sometimes those who rejected the Christian message aroused vehement opposition.

These and other disturbances motivated Roman authorities to do something about the Christians. Christians were rounded up and commanded to deny Christ, bow down to the gods of the Roman Empire, and burn incense to them. Christians who would not were tortured and put to death. Thousands were burned alive or fed to starved lions in the Colosseum at Rome, all for the "amusement" of the people. It is hard to imagine an arena full of high-class Romans cheering wildly, as at a spectator sport, while other human beings were being slaughtered, burned or torn apart before their eyes.

It began, of course, with the original apostles. Tradition tells us that many of Jesus' apostles and almost all of the New Testament writers were martyred for their faith. They chose death at the hands of persecutors rather than deny the facts of the life of Jesus which they were passing on to a new generation of Christians. Eusebius, considered to be generally accurate in what he reports, records the martyrdoms of Peter (crucified upside down), Paul (beheaded), James the brother of Jesus (stoned and clubbed), and James the brother of John (killed by the sword). Acts 12:2 is a much earlier source for the death of James the brother of John, and Josephus is a much earlier source for the death of James the brother of Jesus. Tradition holds that Thomas was killed by a spear and that Thaddeus was put to death by arrows. Bartholomew is reported to have been flayed alive and crucified upside down. Tradition from the fourth century holds Luke to be a martyr. Other tradition has Mark dying a martyr's death in the eighth year of Nero. John is reported to have been boiled in oil but miraculously survived.

For Christians, however, suffering through tragedy actually became an opportunity which eventually secured victory for Christianity over the entire Roman Empire. The martyrdom, torture and threats of death suffered by Christians actually attracted others to the Christian faith. Those who witnessed their peaceful surrender to, and in some cases eager anticipation of, suffering for Jesus were confronted with the reality of what it meant to know the true God personally. Historian Philip Schaff states:

> The final victory of Christianity over Judaism and heathenism, and the mightiest empire of the ancient world, a victory gained without physical force but by the moral power of patience and perseverance, of faith and love, is one of the sublimest spectacles in history, and one of the strongest evidences of the divinity and indestructible life of our religion. (ScP.HCC 2:8)

It does not appear to have been a conscious realization at the time, but the willing suffering of the Christians also verified for succeeding generations their solid conviction that the writings and oral testimony passed to them about Jesus were the truth.

Though Christianity spread rapidly among the uneducated, some of the greatest academic minds in history also were attracted to Jesus during that time. Surely the question uppermost in their minds as they considered the claims of Jesus' birth, miracles, teaching, death and resurrection had to be, *Did these things truly happen?* To understand how these educated Christians answered that question for their generation, and for those to follow, we need some background. Let's look at both weaknesses and strengths of the post-apostolic writers, the church leaders who followed in the footsteps of the apostles.

WEAKNESSES OF POST-APOSTOLIC WRITERS

Schaff introduces these post-apostolic writers as follows:

> We now descend from the primitive apostolic church to the Graeco-Roman; from the scene of creation to the work of preservation; from the fountain of divine revelation to the stream of human development; from the inspirations of the apostles and prophets to the productions of enlightened but fallible teachers. (ScP.HCC 2:7)

Comparing these writers to New Testament writers, he states:

> Not one compares for a moment in depth and spiritual fullness with a St. Paul or St. John; and the whole patristic literature, with all its incalculable

value, must ever remain very far below the New Testament. The single epistle to the Romans or the Gospel of John is worth more than all commentaries, doctrinal, polemic, and ascetic treatises of the Greek and Latin fathers, schoolmen, and reformers. (ScP.HCC 2.629)

The greatest weakness of the post-apostolic writers could probably be described by the word *excess*. If a particular writer thought he saw an allegory used in the apostles' writings, he might be prone to use that method of interpretation to an increased or extreme degree. Justin, for example, interpreted the twelve bells on the robe of the high priest as a type of the twelve apostles, whose sound goes forth into all the world. Because the apostles wrote of events as fulfilling Old Testament prophecies, some of the post-apostolic writers tended to draw unusual parallels between certain events in the life of Jesus or the church and particular Old Testament statements. These are primarily matters of interpretation, though, not faithfulness in reporting historical details which had been passed to them.

Occasionally, however, we do find these writers using questionable sources, quoting apocryphal works as Scripture, or distorting information recalled from memory. For example, both Origen and Eusebius say that Josephus attributes the fall of Jerusalem to the harsh treatment of the Jews toward James the brother of Jesus.[1] But this statement does not appear in our copies of Josephus today, and the modern scholar has to wonder, did Origen and Eusebius have better manuscripts, corrupt manuscripts or lapses of memory? Perhaps Origen, followed by Eusebius, was thinking of Josephus' statement concerning the defeat of Herod's army being attributed by some to John the Baptist's death at the hands of Herod.[2]

It is easy for us to look back over nineteen hundred years of theological debate and clarification, and pass judgment on the errors of certain post-apostolic writers. What we have to remember is that they were the first to grapple with some difficult issues of interpretation inherent in the works of the apostles. Though these men may have erred in some interpretations, for the most part they demonstrated a determined faithfulness to accurately report historical facts which had been passed to them.

STRENGTHS OF POST-APOSTOLIC WRITERS

The early church spokesmen had a wide variety of strengths and abilities. Schaff writes:

Polycarp is distinguished, not for genius or learning, but for patriarchal simplicity and dignity; Clement of Rome for the gift of administration; Ignatius for impetuous devotion to episcopacy, church unity, and Christian martyrdom; Justin for apologetic zeal and extensive reading; Irenaeus for sound doctrine and moderation; Clement of Alexandria for stimulating fertility of thought; Origen for brilliant learning and bold speculation; Tertullian for freshness and vigor of intellect and sturdiness of character; Cyprian for energetic churchliness; Eusebius for literary industry in compilation; Lactantius for elegance of style. (ScP.HCC 2:629)

More important than gifts or abilities, the Christian literature of the first two centuries clearly reveals the exemplary character of the early Christians. Over and over again these writers tell how non-Christians were attracted to the faith by observing how confidently and innocently the Christians faced their persecutors. Schaff writes:

> These suffering virtues are among the sweetest and noblest fruits of the Christian religion. It is not so much the amount of suffering which challenges our admiration, although it was terrible enough, as the spirit with which the early Christians bore it. Men and women of all classes, noble senators and learned bishops, illiterate artisans and poor slaves, loving mothers and delicate virgins, hoary-headed pastors and innocent children approached their tortures in no temper of unfeeling indifference and obstinate defiance, but, like their divine Master, with calm self-possession, humble resignation, gentle meekness, cheerful faith, triumphant hope, and forgiving charity. Such spectacles must have often overcome even the inhuman murderer. (ScP:HCC 2:75-76)

Origen wrote in the preface to his first book, *Against Celsus:*

> When false witness was brought against our blessed Saviour, the spotless Jesus, he held his peace, and when he was accused, returned no answer, being fully persuaded that the tenor of his life and conduct among the Jews was the best apology that could possibly be made in his behalf.... And even now he preserves the same silence, and makes no other answer than the unblemished lives of his sincere followers; they are his most cheerful and successful advocates, and have so loud a voice that they drown the clamors of the most zealous and bigoted adversaries.[3]

It was a well-known saying among those early Christians that the blood of the martyrs was the seed of the church. For all who fell, more came to take their place. Tertullian even challenged the heathen governors:

> But go zealously on.... Kill us, torture us, condemn us, grind us to dust.... The oftener we are mown down by you, the more in number we grow; the blood of Christians is seed.... For who that contemplates it, is not excited to inquire what is at the bottom of it? who, after inquiry, does not embrace our doctrines? and when he has embraced them, desires not to suffer?[4]

Others confessed Jesus under the threat of death but were not executed. These were held in honor as "confessors."

Some have questioned whether there were all that many who died martyrs' deaths. To this Schaff answers:

> Origen, it is true, wrote in the middle of the third century, that the number of Christian martyrs was small and easy to be counted; God not permitting that all this class of men should be exterminated. But this language

must be understood as referring chiefly to the reigns of Caracalla, Helioga-balus, Alexander Severus and Philippus Arabs, who did not persecute the Christians. Soon afterwards the fearful persecution of Decius broke out, in which Origen himself was thrown into prison and cruelly treated. Con-cerning the preceding ages, his statement must be qualified by the equally valid testimonies of Tertullian, Clement of Alexandria (Origen's teacher), and the still older Irenaeus, who says expressly, that the church, for her love to God, "sends in all places and at all times a multitude of martyrs to the Father." Even the heathen Tacitus speaks of an "immense multitude" *(ingens multitudo)* of Christians, who were murdered in the city of Rome alone during the Neronian persecution in 64.

To this must be added the silent, yet most eloquent testimony of the Roman catacombs, which, according to the calculation of Marchi and Northcote, extended over nine hundred English miles, and are said to con-tain nearly seven millions of graves, a large proportion of these including the relics of martyrs, as the innumerable inscriptions and instruments of death testify. The sufferings, moreover, of the church during this period are of course not to be measured merely by the number of actual execu-tions, but by the far more numerous insults, slanders, vexations, and tor-tures, which the cruelty of heartless heathens and barbarians could devise, or any sort of instrument could inflict on the human body, and which were in a thousand cases worse than death. (ScP.HCC 2:79-80)

Certainly it is true that many people throughout history have died for what they thought to be true, even though it may not have been. But the Christian martyrs of the first two centuries AD confirm at least three important facts. First, whatever doubts might be raised from late tradition being unreliable as to whether certain apostles endured martyrdom, the testimony of second- and third-generation martyrs indicates that most of the apostles before them died for their testimony. If the students were willing to die for their faith, how much more the teachers? We need not expect that all of the apostles except John were martyred if tradition gives a weak testimony to that fact. But we can be confident that second- and third-generation believers followed the example of martyrdom set by the original apostles. Further, the voluntary sufferings and deaths of the original eyewitnesses and disciples of Jesus confirm that the basic his-torical information they passed on was true. If they knew, for example, that Jesus had not performed miracles or had not risen from the dead, because they themselves had stolen the body, what possible motivation would they have had to go out and die mar-tyrs' deaths for spreading these lies?

Second, the continued suffering and martyrdom of second-, third- and fourth-generation Christians confirms that, at the very least, any thinking person would make every possible effort to verify the accuracy of the many historical details in those reports. From the very beginning, such a vast Christian network multiplied out across the empire that it would have been easy enough to verify the historical events of Jesus' life. Even 120 years after the death of Christ, at least one godly Christian, Polycarp, was still living who could verify firsthand what some of the original disciples of Jesus had reported.

A third fact confirmed by the early reports is that the early Christians considered moral and ethical integrity more important than life itself. These Christians do not appear to be wild-eyed fanatics. Nor are they simply zealously devoted to a particular philosophy of life. They are men and women who at the very least are saying by their shed blood, "I cannot deny that Jesus of Nazareth lived, taught and died, and that he has been raised from the dead to demonstrate that he is Messiah and Lord and God."

LIVES AND TEACHINGS OF POST-APOSTOLIC WRITERS

Church historians usually divide the Christian writers of the first two centuries into three categories: (1) the post-apostolic "fathers" (first and early second century); (2) the apologists (second century); and (3) the controversialists against heresies (late second and third century). Schaff says concerning the first group that they

> were the first church teachers after the apostles, who had enjoyed in part personal intercourse with them, and thus form the connecting link between them and the apologists of the second century. This class consists of Barnabas, Clement of Rome, Ignatius, Polycarp, and, in a broader sense, Hermas, Papias, and the unknown authors of the Epistle to Diognetus, and of the Didache.
>
> ...They were faithful practical workers, and hence of more use to the church in those days than profound thinkers or great scholars could have been. (ScP:HCC 2:633)

The second group, the apologists, addressed their writings to emperors (Hadrian, Antoninus Pius, Marcus Aurelius), to various governors, or to the general public who were literate. They wanted to refute the false charges against the Christians and to alleviate the persecution brought against them. They included Quadratus, Aristides, Justin Martyr, Irenaeus, Tertullian and Origen. The last three also can be placed in the third group, the controversialists.

The controversialists sought to answer various questionable or false doctrines being spread within and without the church. In none of these questionable doctrines, however, was there a denial that Jesus lived the life reported by the apostles. The questions focused more on how he could be both God and man at the same time.

The quotes documented in the next ten pages show early church leaders, martyrs and confessors speaking of the convictions for which they were prepared to die. Their words confirm their trust in the kind of life Jesus lived and the historical veracity of the gospels. As we briefly describe the following writers and what they said about the historical Jesus, you may wish to refer to the chart at the end of this chapter to see how each one relates with the others.

Clement of Rome (died c. AD 102)

He may be the Clement mentioned by Paul in Philippians 4:3. Origen calls him a disciple of the apostles.[5] According to Eusebius, he was bishop of Rome from AD 92 to AD 101. Tertullian writes that he was appointed by Peter. Late tradition says he was a martyr, but the earliest writers up to Eusebius and Jerome mention nothing of it. At the very least he would have felt the pressure of leadership over a *religio illicita,* or unlicensed religion, in the Roman Empire. He would have been the congregation's leader during the persecutions under Domitian. "In striking contrast with the bloody cruelties practiced by Domitian, he exhorts to prayer for the civil rulers, that God 'may give them health, peace, concord, and stability for the administration of the government he has given them.'" (ScP.HCC 2:643)

Clement's letter to the Corinthians is the only extant work from him which is accepted as genuine. It was written about AD 95 or 96. In it he tells of the martyrdom of Paul and Peter. Significantly, he also quotes from Matthew, Mark, Luke and Acts, as well as 1 Corinthians, 1 Peter, Hebrews and Titus.

Clement verifies several historical details of Jesus' life. In paragraph 32 he speaks of Jesus as a descendent of Jacob—in other words, Jesus was born into the race of the Jews. In paragraphs 21 and 49 he speaks of "the blood of Christ shed for our salvation."[6] Paragraph 13 confirms some of Jesus' teaching:

> Most of all remembering the words of the Lord Jesus which He spake teaching forbearance and long-suffering: for thus He spake; "Have mercy, that ye may receive mercy: forgive, that it may be forgiven you. As ye do, so shall it be done to you. As ye give, so shall it be given unto you. As ye judge, so shall ye be judged. As ye show kindness, so shall kindness be showed unto you. With what measure ye mete, it shall be measured withal to you."

Paragraph 24 speaks of Jesus' resurrection and reflects his teaching about a grain of wheat which must fall into the earth and die before it can bear fruit. The only gospel account reporting this teaching is the one from John, but Paul also uses it in 1 Corinthians 15:36,37. Clement therefore confirms not only the bodily resurrection of Jesus but also some of Jesus' teaching which was passed on through John and Paul.

Clement, as well, was an eyewitness to the transition in leadership from Jesus' original apostles to disciples of these apostles. He reports in paragraph 42:

> The apostles received the gospel for us from the Lord Jesus Christ; Jesus Christ was sent forth from God. So then Christ is from God, and the apostles are from Christ. Both therefore came of the will of God in the appointed order. Having therefore received a charge, and having been fully assured through the resurrection of our Lord Jesus Christ and confirmed in the word of God with full assurance of the Holy Ghost, they went forth with the glad tidings that the kingdom of God should come. So preaching everywhere in country and town, they appointed their first-fruits, when

they had proved them by the Spirit, to be bishops and deacons unto them that should believe.

Clement confirms other teachings of Jesus:

Remember the words of Jesus our Lord: for He said, "Woe unto that man; it were good for him if he had not been born, rather than that he should offend one of Mine elect. It were better for him that a mill-stone were hanged about him, and he cast into the sea, than that he should pervert one of Mine elect."[7]

Clement of Rome probably wrote more than just this one letter which has survived. This letter was written for the specific purpose of healing a division in the Corinthian church, but it clearly demonstrates that Clement's faith was based on facts of history: Jesus was born a Jew, preached and taught, died, was literally raised from the dead, and his disciples carried the message of his life and teaching throughout the surrounding lands.

Ignatius (died c. AD 117)

On his way to certain martyrdom at Rome, Ignatius wrote seven letters, six to churches and one to his friend Polycarp. He had been the bishop of the church at Antioch before his arrest and condemnation to death. His letters reflect a victorious faith which looks forward to the opportunity of suffering for Christ. Some details of his martyrdom are questioned, but the fact of his martyrdom is not. Polycarp's report of it around AD 135 confirms that he was thrown to the lions in the Colosseum at Rome for the amusement of the people. Tradition calls him a disciple of Peter, Paul and John.

Ignatius writes of a number of historical facts, and quotes from Matthew, John and Acts as well as many of Paul's letters, James and 1 Peter. Notice the concentration of historical detail:

The Lord received ointment on His head.[8]

For our God, Jesus the Christ, was conceived in the womb by Mary according to a dispensation, of the seed of David but also of the Holy Ghost; and He was born and was baptized.[9]

But be ye fully persuaded concerning the birth and the passion and the resurrection, which took place in the time of the governorship of Pontius Pilate; for these things were truly and certainly done by Jesus Christ our hope; from which hope may it not befall any of you to be turned aside.[10]

Jesus Christ, who was of the race of David, who was the Son of Mary, who was truly born and ate and drank, was truly persecuted under Pontius Pilate, was truly crucified and died in the sight of those in heaven and those on earth and those under the earth; who moreover was truly raised from the dead, His Father having raised Him.[11]

For I have perceived that ye are…fully persuaded as touching our Lord that He is truly of the race of David according to the flesh, but Son of God by the Divine will and power, truly born of a virgin and baptized by John that all righteousness might be fulfilled by Him, truly nailed up in the flesh for our sakes under Pontius Pilate and Herod the tetrarch.[12]

For He suffered all these things for our sakes [that we might be saved]; and He suffered truly, as also He raised Himself truly: not as certain unbelievers say, that He suffered in semblance.[13]

For I know and believe that He was in the flesh even after the resurrection; and when He came to Peter and his company, He said to them, "Lay hold and handle me, and see that I am not a demon without body." And straightway they touched Him, and they believed, being joined unto His flesh and His blood. Wherefore also they despised death, nay they were found superior to death. And after His resurrection He both ate with them and drank with them as one in the flesh, though spiritually He was united with the Father.[14]

For if these things were done by our Lord in semblance, then am I also a prisoner in semblance. And why then have I delivered myself over to death, unto fire, unto sword, unto wild beasts? But near to the sword, near to God; in company with wild beasts, in company with God. Only let it be in the name of Jesus Christ, so that we may suffer together with Him. I endure all things, seeing that He Himself enableth me, who is perfect Man.[15]

As you can see, the foundation of faith for Ignatius was the undeniable historical facts of Jesus' birth, life, death and bodily resurrection. Ignatius, like Clement of Rome and Polycarp, was close enough to the apostles to get at least these basic facts straight. He was sure enough about them to die for them.

Papias (c. AD 60 or 70 to 130 or 140)

Papias was bishop of Hierapolis in Phrygia and, according to Irenaeus, a hearer of John and companion of Polycarp.[16] Eusebius remarks that Papias wrote five books entitled *Expositions of Oracles of the Lord,* and these were still extant in Eusebius' time. They have since been lost, and what a tremendous loss that is. Their contents can be imagined by the following comment of Papias preserved by Eusebius:

On any occasion when a person came (in my way) who had been a follower of the Elders, I would inquire about the discourses of the Elders—what was said by Andrew, or by Peter, or by Philip, or by Thomas or James, or by John or Matthew or any other of the Lord's disciples, and what Aristion and the Elder John, the disciples of the Lord, say. For I did not think that I could get so much profit from the contents of books as from the utterances of a living and abiding voice.[17]

From fragments surviving in Eusebius and Irenaeus, it appears that Papias included in these books various unwritten traditions from those mentioned above and from the daughters of Philip, the apostle in Hierapolis, as well as others. Eusebius does preserve what Papias reported concerning the formation of the gospels of Mark and Matthew. Concerning Mark, Papias wrote:

> And the Elder said this also: Mark, having become the interpreter of Peter, wrote down accurately everything that he remembered, without however recording in order what was either said or done by Christ. For neither did he hear the Lord, nor did he follow Him; but afterwards, as I said, (attended) Peter, who adapted his instructions to the needs (of his hearers) but had no design of giving a connected account of the Lord's oracles. So then Mark made no mistake, while he thus wrote down some things as he remembered them; for he made it his one care not to omit anything that he heard, or to set down any false statement therein.[18]

And regarding Matthew: "So then Matthew composed the oracles in the Hebrew language, and each one interpreted them as he could."

Critics have speculated whether Papias meant literal Hebrew or Aramaic when he used the term "Hebrew." Other reported historical reminiscences from Papias include the complete story of the woman caught in adultery found in John 8:1-11.[19] Since the story is not found in most of the oldest manuscripts of John's gospel, Papias' report is an important early documentation of this historical detail of Jesus' life.

Polycarp (c. AD 69–155)

Polycarp, a disciple of John, maintained an unflagging devotion to Christ and the Scriptures. His famous death as a martyr demonstrated his trust in the accuracy of the Scriptures. He was the chief presbyter (bishop) over the church at Smyrna and the teacher of Irenaeus of Lyons. The account of his martyrdom is given in a letter from the church at Smyrna to other churches. Except for a few insertions, the letter is held by scholars to be genuine and substantially correct in what it reports. At one point it tells of Polycarp being led into the stadium and questioned before the proconsul. The crowds were said to be in a great tumult, hearing that it was "the atheist" Polycarp.

The proconsul demanded that he "swear by the genius of Caesar; repent and say, Away with the Atheists."

Polycarp looked out on the masses, gestured toward them with his hand and looking up to heaven said, "Away with the atheists." When it was demanded that he revile Christ, Polycarp responded "Fourscore and six years have I been His servant, and He has done me no wrong. How then can I blaspheme my King who saved me?" After further threats Polycarp responded, "You threaten that fire which burns for a season and after a while is quenched: for you are ignorant of the fire of the future judgment and eternal punishment, which is reserved for the ungodly. But why do you delay? Come, do what you will."[20] At this point Polycarp was burned at the stake and thrust through with a sword.

Our only surviving work of Polycarp is a letter to the Philippians written c. AD 110. In the letter, he quotes various New Testament writings approximately sixty times. At one point he states:

> Let us therefore without ceasing hold fast by our hope and by the earnest of our righteousness, which is Jesus Christ who took up our sins in His own body upon the tree, who did no sin, neither was guile found in His mouth, but for our sakes He endured all things, that we might live in Him. Let us therefore become imitators of His endurance; and if we should suffer for His name's sake, let us glorify Him. For He gave this example to us in His own person, and we believed this.[21]

The Didache (c. AD 95)

A church manual, the Didache was written toward the end of the first century. It quotes from the Sermon on the Mount and the Lord's prayer, and gives other instruction based on material in the gospels. The Didache evidences that the early church, within seventy years of the crucifixion, believed that the gospel accounts were accurate descriptions of the life of the historical Jesus.

The Epistle of Barnabas (between AD 70 and 135)

Within this letter itself, the name Barnabas is never given. The author, therefore, is unknown. Scholars have consistently denied that the New Testament Barnabas was its author. From the content of the letter it can be determined that its date of origin probably falls between the first and second Jewish rebellions against Rome, i.e., between AD 70 and 135. (This letter is different from a late forgery, the "Gospel of Barnabas," of which Muslims are particularly fond.)

The writer of the epistle is a strong antagonist against those who wanted to require Christians to keep the Old Testament Law. He strongly upholds the agreement of the New Testament teachings with those of the Old Testament, but charges that the Judaizers do not interpret the Law and the Prophets correctly. While the letter is genuine and accurate on a number of points, typology and allegory are used to an extreme degree in some interpretations of the Old Testament. But the letter is a valuable source, confirming again what the first- and second-century Christians knew about Jesus. In section 5 it states:

> But He Himself endured that He might destroy and show forth the resurrection of the dead, for that He must needs be manifested in the flesh; that at the same time He might redeem the promise made to the fathers, and by preparing the new people for Himself might show, while He was on earth, that having brought about the resurrection He will Himself exercise

judgment. Yea and further, He preached teaching Israel and performing so many wonders and miracles, and He loved him [Israel] exceedingly. And when He chose His own apostles who were to proclaim His Gospel, who, that He might show that He came not to call the righteous but sinners, were sinners above every sin, then He manifested Himself to be the Son of God.

In section 7 he adds, "But moreover when crucified He had vinegar and gall given Him to drink."

Quadratus (AD 138?)

Schaff states that Quadratus was a disciple of the apostles and bishop of the church at Athens. He was one of the earliest "apologists." His defense of the Christian faith, addressed to Hadrian, c. AD 125, is not extant except for a few lines preserved by Eusebius:

> The deeds of our Saviour were always before you, for they were true miracles; those that were healed, those that were raised from the dead, who were seen, not only when healed and when raised, but were always present. They remained living a long time, not only whilst our Lord was on earth, but likewise when he had left the earth. So that some of them have also lived to our own times.[22]

Aristides (second century)

Eusebius says Aristides was a contemporary of Quadratus and that he also addressed a defense of the Christian faith to the Emperor Hadrian. The work was lost until the nineteenth century (but has since been found in three separate versions, one Armenian, one Syriac and one Greek "taken over almost wholly into a popular Oriental Christian romance, 'Barlaam and Josaphat.'"[23] The extant versions are addressed to Antoninus Pius (reigned AD 138–161), who succeeded Hadrian. One portion describes Christ as

> the Son of the most high God, revealed by the Holy Spirit, descended from heaven, born of a Hebrew Virgin. His flesh he received from the Virgin, and he revealed himself in the human nature as the Son of God. In his goodness which brought the glad tidings, he has won the whole world by his life-giving preaching.... He selected twelve apostles and taught the whole world by his mediatorial, light-giving truth. And he was crucified, being pierced with nails by the Jews; and he rose from the dead and ascended to heaven. He sent the apostles into all the world and instructed all by divine miracles full of wisdom. Their preaching bears blossoms and fruits to this day, and calls the whole world to illumination. (ScP.HCC 2. 709-10)

Justin Martyr (c. AD 100–166)

Born in Flavius Neapolis, formerly Shechem, Justin grew up well educated but ignorant of Moses and Christianity. He called himself a Samaritan. During his early manhood he sought successively to become a Stoic, a Peripatetic, a Pythagorean and finally a Platonist. When almost convinced of the truth of Platonism, he met a dignified and gentle old Christian man on a walk not far from the coast. He reports that as he investigated the Christian faith, he was moved by the fearless courage of the Christians and their steadfastness in the face of death. After becoming a Christian he became a fearless and energetic defender of the Christian faith at a time when it was most under attack. Schaff judges that as a lay preacher he "accomplished far more for the good of the church than any known bishop or presbyter of his day." (ScP.HCC 2.714) In AD 166, along with six others in Rome, he sealed his testimony with his own blood. There he was scourged and beheaded at the instigation of a Cynic philosopher, Crescens, whom he had confronted with the truth of the gospel. (ScP.HCC 2.715)

The genuine works of Justin Martyr "everywhere attest his honesty and earnestness, his enthusiastic love for Christianity, and his fearlessness in its defense against assaults from without and perversions from within." (ScP.HCC 2.715) In his *Dialogue with Trypho,* Justin challenges his friendly opponent regarding the Christian faith not being an empty myth:

> But if you are willing to listen to an account of Him, how we have not been deceived, and shall not cease to confess Him—although men's reproaches be heaped upon us, although the most terrible tyrant compel us to deny Him—I shall prove to you as you stand here that we have not believed empty fables, or words without any foundation. [24]

In all of his works he supports the historical facts given in the gospel accounts (he calls them "Memoirs by the Apostles"). From these he quotes various events in the life of Christ and defends them. Like other early Christian writers, he appeals to the Old Testament as prophetic of events which occurred in Jesus' life. But if those events never occurred, it would have been useless to look for prophecies in the Old Testament which allegedly point to events described in the gospels.

Justin also appealed to the knowledge of his hearers and to non-Christian sources available to them if they wanted to verify his claims. Regarding Jesus' birth he says, "Now there is a village in the land of the Jews, thirty-five stadia from Jerusalem, in which Jesus Christ was born, as you can ascertain also from the registers of the taxing made under Cyrenius, your first procurator in Judea." [25] Regarding Jesus' death he writes:

> And the expression, "They pierced my hands and my feet," was used in reference to the nails of the cross which were fixed in His hands and feet. And after he was crucified they cast lots upon his vesture, and they that crucified Him parted it among them. And that these things did happen you can ascertain from the Acts of Pontius Pilate. [26]

These "Acts of Pilate" were destroyed, possibly as a result of the appeal of Christians to them or just due to their seeming insignificance to a later Roman administration. As we mentioned earlier, an apocryphal "Acts of Pilate" which now exists was forged by churchmen of the fourth or later centuries.

It is very unlikely that a man of Justin's academic ability, living within 100 years of the life of Jesus, would die a martyr's death for historical facts which could not be verified. Modern critics and scholars, removed 1,950 years from the life of Jesus and having nothing to lose (they think), may seek to explain away the life of Jesus as a myth or a legend. For Justin, the ample evidence that was available in his day forced him to the conclusion that the gospel accounts of Jesus' life were reliable. More, that they were worth dying for.

Hegesippus (mid second century)

Eusebius concludes that Hegesippus was a Jewish Christian and states also that he produced a five volume "Memoirs." He apparently traveled extensively through Syria, Greece and Italy collecting the "memorials" of the apostles. He valued both written and oral traditions. His books are known to have survived until the sixteenth century but are now lost. If found, they would likely place him in front of Eusebius as the father of church history. During his travels, he seems to have been intent on determining if the true story had been passed from the apostles down through their successors. Eusebius quotes him as saying:

> The Corinthian church continued in the true doctrine until Primus became bishop. I mixed with them on my voyage to Rome and spent several days with the Corinthians, during which we were refreshed with the true doctrine. On arrival at Rome I pieced together the succession down to Anicetus, whose deacon was Eleutherus, Anicetus being succeeded by Soter and he by Eleutherus. In every line of bishops and in every city things accord with the preaching of the Law, the Prophets, and the Lord.[27]

Irenaeus (c. AD 120? to 190+)

Irenaeus is generally accepted as the most orthodox of the Ante-Nicene fathers (early church leaders prior to the council of Nicaea in AD 325). He is a valuable source of information on the life of Jesus since he was a pupil of Polycarp, a disciple of the original apostles. Think of it. He could say, "My teacher was a disciple of a man who walked with Jesus." He probably grew up in Smyrna, perhaps studied and taught in Rome and was presbyter of the church in Lugdunum and Vienne during the persecutions of Marcus Aurelius. Irenaeus succeeded Bishop Pothinus when he died in the persecution of AD 177–178. In his ministry he was a missionary, writer and church statesman.

In his works he relies heavily on the Old Testament, all the gospels and nearly all the Epistles. Of the origin of the gospels he writes:

> Matthew also issued a written Gospel among the Hebrews in their own dialect, while Peter and Paul were preaching at Rome, and laying the

foundations of the Church. After their departure, Mark, the disciple and interpreter of Peter, did also hand down to us in writing what had been preached by Peter. Luke also, the companion of Paul, recorded in a book the Gospel preached by him. Afterwards, John, the disciple of the Lord, who had leaned upon his breast, did himself publish a Gospel during his residence at Ephesus in Asia.[28]

Notice that Irenaeus, like other early writers, is concerned that the reports about Jesus handed down by the apostles are reliable. He continues by saying that those who deny the teachings of the apostles "blaspheme their Creator after a most imprudent manner!"[29]

Tertullian (c. AD 160/79–215/20)

An African moralist, apologist, theologian and lawyer, Tertullian quotes the New Testament more than 7,000 times, of which 3,800 quotes are from the gospels. He also reports that Tiberius at one time seems to have been impressed with what he had discovered about the Christ of the Christians. Tertullian writes:

> Tiberius accordingly, in whose days the Christian name made its entry into the world, having himself received intelligence from Palestine of events which had clearly shown the truth of Christ's divinity, brought the matter before the senate, with his own decision in favour of Christ. The senate, because it had not given the approval itself, rejected his proposal. Caesar held to his opinion, threatening wrath against all accusers of the Christians.[30]

If this confrontation did take place, it does not mean that Tiberius had necessarily become a Christian. He may have wished only to add this "new god" to the already long list of Roman gods.

Origen (AD 185–c. 254)

Origen lived one of the most intense Christian lives of history. He was born in Egypt and educated by his father, Leonides, probably a rhetorician. While still a boy, Origen had memorized vast portions of Scripture. In AD 202 his father was martyred under the persecution of Septimus Severus. Origen wanted to die with his father but was prevented from leaving his house when his mother hid his clothes during the night. Origen went on to a brilliant career as a writer, teacher and preacher. One opponent of his said that he had written six thousand books. Jerome says he wrote more books than others could read. Admittedly many were tracts, letters and homilies, as well as lectures which others recorded and published. In his writings, he quotes the New Testament over eighteen thousand times.

Origen, intense defender of the Christian faith, took the words of Jesus literally and seriously. He owned only one set of clothes and no shoes. He took no thought for the morrow. During the persecution of Decius in AD 250, Origen was "put in chains and tortured, suffered the experience of the iron collar, was placed in stocks and confined to a dungeon."[31] He died shortly after—at least a "confessor" if not a martyr.

Eusebius (died 341 or 342)

We close with Eusebius because of his work of gathering the early sources together in the earliest extant *History of the Christian Church*. Though some of his scriptural interpretations are questionable, his work as a historian is invaluable. Schaff writes:

> Whatever may be said of the defects of Eusebius as an historical critic and writer, his learning and industry are unquestionable, and his *Church History* and *Chronicle* will always remain an invaluable collection of information not attainable in any other ancient author. (ScP.HCC 2.5)

EVALUATING THE EVIDENCE

The early church writers, both by their lives and words, certified that the historical details of Jesus' life, as presented in the gospel accounts, are correct and may be trusted. But there are two objections which critics may raise to the historical value of their testimony.

First, since these writers obtained their historical information from the gospel accounts, how can they be used as extrabiblical evidence for historical details about Jesus? This question is actually somewhat misleading. Consider these perspectives:

- The early writers didn't always use the gospels as their sources. You may have noticed it was the later writers who more specifically quoted the gospel accounts as *written* sources. The earliest writers, for example Papias, obtained their information from a wide variety of sources and even considered the "living and abiding voice" of the apostles through their disciples as more valuable than the written sources which could be corrupted. That's only normal. If you wanted the best information about your great-grandfather, you'd probably regard your grandfather's words as more valuable than any newspaper account telling about your great-grandfather. If there were a conflict, you would be prone to side with your grandfather's story, assuming that you knew him to be a truthful man. As for the disciples, they risked everything in their commitment to the truth of the gospel accounts which they left behind.

- A vast network of multiplication sprang from Jesus and the first apostles. If any had included historical errors in their reports, the early literature would reflect controversy over matters of fact concerning what actually took place. We find this type of controversy nowhere in the early literature. There was controversy over how to interpret the facts, the details of Jesus' life, but not over the facts themselves as actual events of history. The fact that the early literature does reveal controversy over interpretation of the life of Jesus also shows that no one would have been able to suppress controversy over the fact of his existence if such a controversy had ever occurred.

- The early writers consistently appealed to the availability of evidence for anyone who wanted to check it out. They cited the existence of government records. The earliest writers appealed to eyewitnesses who could confirm or deny the facts. Finally, they appealed to the moral integrity of their own lives. They had nothing to gain by spreading lies. They gave up their possessions and even their very lives standing for the truth.

But, the critic may ask, and this is the second possible objection, was the testimony of the early Christians based on historical facts or just their own psychological experience of a mystical "Christ" which compelled them to establish Jesus as a figure of history? To this question we answer with another question: Would you give up everything, suffer hardship, torture and death in order to spread lies, fabrications or even just beliefs you had some doubts were true?

What critics so often overlook, especially when criticizing the gospel accounts, is that if these reports are false, then those who wrote them were not just misguided. They were deceivers of the worst kind, who knew the documents were fabricated. The early church writings are so dominated by the themes of moral integrity and ethical consistency that for them to propagate known falsehoods would have been a psychological impossibility. Similarly, it is doubtful that so many people following the disciples would have blindly submitted to a mystical experience without first assuring themselves that the historical reports upon which that experience was based, were beyond question.

There were those, however, who had motive enough to produce distorted accounts. And this is the subject of our next chapter.

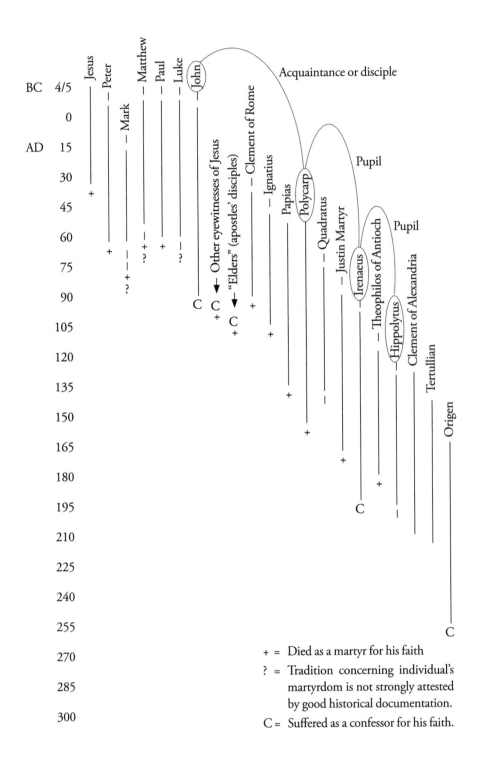

BC 4/5

AD

Jesus
Peter
Mark
Matthew
Paul
Luke
John

0
15
30
45
60
75
90
105
120
135
150
165
180
195
210
225
240
255
270
285
300

Acquaintance or disciple

Other eyewitnesses of Jesus
"Elders" (apostles' disciples)
Clement of Rome
Ignatius
Papias
Polycarp
Quadratus
Justin Martyr
Irenaeus
Theophilos of Antioch
Hippolytus
Clement of Alexandria
Tertullian
Origen

Pupil

Pupil

+ = Died as a martyr for his faith

? = Tradition concerning individual's martyrdom is not strongly attested by good historical documentation.

C = Suffered as a confessor for his faith.

AGRAPHA, APOCRYPHA
AND PSEUDEPIGRAPHA

That Jesus actually lived in history should be obvious by now. And, as we said in the introduction, the fact of Jesus' existence in history is not much doubted among critical scholars. What is debated is whether or not the gospel accounts of the New Testament accurately describe the Jesus who lived in history.

Some of the most popular critics and life-of-Jesus reconstructionists today, by appealing to apocryphal and pseudepigraphal writings, attempt to show that the Jesus of history was much different from the Jesus of the gospels. Therefore, one who has limited understanding of these noncanonical writings will have difficulty discerning the errors contained within the works of many today who promote a nonbiblical historical Jesus. But before we can evaluate whether these "extracanonical" sources can tell us much about the historical Jesus, we first need to define some terms.

DEFINITIONS

1. Agrapha. This is a Greek word meaning "unwritten things." In New Testament studies it refers to alleged sayings of Jesus not found in the canonical gospels—Matthew, Mark, Luke or John.

2. Apocrypha. This word is derived from a Greek word meaning "hidden things." By itself, the Apocrypha normally refers to the fourteen (or fifteen)[1] books of doubtful authenticity and authority, most of which were written between 250 BC and the time of Jesus. These books also are called the Old Testament Apocrypha. Our concern here will be with another group of writings often called the New Testament Apocrypha. The term *apocrypha* is appropriate for many of these works for they often purport to tell of secret or hidden details of the lives and teachings of Jesus and his disciples.

3. Pseudepigrapha. The name comes from a Greek word meaning "false writings." It normally applies to books related to the Old Testament but also has been used to apply to a number of New Testament apocryphal works and other works which falsely attribute their contents to an apostolic author. The term *pseudonymous,* meaning "false name," is used also for these works since they falsely claim to be written by true prophets or apostles.

4. Canon. Skeptics often charge: How can Christians believe to be the word of God twenty-seven books designated as Scripture by fallible men at a fourth-century council? But this question presents a distorted view of the New Testament canon. The word *canon* is a transliteration of a Greek word having the primary meaning of "rod" or "rule." It came to have the meaning of a rule of faith, and later, a list or catalog of authorized New Testament books. Long before councils were ever convened, however, Christians, especially local church elders, were constantly collecting, evaluating and deciding which of the many writings of their day carried the authority of the apostles.[2] The question asked of any writing to be read in the churches was: To what extent is this book (epistle, narrative, apocalypse or gospel) an authentic and pure representation of the life and teachings of Jesus and his apostles? Thus, as Donald Guthrie puts it, "The content of the canon was determined by general usage, not by authoritarian pronouncement."[3] F. F. Bruce states that

> when at last a Church Council—The Synod of Hippo in AD 393—listed the twenty-seven books of the New Testament, it did not confer upon them any authority which they did not already possess, but simply recorded their previously established canonicity. (The ruling of the Synod of Hippo was repromulgated four years later by the Third Synod of Carthage.) (BrF.BP 113)

Geisler and Nix conclude, "Canonicity is *determined* or fixed authoritatively by God; it is merely *discovered* by man." (GeN.GIB 221) First century Christians saw in the words of Jesus and the writings of the apostles an authority of divine inspiration equaling that of the Old Testament Scriptures. This was only natural, for if Jesus was the long-awaited Messiah, then his words should be every bit as authoritative as those of Moses and the prophets of old. Thus, the gospel records which contained the reports of his words and actions gained credibility over the first century as eyewitnesses could orally verify the truth of what was written. Further, the deaths of the apostles elevated the importance of their writings as Christians saw the need to preserve what the apostles had reported. Prior to this time, in accordance with common Jewish practice, "Oral teaching was regarded more highly than written testimony."[4]

As time passed, an increasing circulation of books recognized as either not in accordance with the apostles' teachings (i.e., heretical) or not written by them, even though an apostle's name may have been attached to them (i.e., pseudonymous), motivated the believers to become increasingly concerned about identifying the authentic works of the apostles or those entrusted with their teachings (namely Mark for Peter and Luke for Paul). The very fact that many heretical or unauthentic writings falsely attached the names of various apostles as their authors demonstrates how eager the early Christians were to know that the teaching they received from books read in their churches actually did come from the apostles of Jesus.

Christians today can be thankful that the final formation of the New Testament canon was such a long and difficult process. It was so difficult, in fact, that there was heated debate over whether Hebrews, James, 2 and 3 John, 2 Peter, Jude and Revelation were truly canonical. But the close scrutiny to which the New Testament books were subjected before being universally accepted as authentic should give readers today increased confidence in the reliability of these books and the things which they report and teach.

We will quote from several apocryphal and pseudepigraphal works by name below. For now, you may find it helpful to distinguish between the terms this way: Both *pseudepigrapha* (writings with false superscriptions) and *apocrypha* (writings containing hidden things) may characterize a particular work, but such a work necessarily falls outside the *canon* since it is an unauthentic or, at the very least, a doubtful work of an apostle. Also, both *pseudepigrapha* and *apocrypha* may contain *agrapha,* alleged sayings of Jesus, but still outside the canonical gospels.

VALUE

Are writings of doubtful authenticity at all valuable in the quest for the historical Jesus? We believe they are and will give examples below. First, though, here are several reasons the apocryphal and pseudepigraphical writings are of some value:

- It is clear that many of these documents are counterfeits. In order to have a counterfeit you must first have an authentic original. Thus even some of the most doubtful writings confirm the canonical writings. Guthrie remarks:

  > During the early period some evidence regarding the NT canon may be culled from heretical sources. When heterodox writers cite canonical books, it is evidence that these books must have been regarded first as authoritative in orthodox circles before being taken over and reinterpreted by deviating sects.[5]

- A comparison between the false writings and the canonical ones often immediately confirms the obvious superiority and authenticity of the canonical gospels. Conversely, a comparison is sufficient to show, according to Guthrie, that the "inferiority and lack of true apostolicity of the false writings…is self-evident. The mere ascription of the books to apostles could not hide this fundamental distinction, and this shows why the orthodox churches were not misled."[6] Yamauchi states: "The study of the agrapha, particularly in the apocryphal gospels, reveals the relative poverty and inferiority of the mass of the extracanonical literature, and by contrast highlights the precious value of the canonical gospels."[7]

- Many of the apocryphal works quote the canonical gospels verbatim or almost verbatim at certain points. It is often clear that the canonical gospels were the jumping off point for those who wished to promulgate a false doctrine. Thus the false writings help to confirm the authenticity of the canonical ones.

- The lengths to which the early church went to weed out the false writings from the true ones indicate the church's very early and vigilant concern that the words of Jesus be accurately preserved. Daniel-Rops puts it:

> As doctrinal deviations, "heresies," appeared very early in the Church, there was a temptation to try to support them with texts alleged to be genuinely apostolic. The church avoided these snares. She retained only those texts which enjoyed the practically unanimous trust of the churches and could exhibit the guarantee of apostolic origin or approval as proof of their inspired character, and she rejected all the rest. (AmF.SLC 41)

- Some possible reliable agrapha, while not quoting from the gospel accounts, do agree in principle or context with other things Jesus is reported as saying in the gospels, thus providing limited evidence to the kinds of things he said.

- The origin of certain apocryphal works within various other groups such as Judaizers, anti-Semites, gnostics, and ascetics provides further evidence for the type of material added or changed from apostolic writings and thereby gives evidence of what was reliable. "The Gospel of Peter," for example,

> is significant in the way it reflects the rising tide of militant anti-Semitism in the second-century Church, as evidenced by the way in which the gospel writer systematically altered his narrative (assuming he relied on the canonical gospels) to intensify the Jewish elders' fierce desire to exterminate Jesus, while at the same time altering Pilate's role to one of innocent helplessness. (CaDR.DSG 83)

We turn now to specific examples of statements made in the spurious writings which illustrate the points above concerning the value of these writings. The statements fall into three categories: (1) material confirming the gospel accounts; (2) possibly reliable agrapha; and (3) unreliable additions to the gospel accounts.

MATERIAL CONFIRMING THE GOSPEL ACCOUNTS

"The Gospel of Thomas," not really a narrative type gospel, is a collection of 114 sayings which it alleges that the "living Jesus" dictated to Judas Thomas. Some set the date of composition as early as AD 140, some even into the first century. It was probably composed in Syria where traditions about Thomas flourished and where the Encratite heresy, an ascetic heresy, was accepted fairly early. Even though much in the writing is unreliable, there are a number of sayings which confirm reports in the canonical gospels and Acts. Saying 9, for example, is a very close version of the parable of the sower:

> Jesus said: "See, the sower went out, he filled his hand and scattered (the seeds). Some fell on the road; the birds came and picked them up. Some fell on the rock; they were quite unable to take root in the earth and sent forth no ears up to heaven. Some fell among thorns; they choked the seeds and the worm devoured them. But some fell on good ground, and it brought forth good fruit; it yielded sixtyfold and a hundred and twentyfold."

Saying 12, with some legendary embellishment, confirms what we already know from Josephus and Acts about James being head of the Jerusalem church: "Jesus said to them: 'In the place to which you go, betake yourselves to James the Just, on whose behalf heaven and earth alike were made.'"

Saying 20 confirms Mark 4:30-32, Matthew 13:31ff. and Luke 13:18ff.

> The disciples said to Jesus: "Tell us what the kingdom of heaven is like." He said to them: "It is like a mustard seed, smaller than all seeds. But when it falls on the cultivated ground, it puts forth a large branch and provides shelter for (the) birds of heaven."

Saying 26 confirms Matthew 7:3-5 and Luke 6:41ff.:

> Jesus said: "You see the splinter which is in your brother's eye, but you do not see the plank which is in your own eye. When you have removed the plank from your own eye, then you will see to remove the splinter from your brother's eye."

Saying 54 confirms Luke 6:20: "Jesus said: 'Happy are the poor; for yours is the kingdom of heaven.'"

Saying 63 summarizes the parable in Luke 12:16-21:

> Jesus said: "There was a rich man who had much money. He said: 'I will use my money to sow and reap and plant and fill my storehouses with fruit, so that I may lack nothing.' So he thought in his heart. But during that night he died. He who has ears to hear, let him hear!"

Saying 90 abbreviates Matthew 11:28-30: "Jesus said, 'Come to me, for my yoke is easy and my rule is gentle, and you will find rest for yourselves.'"

"The Gospel of Truth," possibly written by the gnostic Valentinus, dates from the mid to late second century. This book confirms certain historical details reported in the canonical gospels:

Jesus, was patient in accepting sufferings…he was nailed to a tree…

For when they had seen him and had heard him, he granted them to taste him and to smell him and to touch the beloved Son. When he had appeared instructing them about the Father…. For he came by means of fleshly appearance. (RoJM.NHL 20:11-14, 25-34; 30:27-33; 31:4-6)

"The Gospel According to the Hebrews," says F. F. Bruce, "appears to have been a paraphrase of the Gospel of Matthew." (BrF.JCO 99) Origen knew of it, as did Hegesippus (c. AD 170).[8] Matthew 18:15-22 is reflected in the following dialogue:

"If your brother sins in word and makes amends to you, receive him," said he, "seven times a day." His disciple Simon said to him: "Seven times a day?" The Lord replied: "Yes, I tell you, and seventy times seven."[9]

"The Egerton Gospel" (Egerton Papyrus 2) is part of a collection of papyri acquired by the British Museum in 1934, and dates to no later than AD 150. "Its handwriting is closest in appearance to that of a non-Christian document datable precisely to AD 94." (WiL.JTE 29) One segment reproduces Mark 1:40-45 with some embellishment included:

And see, a leper approached him and said: "Teacher Jesus, while journeying with lepers and eating with them in the inn, I myself also became a leper. If, therefore, you are willing, I am cleansed."

The Lord said to him: "I am willing: be cleansed." And immediately the leprosy departed from him, and the Lord said: "Go, show yourself to the priests." (BeH.FU)

"The Gospel of Peter" was highly esteemed by the church at Rhosus (near Antioch) near the end of the second century. It was marked with docetic teaching, but clearly draws on all four canonical gospels. (See BrF.JCO 8.) One portion describes the burial of Jesus:

Then they drew out the nails from the Lord's hands and laid him on the ground. The whole earth quaked and great fear fell on them. Then the sun shone out and it was found to be the ninth hour (3 P.M.). The Jews rejoiced, and gave his body to Joseph to be buried, since he had beheld all the good things he had done. So, taking the Lord, he washed him, wrapped him in linen and brought him into his own tomb, called Joseph's Garden.

"The Treatise on Resurrection" dates from the late second century AD. Gnostic teaching permeates the book, but it once again points back and confirms the original reports about Jesus. The texts in 46:14-21 and 48:10-19 confirm the canonical gospel teaching regarding the resurrection of Jesus:

For we have known the Son of Man, and we have believed that he rose from among the dead.

Do not think the resurrection is an illusion. It is no illusion, but it is a truth. Indeed, it is more fitting to say that the world is an illusion, rather than the resurrection which has come into being through our Lord the Savior, Jesus Christ.

We need to emphasize that any one quote from any apocryphal writing carries little weight in confirming the historical life of Jesus. But when faced with the mass of sayings of and about Jesus in the apocryphal writings, the honest investigator must ask, "Where did all this material originate?" Again and again it becomes clear that the only logical explanation is that it originated from the early firsthand accounts of the apostles themselves which others with different viewpoints felt to be reliable enough to use as the cornerstone of their own, in many cases, quite heretical teachings.

POSSIBLY RELIABLE AGRAPHA

The apostle John wrote in his gospel account, "And there are also many other things which Jesus did, which if they were written in detail, I suppose that even the world itself would not contain the books which were written."[10] It is therefore normal to think that there might possibly be other things Jesus said while on earth which could be preserved outside the canonical gospels. In fact, for those who accept the inspiration of all of the New Testament, there is at least one saying of Jesus, preserved in Acts 20:35, which is not found in the gospel accounts. There, Paul says to the Ephesian elders, "In everything I showed you that by working hard in this manner you must help the weak and remember the words of the Lord Jesus, that he Himself said, 'It is more blessed to give than to receive.'" Since *agrapha* are defined as sayings of Jesus outside the canonical gospels, Christians accept Acts 20:35 as a truly authentic agraphon (singular form of *agrapha*).

Many scholars consider John 7:53–8:11, the story of the woman caught in adultery, to be an agraphon. The passage occurs only in John and even there it is not supported by the oldest manuscripts. The textual evidence is strong enough, though, that almost all Bible versions include it as part of their text. If it is not accepted as part of the text, most scholars would accept it as an authentic agraphon. As we saw in the last chapter, Papias quoted the passage early in the second century.

Scholars use three primary criteria to evaluate the authenticity of an agraphon (Law. CPAA 30-31): (1) Multiplicity of witnesses: How many witnesses report that Jesus said the saying in question? (2) Authority of the witnesses: How qualified is the witness to attribute the saying to Jesus? This may be determined by the proximity of the witness to early tradition and how much care the witness displays in recording the words of Jesus. (3) Degree of agreement between the witnesses and the canonical gospels. However, if an agraphon simply appears to be a loose paraphrase of a statement in the canonical gospels then it cannot be said to be an authentic agraphon. It simply confirms what is already in the previously written canonical gospels.

Between verses 4 and 5 of Luke 6, one manuscript, Codex D (called Bezae), adds:

> On the same day, seeing one working on the Sabbath day, he [Jesus] said
> to him, "Man, if you know what you are doing, you are blessed; but if you
> do not know, you are accursed and a transgressor of the law." (MeB.TNT 50)

The passage does seem to reflect Jesus' practice and teaching regarding the Sabbath, especially that the Sabbath was made for man and not man for the Sabbath (Mark 2:27). Metzger concludes:

> Although this sentence, which is found in no other manuscript, cannot
> be regarded as part of the original text of Luke, it may well embody a first-
> century tradition, one of the "many other things which Jesus did" but
> which were not written in the gospels (see John 21:25). (MeB.TNT 50)

One agraphon quoted approximately seventy times by church fathers is the command, "Be approved money-changers." It carries the idea of being like skilled money-changers who can detect counterfeit coins among the genuine coins. The agraphon is often found coupled with Paul's statement, "But examine everything carefully; hold fast to that which is good" (1 Thessalonians 5:21). It is conceivable that someone originally heard Jesus say this and later wrote it in the margin of a copy of Paul's first letter to the Thessalonians which was then passed on to the early church fathers. We know that Papias was fond of collecting these kinds of reminiscences from "the Elders" whom he met.

Oxyrhynchus Papyrus 840 may preserve a confrontation between Jesus and a self-righteous high priest:

> Woe to you blind that see not. Thou hast bathed thyself in water that is
> poured out, in which dogs and swine lie night and day and thou hast
> washed thyself and hast chafed thine outer skin, which prostitutes also and
> flute-girls anoint, bathe, chafe and rouge, in order to arouse desire in men,
> but within they are full of scorpions and of badness of every kind. But I
> and my disciples of whom thou sayest, that we have not immersed our-
> selves, have been immersed in the living…water.

It is conceivable that Jesus might have said something similar to the above. Archaeologists have uncovered numerous mikvah baths in Jerusalem and elsewhere. These baths verify the many ritual washings of the devout religious leaders in Jesus' day. The gospels reflect often that Jesus was more concerned with inner purity than with external ritual purity.

Oxyrhynchus Papyrus 655 has Jesus saying, "He himself will give you your raiment," a saying consistent with Matthew 6:25-34. The apocryphal "Acts of Peter" may preserve an occasion where Jesus said, "They that are with me have not understood me." The canonical gospels often record times when the disciples had not understood Jesus.

Because so many agrapha are in doubt as to their origin, there is no devotional value in any of these sayings. But there is evidential value in that they show a widespread early desire to preserve the words of Jesus. William White emphasizes:

> The canonical gospels never state that they are either exhaustive or comprehensive, but indicate only that they are sufficient to elicit faith in Christ and His atonement. (Cf. John 21:25, et al.) In the light of such texts and the allusions to teachings of the Lord not mentioned in the gospels…it is highly likely that fragments of noncanonical discourses and sermons would be found extant in extrabiblical literature.[11]

On the other hand, White cautions against trying to use agrapha to form an impression of Jesus which is not consistent with the biblical accounts:

> To assume that these represent lost documents which are the true and authoritative sources of the canonical writings is a specious and highly subjective judgement.[12]

White's conclusion is fully justified in view of the findings presented next.

UNRELIABLE ADDITIONS TO THE GOSPELS

Most of the material in the apocryphal and pseudepigraphal writings is clearly unreliable. These works contain teachings which deviate from those of the apostles, and which are often supported by "historical" details of Jesus' life which are fanciful beyond credible belief. France reveals:

> The one feature which quickly becomes obvious as one reads what remains of these apocryphal "gospels" is that a high proportion of them are clearly angled towards a gnostic interpretation of Jesus' life and teaching. This is true, for instance, of all the "Christian" material from Nag Hammadi, which clearly represents the library of a gnostic group. And much that is not gnostic is equally clearly designed to promote other doctrinal tendencies which are known to have developed in second-century and later Christianity, such as the doctrine of the "harrowing of hell" or the perpetual virginity of Mary. (FrR.E 62)

It is, therefore, highly speculative to try to reconstruct the details of the life of the historical Jesus from these stories. This is where many of the popularistic lives of Jesus err. By virtually ignoring the canonical gospels and using apocryphal material as a foundation, they construct an image of Jesus which, in view of the best historical evidence, takes more "faith" to believe than that required for accepting the New Testament accounts.

"The Infancy Gospel of Thomas," written about AD 125, contains stories that serve as examples of questionable history:

> 3.1. The son of Annas the scribe was standing there with Joseph. He took

a branch of a willow and scattered the water which Jesus had arranged. 2. Jesus saw what he did and became angry and said to him, "You unrighteous, impious ignoramus, what did the pools and the water do to harm you? Behold, you shall also wither as a tree, and you shall not bear leaves nor roots nor fruit." 3. And immediately that child was all withered.

4.1. Once again he was going through the village, and a child who was running banged into his shoulder. Jesus was angered and said to him, "You shall go no further on your way." And immediately the child fell down dead. Some people saw this happen and said, "From whence was this child begotten, for his every word is an act accomplished?" 2. The parents of the dead boy went to Joseph and blamed him: "Because you have such a boy, you cannot live with us in the village; your alternative is to teach him to bless and not to curse, for he is killing our children."

5.1. Joseph took the child aside privately and warned him, saying, "Why do you do such things? These people are suffering and they hate us and are persecuting us!" Jesus said, "I know that these are not your words, but on account of you I will be silent. However, they shall bear their punishment." Immediately, those who accused him were blinded. (CaDR.DSG 92-93)

Unlike the canonical gospels, and completely contradictory to the character of Jesus in them, there is no point to these stories. F. F. Bruce states, "The embellishments with which these 'Infancy Gospels' fill out the sparse details of the birth stories in Matthew and Luke are all fabricated out of whole cloth." (BrFJCO 87) France adds that the apocryphal writings "represent not additional historical information about Jesus, but pious (or sometimes rather secular!) imagination filling in the gap left by the canonical writers' relative lack of story-telling for its own sake." (FrR.E 75) The very fact that these apocryphal writings supplied abundant details of Jesus' childhood contributes to their lack of credibility, for first century writings normally omitted most childhood details of even the greatest people.

"The Secret Gospel of Mark." In 1958, Professor Morton Smith of Columbia University discovered a partial document now known as "The Secret Gospel of Mark." (See SmM.CA and SmM.TSG) More accurately, it was part of the text of this "Secret Gospel" being quoted by a writer purporting to be Clement of Alexandria.[13] This Clement wrote toward the end of the second century, but this particular copy of the letter is removed from his time by about sixteen centuries. It was found written into the back of a seventeenth-century book by an eighteenth-century hand.

The letter, according to Ian Wilson in *Jesus: The Evidence*, "raises some intriguing questions concerning the founder of Christianity." (Wil.JTE 27) They are intriguing to those who would like to hypothesize that Jesus might have been a homosexual. The letter describes how Jesus raised a rich young man from the dead, obviously drawing on the account of Jesus' raising of Lazarus in the Gospel of John. It continues:

But the youth, looking upon him, loved him and began to beseech him that he might be with him. And going out of the tomb they came into the house of the youth, for he was rich. And after six days Jesus told him what to do and in the evening the youth comes to him, wearing a linen cloth over [his] naked [body]. And he remained with him that night, for Jesus taught him the mystery of the kingdom of God. And thence, he returned to the other side of the Jordan. (Wil.JTE 27)

Ian Wilson summarizes Morton Smith's conclusions that since this version of Mark contains "the Lazarus story," and since the Gospel of Mark was written before that of John, then this "Secret Gospel of Mark" must be the earliest version of Mark. In other words, the biblical Mark deleted this story from the secret version.

This scenario misrepresents the facts and is a good example of how questionable evidence about Jesus is often distorted for sensational purposes. In the first place, if this text really is an apocryphal gospel of the first two centuries, there is so little of it that it is speculative to conclude that it was a longer document which Mark condensed to produce his canonical gospel. It is almost certain that the reverse is true. In other words, the Lazarus story from John was embellished and written into "The Secret Gospel of Mark." In fact, this Clement, whoever he really is, even states in the document that Mark wrote this longer version of his canonical gospel when he came to Alexandria, "thus producing a 'more spiritual gospel for the use of those who were being perfected,' designed to 'lead the hearers into the innermost sanctuary of that truth hidden by seven veils.'" (FrR.E 81) The language is obviously gnostic, which we would expect, for gnosticism flourished at an early date in Alexandria.

Clement of Alexandria, as many scholars accept, very well may be the author of this letter. And this is one more reason the letter suffers a lack of credibility. France states:

Clement's other writings show him to be both a lover of ideas of secrecy, esoteric teaching, mystical experiences and the like…. Keen as Clement was on opposing what he regarded as heretical, he seems to have been uncritical almost to the point of gullibility in accepting material which chimed in with his own predilections. (FrR.E 83)

One more problem with "The Secret Gospel of Mark" is that its genuineness is still doubted. Professor James D. G. Dunn, professor of New Testament at the University of Durham, writes that, though many scholars have accepted the letter as being from Clement, "until more experts have been able to examine and subject the original to appropriate tests, the possibility of some elaborate hoax cannot finally be ruled out." (DuJ.E 51)

In view of the evidence against the claims of "The Secret Gospel" being historical, Professor Henry Chadwick of Cambridge University describes Morton Smith's hypothesis as: "Marvelously implausible, delightful to read; and there is not the slightest chance that it is true."[14] The same could thus be said for the popular *Holy Blood, Holy*

Grail, which relies on the views of Morton Smith and others like him who elevate questionable texts of this kind to a level of historical reliability. (BaM.HB)

"The Gospel of Philip" is another apocryphal writing which is highly gnostic and historically unreliable. The authors of *Holy Blood, Holy Grail* also rely on this work for historical details to support their elaborate hypothesis. (BaM.HB 382) But even Ian Wilson recognized the need to disclaim the accuracy of "The Gospel of Philip" by saying, "It should be recognized, however, that 'The Gospel of Philip'...has no special claim to an early date, and may be merely a fantasy of a type not at all uncommon among Christian apocryphal literature of the third and fourth centuries." (Wil.JTE 96-97)

Some apocryphal gospels were written very late and therefore cannot provide any new historical evidence about Jesus. For example, "The Gospel of Pseudo-Matthew" was written possibly as late as the eighth or ninth century, though some think it is from an earlier period. (CaDR.DSG) It relies heavily on "The Gospel of James" and "The Infancy Gospel of Thomas."

"The Gospel of Peter," an earlier work, was known by about AD 200. It appears to rely on the canonical gospels but changes details to fit the author's purpose. Not only is it docetic (following the heresy that Jesus' body was not real flesh and blood), but it also seeks at every possible point to remove blame from Pilate for Jesus' death and place the blame solely on the Jews.

"The Gospel of Thomas." The sensational TV series "Jesus: The Evidence," aired on London Weekend Television in 1984, claimed that gnostic Christianity was one of the oldest forms of Christianity. The implication is that it is therefore at least an equal competitor for the original and true form of the Christian faith. But this contention, based primarily on "The Gospel of Thomas," does not hold up under investigation.

"The Gospel of Thomas," probably first compiled c. AD 150, is a collection of 114 alleged sayings of Jesus (agrapha). It begins on a gnostic note: "These are the secret words which the living Jesus spoke, and which Didymus Judas Thomas wrote." You can also taste the obvious gnostic flavor of this work in the following segments:

> 70. Jesus said: When you beget in yourselves him whom you have, he will save you. If you do not have him within yourselves, he whom you do not have within yourselves will kill you.

> 77. Jesus said: I am the light which is over everything. I am the All; the All came forth from me and the All has reached to me. Split the wood; I am there. Lift up the stone, and you will find me there.

> 82. Jesus said: He who is near me is near the fire, and he who is far from me is far from the kingdom.

> 114. Simon Peter said to them: Let Mary go away from us, for women are not worthy of life. Jesus said: Lo, I shall lead her, so that I may make her a

male, that she too may become a living spirit, resembling you males. For every woman who makes herself a male will enter the kingdom of heaven.

(Compiled by R. T. France in FrR.E 75-76)

Some scholars, more recently Joachim Jeremias and much earlier, Origen, have recognized some sayings in "The Gospel of Thomas" (for example #82 above) as authentic agrapha. Origen, however, rejected "The Gospel of Thomas" as a whole from being an authentic gospel. He appears to have had good reason for doing so. Approximately one fourth of "The Gospel of Thomas" preserves early tradition found in the Gospels of Matthew and Luke.

But even the original "Gospel of Thomas" was subjected to a definite later gnosticizing process. The manuscript version found at Nag Hammadi is a Coptic work written after the beginning of the fourth century. Another discovery, the Oxyrhynchus Papyri, contains what appears to be one or more earlier editions (late second and early third century) of the same work. (See DuJ.E 101.)

As Dunn illustrates, we can trace the gnostic additions by examining certain sayings. The earliest version of Saying 2, for example, was probably Matthew 7:7-8 and 11:28, "Seek and you will find…he who seeks finds…. Come to me…and I will give you rest." By the late second or early third century, the Oxyrhynchus Papyri 654.5-9 has altered the text to read:

> (Jesus says:) Let him who see(ks) not cease (seeking until) he finds; and when he finds (he will) be astounded, and having been (astoun)ded, he will reign; an(d reigning), he will (re)st.

By the time of the fourth-century "Gospel of Thomas," the saying reads:

> Jesus said: He who seeks should not stop seeking until he finds; and when he finds, he will be bewildered (beside himself); and when he is bewildered, he will marvel, and will reign over the All.

The thoroughly gnostic feature, "The All," is the last element that has been added, confirming that the gnostic features of the saying were not original but late. By using this kind of analysis scholars have determined that far from being the original form of Christianity, the gnosticism that developed corrupted the Christian faith. Therefore, popularistic works which build their concept of Jesus on gnostic or other apocryphal traditions are certainly on shaky ground.

CONCLUSIONS

Critics of the gospel accounts often declare they are legendary, not historical. It is therefore incredible that these very detractors, such as the authors of *Holy Blood, Holy Grail,* will so uncritically accept the historical reliability of apocryphal gospels. These works were produced later and with much more of an obvious theological bias (gnostic, docetic, etc.) than the canonical gospels.

In this chapter we have seen that some agrapha simply confirm material already in the canonical gospels. Of the remaining agrapha very small portions may present genuine historical information about Jesus, but the vast majority should be considered historically unreliable.

Some may wonder if the development of legends about Jesus in the apocryphal gospels shows that the canonical gospels are also legendary. F. F. Bruce answers:

> A parallel case is that of Alexander the Great, around whose name a cycle of romantic stories took shape from the early third century AD to the fifteenth century, from Britain to Malaya. This cycle bears but little relation to the historical facts of Alexander's career, but its existence in no way impairs the credibility of the historical facts; rather it testifies to the exceptional impact which the memory of Alexander and his exploits made throughout Europe and Asia. Similarly the proliferation of legends about Jesus, in the apocryphal gospels and elsewhere, in no way impairs the historical validity of his life and ministry; rather it bears witness to the increasing impact of his person and achievement both within Christendom and beyond its frontiers, even among people who had no experience of his redeeming grace. (BrEJCO 204)

You probably have asked or been asked, "How can we trust gospel accounts written years after Jesus' death? After all, everyone knows what happens to a message when you whisper it around a circle." The apocryphal and pseudepigraphal writings demonstrate that much was being said and written about Jesus in the first four centuries. Some of it was true. Some was not. It is as though a handful of people in an auditorium are given the same message to spread to everyone else in the auditorium. Each person has the freedom to verify with others what the true, original message was. Under these circumstances, one would expect that those who wanted to get the message right certainly could.

France, speaking of the noncanonical writings about Jesus, summarizes:

> In assessing how much historical value may be attributed to this later material, we are therefore thrown back on a fundamental choice between two approaches. One is to take the New Testament evidence (which after all is unquestionably the earliest) as our starting-point, and to use the portrait of Jesus which it offers as our criterion for judging the plausibility of the later accounts. In that case, as we have already noted, the scales are clearly weighted against any significant alteration to our knowledge of Jesus, since any data which do not conform to the New Testament pattern will be automatically suspect.
>
> The other approach is to assume that the New Testament evidence is itself tendentious and unreliable, representing a deliberate reinterpretation of Jesus in the direction of what later became "orthodox" Christianity, and that

the "gnostic" Jesus of the second-century writings is the historical figure who underlies this early distortion. In that case, the search for "suppressed evidence" becomes the essential means of progress in our knowledge of the real Jesus, in order to penetrate behind the ruthless and remarkably successful cover-up operation carried out by the victorious "orthodox party."

This second approach is the one adopted, in various ways, by those who are now advocating a reinterpretation of Jesus as a Zealot, a magician, a practitioner of esoteric cultic initiation, and so on. (FrR.E 84-85)

It is interesting to note that these authors will go to almost any extreme in order to explain away or ignore the historical reliability of the canonical gospels, which are attested by much more and much better evidence, and will so eagerly embrace the more questionable apocryphal accounts.

But is there enough evidence to justify our acceptance of the canonical gospels as historically reliable? Part II of this book discusses the evidence for the historical reliability of the description of Jesus given in the New Testament.

PART II

THE HISTORICAL RELIABILITY *of* NEW TESTAMENT EVIDENCE

ARE THE BIBLICAL
RECORDS RELIABLE?

I was speaking at Arizona State University and a professor who had brought his literature class with him approached me after a "free-speech" lecture outdoors. He said,
"Mr. McDowell, you are basing all your claims about Christ on a second-century
document that is obsolete. I showed in class today how the New Testament was written
so long after Christ that it could not be accurate in what it recorded."

I replied, "Your opinions and conclusions about the New Testament are twenty-
five years out of date."

That professor's opinions about the records concerning Jesus found their source
in the conclusions of a German critic, F. C. Baur. Baur assumed that most of the New
Testament Scriptures were not written until late in the second century AD. He concluded that these writings came basically from myths or legends that had developed
during the lengthy interval between the lifetime of Jesus and the time these accounts
were set down in writing.

By the twentieth century, however, archaeological discoveries had confirmed the
accuracy of the New Testament manuscripts. Discoveries of early papyrus manuscripts
(the John Rylands Papyrus, AD 130; the Chester Beatty Papyri, c. AD 155 and the Bodmer Papyri II, AD 200) bridged the gap between the time of Jesus and existing manuscripts from a later date.

Millar Burrows of Yale says, "Another result of comparing New Testament Greek
with the language of the papyri [discoveries] is an increase of confidence in the accurate
transmission of the text of the New Testament itself." (BuM.WM 52.) Such findings as these
have increased scholarly confidence in the reliability of the Bible. *

William Albright, at one time the world's foremost biblical archaeologist, writes:
"We can already say emphatically that there is no longer any solid basis for dating any
book of the New Testament after about AD 80, two full generations before the date

---

* This chapter is adapted from chapters 4, 5 and 6 of *More Than a Carpenter* by Josh McDowell, Tyndale House
Publishers, Carol Stream, IL.

between 130 and 150 given by the more radical New Testament critics of today." (AIW.RD 136) He reiterates this view in an interview for *Christianity Today:* "In my opinion, every book of the New Testament was written by a baptized Jew between the forties and the eighties of the first century AD (very probably sometime between about AD 50 AND 75)."[1]

Sir William Ramsay is regarded as one of the greatest archaeologists ever to have lived. He was a student of the German historical school that taught that the Book of Acts was a product of the mid-second century AD and not the first century as it purports to be. After reading modern criticism about the Book of Acts, he became convinced that it was not a trustworthy account of the facts of that time (AD 50) and therefore was unworthy of consideration by a historian. So in his research on the history of Asia Minor, Ramsay paid little attention to the New Testament. His investigation, however, eventually compelled him to consider the writing of Luke. He observed the meticulous accuracy of the historical details, and his attitude toward the Book of Acts began to change. He was forced to conclude that "Luke is a historian of the first rank... this author should be placed along with the very greatest of historians." (RaW.BRD15 222) Because of the accuracy of the most minute detail, Ramsay finally conceded that Acts could not be a second-century document but was rather a mid-first-century account.

Many liberal scholars are being forced to consider earlier dates for the origination of the New Testament. British theologian and New Testament scholar John A. T. Robinson reveals some startlingly radical conclusions in his book *Redating the New Testament.* His research led him to the conviction that the whole of the New Testament was written before the fall of Jerusalem in AD 70. (RoJA.BNT)

"As a Western Scripture scholar," observes Dr. Peter Stuhlmacher of Tübingen, "I am inclined to doubt these [gospel] stories but as a historian I am obliged to take them as reliable."[2]

Stuhlmacher now confesses, "The biblical texts as they stand are the best hypothesis we have until now to explain what really happened."[3]

Today the form critics say that the material was passed by word of mouth until it was written down in the form of the gospels. Even though the period was much shorter than previously believed, they still conclude that the gospel accounts took on the forms of folk literature (legends, tales, myths and parables).

One of the major criticisms of the form critics' concept of oral tradition development is that the period of oral tradition (as defined by the critics) is not long enough to have allowed the alterations in the tradition. Speaking of the brevity of the time element involved in the writing of the New Testament, Simon Kistemaker, professor of Bible at Dordt College, writes:

> Normally, the accumulation of folklore among people of primitive culture takes many generations; it is a gradual process spread over centuries of time. But in conformity with the thinking of the form critic, we must conclude that the gospel stories were produced and collected within little

more than one generation. In terms of the form-critical approach, the formation of the individual gospel units must be understood as a telescoped project with accelerated course of action. (KiS.G 48-49)

A. H. McNeile, former Regius Professor of Divinity at the University of Dublin, challenges form criticism's concept of oral tradition. He points out that form critics do not deal with the tradition of Jesus' words as closely as they should. A careful look at 1 Corinthians 7:10, 12 and 25 shows the careful preservation and the existence of a genuine tradition of recording these words. In the Jewish religion it was customary for a student to memorize a rabbi's teaching. A good pupil was like "a plastered cistern that loses not a drop" (Mishnah Aboth, 2,8). If we rely on C. F. Burney's theory (in *The Poetry of Our Lord*, 1925), we can assume that much of the Lord's teaching is in Aramaic poetical form, making it easy to be memorized. (McA.IS 64)

Analyzing form criticism, Albright wrote: "Only modern scholars who lack both historical method and perspective can spin such a web of speculation as that with which form critics have surrounded the gospel tradition." Albright's own conclusion was that "a period of twenty to fifty years is too slight to permit of any appreciable corruption of the essential content and even of the specific wording of the sayings of Jesus." (AIW.FSA 297-98)

Often when I am talking with someone about the Bible they sarcastically reply that you can't trust what the Bible says. Why, it was written almost two thousand years ago. It's full of errors and discrepancies. I reply that I believe I can trust the Scriptures. Then I describe an incident that took place during a lecture in a history class. I made the statement that I believed there was more evidence for the reliability of the New Testament than for almost any ten pieces of classical literature put together. The professor sat over in the corner snickering, as if to say, "Oh, gee—come on."

I said, "What are you snickering about?"

He said, "The audacity to make the statement in a history class that the New Testament is reliable. That's ridiculous."

Well, I appreciate it when somebody makes a statement like that because I always like to ask this one question (and I've never had a positive response), "Tell me, sir, as a historian, what are the tests that you apply to any piece of literature of history to determine if it's accurate or reliable?"

The amazing thing was he didn't have any tests.

I answered, "I have some tests."

I believe that the historical reliability of the Scripture should be tested by the same criteria used on all historical documents. Military historian C. Sanders lists and explains the three basic principles of historiography. They are (1) the bibliographical test; (2) the internal evidence test; and (3) the external evidence test. (SaC.IR 143ff.)

BIBLIOGRAPHICAL TEST

The bibliographical test is an examination of the textual transmission by which documents reach us. In other words, not having the original documents, how reliable are the copies we have in regard to the number of manuscripts (MSS) and the time interval between the original and extant copy?

We can appreciate the tremendous wealth of manuscript authority of the New Testament by comparing it with textual material from other notable ancient sources.

The history of Thucydides (460–400 BC) is available to us from just eight manuscripts dated about AD 900, almost 1,300 years after he wrote. The manuscripts of the history of Herodotus are likewise late and scarce, and yet, as F. F. Bruce, former Rylands Professor of Biblical Criticism and Exegesis at the University of Manchester, comments, "No classical scholar would listen to an argument that the authenticity of Herodotus or Thucydides is in doubt because the earliest manuscripts of their works which are of use to us are over 1,300 years later than the originals." (BrF.NTD 16ff.)

Aristotle wrote his Poetics c. 343 BC, and yet the earliest copy we have is dated AD 1100, nearly a 1,400-year gap, and only five manuscripts are in existence.

Caesar composed his history of the Gallic Wars between 58 and 50 BC and its manuscript authority rests on nine or ten copies dating a thousand years after his death.

When it comes to the manuscript authority of the New Testament, the abundance of material is almost embarrassing in contrast. After the early papyri manuscript discoveries that bridged the gap between the times of Jesus and the second century, an abundance of other manuscripts came to light. Over 22,000 copies of New Testament manuscripts are in existence today. The *Iliad* has 643 manuscripts and is second in manuscript authority after the New Testament.

Sir Frederic Kenyon, who was the director and principal librarian at the British Museum and second to none in authority for issuing statements about manuscripts, concludes:

> The interval then between the dates of original composition and the earliest extant evidence becomes so small as to be in fact negligible, and the last foundation for any doubt that the Scriptures have come down to us substantially as they were written has now been removed. Both the authenticity and the general integrity of the books of the New Testament may be regarded as finally established. (KeF.BA 288-89)

The New Testament Greek scholar J. Harold Greenlee adds:

> Since scholars accept as generally trustworthy the writings of the ancient classics even though the earliest MSS were written so long after the original writings and the number of extant MSS is in many instances so small, it is clear that the reliability of the text of the New Testament is likewise assured. (GrJ.116)

The application of the bibliographical test to the New Testament assures us that it has more manuscript authority than any piece of literature from antiquity. Adding to that authority the more than 100 years of intensive New Testament textual criticism, one can conclude that an authentic New Testament text has been established.

INTERNAL EVIDENCE TEST

The bibliographical test has determined only that the text we have now is essentially what was originally recorded. One has still to determine whether that written record is credible and to what extent. That is the problem of internal criticism, which is the second test of historicity listed by C. Sanders.

At this point the literary critic continues to follow Aristotle's dictum: "The benefit of the doubt is to be given to the document itself, and not arrogated by the critic to himself."[4] In other words, as John Montgomery summarizes: "One must listen to the claims of the document under analysis, and not assume fraud or error unless the author disqualified himself by contradictions or known factual inaccuracies."[5]

Dr. Louis Gottschalk, former professor of history at the University of Chicago, outlines his historical method in a guide used by many for historical investigation. Gottschalk points out that the ability of the writer or the witness to tell the truth is helpful to the historian to determine credibility "even if it is contained in a document obtained by force or fraud, or is otherwise impeachable, or is based on hearsay evidence, or is from an interested witness." (GoL.UH69 160-161, 168)

This "ability to tell the truth" is closely related to the witness's nearness both geographically and chronologically to the events recorded. The New Testament accounts of the life and teaching of Jesus were recorded by men who had been either eyewitnesses themselves or who related the accounts of eyewitnesses of the actual events or teachings of Jesus.

> Luke 1:1-3: Inasmuch as many have undertaken to compile an account of the things accomplished among us, just as those who from the beginning were eyewitnesses and servants of the Word have handed them down to us, it seemed fitting for me as well, having investigated everything carefully from the beginning, to write it out for you in consecutive order, most excellent Theophilus.

> 2 Peter 1:16: For we did not follow cleverly devised tales when we made known to you the power and coming of our Lord Jesus Christ, but we were eyewitnesses of His majesty.

> 1 John 1:3: What we have seen and heard we proclaim to you also, that you also may have fellowship with us; and indeed our fellowship is with the Father, and with His Son Jesus Christ.

> John 19:35: And he who has seen has borne witness, and his witness is true; and he knows that he is telling the truth, so that you also may believe.

> Luke 3:1: In the fifteenth year of the reign of Tiberius Caesar, when Pontius Pilate was governor of Judea, and Herod was tetrarch of Galilee, and his brother Philip was tetrarch of the region of Ituraea and Trachonitis, and Lysanias was tetrarch of Abilene...

This closeness to the recorded accounts is an extremely effective means of certifying the accuracy of what is retained by a witness. The historian, however, also has to deal with the eyewitness who consciously or unconsciously tells falsehoods even though he is near to the event and is competent to tell the truth.

The New Testament accounts of Jesus began to be circulated within the lifetimes of those alive at the time of his life. These people could certainly confirm or deny the accuracy of the accounts. In advocating their case for the gospel, the apostles had appealed (even when confronting their most severe opponents) to common knowledge concerning Jesus. They not only said, "Look, we saw this"; or "We heard that"; but in addition they turned the tables around and right in front of adverse critics said, "You also know about these things.... You saw them; you yourselves know about it." One had better be careful when he says to his opposition, "You know this also," because if he isn't right in the details, it will be shoved right back down his throat.

> Acts 2:22: Men of Israel, listen to these words: Jesus the Nazarene, a man attested to you by God with miracles and wonders and signs which God performed through Him in your midst, just as you yourselves know.

> Acts 26:24-28: And while Paul was saying this in his defense, Festus said in a loud voice, "Paul, you are out of your mind! Your great learning is driving you mad." But Paul said,

> "I am not out of my mind, most excellent Festus, but I utter words of sober truth. For the king knows about these matters, and I speak to him also with confidence, since I am persuaded that none of these things escape his notice; for this has not been done in a corner."

Concerning the primary-source value of the New Testament records, F. F. Bruce, says:

> And it was not only friendly eyewitnesses that the early preachers had to reckon with; there were others less well disposed who were also conversant with the main facts of the ministry and death of Jesus. The disciples could not afford to risk inaccuracies (not to speak of willful manipulation of the facts), which would at once be exposed by those who would be only too glad to do so. On the contrary, one of the strong points in the original apostolic preaching is the confident appeal to the knowledge of the hearers; they not only said, "We are witnesses of these things"; but also, "As you yourselves know" (Acts 2:22). Had there been any tendency to depart from the facts in any material respect, the possible presence of hostile witnesses in the audience would have served as a further corrective. (BrF.NTD 16 ff., 33)

Lawrence J. McGinley of Saint Peter's College comments on the value of hostile witnesses in relationship to recorded events:

> First of all, eyewitnesses of the events in question were still alive when the tradition had been completely formed; and among those eyewitnesses were bitter enemies of the new religious movement. Yet the tradition claimed to

narrate a series of well-known deeds and publicly taught doctrines at a time when false statements could, and would, be challenged. (McL.FC 25)

New Testament scholar Robert Grant of the University of Chicago concludes:

> At the time they [the synoptic gospels] were written or may be supposed to have been written, there were eyewitnesses and their testimony was not completely disregarded…This means that the gospels must be regarded as largely reliable witnesses to the life, death, and resurrection of Jesus. (GraR.HI 302)

Historian Will Durant, who has spent his life analyzing records of antiquity, says the literary evidence indicates historical authenticity regarding the New Testament:

> Despite the prejudices and theological preconceptions of the evangelists, they record many incidents that mere inventors would have concealed— the competition of the apostles for high places in the Kingdom, their flight after Jesus' arrest, Peter's denial, the failure of Christ to work miracles in Galilee, the references of some auditors to his possible insanity, his early uncertainty as to his mission, his confessions of ignorance as to the future, his moments of bitterness, his despairing cry on the cross; no one read- ing these scenes can doubt the reality of the figure behind them. That a few simple men should in one generation have invented so powerful and appealing a personality, so lofty an ethic, and so inspiring a vision of human brotherhood, would be a miracle far more incredible than any recorded in the gospels. After two centuries of higher criticism the outlines of the life, character, and teaching of Christ remain reasonably clear, and consti- tute the most fascinating feature in the history of Western man. (DuW.SC 3:557)

EXTERNAL EVIDENCE TEST

The third test of historicity is that of external evidence—whether other historical material confirms or denies the internal testimony of the documents themselves. In other words, what sources are there, apart from the literature under analysis, that sub- stantiate its accuracy, reliability and authenticity?

Gottschalk argues that *"conformity* or *agreement* with other known historical or sci- entific facts is often the decisive test of evidence, whether of one or of more witnesses." (GoL.UH50 168)

Two friends of the apostle John confirm the internal evidence from John's accounts. The historian Eusebius, as previously cited, preserves writings of Papias, bishop of Hier- apolis (AD 130):

> The Elder [apostle John] used to say this also: "Mark, having been the interpreter of Peter, wrote down accurately all that he [Peter] mentioned, whether sayings or doings of Christ, not, however, in order. For he was neither a hearer nor a companion of the Lord; but afterwards, as I said, he

accompanied Peter, who adapted his teachings as necessity required, not as though he were making a compilation of the sayings of the Lord. So then Mark made no mistake, writing down in this way some things as he mentioned them; for he paid attention to this one thing, not to omit anything that he had heard, not to include any false statement among them."[6]

Irenaeus, Bishop of Lyons AD 180, was a student of Polycarp, Bishop of Smyrna (who had been a Christian for eighty-six years and was a disciple of John the Apostle), wrote:

> Matthew published his gospel among the Hebrews [i.e., Jews] in their own tongue, when Peter and Paul were preaching the gospel in Rome and founding the church there. After their departure [i.e., death, which strong tradition places at the time of the Neronian persecution in 64], Mark, the disciple and interpreter of Peter, himself handed down to us in writing the substance of Peter's preaching. Luke, the follower of Paul, set down in a book the gospel preached by his teacher. Then John, the disciple of the Lord, who also leaned on his breast [this is a reference to John 13:25 and 21:20], himself produced his gospel, while he was living at Ephesus in Asia.[7]

Archaeology often provides some extremely powerful external evidence. It contributes to biblical criticism, not in the area of inspiration and revelation, but by providing evidence of accuracy about events that are recorded. Archaeologist Joseph Free writes: "Archaeology has confirmed countless passages which have been rejected by critics as unhistorical or contradictory to known facts." (FrJP.A 1)

We already have seen how archaeology caused Sir William Ramsay to change his initial negative convictions about the historicity of Luke and come to the conclusion that the Book of Acts was accurate in its description of the geography, antiquities and society of Asia Minor.

F. F. Bruce notes: "Where Luke has been suspected of inaccuracy, and accuracy has been vindicated by some inscriptional [external] evidence, it may be legitimate to say that archaeology has confirmed the New Testament record." (BrF.AC 331)

A. N. Sherwin-White, a classical historian, writes that "for Acts the confirmation of historicity is overwhelming." He continues by saying that "any attempt to reject its basic historicity even in matters of detail must now appear absurd. Roman historians have long taken it for granted." (ShA.RS 189)

After personally trying, as a skeptic myself, to shatter the historicity and validity of the Scriptures, I had to conclude that they actually are historically trustworthy. If a person discards the Bible as unreliable in this sense, then he or she must discard almost all the literature of antiquity. One problem I constantly face is the desire on the part of many to apply one standard or test to secular literature and another to the Bible. We need to apply the same test, whether the literature under investigation is secular or religious. Having done this, I believe we can say, "The Bible is trustworthy and historically reliable in its witness about Jesus."

Dr. Clark H. Pinnock states:

> There exists no document from the ancient world witnessed by so excellent a set of textual and historical testimonies and offering so superb an array of historical data on which an intelligent decision may be made. An honest [person] cannot dismiss a source of this kind. Skepticism regarding the historical credentials of Christianity is based upon an irrational [i.e., antisupernatural] bias. (PiC.SF 58)

WHO WOULD DIE FOR A LIE?

One area which is often overlooked in challenges to Christianity is the transformation of Jesus' apostles. Their changed lives provided solid testimony for the validity of his claims. Since the Christian faith is historical, to investigate it we must rely heavily upon testimony, both written and oral.

There are many definitions of "history," but the one I prefer is "a knowledge of the past based upon testimony." If someone says, "I don't believe that's a good definition," I ask, "Do you believe that Napoleon lived?"

They almost always reply, "Yes."

"Have you seen him?" I ask, and they confess they haven't. "How do you know, then?" Well, they are relying on testimony.

This particular definition of history has one inherent problem. The testimony must be reliable or the hearer will be misinformed. Christianity involves knowledge of the past based upon testimony, so now we must ask, "Were the original oral testimonies about Jesus trustworthy? Can they be trusted to have conveyed correctly what Jesus said and did?" I believe they can be.

I can trust the apostles' testimonies because, of those twelve men, eleven died martyrs' deaths on the basis of two things: (1) the resurrection of Jesus; and (2) their belief in him as the Son of God. Reliable tradition shows they were tortured and flogged, and then finally faced death by some of the crudest methods then known:

1. Peter—crucified

2. Andrew—crucified

3. Matthew—the sword

4. John—natural

5. James, son of Alphaeus—crucified

6. Philip—crucified

7. Simon—crucified

8. Thaddaeus—killed by arrows

9. James, brother of Jesus—stoned

10. Thomas—spear thrust

11. Bartholomew—crucified

12. James, son of Zebedee—the sword

The response that is usually chorused back is this: "Why, a lot of people have died for a lie; so what does it prove?"

Yes, a lot of people have died for a lie, but they thought it was the truth. Now if the resurrection didn't take place (i.e., was false), the disciples knew it. I find no way to demonstrate that they could have been deceived. Therefore these eleven men not only died for a lie—here is the catch—but they knew it was a lie. It would be hard to find eleven people in history who died for a lie, knowing it was a lie.

We need to be cognizant of several factors in order to appreciate what the apostles did.

First, as we have already seen, when the apostles wrote or spoke, they did so as eyewitnesses of the events they described. The main content of these eyewitness testimonies concerned the resurrection. The apostles were witnesses of the resurrected life of Jesus:

Luke 24:48	Acts 5:32	Acts 26:16
John 15:27	Acts 10:39	1 Corinthians 15:4-9
Acts 1:8	Acts 10:41	
Acts 2:24,32	Acts 13:31	1 Corinthians 15:15
Acts 3:15	Acts 22:15	
Acts 4:33	Acts 23:11	1 John 1:2

Second, the apostles themselves had to be convinced that Jesus was raised from the dead. At first they hadn't believed. They went and hid (Mark 14:50). They didn't hesitate to express their doubts. Only after ample and convincing evidence did they believe. There was Thomas, who said he wouldn't believe that Jesus was raised from the dead until he had put his finger in the nail prints. Thomas later died a martyr's death for Jesus. Was he deceived? He bet his life he wasn't.

Then there was Peter. He denied Jesus several times during his trial. Finally he deserted him. But something happened to this coward. Just a short time after Jesus' crucifixion and burial, Peter showed up in Jerusalem preaching boldly, though threatened with death, that Jesus was the Christ and had been resurrected. Finally, Peter was crucified upside down. Was he deceived? What had happened to him? What had transformed him so dramatically into a bold lion for Jesus? Why was he willing to die for him? The only explanation I am satisfied with is 1 Corinthians 15:5—"and then He appeared to Cephas [Peter]" (John 1:42).

The classic example of a man convinced against his will was James, the brother of Jesus (Matthew 13:55; Mark 6:3). Although James wasn't one of the original twelve

(Matthew 10:2-4), he was later recognized as an apostle (Galatians 1:19), as were Paul and Barnabas (Acts 14:14). When Jesus was alive, James didn't believe in his brother Jesus (John 7:5). He, as well as his other brothers and his sisters, even may have mocked Jesus. "You want people to believe in you? Why don't you go up to Jerusalem and do your thing?" For James it must have been humiliating for Jesus to go around and bring ridicule to the family name by his wild claims ("I am the way, and the truth, and the life; no one comes to the Father, but through Me"—John 14:6; "I am the vine, you are the branches"—John 15:5; "I am the good shepherd…and My own know Me"—John 10:14). What would *you* think if your brother said such things?

But something happened to James. After Jesus was crucified and buried, James was preaching in Jerusalem. His message was that Jesus died for sins and was resurrected and was alive. Eventually, James became one of the leaders of the Jerusalem church and wrote a book, the epistle of James. He began it by writing, "James, a servant of God and of the Lord Jesus Christ, his brother." Eventually James died a martyr's death by stoning at the hands of Ananias the high priest (according to Josephus). Was James deceived? No, the only plausible explanation is 1 Corinthians 15:7—"then He appeared to James."

If the resurrection was a lie, the apostles knew it. Were they perpetuating a colossal hoax? That possibility is inconsistent with what we know about their lives. They personally condemned lying and stressed honesty. They encouraged people to know the truth. Historian Edward Gibbon, in his famous work *The History of the Decline and Fall of the Roman Empire,* gives the "purer but austere morality of the first Christians" as one of five main reasons for the rapid success of Christianity. Michael Green, principal of St. John's College, Nottingham, observes that the resurrection

> was the belief that turned heartbroken followers of a crucified rabbi into the courageous witnesses and martyrs of the early church. This was the one belief that separated the followers of Jesus from the Jews and turned them into the community of the resurrection. You could imprison them, flog them, kill them, but you could not make them deny their conviction that "on the third day he rose again." (LaGE.IBR, Editor's Preface)

Third, the bold conduct of the apostles immediately after they were convinced of the resurrection makes it unlikely that it all was a fraud. Peter, who had denied Jesus, stood up—even at the threat of death—and proclaimed Jesus alive after the resurrection. The authorities arrested the followers of Jesus and beat them, yet they were soon back in the street speaking about him (Acts 5:40-42). Their friends noticed their buoyancy and their enemies noticed their courage. Nor did they preach in obscure towns, but in Jerusalem.

Jesus' followers couldn't have faced torture and death unless they were convinced of his resurrection. The unanimity of their message and course of conduct was amazing. The chances against any large group being in agreement are enormous, yet they all agreed on the truth of the resurrection. If they were deceivers, it's hard to explain why one of them didn't break down under pressure. Pascal, the French philosopher, writes:

> The allegation that the apostles were impostors is quite absurd. Let us follow the charge to its logical conclusion: Let us picture those twelve men, meeting after the death of Jesus Christ, and entering into conspiracy to say that He has risen. That would have constituted an attack upon both the civil and the religious authorities. The heart of man is strangely given to fickleness and change; it is swayed by promises, tempted by material things. If any one of those men had yielded to temptations so alluring, or given way to the more compelling arguments of prison [or] torture, they would have all been lost. (Quoted in G1R.EP 187)

"How have they turned, almost overnight," asks Michael Green, "into the indomitable band of enthusiasts who braved opposition, cynicism, ridicule, hardship, prison, and death in three continents, as they preached everywhere Jesus and the resurrection?" (GreM.MA 23-24)

One of the greatest church historians ever to have lived, Kenneth Scott Latourette, at first a missionary to China, then a professor at Yale University until 1953, wrote:

> The effects of the resurrection and the coming of the Holy Spirit upon the disciples were…of major importance. From discouraged, disillusioned men and women who sadly looked back upon the days when they had hoped that Jesus "was he who should redeem Israel," they were made over into a company of enthusiastic witnesses. (LaK.HC 1:59)

Writer, professor and Christian activist Paul Little asks, "Are these men, who helped transform the moral structure of society, consummate liars or deluded madmen? These alternatives are harder to believe than the fact of the resurrection, and there is no shred of evidence to support them." (LiP.KW 63)

The steadfastness of the apostles even to death cannot be explained away. According to the *Encyclopedia Britannica,* Origen records Peter's head-downward crucifixion. British scholar Herbert Workman describes Peter's death:

> Thus Peter, as our Lord had prophesied, was "girt" by another, and "carried" out to die along the Aurelian Way, to a place hard by the gardens of Nero on the Vatican hill, where so many of his brethren had already suffered a cruel death. At his own request he was crucified head downward, as unworthy to suffer like his Master. (WoH.MEC 18-19)

Tertullian wrote that "no man would be willing to die unless he knew he had the truth." (FoG.TT 12)

Dr. Simon Greenleaf, former Royal Professor of Law at Harvard and author of a three-volume series on laws of legal evidence, a man who lectured for years on how to break down a witness and determine whether or not a witness was lying, observed that the annals of military warfare afford scarcely an example of the like heroic constancy, patience, and unflinching courage. They had every possible motive to review carefully the grounds of their faith, and the evidences of the great facts and truths which they asserted. (GrS.ET 29)

The apostles went through the test of death to verify what they were proclaiming. I believe I can trust their testimony more than that of most people I meet today, people who aren't willing to walk across the street for what they believe, let alone die for it.

WHAT GOOD IS A DEAD MESSIAH?

A lot of people have died for a good cause. Look at the student in San Diego who burned himself to death protesting the Vietnam war. In the 1960s many Buddhists burned themselves to death in order to bring world attention to Southeast Asia.

The problem with the apostles is that their good cause died on the cross. They believed Jesus to be the Messiah. They were convinced that he was the one to set up the kingdom of God and to rule over the people of Israel. They didn't think he could die.

In order to understand the apostles' relationship with Jesus and to understand why the cross was so incomprehensible to them, you have to grasp the attitude about the Messiah at that time.

The life and teachings of Jesus were in tremendous conflict with the Jewish messianic speculation of that day. From childhood a Jew was taught that when Messiah came, he would be a reigning, victorious, political leader. He would release the Jews from bondage and restore Israel to its rightful place. A suffering Messiah was "completely foreign to the Jewish conception of messiahship."[8]

E. F. Scott, former Professor of Biblical Theology at Union Theological Seminary in New York, gives his account of the historical setting of the time of Jesus:

> The period was one of intense excitement. The religious leaders found it almost impossible to restrain the ardour of the people, who were waiting everywhere for the appearance of the promised Deliverer. This mood of expectancy had no doubt been heightened by the events of recent history.
>
> For more than a generation past the Romans had been encroaching on Jewish freedom, and their measures of repression had stirred the spirit of patriotism to fiercer life. The dream of a miraculous deliverance, and of a messianic king who would effect it, assumed a new meaning in that critical time; but in itself it was nothing new. Behind the ferment of which we have evidence in the gospels, we can discern a long period of growing anticipation.
>
> To the people at large the Messiah remained what he had been to Isaiah and his contemporaries—the Son of David who would bring victory and prosperity to the Jewish nation. In the light of the gospel references it can hardly be doubted that the popular conception of the Messiah was mainly national and political. (ScEF.KM 65)

Jewish scholar Joseph Klausner writes: "The Messiah became more and more not only a preeminent political ruler but also a man of preeminent moral qualities." (KlJ.MI 23)

Jacob Gartenhaus reflects the prevailing Jewish beliefs of the time: "The Jews awaited the Messiah as the one who would deliver them from Roman oppression... the messianic hope was basically for a national liberation." (GaJ.JCM 8-10)

The *Jewish Encyclopedia* states that the Jews "yearned for the promised deliverer of the house of David, who would free them from the yoke of the hated foreign usurper, would put an end to the impious Roman rule, and would establish His own reign of peace and justice in its place."[9]

At that time the Jews were taking refuge in this promised Messiah. The apostles held the same beliefs as the people around them. As Millar Burrows stated, "Jesus was so unlike what all Jews expected the son of David to be that His own disciples found it almost impossible to connect the idea of the Messiah with Him." (BuM.ML 68) The grave communications by Jesus about being crucified were not at all welcomed by his disciples (Luke 9:22). There "seems to have been the hope," observes Scottish theologian A. B. Bruce,

> that He had taken too gloomy a view of the situation, and that His apprehensions would turn out groundless...a crucified Christ was a scandal and a contradiction to the apostles; quite as much as it continued to be to the majority of the Jewish people after the Lord had ascended to glory. (BrA.TT 177)

One can detect in the New Testament the apostles' attitude toward Jesus: They expected a reigning Messiah. After Jesus told his disciples that he had to go to Jerusalem and suffer, James and John asked him to promise that in his kingdom they could sit on his right and left hands (Mark 10:32-38). What type of Messiah were they expecting? A crucified Messiah? No, a political ruler. Jesus indicated that they misunderstood what he had to do; they didn't know what they were asking. When Jesus predicted his crucifixion, the twelve apostles couldn't figure out what he meant (Luke 18:31-34). Because of their background and training they believed they were in on a good thing. Then came Calvary. All their hopes were gone. They returned to their homes deeply discouraged.

Dr. George Eldon Ladd, professor of New Testament at Fuller Theological Seminary, writes:

> This is also why his disciples forsook him when he was taken captive. Their minds were so completely imbued with the idea of a conquering Messiah whose role it was to subdue his enemies that when they saw him broken and bleeding under the scourging, a helpless prisoner in the hands of Pilate, and when they saw him led away, nailed to a cross to die as a common criminal, all their messianic hopes for Jesus were shattered. It is a sound psychological fact that we hear only what we are prepared to hear. Jesus' predictions of his suffering and death fell on deaf ears. The disciples, in spite of his warning, were unprepared for it. (LaGE.IBR 38)

But a few weeks after the crucifixion, contrary to their former doubting, the disciples were in Jerusalem proclaiming Jesus as Savior and Lord, the Messiah. The only reasonable explanation of this change is 1 Corinthians 15:5—"He appeared...to the twelve." How else could those despondent disciples have gone out and suffered and died for a crucified Messiah? He certainly must have "presented Himself alive, after His suffering, by many convincing proofs, appearing to them over a period of forty days" (Acts 13)

Yes, a lot of people have died for a good cause, but, for the apostles, the good cause itself died on the cross. Only his resurrection and resultant contact with his followers would convince them Jesus was the Messiah. To this they testified, not only with their lips and lives but also with their deaths.

HIGHER CRITICISM: HOW "ASSURED" ARE THE RESULTS?

In the British television series "Jesus: The Evidence," a plaster image of a traditional white-faced Jesus (complete with long, wavy hair) was shown repeatedly—exploding—in slow motion. The basic message of the series was that modern scholarship has shattered the traditional Jesus of Christianity. True, the Jesus who lived in history almost surely was not the meek and mild person often portrayed in religious literature. Many modern critics, however, have gone beyond these cultural distortions and collectively have thrown out nearly all the historical references to Jesus in the gospel accounts.

Logically, it makes sense that our best source of knowledge about Jesus would be those who knew him or heard about him from eyewitnesses. We would expect, then, that the most detailed knowledge about him would be in the four gospel accounts of the New Testament.

In the last several centuries, however, a number of scholars have questioned the historical reliability of the New Testament portrayal of Jesus. They call the basis for their skepticism "the assured results of higher criticism." Almost all popular and scholarly "lives of Jesus" on the market today rely upon the results obtained by those higher critics.

Higher criticism is found in various forms and has been promoted primarily by German scholarship. Its influence in recent times has dominated the reporting in popular media on biblical subjects.

What is higher criticism? What are its divisions and distinctives? How does it affect our knowledge of Jesus as a historical person?

The subject is broad, but the following condensation and evaluation of several main distinctives of higher criticism should help answer the questions as to why discovering the historical Jesus has become an impossible task for the higher critic.

WHAT IS HIGHER CRITICISM?

Higher criticism is a division of biblical criticism. *Harper's Bible Dictionary* defines biblical criticism as "the study and investigation of biblical writings that seeks to make discerning and discriminating judgments about these writings."[1] It is meant to be neither positive nor negative.

Biblical criticism may be divided into lower and higher criticism as indicated on this chart:

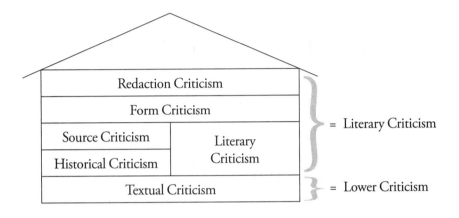

Lower criticism is identified with textual criticism since textual criticism is foundational to all other forms of biblical criticism. Textual criticism seeks to determine the original wording of the biblical text, especially since we do not have the original documents (called "autographs") themselves. Anyone who can read engages in textual criticism. If, for example, you noticed a typographical error while reading this page, you would correct the error in your mind, knowing that it was not originally intended by the authors. This process is essentially textual criticism.

Building upon lower or textual criticism, higher criticism uses other means to evaluate the text which lower criticism establishes as the most authentic version of the original. Thus, as in building a house, higher criticism builds on top of the foundation established by lower criticism.

Higher criticism can be divided into two broad disciplines, historical criticism and literary criticism. (McJ.ME/81)[2] Literary criticism seeks to analyze the text as a finished piece of literature. It evaluates the meanings of words, the grammar and the style of the text; it also seeks to determine the meaning of the text, and has been used to speculate about the life setting and circumstances of the writer.

Historical criticism studies the historical setting surrounding the composition of the text. It seeks to answer such questions as: (1) When and where was it written? (2) Who wrote it? (3) What circumstances surrounded the author or authors? (4) To whom was it written?

Growing out of historical criticism, source criticism emerged to a position of prominence among higher critics in the nineteenth century as many critical scholars rallied around the documentary hypothesis. This theory proposed that at least four sources (tagged "J," "E," "P," and "D") lay behind the formation of the first five books of the Old Testament. The same methodology was then applied to the gospels during the nineteenth century to suggest various sources (for example, "Q," "Mark," and "Proto-Luke") behind the gospel accounts.

Form criticism of the New Testament originated in Germany immediately after World War I. Relying much on source criticism, form criticism combined methods from both historical and literary criticism.

The Germans called form criticism *Formgeschichte,* meaning "form history." Its chief early proponents were Karl Ludwig Schmidt, Martin Dibelius and Rudolf Bultmann. Other form critics include R. H. Lightfoot and D. E. Nineham. Some of the more moderate form critics are Frederick Grant, B. S. Easton and Vincent Taylor.

New Testament form critics generally hold that the gospels were composed of small independent units or episodes. These small single units (*pericopes*) were circulated independently. The critics teach that the units gradually took on the form of various types of folk literature, such as legends, tales, myths and parables.

According to form criticism, the formation and preservation of the units were determined by the needs of the Christian community. In other words, when the community had a problem, they either created or preserved a saying or episode of Jesus to meet the needs of that particular problem. Therefore these units are not basically witnesses to the life of Jesus but reflections of the beliefs and practices of the early church.

The task of form criticism, then, is to discover the "laws of tradition" which governed the collection, development and writing down of the isolated units. Then with the removal of the alleged artificial (editorial) framework of chronology or other additions provided by the community, form critics believe they can recover the original of the units (pericopes) and determine for what practical purpose *(Sitz im Leben)* the early Christians preserved them. By this method it is thought one can "pierce back beyond written sources into the period of oral transmission and account for the rise of the different types of episodes which eventually became a part of the gospels." (FiJA.MM 23:446)

Where form criticism postulated the work of the "creative community" to formulate all the various pericopes, redaction criticism, growing out of form criticism, focused on the final redactors (or compilers) of the gospels as authors in their own right. Norman Perrin, a redaction critic, defines it as "concerned with studying the theological motivation of the author as this is revealed in the collection, arrangement, editing, and modification of traditional material, and in the composition of new material or the creation of new forms within the traditions of early Christianity." (PeN.WRC I)

There are newer forms of higher criticism emerging, but because almost every recent nonbiblical treatment of the historical Jesus relies on the conclusions of form and redaction criticism, we will use the remainder of this chapter to investigate the validity of the main distinctives or areas of concentration within these two disciplines. As we do, keep in mind that form and redaction critics will disagree among themselves on particulars. What we present here is what these critics postulate in general.

Distinctive #1: Oral Tradition

The British New Testament scholar James D. G. Dunn has observed that a positive feature of the form-critical approach is that it "has made us much more conscious of the period of oral tradition which lies behind the written gospels, the tradition as it was being used before it was written down." (DuJ.HSG 9) Oral tradition has been defined as "any teaching or similar material transmitted from person to person or generation to generation by word of mouth rather than by use of writing; also the process of such transmission." (SpR.ANT 463-66)

The next chapter will discuss in greater detail the oral period, the time between Jesus' resurrection and when the accounts about him were recorded. Here, we need to call attention to some of the ways form criticism has distorted an accurate view of this period.

Form criticism holds that the first gospels were not completed until some fifty or more years after Jesus' crucifixion. In the middle of the last century, the Tübingen school in Germany postulated that the synoptic gospels were second-century documents, removed from the life of Jesus by a hundred or more years. But scholars are increasingly opting for earlier dates of composition for the gospel accounts. In particular, John A. T. Robinson, not a conservative theologian, has recently forcefully argued that it is possible that every book in the New Testament was completed by AD 70 with Matthew, Mark and Luke all completed by c. AD 60. (See RoJA.RNT) The book of Acts, written by Luke, breaks off with the events of AD 62, leading scholars to believe that this was the date of composition of Acts. Since Acts 1:1,2 indicate that Luke had already written his gospel account, then it must have been finished by AD 60 at the latest. Lawrence McGinley has written, "The fact that the whole process took less than thirty years, and that its essential part was accomplished in a decade and a half, finds no parallel in any tradition to which the synoptic gospels have been compared." (McL.FC 25)

Critics like to have as long a formative period as possible in order to substantiate their belief that error, legend and myth gradually overtook the gospel accounts. But Simon Kistemaker observes, "Normally the accumulation of folklore among people of primitive culture takes many generations: It is a gradual process spread over centuries of time." (KiS.G 48-49)

In regard to the late dating of the gospels by certain critics, R. T. France has commented, "It is interesting to observe that the lateness of the date proposed is often in proportion to the degree of a scholar's skepticism as to their historical value; the cynic might wonder which comes first!" (FrR.E 101)

Rudolf Bultmann, probably the most influential form critic of all, further distorts the truth regarding the oral tradition behind the gospels when he lists his four laws governing narrative and tradition. Summarizing, they are: (1) Narrators do not give long, unified accounts, but rather, small, single pictures of utmost simplicity. (2) As narratives pass from mouth to mouth, their fundamental character remains the same, but the details are subject to the control of fancy and are usually more explicit and definite. (3) Indirect discourse tends to become direct discourse during the process of transmission. (4) There was an inclination to impose a schematic idea of the course of Jesus' activity on the tradition. (See BuR.FC)

Dibelius adds that

> these Christians believed themselves to be more faithful to their Master when they explained His sayings by expanding them and then followed them with understanding, than if they had abhorred any addition and passed on the original form of His words. (DiM.FA 34-35)

The problem with these views is that they apply more to a Greek rather than a Hebrew culture. Geza Vermes, the renowned Jewish scholar and not a Christian, states:

> The system's chief weakness lies, I think, in the absence among its developers and practitioners of any real familiarity with the literature, culture, religion and above all spirit, of the post-biblical Judaism from which Jesus and his first disciples sprang. Instead, it is in the Hellenistic world of early Christianity that Bultmann and his pupils are at home. (VeG.JWJ 19)

In addition, form critics often overlook the fact that the reports about Jesus were circulated openly, not in secret. In the early church services, the stories of Jesus were repeated so often that they had to be well known. Some scholars believe that much of Jesus' teaching was given in Aramaic or Hebraic poetical form making it easy to be memorized. Since the early church was originally mostly Jewish in composition, it is reasonable to believe that the period of oral tradition accurately preserved the words and deeds of Jesus just as the Hebrew culture had done for centuries with its own religious writings.

Combining the presence of eyewitnesses with the short time period, E. B. Redlich, himself a form critic, states:

> In point of fact, it is another weakness of form criticism that it sits too lightly on the results of literary criticism and assumes that the formative period lasted about two generations of forty years. Thus, in their investigations there is a tendency to overlook the presence and influence of those who were eyewitnesses and earwitnesses of the events of the life, death, and resurrection of Jesus, and could therefore guarantee the historical value of the tradition. (ReE.FC 15-16)

James Martin, New Testament professor at Union Theological Seminary, Richmond, Virginia, emphasizes:

> There was no time for the gospel story of Jesus to have been produced by legendary accretion. The growth of legend is always a slow and gradual

thing. But in this instance the story of Jesus was being proclaimed, substantially as the gospels now record it, simultaneously with the beginning of the Church. (MarJ.RG 103-4)

Distinctive #2: Pericopes, or Self-Contained Units

Form criticism assumes that during the oral period almost all of the narratives and sayings circulated mainly as single, self-contained, detached units, complete in themselves. These units are labeled *pericopes*. Dibelius says it this way:

> When, however, we trace the tradition back to its initial stage we find no description of the life of Jesus, but short paragraphs or pericopes. This is the fundamental hypothesis of the method of form criticism *(formgeschichtliche Methode)* as a representative of which I am speaking here. (DiM.GCC 27)

In response to the form critics' assertion that the chronological framework of the life of Jesus was almost entirely lost during the oral period, C. H. Dodd, probably the most influential figure in British New Testament scholarship during the middle decades of the twentieth century, countered that "none of the gospels would ever have come into being, were it not for the fact that the individual pieces of the oral tradition were proclaimed from the beginning as elements of a coherent story." (DoC.AP 66) The work which Mark did in his gospel was done "not arbitrarily or irresponsibly," added Dodd,

> but under such guidance as he could find in tradition. It is hazardous to argue from the precise sequence of the narrative in detail; yet there is good reason to believe that in broad lines the Marcan order does represent a genuine succession of events, within which movement and development can be traced. (DoC.FGN 43:400)

L. J. McGinley observes concerning Matthew, Mark and Luke that

> were the gospels mere compilations, their heterogeneous origins should be conspicuous in the tenor of their story. Yet it is a striking fact that in these three converging and diverging narratives there reigns a simple but unmistakable consistency; there is no contradiction in Jesus' doctrine nor in His deeds, no inconsistency of word with action; the story of His success and failure flows logically to its end; the description of the land in which He lived and the people whom He encountered—a land and people never seen by many of the early Christians—has never been convicted of inaccuracy. Such unanimity of presentation would be impossible in a collection of isolated units. (McL.FC 10)

Distinctive #3: Classification According to Form

When form critics speak of "forms," what specifically do they mean? It is probably easier to get a feel for particular kinds of forms than to precisely define "forms." Following are five classifications of forms which Vincent Taylor has delineated. Other form critics use similar classifications, though possibly with different terminology and some differences in categories defined.

1. *Pronouncement Stories:* Bultmann tagged them "apophthegmata"; Dibelius called them "paradigms." They are usually brief episodes ending with a famous saying such as "Render to Caesar the things that are Caesar's, and to God the things that are God's" (Mark 12:17).

2. *Sayings and Parables:* This classification includes words of wisdom, prophetic sayings (almost always put in Jesus' mouth by a later writer after the prophesied event had occurred), teaching on various aspects of the believer's life, "I" sayings and parables. Form critics differ as to how much of the content can be attributed to Jesus, usually holding that the later church was the original source for much of the material.

3. *Miracle Stories:* Bultmann attributed the miracle stories to later churchmen who were influenced by the miracle stories in Greek literature.

4. *Stories about Jesus:* Everett F. Harrison explains that they

> have considerable variety and therefore are not easy to classify. It is readily admitted by the form critics that there are mythological elements in the portrayal of Jesus, for example, in the transfiguration. The tendency is regarded as full-blown in the fourth gospel. The category of myth is applied to those elements of the gospel exposition of Jesus that present him in a guise transcending the human and the natural. (BePJG 148-49)

5. *The Passion Story:* Form critics differ as to whether this is primarily a cohesive, self-contained narrative or a patchwork of several fragments woven together.

It is one thing to say that a particular gospel pericope has a certain literary form about it. It is another to say that because it does have a certain literary form it cannot be original and must have been borrowed from somewhere else. Yet this is what the radical form critics routinely do. Bultmann, for example, has the gospel writers and editors depending on written gnostic sources, making additions to the texts they received, and rearranging the content of the gospels. (MuF.BR 207) Bultmann's assumptions have been justly criticized as unfounded since he rules out, a priori (beforehand), the possibility that the pericope, regardless of its form, accurately preserved an actual historical occurrence.

The weakness of classification according to form is probably best seen in the criticism of it posed by form critics themselves. For example, Dibelius concedes, "Because the eyewitnesses could control and correct, a relative trustworthiness of the paradigms is guaranteed." (DiM.FTG 62) One wonders why he does not conclude that eyewitnesses actually wrote narrative stories, rather than form classified pieces of literature.

Some of the more moderate form critics recognize how subjective form criticism is. Vincent Taylor, for example, questions pronouncement stories as being products of imagination:

> The distribution of the Pronouncement-Stories has some bearing on the question of their early currency and genuineness. There are at least twenty in Mark seven or nine in Luke's special source, four or five in Q [the supposed document behind common material in Matthew and Luke], one in Matthew, and none in John. If the stories are products of Christian imagination, why do they not increase in number as time passes, and as new problems confront the growing Church? Why is there no Pronouncement-Story about the necessity of the Cross, or the Gentile Mission, or the foundation and organization of the Church?...If Bultmann is right, Christian imagination was potent where it was least needed, feeble or wanting where silence called for its exercise; it left undone the things which it ought to have done, and did the things it had no need to do. (TaV.FGT 86-87)

About myths and legends, Taylor frankly admits, "'Myths' and 'Legends' are terms which do not define any particular structural forms." (TaV.FGT 31-32)

Another form critic, Burton Scott Easton, comments on the countless forms which have been invented by form critics to suit the needs of their theory:

> Paradigms, stories, legends, cult-legends, epiphanies, apothegms, miracles, parables, folk-tales, controversies, dialogues, parenesis, logia, prophetic and apocalyptic utterances, church rules, sayings in the first person, allegories, poem stanzas—the research of the past decade has exhibited no poverty of terminology! But how profitable is it all? Can we really analyze forms with such precision as to make form criticism a true discipline?
>
> (EaB.GBG 61)

Other scholars outside the form critical school have revealed the faults of form classification as well. Because Bultmann was prone to reject as a later corruption of the text any portion that did not fit a form classification, McGinley charges that ultimately Bultmann

> rejects as secondary corruptions of the primitive type almost all details of time and place, all initiative by Jesus, all definite names and characterization, the constant opposition of the Scribes and Pharisees. In so doing, he constructs a typical apothegm but destroys its reason for existence. Jesus lives at no time and in no place. He does nothing of His own account; He moves in a world of impersonal shadows; there is no reason for His rejection, trial, execution. While being molded to fit the theory, the facts have disappeared. (McL.FC 43)

C. S. Lewis, former professor of Medieval and Renaissance Literature at Cambridge University, has written a classic response to modern biblical criticism. The following excerpt is especially appropriate with regard to the subjectivity of much of form classification:

> First then, whatever these men may be as biblical critics, I distrust them as critics. They seem to me to lack literary judgment, to be imperceptive about the very quality of the texts they are reading. It sounds a strange charge to bring against men who have been steeped in those books all their lives. But that might be just the trouble. A man who has spent his youth and manhood in the minute study of New Testament texts and of other people's studies of them, whose literary experiences of those texts lacks any standard of comparison such as can only grow from a wide and deep and genial experience of literature in general, is, I should think, very likely to miss the obvious things about them. If he tells me that something in a gospel is legend or romance, I want to know how many legends and romances he has read, how well his palate is trained in detecting them by the flavour; not how many years he has spent on that gospel. (LeC.CR 154)

Referring to the Gospel of John, Lewis goes on to say:

> I have been reading poems, romances, vision-literature, legends, myths all my life. I know what they are like. I know that not one of them is like this.
>
> …These men ask me to believe they can read between the lines of the old texts; the evidence is their obvious inability to read (in any sense worth discussing) the lines themselves. They claim to see fern-seed and can't see an elephant ten yards away in broad daylight. (LeC.CR 155)

It should not be surprising to find many of Jesus' discourses or sayings in a particular form. Robert Thomas and Stan Gundry have commented:

> As for the poetic form of many of Jesus' sayings, what would have been more natural for Him, speaking to Jews, than to cast His declarations in poetic form? Such, in fact, was normal Semitic style. This practice would have made it easier for His followers, whether Jews or not, to remember His words. It makes just as much sense, perhaps more, to say that the real originator of the forms of those sayings attributed to Jesus is Jesus Himself. (ThR.H 285-86)

Form classification by itself is not unjustified. It is when form classification is used as a measure of authenticity that it oversteps its boundaries. A. M. Hunter, Scottish New Testament scholar, says that one

> must never forget that the form in which a story is told can never tell us whether the substance of the story is true or false. The whole method is too subjective and speculative to afford us much sure guidance. (HuA.INT 40)

"Form criticism," says Talbot Seminary New Testament professor Robert Mounce, sounds like a scientific method. If it were, you would find consistency of interpretation. But the interpretations of a single saying vary widely. Not only are interpretations widespread but form critics often can't agree whether a pericope is a miracle story or a pronouncement story—the two can be woven together. One would expect consistency in historical reconstruction if form criticism were a true science.[3]

Distinctive #4: Creative Community

If form classification is one of the most subjective elements of form criticism, the concept of a creative community is one of its most unrealistic elements. The central recurring phrase here is *Sitz im Leben,* meaning literally "seat in life" or life situation. Form criticism generally espouses that the story of Jesus developed through the influence of the early Christian community and its need to explain Jesus in terms of its own needs or life situation. The more radical form critics postulate that the influence of this early creative community was so great that we can know virtually nothing of the actual historical Jesus, only what the early church wanted him, the Christ of faith, to be for them in view of the needs they faced. Moderate form critics believe we can know something about the historical Jesus but that the creative community exerted enough influence on the formation of the gospel accounts that at least some of the story is distorted. For example, Vincent Taylor teaches that

> every consideration bearing on the life of the first Christians must be taken into account—the practical demands arising from daily life, the need to explain the new faith to themselves and to others, the necessities of defence against objections and slanders from unfriendly and hostile neighbors. These and other considerations have determined the form which the tradition now has, and the changes it has undergone, and by taking them into account it is often possible to explain why this or that element in the tradition has survived and why much we should greatly desire to know has not been handed down to us. (TaV.FGT 36)

Bultmann, the most radical and influential form critic, displays the greatest skepticism as you can see from the following dogmatic statements by him:

> In the synoptic tradition a series of sayings shows that Jesus' work was conceived as decisive happening, especially such as speak of him as having come or having been sent. They are scarcely (at least in the majority of cases) original words of Jesus, but mostly products of the Church. (BuR.TNT 44)

> Not only have many of the older sayings of Jesus been modified in the course of tradition, but not seldom words have been placed in Jesus' mouth which in reality were either spoken by other Jewish teachers or first arose in the Christian community. (BuR.FC 42)

Remember that all of this is based on literary analysis (or should we say, conjecture), not on external historical evidence. As can be imagined, form criticism could be a mighty handy tool for getting rid of anything a person might not want Jesus to be saying to them!

The idea of a creative community is perhaps the most criticized aspect of form criticism. The New Testament scholar James D. G. Dunn has said that "the idea that the first Christians were not interested in the pre-Easter Jesus is little short of ludicrous." (DuJ.HSG 11) Can you imagine an early Christian telling a friend about Jesus, and his friend asking, "Wait a minute, who is this Jesus?"

If the form critics are right and the Christian responded truthfully, he would have to say something like, "Well, we're not really sure, but if he did live, we thought it would be nice if he was like this."

The friend would likely respond, "You're asking me to die a martyr's death for that?" Perhaps this is why the noted Tübingen professor of New Testament, Gerhard Kittel, countered:

> The Christ of faith has no existence, is mere noise and smoke, apart from the reality of the Jesus of history. These two are utterly inseparable in the New Testament. They cannot even be thought apart. There is no word about Christ which is not referred to Him who suffered under Pontius Pilate, and which is not at the same time intended as the gospel applicable to all men of every time and place. Anyone who attempts first to separate the two and then to describe only one of them has nothing in common with the New Testament. (KiG.JH 49)

In order to bridge the supposed gap between the Christ of faith and the Jesus of history, form critics made a critically faulty assumption. They assumed that communities create. German New Testament professor Alfred Wikenhauser responds:

> It is false to ascribe the making of tradition to anonymous forces, to say that it was the community and the faith of the community which formed and handed on the tradition about Jesus. Creative power belongs not to a mass but only to individuals who tower over the mass. (WiA.NTI 277)

Philosophy and church history professor Stephen Neill, for twenty years a missionary in India before returning to Europe and Nairobi to teach, adds:

> To sum up so much spiritual truth so simply, so briefly, and in such unforgettable images demands creative genius of the highest possible calibre. Who in the early Christian groups had such genius? Paul, on occasion, is capable of flights of lyric splendour; but he has not a plastic, visual imagination of the kind that expresses itself in such forms as the story of the temptation. In the first century we know of one man, and one only, who had that kind of imagination, and that kind of power over words. His name was Jesus of Nazareth. (NeS.INT 251)

The work of the early Christian community, then, was to *communicate,* not to *create,* the words and deeds of Jesus. In this communication process, as noted University of Cambridge New Testament scholar C. F. D. Moule recognized, "the synoptic gospels represent primarily the recognition that a vital element in evangelism is the plain story of what happened in the ministry of Jesus." (MoCF.IE 176-76) Thus, the role of eyewitnesses became extremely important and it has been overlooked or ignored by most form critics. Biblical studies professors Robert Thomas and Stan Gundry charge:

> In effect form critics see Christianity as cut off from its founder and His disciples by an inexplicable ignorance. The new sect had to invent situations for the words of Jesus and put into His mouth words that memory could not check and that He may not have said. But still living in those early days were leaders and disciples who had heard and seen what they recounted (Acts 2:1-4). The form critic either forgets or ignores the fact that Jesus had a surviving mother and followers who had many vivid memories of His life and ministry. There is no reason to suppose that the individuals mentioned in Mark 3:31-35; 4:10; 15:40; and 16:1-8 would not have remembered these things. (ThR.H 282)

Vincent Taylor recognized:

> If the form critics are right, the disciples must have been translated to heaven immediately after the resurrection. As Bultmann sees it, the primitive community exists in vacuo, cut off from its founders by the walls of an inexplicable ignorance. (TaV.FGT/33 41)

There are several points of evidence which contradict the form critic's view of a creative community. One is the existence of the gospels themselves. Since form critics claim that the teaching or didactic needs of the early church shaped the caricature of the Jesus it created, Geza Vermes asks:

> If the evangelists were primarily preoccupied with teaching Christian doctrine, how are we to explain their choice of biography as their medium? They cannot have been influenced by tradition; no Jewish convention exists that the sayings of the sages should be transmitted in this way. (VeG.JWJ 20)

Norman Anderson questions:

> Was it not rather inept to adopt a biographical literary style, which provides liveliness and colour but at the expense of simplicity and clarity? Their story of Jesus is replete with Palestinian ideas, customs, linguistic peculiarities and realia of all sorts, incomprehensible to non-Jewish readers and demanding continuous interpretative digressions which were bound to be catechetically harmful.... Early teachers such as Paul, James, the author of Didache, found in any case no advantage in "biography" for the transmission of

theological expositions, moral exhortations, and disciplinary or liturgical rules, and opted sensibly for a direct method of communication. (AnN.JC 29)

The uniqueness of Jesus' teaching and life is a second point of evidence against the influence of a creative community. "The New Testament," says W. D. Davies, Duke University Professor of Advanced Studies and Research in Christian Origins,

> witnesses to virile, expanding Christian communities, it is true, but also to confused and immature ones. It is more likely that the trust, the creativity, the originality which lies behind the gospel tradition of the works and words of Jesus should be credited to him rather than to the body of Christians. The kind of penetrating insight preserved in the gospels points not to communities—mixed and often muddled in their thinking—but to a supreme source in a single person, Jesus, Rabbi and prophet. (DaW.IN 115)

Floyd V. Filson, McCormick Theological Seminary professor and dean emeritus in New Testament literature, exegesis and history, points out, for example, the uniqueness of the parables:

> Finally, all attempts to make the apostolic age responsible for the creation of any considerable amount of the gospel material shatter upon the evidence of the parables. This is the characteristic teaching form in the synoptic gospels. It is noticeably absent from the rest of the New Testament and from other early Christian literature. If the apostolic age had created these masterly mediums of teaching, other writings of that time would naturally have reflected the same method. But they do not. (FiF.OG 109)

A third point of evidence against the influence of a creative community is that within the gospels there exists "counterproductive" material which the creative community had every reason to exclude from the gospels had they formed them. Philosophy and Theology Professor J. P. Moreland details:

> Jesus' denial of being good is an example. Jesus' attitudes toward legalism, fasting, divorce, sinners, and women were radical and somewhat embarrassing. Several features of Jesus' character were stumbling blocks, including his displays of anger, his baptism, his death on a cross, and the fact that he was a carpenter from Nazareth. To this could be added the opposition to Jesus from his family. Also, the portrayal of the disciples is often embarrassing (e.g., when they are in unbelief, show cowardice, or have difficulty with Jesus' teaching). The request of the sons of Zebedee is surely authentic, as is Matthew 23:8,10 which would seem to condemn the churches' own practice of having official teachers. (MoJP.S 145-46)

In view of the "doctrinally embarrassing" material in the gospels, the Jewish scholar Geza Vermes concluded: "Bultmann's dictum about the impossibility of knowing anything about Jesus or his personality, 'because the early Christian sources show no interest in it either,' becomes a plain misjudgment." (VeG.JWJ 21)

Moreland also calls attention to the presence of "irrelevant" material which the Gentile creative community would have neglected:

> Especially noteworthy is Jesus' attitude of favor to Israel. To this could be added Jesus' use of the phrases the kingdom of God and the son of man. Jesus' controversies with the Pharisees (e.g., about keeping the Sabbath) and his comments on Corban practices were not relevant at the same time the Gospels were written. (MoJP.S 146)

If, then, the early Christians preserved what was irrelevant to them, how much more that which was relevant. And they adapted their lives to the teaching rather than adapting the teaching to their lifestyles. This truth can again be seen in "the lack of relevant material" in the gospels—material which the creative community could have included but didn't. For example, the alleged editors of the gospels failed to put into Jesus' mouth any teaching on "circumcision, charismatic gifts, baptism, food laws, Gentile missions (Paul could not appeal to a saying of the historical Jesus to justify his Gentile mission), several ministries of the Holy Spirit, rules governing assembly meetings, and church-state relations." (MoJP.S) One very significant body of relevant material which the "creative community" failed to include was that given by its forceful activist and spokesman, the apostle Paul. T. W. Manson, former Rylands Professor of Biblical Criticism at the University of Manchester, has proposed that if there is little or nothing of what the apostle Paul wrote that is found in the mouth of Jesus in the gospel accounts, we cannot expect that "the tradition about Jesus is in any considerable degree the creation of the Christian community." (MaT.QHJ 7)

We must conclude, then, that it is an unrealistic assumption of form criticism that an early creative community shaped the story of Jesus out of its own needs.

Distinctive #5: Absence of Biographical Interest

Most form critics hold that the early Christian community had no real biographical interest, so the gospels have little, if any, biographical, chronological or geographical value. Dibelius proclaims:

> The oldest traditions of Jesus came into existence because the community was in need of them—a community which had no thought of biography or of world history but of salvation—a community which had no desire to write books but only to preserve all that was necessary for preaching. (DiM.GCC 30)

Dibelius also wrote, "The fact that Jesus was a man is decisive for faith; how this earthly life was lived seems to be of no importance." (DiM.GCC 30) Bultmann was even more skeptical:

I do indeed think that we can now know almost nothing concerning the life and personality of Jesus, since the early Christian sources show no interest in either, are moreover fragmentary and often legendary; and other sources about Jesus do not exist. (BuR.JW 8)

Part of the form critic's problem is that the term *biographical* is not very well defined. In answer to Bultmann's charge that the gospels are not biographies, James Dunn counters:

What he meant or should have said was that they are not *modern* biographies. Unfortunately this qualification was not recognized and the blanket dictum (the gospels are not biographies) became a basic axiom in most form-critical studies for the next two generations...

In fact, however, the synoptic gospels conform quite closely to the form and function of the *ancient* biography. The nearest parallel in the Greco-Roman world to the genre of gospel is the *bios* or *vita* (life). Whereas modern biography has a central concern with personality development and the chronological framework within which it occurs, ancient biography had a much more static concept of personality and only rarely expressed interest in such development. On the contrary, human personality was thought of as fixed and unchanging. Moreover a deeply rooted assumption of the ancients was that a person's character was clearly revealed in his actions and words. Consequently it was the principal task of the biographer to portray his subject by relating things he did and said and thus to depict his character. (DuJ.HSG 8)

Scholars have long recognized that plenty of evidence exists to show that the gospel writers did have a biographical interest, in the ancient sense of the word. Stan Gundry lists the following evidence from the words of Paul and Luke:

1. If there were no biographical interest in the early church, why did Paul distinguish between his words and the Lord's words (1 Corinthians 7:10,12, 25)?

2. If the early church had no biographical interest, why had many taken in hand to draw up narratives of the events of Jesus' life (Luke 1:1-3)?

3. And why had they used the material of eyewitnesses (Luke 1:1,2)? If such were the case, why did Luke add to this collection an accurate account of the Lord's ministry after having done his own careful research (Luke 1:3,4)?

4. If these early Christians had no biographical interest, why did they bother to appeal constantly to the fact that they were eyewitnesses of those events concerning which they spoke?

5. The form critics must discredit the book of Acts and Luke's prologue if they

are to claim seriously that the early church had no biographical interest.
(GuS.C 489:38)

Distinctive #6: Laws of Tradition

By comparing the preliterary forms of oral tradition in other societies with those of the gospel, form critics believe they can discover "the laws which operate as formative factors in popular tradition." (DiM.FTG 7) New Testament scholar W. S. Taylor, former Principal of Union College of British Columbia, lists these laws:

> (1) As time goes on, the oral tradition becomes embellished by the elaboration of simple themes and by the addition of new detail. It becomes both longer and more complex. Consequently, it can be taken as virtually axiomatic that "the simpler version represents the original."

> (2) As time goes on, there is a tendency for the particular to become general, and for a statement with local significance to become a statement with universal significance. In the situation faced by the expanding church, this tendency was accentuated.

> (3) As time goes on, the material often changes in form, becoming more dramatic by the addition of vivid detail, by the transformation of indirect into direct narration, etc.

> (4) And, as time goes on, concepts are added which would have been unfamiliar and unnatural in the original situation. (TaW.MGT 15:471)

Notice that each law begins with, "As time goes on." As we noted earlier, the amount of time refers to several centuries in other stories (myths and legends) compared to thirty, twenty or even fewer years for the gospel reports. The time factor, combined with the presence of eyewitnesses, fatally flaws form critical methodology. Still, as Stan Gundry notes:

> The form critic ignores the possibility of eyewitnesses, for he is totally occupied with forms and the smooth working of a theory. He has not taken the time to examine the historical evidence. (GuS.C 34-35)

F. F. Bruce notes the additional factor of hostile witnesses as a further preventative for any "laws of tradition" to distort the gospel testimony:

> One of the strong points in the original apostolic preaching is the confident appeal to the knowledge of the hearers; they not only said, "We are witnesses of these things," but also, "As you yourselves also know" (Acts 2:22). Had there been any tendency to depart from the facts in any material respect, the possible presence of hostile witnesses in the audience would have served as a further corrective. (BrF.NTD 45-46)

James Martin adds:

There can be little doubt that, if the Christians had been guilty of inconsistency in the repetition of their tradition, their enemies would have been able to rout them ignominiously from the field, making them a public laughingstock and effectively ensuring that their preaching would have no impact on the minds of any who heard it. (MarJ.RG 68)

Distinctive #7: Criteria for Establishing Authenticity

Not only does the form critic use a faulty methodology in applying "laws of tradition" to the gospels, but he also employs a faulty methodology in analyzing the gospels for authentic and non-authentic sayings of Jesus. Form criticism postulates several criteria to be used in determining whether or not a saying of Jesus found in the gospels should be accepted as actually having come from Jesus.

The most widely used of these criteria is the principle of dissimilarity. Norman Perrin states this principle in this form: "By definition it will exclude all teaching in which Jesus may have been at one with Judaism or the early church at one with him." (PeN.RTJ 43) Obviously, this is putting the horse *behind* the cart. Shouldn't we expect the early followers of Jesus to be saying much that sounds like Jesus? And if they are, then are we not disqualifying Jesus a priori for the faithfulness of his disciples to accurately reflect his teachings?

Again, as Perrin reflects in the previous quote, the same principle would say, "If it sounds like ancient Judaism, then you can't trust it either, as being originally from Jesus."

"The gospel, however," says Robert Mounce, "got underway in a Jewish setting. How else could Jesus talk but like a Jew?" [4]

Geza Vermes makes clear why many Christian as well as Jewish scholars have become disenchanted with various form critical applications:

> Even such a moderate writer as Norman Perrin proclaims his overall principle to be, "When in doubt, discard," and states categorically that "the burden of proof always lies on the claim of authenticity"; that is to say, whatever is not proved to be genuine is to be presumed unauthentic (*Rediscovering the Teaching of Jesus,* pp. 11-12). Bearing in mind the basic Jewish respect of tradition in general, and attachment to the words of a venerated master in particular, I myself would advocate *a priori* an open mind, and would not tip the balance in favor of inauthenticity. (VeG.JWJ 150)

France comments, "The inevitable result is a Jesus who agrees neither with current Jewish piety nor with subsequent Christian faith, a Jesus whose teaching his followers at least failed to grasp or even actively disapproved of." (FrR.E 105)

Moreland adds:

> It is odd, to say the least, if a preacher does not preach in the idioms of his day. And it is also odd to say that such a discontinuity should be seen between Jesus and the early church. (MoJ.PS 154)

Distinctive #8: Historical Skepticism

Prominent among most form critics is a historical skepticism rooted in an antisupernatural bias. In Bultmann, this predisposition against anything supernatural is clear:

> This closedness means that the continuum of historical happenings cannot be rent by the interference of supernatural, transcendent powers and that therefore there is no "miracle" in this sense of the word. Such a miracle would be an event whose cause did not lie within history.... It is in accordance with such a method as this that the science of history goes to work on all historical documents. And there cannot be any exceptions in the case of biblical texts if the latter are at all to be understood [as] historical. (BuR.EF 291-92)

Though his argument probably comes straight from David Hume, Bultmann was deeply influenced by Martin Heidegger and existential philosophy. It was likely this philosophical bent, not historical evidence, which caused Bultmann to discount so many of the historical events reported in the New Testament.

Jerusalem-based French New Testament scholar, Pierre Benoit, argues against Bultmann when he asks:

> Is it credible that the converts accepted so novel a faith, which demanded so much of them, on the strength of mere gossip sessions, at which Dibelius and Bultmann's preachers invented sayings and actions which Jesus never uttered and never performed, merely to suit themselves? (BeP.JG 32)

If Bultmann and other form critics were truly interested in the historicity of what the gospels report, one would expect them to deal with historical evidence. But, McGinley observes:

> External testimony such as Irenaeus, Tertullian, and Origen is noticeably not referred to. Justin's observation that the gospels are merely apostolic memoirs...is mentioned only to be rejected as misleading.... Papias' testimony...of Matthew and Mark fares no better. Bultmann refers to Papias' reference to Mark as the interpreter of Peter—as an error; Dibelius refers to Papias' testimony on the authorship of Matthew and Mark but concludes that he has been misled by thinking that the evangelists were really authors.... This neglect of historical testimony seems to show a lack of completeness and perspective.
>
> ...As De Grandmaison remarks, "It is the wisest method in these matters to prefer an ounce of ancient information which is authentic to a bookful of learned conjectures."[5]

Form critics argue that since, in their estimation, oral traditions about Jesus circulated in small units (pericopes), most chronological, geographical, historical and biographical references are fictional additions made by the evangelists. "However," say Thomas and Gundry,

> an examination of the references to place, time, sequence, and persons shows these to be so interwoven with the other material of the units, and to present such a natural ordered sequence when considered separately, that to view them as editorial creations of the evangelists is highly speculative. The contexts, as well as the sayings and events, are rooted in history. (ThR.H 285)

The most often heard argument of form critics against historical accuracy in the gospels is that since the early church was interested only in preaching salvation, it was not interested in handing down an accurate portrait of the historical Jesus. Dibelius states:

> The first Christians had no interest in reporting the life and passion of Jesus objectively to mankind.... They wanted nothing else than to win as many as possible to salvation in the last hour just before the end of the world, which they believed to be at hand. Those early Christians were not interested in history. (DiM.GCC 16)

We admit with France:

> No one who has read the gospels with any sensitivity would want to argue that they are plain, disinterested records of facts, written with the clinical objectivity of a modern scientific report or a legal deposition. The gospel writers were men with a message. They wrote in order to persuade, to convert, to encourage. (FrR.E 102)

But J. P. Moreland, author of *Scaling the Secular City*, argues:

> It is a false dichotomy to say something has to be either history or a document which promotes a message. The fact that the gospels are kerygmatic [have to do with the preaching of the gospel] does not rule out their historical dimension, especially when they emphasize the inseparability of the historical and the theological in understanding the incarnation. (MoJP.S 140)

The late Harold W. Hoehner, former chairman of the New Testament Department at Dallas Theological Seminary, and PhD in New Testament from Cambridge University, liked to tell his classes that it was a good thing Bultmann had never had to rely on him or any other Christian as a witness to an auto accident. If a theological conviction cancels out a person's historical accuracy, Christians [or for that matter, any theist] cannot be relied upon for much of anything. The real problem of form critics' approach to history, writes Hoehner, is that

> they will not let the text speak on its own terms. Certainly the modern theologians would not want us to read their books the way they want us to read the New Testament![6]

REDACTION CRITICISM

Norman Perrin summarizes the origins of redaction criticism:

> Redaction criticism burst into full flower immediately after the Second
> World War in Germany. Just as three scholars emerged with independent
> works marking the beginning of form criticism proper after the hiatus
> caused by the First World War, so three scholars came forward with inde-
> pendent works denoting the beginning of redaction criticism proper after
> the hiatus caused by the Second World War. After the First World War it
> was Karl Ludwig Schmidt, Martin Dibelius, and Rudolf Bultmann, as we
> have already noted; after the Second World War it was Günther Bornkamm,
> Hans Conzelmann, and Willi Marxsen. Though working independently of
> one another—Bornkamm on Matthew, Conzelmann on Luke, and Marx-
> sen on Mark—they moved in the same general direction. (PeN.WRC 25) [7]

Redaction criticism takes form criticism one step further. Whereas form critics postulate the work of the creative community to form the content of individual pericopes,
redaction critics set forth the work of the gospel writers to edit, arrange, compose and
change the material in the pericopes to support their particular theological purpose.
Redaction criticism, then, seeks to determine the theological viewpoint of the evan-
gelist who wrote the gospel. The critics attempt to ascertain what sources the gospel
writers chose and why, and where these fit together in his particular account (known
as "seams"). The critics want to find the specific theological "glue" the authors used to
build their gospels.

But as the redaction critic attempts to determine why each author chose to develop
his gospel as he did, he completely ignores the author's own claims and reasons for writing. The critics also do not view the gospels as historical accounts in any accepted sense of
the idea. The critics pass judgment on the documents before the documents are allowed
to speak for themselves. A typical redaction critical approach to the narrative connected
with Caesarea Philippi (Mark 8:27–9:1) is summarized here by Thomas and Gundry.

> The writer reports questions and answers as from the lips of Jesus and Peter.
> In reality, redaction criticism alleges, the titles are from the christological
> vocabulary of the early Christian community. Furthermore, though persons
> bear the names of individuals and groups connected with Jesus' ministry,
> the principal reference is to circumstances in the church of the late six-
> ties. "Jesus" and His sayings represent the Lord from heaven and His mes-
> sage to this church. "Peter" pictures misled believers who confess correctly
> but interpret their own confession erroneously. "The multitude" stands for
> the total church membership for whom the teaching is intended. In other
> words, redaction criticism sees this story as bearing the form of a history
> about Jesus, but its actual purpose was the conveying of the risen Lord's
> message to His church, as conceived by Mark. The historical impression is
> only a vehicle and is not to be equated with actual happenings. (ThR.H 289-90)

Because redaction criticism depends so heavily on the methodology and conclusions of form criticism, many scholars have expressed the same kinds of doubts toward it as they have toward form criticism. Redaction critics almost universally hold to a rigid supposedly scientific worldview where the supernatural is ruled out a priori. Contrary to the claims of first- and second-century church leaders and even the gospel writers themselves, redaction critics presuppose that the theological viewpoint of the author, and not actual historical events, shaped the content of his gospel. They ignore the Jewish cultural background of the gospels, failing to see that the Jewish mind-set beheld God as a God who *does*, thus making it vital for the Jewish people to preserve the historical acts of God precisely as they happened.

Professor Hoehner makes the following summary assessments, all of which have been leveled against form criticism also:

1. The *Sitz im Leben* position is not historically substantiated. The evidence points to the fact that the gospels created the Christian community rather than the idea that the communities created the gospel.

2. The role of eyewitnesses is forgotten. Their testimony is clear in the gospels, and if one of the gospel writers was wrong the eyewitnesses could have corrected him. The critics believe that theologians would distort history to fit their theology. This is not necessarily the case. The critics attempt to reconstruct the gospel accounts totally apart from the eyewitnesses, who were actually present.

3. The uniqueness of Jesus is minimized. The critics assume the gospel writers made the brilliant statements in the gospels rather than Jesus.

4. Christian ethics are minimized. Christ emphasized the truth, yet the gospel writers fabricated a story. They told us that the story of Christ happened a certain way, yet in reality it did not. It was a community creation. A small lie may have small consequences, yet here their lie is believed by thousands, and thousands thus have even died for a lie.

5. There is no room for the Holy Spirit. Their naturalistic theology almost excludes the work of God in the believer's life.

6. Simply because the authors have a theological purpose in writing does not negate authenticity or historical accuracy.[8]

In concluding this short section on redaction criticism, there is one argument which also applies to form criticism, which we feel needs particular emphasis. Hoehner mentioned it above (#4), and Thomas and Gundry allude to it in their description of redaction criticism here:

> The writers, then, were theologians or theological editors, not historians. It was quite inconsequential to them that they falsely attributed to Jesus and

His associates many things they never said or did. Their prime concern was to construct a theology that would meet the needs of the church, even if doing so successfully meant fabricating a life of Jesus in order to give the system more credibility. (ThR.H 290)

Does it seem at all likely—in fact, does it seem at all possible—that the gospel writers could preach such a high ethical standard through their portrait of Jesus and then, when there existed no economic or social benefit for doing so, blatantly misrepresent the facts concerning Jesus' life? In addition, how could these writers ask their audience to risk their lives for this distorted message? And, finally, why, if they knew their portrait of Jesus was a fabrication, would they themselves be willing to risk their lives for such a perversion?

SCHOLARLY CONCLUSIONS TO HIGHER CRITICISM

As long as "life of Jesus" reconstructionists employ speculative form and redaction criticism, they cannot persuade knowledgeable Christians that the gospel accounts of Jesus' life are historically inaccurate. Knowledgeable Christians have long since learned that, as C. S. Lewis reminded us, it is a fallacy to read between the lines without reading the lines themselves! And yet this seems to be the common practice of most higher critics.

Other scholars, however, have spoken out against the higher critical approach to the study of the gospels. McGinley summarizes:

> It has failed to work out a position in independence of the Two-Source theory. It has neglected the essential differences between the gospels and *Klein-literatur* [folk literature]. It has accepted the discredited theory of collective creation and applied it to a community in which it did not and could not exist. It has mistaken simplicity of style for patchwork compilation. Forms have been too sharply defined and at the price of much excision of the text. A *Sitz im Leben* has been sought in every phase of primitive Christian life except the most important one: the Christian's desire to know the life of Jesus. Throughout, no place is given to historical testimony; substance is neglected in preoccupation with form; the controlling factor of time is disregarded; there is prejudice against the historical value of the whole gospel story. (McL.FC 154)

Filson includes the following points:

> It does not do justice to the historical sense, intelligence and integrity of the early Christians; while it rightly recognizes the extensive topical grouping of material in the gospels, it goes too far in discrediting their basic outline of Jesus' ministry; while it correctly sees the importance of the early oral period, it hardly gives adequate weight to the fact that within some twenty years the writing of written sources began, and so the process of oral tradition was not so long as in folk tales and in the earliest Old Testament stories;

its tendency to assume radical distortion of the tradition in the Hellenistic church is refuted by the prevailing Semitic character of the common synoptic tradition; and its results are warped by unexamined assumptions, such as that miracle stories are largely late creations and that explicit Christology arose first in the church rather than in the mind of Jesus. (FiF.FC 1:436-37)

A M. Hunter criticizes:

(1) The critics assumed that all the early tradition about Jesus was quite unfixed and relatively unreliable, though the first Christians, who were Jews, had a serious care for the faithful and controlled transmission of their Lord's words and deeds.

(2) They drew dubious parallels between oral tradition in other cultures, where the time of transmission runs into centuries, and oral tradition in the gospels, where it is a matter of two or three decades.

... They were prone to assume that the form of a gospel story or saying was a reliable criterion of its authenticity, which of course it is not. (HuA.WWJ 34)

F. G. Kenyon, a proven scholar, questions the time element required by the form critical hypothesis:

There is simply not time for the elaborate processes required for Dibelius' *Formgeschichte,* which has won rather surprising popularity, but which presupposes, first the dissemination of stories of the life and teachings of Jesus, then their collection and classification into groups according to their character, and then the formation of continuous narratives in which they were utilized. (KeF.BMS 52)

Kistemaker, writing of those at Pentecost who received the Holy Spirit, says, "These people did not vanish but were active in many communities throughout Palestine, preaching the word which they had received from Jesus." (KiS.G 48-49)

E. M. Blaiklock notes the difference between classical scholars and higher critics in their approach to the gospel texts:

A classical scholar finds it difficult to be patient with some of the exotic theories of literary criticism which have bedeviled New Testament studies. Classical historians have been a little ironical in recent decades over the calculated skepticism of New Testament scholars who refuse to see what the classicists so naturally see—a record of life in the first century, if no more than that, which must at least be accorded its unique value as historical material.

Had the so-called form critics confined their activities to that which may be a demonstration of the obvious—the part played by the experience and practice of the church in determining the stresses and emphases in material which was necessarily and admittedly selective—they might conceivably have thrown some light on the mind of the first communities of Christians. Even the rude art of the catacombs picked and chose the themes which most appealed to the embattled Christians of Italy. But when critical theory seeks to persuade that liturgical and spiritual needs and aspirations, taking shape from nowhere, and within the lifetime of those who had known the first half of the first century, themselves created a supporting literature, the narratives and sayings which form the gospels, fantasy is propounded which would provoke ridicule in any less confined and introverted sphere of literary criticism. (BIE.MM 34-35)

R. T. France likewise questions the excessive skepticism of the higher critics:

At the root of such skepticism is a general understanding of the early church, and of its methods of transmitting the traditions of Jesus, which other scholars have seriously questioned. How likely is it, in the milieu of first-century Palestinian Judaism, that such a lack of concern for historicity, such a freely creative oral tradition, and such rapid loss of a historical perspective on Jesus could have occurred? Is this not to read into the early church the values of quite alien cultures, not least that of twentieth-century existentialist philosophy? Is this how we might reasonably expect first-century Jewish Christians to think and behave? (FrR.E 106)

If higher criticism was to be a magnificent edifice built on the foundation of lower criticism, we must conclude that the building is not structurally sound. We have surveyed eight of its primary pillars and found each one called into question by knowledgeable scholars. We must conclude that the "assured results of higher criticism" are not very assured.

8

THE GOSPEL
BEFORE THE GOSPELS

We noted in the last chapter that one of the positive effects of form criticism was to focus attention back on the period of oral transmission of the gospel before it was recorded in the four gospel accounts of the New Testament. François Amiot, along with several others, observed:

> Long before it became that great leather-bound volume carried around by the altar boy, the gospel was a spoken word. It was spoken, repeated, recited, for men to whom it brought a revelation, by men who had devoted their whole lives to the task of handing it on. In very truth, this direct message, this eternally overwhelming news, is something we must never allow to become buried under the dust of routine and mumbling monotony; we must ever be recovering that trembling expectation, that fresh and devouring curiosity which, when to belong to Christ was fraught with peril, made those who gave themselves to him as loving slaves. (AmF.SLC 33)

In this chapter, we want to look at the state of the gospel before the gospels were recorded. Our goal is to determine if the gospel writers have given to us an accurate historical record of the things Jesus did and said, despite the period of time between the end of Jesus' life and the formation of the first written records about him.

We know that it is simplistic, even inaccurate, to picture Matthew, Mark, Luke and John following Jesus around the countryside of Palestine, jotting down things that Jesus did or said as they were happening, and eventually writing out their narratives in four separate continuous accounts. While some notes may have been taken, the similarities (often word for word) as well as the differences in these four accounts are so striking that scholars have debated for centuries various explanations for the origins of the gospel accounts. Did one gospel writer copy from another? Did later writers put the final accounts together after changing the original accounts? How can we have any confidence that these are accurate historical reports? For example, since none of them were even there, how do any of the writers even know what went on during Jesus' trials? How *were* the gospels formed?

First, it is important to understand that the plural word *gospels* is foreign to the New Testament. F. F. Bruce explains:

> Our word *gospel* is a simplified form of the Old English *godspell*, which meant "good story" in the sense of "good news." The Old English word was designed to be the equivalent of the Latin *evangelium*, which in turn was derived from the Greek *euangelion*. In Greek the prefix *eu-* means "well" or "good," while the second part of the word is related to the verb *angello*, "report," "bring a message," and to the noun *angelos*, "messenger."...The Greek compound *euangelion* thus appears in the New Testament in the sense of "good news" or "good tidings." (BrF.DG 1,4)

Originally, there were not four gospels, only the one gospel or good news about Jesus Christ. As the four gospel accounts came to be seen as distinctively authoritative, Christians still recognized only one gospel, yet as stated by four separate evangelists. The French scholar Henri Daniel-Rops comments:

> St. Irenaeus spoke very accurately of the tetramorphic gospel, the gospel, that is, which is under four forms. And from the middle of the second century, with Clement of Alexandria and the Muratorian Canon, it was the practice—and the only right practice—to say, the Gospel according to St. Matthew, according to St. Mark, according to St. Luke, according to St. John, to make it clear that here is a body of truth, substantially one and unique, communicated to men in different modes. (AmF.SLC 39)

For centuries, scholars have struggled to explain how the various gospel accounts came into existence. In his excellent book *The Roots of the Synoptic Gospels,* Bo Reicke, the late professor of New Testament at the University of Basel, summarizes the various theories which have been proposed up to the present day: (ReB.RSG I)[1]

> First, since the middle of the nineteenth century, most scholars have based their synoptic investigations on the assumption that texts were used by the evangelist as *literary* sources.
>
> 1. Widely dominant today is the two-source theory, according to which Mark and a presumed document called Q were the common sources of Matthew and Luke.
>
> 2. Some contemporary scholars, however, reject this position and return to an older tradition which reserved a priority for Matthew.
>
> 3. Others prefer to reconstruct a number of different sources behind the Gospels by separating a proto-Luke from Luke, a pre-Mark from Mark, or by dividing the so-called Q into various documents.

These literary approaches contradict each other, and their advocates have not yet been able to convince the adherents of the other theories. (ReB.RSG, Preface)

Why is it that after centuries of debate we seem to have come no closer to determining how the gospel accounts came to be written? We believe it is because modern man is trapped in a literary culture. What do we mean?

TRAPPED IN A LITERARY CULTURE

Try to imagine being born into a culture where there are no written documents. All you know about the past is communicated to you by your parents or other elders in your village. You have no documents or written sources which can refresh your memory as to actual events that have occurred and things that have been said in the past. How would you pass on to your children the things that have been passed on to you?

What happens in a culture of this kind is that certain means of expression become standardized in the process of storytelling. In a literary culture such as our own, whenever we do communicate a story orally rather than in written form, we tend to tell the story a little differently every time we tell it in order to make it more interesting. This is taboo in an oral culture. You grow up knowing that the only way your children are going to understand their past is by hearing from you the exact story in the exact wording in which it was conveyed to you. It is difficult for us to imagine such a culture, but such cultures have been common since the beginning of human history. The culture into which Jesus was born did use literary documents, but it was primarily an oral-tradition-based culture. "To understand this," says Daniel-Rops,

> we must rid ourselves for the moment of our habits as modern men, men of a paper civilization. For us, reading and writing are two such automatic operations that we can scarcely imagine how some societies have almost managed to do without them. Our memories, in consequence, have become anaemic and stiff, but it is not so among many eastern peoples who make more demands on it; it was not so in the time of Christ. To learn by heart and recite were the two normal operations for the transmission of a text. The great writers of Israel were no doubt, quite literally, great speakers; thus the prophecies of Jeremias were spoken over a period of twenty-two years before being written down. Later, in the same way, the Mishna, the most essential part of the Talmud, was only written down after centuries of oral transmission. "A good disciple," said the rabbis, "is like a well-built cistern: He does not let fall one drop of water from his master's teaching." We must imagine the first instruction in the gospel in the same fashion; what the apostles stored up in their memory, they taught infallibly to their own disciples, who in their turn would repeat it to their hearts. (AmESLC 35)

Was this dependence on oral tradition a hindrance to those who lived in Jesus' day?

They didn't seem to think so. We have already noted how Papias valued the "living and permanent voice" of the apostles and their disciples more than books. The Mishnah upheld oral tradition, warning that written documents could be falsified and thus forever preserve error. Daniel-Rops adds:

> In the same way, St. Irenaeus, bishop of Lyons, recalls the time when he heard St. Polycarp, the great bishop of Smyrna, telling what he had himself remembered of St. John. Here we can feel the human warmth, the very truth of life; when, much later, the written text was definitely imposed, after being long concurrent with the spoken word, can we imagine that in these conditions the two could have differed? The written text preserves, for all who can hear, the moving accent of those living testimonies. (AmF.SLC 37)

THE FORMATIVE PERIOD

The formative period has been designated as that period of time between the crucifixion and the writing of the gospels. During the heyday of the German Tübingen school, it was popular to date the gospel accounts to a hundred or more years after Jesus' crucifixion. Such is no longer the case. As more evidence is found, scholars continue to push the dates of composition into the first century. In 1955 Dr. William F. Albright, recognized as one of the world's outstanding biblical archaeologists, wrote:

> We can already say emphatically that there is no longer any solid basis for dating any book of the New Testament after c. AD 80, two full generations before the date between 130 and 150 given by the more radical New Testament critics of today. (AIW.RD 136)

Eight years later he stated in an interview that the completion date for all the books in the New Testament was "probably sometime between c. AD 50 and 75."[2] With the arrival of John A. T. Robinson's *Redating the New Testament* (1976) which pays greater attention to historical evidence than did the form critics, the date has been pushed back to as early as c. AD 40 for a possible first draft of Matthew.[3] Most scholars who do not hold antisupernatural presuppositions date the synoptic gospels generally in the 60s, some a little earlier. Those who accept the existence of a Q source document behind Matthew and Mark usually date it from before AD 50. (AnC.CQ 78) There is, then, strong evidence that the formative period was no more than seventeen to twenty years in length, possibly as little as seven to ten years for an Aramaic or Hebrew version of Matthew spoken of by Papias.

This conclusion is corroborated by several pieces of evidence all converging together. First, as noted before, it is evident that the Book of Acts was written in approximately AD 62. It does not mention the fall of Jerusalem in AD 70, an event which would have been impossible to omit since Jerusalem is central to much of Acts. Nothing is mentioned of Nero's persecution of AD 64. The book ends with Paul in Rome under the confinement of Nero. Neither does Acts mention the martyrdoms of three central figures of the book: James (AD 62), Paul (AD 64), and Peter (AD 65). Why aren't their deaths mentioned when Acts does record the deaths of Stephen and of James, the brother of John?

If the Book of Acts was written in AD 62, then the Gospel of Luke must be dated earlier, probably in the late 50s, for Luke refers back to his earlier gospel account to Theophilus by saying in Acts, "The first account I composed, Theophilus, about all that Jesus began to do and teach."[4] Luke previously had opened his gospel account by addressing Theophilus at that time as well.[5]

The early church fathers affirm that Matthew wrote his account first. Many modern critics say Mark wrote his first. In either case almost everyone agrees that they both wrote before Luke, which puts their dates of composition no later than the late 50s. Earlier drafts, partial written drafts or collections of things Jesus said or did were likely in circulation for years prior to being used in the gospel accounts as we know them. These reports probably circulated in the 40s and 50s. Thus again, the formative period could have been no longer than seventeen to twenty years. R. T. France, a scholar not given to exaggeration or distortion, concludes:

> It is, I believe, probable that some, and perhaps all, of the gospels were written in substantially their present form within thirty years of the events, and that much of the material was already collected and written a decade or two before that. If that is the case, we are not dealing with a long folk-tradition, but with four parallel records of quite recent events, well within the lifetime of even a middle-aged witness of Jesus' ministry. (FrR.E 121)

The formative period should not be construed as that period of time in which the content of the gospels was being formed by some "creative community." As we will see below, it is rather that period of time when the form of the material was in transition from an oral to a written medium. We concur, then, with Charles Anderson when he writes:

> We would agree with the critics that some transformation such as they claim could have come over the material if the formative period had been two hundred rather than twenty years, but such a transformation in the length of time available was simply impossible. (AnC.CQ 80)

HOW WAS THE INFORMATION PRESERVED?

Recognizing the importance of oral tradition is by no means new. In 1796 and 1797 Johann Gottfried von Herder publicized the oral traditions behind the gospels. He wrote:

> The whole idea that our evangelists had been like scribes *(scribae)* who collected treatises and supplemented, improved, collated, compared each with the other, is...extraordinarily inconsistent and unnatural with regard

to their situation and intention, also to the purpose of their respective gospels….Ultimately, one does not know which evangelists would have copied the other, or supplemented, abbreviated, disrupted, improved, corrupted him or even stolen from him….In fact, not one of them endeavored to surpass and subdue the other, but each simply presented his report.[6]

In 1818 Johann Karl Ludwig Gieseler developed Herder's thesis even further. Concerning the importance of oral tradition behind the gospel accounts, he said:

> Assuming a common oral source is the most convenient means to explain how the following state of things has emerged: The more the stories appeared important to the disciples, the more they were told in a congruous way. It was these units that were most often presented, and being frequently repeated they preserved their original form in a more pure way than did other stories. Concerning the latter it was the matter and not so much the form that was recalled by the individuals. But here, too, the noticeable expressions are more or less identical, while before and after those expressions there is variation in the forms of synonyms. This exactly had to be the natural consequence of an oral prototype.[7]

Modern scholars, however, find it easier to believe that the similarities between the gospel accounts are due to their copying of another source or of common sources. The most widespread theory, the two-source theory, holds that Matthew and Luke (or redactors who were later thought to be Matthew and Luke) composed the accounts by using two primary sources, the gospel account of Mark and another source designated as Q (which stands for the German *Quelle,* meaning "source."). F. F. Bruce summarizes data which they attempt to explain:

> We find, for example, that the substance of 606 out of the 661 verses of Mark appears in Matthew, and that some 350 of Mark's verses reappear with little material change in Luke. Or, to put it another way, out of the 1,068 verses of Matthew, about 500 contain material also found in Mark; of the 1,149 verses of Luke, about 350 are paralleled in Mark. Altogether, there are only 31 verses in Mark which have no parallel either in Matthew or Luke.
>
> When we compare Matthew and Luke by themselves, we find that these two have about 250 verses containing common material not paralleled in Mark. This common material is cast in language which is sometimes practically identical in Matthew and Luke, and sometimes shows considerable divergence. We are then left with some 300 verses in Matthew containing narratives and discourses peculiar to that gospel, and about 550 verses in Luke containing matter not found in the other gospels. (Br:NTD 31)

Thomas and Gundry conveniently summarize here the arguments of the Oxford scholar, B. H. Streeter, in support of Mark's use by Matthew and Luke.[8] In addition they give counterarguments to Streeter's reasonings for Marcan priority and the two-source theory. Because the following material represents the heart of the issue for the formation of the gospels, we quote at some length:

1. Most of the material in Mark (93 percent according to Westcott) is found in Matthew and Luke. Since it seemed inconceivable to him that Mark would have abbreviated the other two, Streeter concluded that Matthew and Luke must have expanded Mark.

   Answers to this argument note that Mark may have had special reason for condensing one or both of the other gospels. Then too, material common to two or three gospels may have come to be there by some means other than copying. For example, it may be traceable to a common oral tradition. In other words, Mark may not have seen the gospels of Matthew and Luke before writing his own, and vice versa.

2. Though agreeing often with Mark in actual words used, Matthew and Luke do not agree with each other when they diverge from Mark. Allowing for exceptions to this generalization, Streeter explained these exceptions as irrelevant or deceptive or agreements made because of an overlap of Mark and Q (Matthew and Luke's other major source), or agreements because of textual corruption. This Matthean-Lucan diversity is taken to prove their dependence on Mark. Like Streeter's first proposition, however, this one, too, can be turned to prove the priority of Matthew or Luke. Depending on the parallel passages chosen and on which two gospels are pitted against the other, one could prove the priority of either Matthew or Luke as well. Though not numerous, agreements between Matthew and Luke where Mark has something different are substantial enough to indicate their independence of Mark in almost all sections where the two-source theory says they were dependent. No convincing explanation that would allow this premise to stand has accounted for these "exceptions."

3. The order of events in Mark is original, for wherever Matthew departs from Mark, Luke supports Mark's order, and wherever Luke departs from Mark, Matthew agrees with Mark's order. This, it is said, demonstrates Marcan priority and that the other two gospels are secondary since they never follow each other when departing from Mark's order. Again, however, the conclusion does not necessarily follow. For example, Mark may have worked from Matthew and Luke; he may have followed their order when they agreed and followed one or the other of them when they disagreed. Other explanations also offer plausible alternatives for the observed phenomena. One option which must remain open is that all three were working from an order dictated by a tradition agreed upon by eyewitnesses

and transmitted in varieties of ways among early Christians. All three writers, then, as occasion arose, deviated from this traditional sequence in their gospels.

4. The primitive nature of Mark as compared with Matthew and Luke demonstrates Mark's priority. To illustrate, Matthew uses *kurie* ("Lord") nineteen times and Luke sixteen times, compared to the word's appearing only once in Mark. This is taken to indicate a more developed reverential attitude and hence a later date for the two longer gospels.

Yet the same type of evidence may be used otherwise. Question may be raised as to a reverential connotation in *kurie* since Matthew uses such an address seven times when referring to mere man (Matthew 13:27; 21:29; 24:27-63; 25:11,20,22). Certainly this was not a form of address Matthew reserved for deity. Consequently, nothing chronological can be built on its use or nonuse in any of the gospels.

The same disposition may be made of other alleged marks of primitivity, such as Mark's Aramaisms. According to most standards of judgment, Matthew is much more Semitic than Mark. Couple this with Mark's Latinisms and his translation of Aramaic expressions for the sake of those who knew no Aramaic, and one has good reason for postulating the priority of Matthew.

5. The distribution of Marcan and non-Marcan material in Matthew and Luke shows their dependence on Mark. Matthew uses Mark as a framework and arranges his material into that structure, while Luke gives Marcan and non-Marcan material in alternate blocks.

It is just as plausible, however, to suppose the opposite procedure. Rather than Matthew's picking words or phrases here and there and weaving them into a smooth polished narrative, Mark, in coming up with his account, just as feasibly may have taken the book of Matthew and added details for vividness. If the assumption of Mark's priority be dropped, it can be shown how Luke could have extracted sections from Matthew and, in turn, Mark could have done the same from Luke. Another possible explanation is that all three could have drawn from a common core of tradition among early Christians. (ThR.H 275-76)

In addition to the Gospel According to Mark, scholars today commonly refer to the Q document, which is held to be the other document from which Matthew and Luke obtained much of their material. The existence of this *literary* document is presumed so strongly by some, that you would think we possess it in hand. In fact, all that we really possess is a collection of various verses from Matthew and Luke which are said to make up the Q document based on present literary criticism. After presenting strong technical arguments against the existence of a literary Q document, Professor Reicke states:

These specific Matthean and Lukan traditions have in no way proven them-selves as deriving from a document or text collection. Mainly comprised of sayings, or logia, they oftentimes contain narratives too. The peculiar dis-persion of the relevant 35 or 31 plus 4 units, among which there are only 2 really contextual parallels, shows that any supposition of a written source behind the Matthean-Lukan double traditions, such as the Logia source or the presumed document Q, is an illusion. (ReB.RSG 27)

Reicke goes on to say:

Only on the assumption of independent, freely circulating, not ordered traditions from which Matthew and Luke took over greater and smaller units of material as occasion demanded, can the constitutive flexibility of the double traditions in Matthew and Luke be explained. (ReB.RSG 28)

In order to explain how large blocks of material within each of the gospels (in par-ticular, Matthew and Luke) describe similar events but occur in different contexts, Reicke states:

The explanation lies in the principle of supply and demand, that is, each synoptic writer had a certain material at his disposal which had been trans-mitted and formulated in various ways among the Christians and which he took up, eventually rearranged, broadened, or limited according to his interests. (ReB.RSG 29)

Reicke is not saying here that the gospel writers used some material to basically make up their own stories, but rather that they fit together oral traditions in a manner that highlighted the particular facets of Jesus' life that they wanted to emphasize. There-fore, whereas we find no contradiction of historical details within the gospel accounts, we will find various rearrangements of the material which helped each gospel writer communicate the life of Christ to the particular audience which he had targeted.

Thus the two-source theory appears to have serious weaknesses in explaining the data. Again, Thomas and Gundry have summarized additional objections to the two-source theory as a whole:

1. The two-source theory cannot account for what has been labeled "The Great Omission." If Luke used Mark as a source, no feasible explanation has as yet come as to why he omitted any reference to Mark 6:45–8:26. This important section includes Jesus' walking on the water, the healing at Gennesaret, a major conflict over the tradition of the elders, the Syrophoenician woman's faith, the healing of a deaf and dumb man, the feeding of the four thousand, the Pharisees' demand for a sign, the instruction regarding the leaven of the Pharisees and that of Herod, and the healing of a blind man at Bethsaida.

2. Recent archaeological findings and increased knowledge about first-century

Palestinian conditions have made it increasingly difficult to sustain the argument for Q as a single written body of tradition.... It is more satisfying to explain Q, if the symbol is to be retained, as gospel material belonging to many different strands of tradition, both written and oral.

3. In sections of triple tradition (i.e., those covered by Matthew, Mark and Luke), a considerable number (about 230) of agreements between Matthew and Luke are different from a parallel portion of Mark. ["Different from" does not mean that Mark contradicts the other two, but that his wording varies.]...For example, Matthew 9:1-8 and Luke 5:17-26 agree with one another verbatim in nine separate expressions, whereas Mark 2:1-12 records different wording. In Matthew 8:1-4 and Luke 5:12-16 seven identical words or expressions are found, whereas Mark 1:40-45 deviates.... The fact of the matter is that the two-source theory cannot account for such agreements between Matthew and Luke when Mark reads differently.

4. The priority of Mark poses a serious challenge to the heretofore unchallenged testimony of early Christianity that Matthew the apostle wrote the first gospel. It necessitates understanding that Matthew, an eyewitness of Jesus' ministry, depended on Mark, a noneyewitness, for his information. This dependence extends even to Matthew's reliance on Mark for a description of his own conversion.

5. The two-source theory takes insufficient notice of personal contacts between the synoptic writers.... Matthew and Mark must have been close associates immediately following Pentecost, while Jerusalem Christians used Mark's home as a meeting place (cf. Acts 12:12). Mark and Luke were associated during Paul's Roman imprisonment (Colossians 4:10,14). Quite likely Luke encountered Matthew during his two-year stay with Paul in Palestine in the late fifties (cf. Acts 24:27). If not, in the process of his gospel research he must have talked to some [who were] very close to Matthew. Personal contacts like these render unnecessary the literary dependence advocated by the two-source theory. (ThR.H 277-78)

How can we explain the similarities and differences in the gospel accounts? The answer is becoming clearer and it is not a simple one. The gospel writers must have used a variety of sources including oral reports standardized through retelling, personal interviews, their own memories, short notes and extended outlines jotted down quickly by eyewitnesses; perhaps one or more saw one or more of the other accounts. And why all this activity? Very simply—to remember! As James D. G. Dunn states:

> The point is this. The gospel traditions themselves show that their present form is the outcome of a well-established practice of oral use. In other words, they bear witness to a strong and widely prevalent concern among

the first Christians to *remember* Jesus, to celebrate their memories, to retain them in appropriate forms, to structure their traditions for easy recall, but above all to remember. (DuJ.HSG 10-11)

The sections which follow contain evidence demonstrating how the gospel writers endeavored to remember Jesus by transferring an accurate and reliable description of Jesus' life from an oral to a written form.

EVIDENCE

Sitz im Leben, *the Real One*

What was the real-life situation of the early church? When we forget about the modern-day trappings and activities of today's churches, how do we envision the early Christian communities?

If we pay any attention at all to the New Testament letters, the book of Acts, and even the gospels themselves, we see quickly that one of the primary activities of the church was the spread of the gospel, the good news. This preaching of the gospel would have made it "probable that relatively comprehensive 'tractates' of Jesus-traditions had to be compiled at a fairly early stage for use of missionaries and teachers who went out from Jerusalem." (AnC.CQ 80) With new believers being added to the church daily, and these in turn spreading the word to others, there would have been a natural demand for accurate information about this Jesus.

The dissemination of material about Jesus, however, was not haphazardly entrusted to unknowledgeable Christians who could distort the message. When a successor was needed for Judas Iscariot, the one qualification accepted by the apostles was that the successor be an eyewitness of the entire ministry of Jesus:

> It is therefore necessary that of the men who have accompanied us all the time that the Lord Jesus went in and out among us—beginning with the baptism of John, until the day that He was taken up from us—one of these should become a witness with us of His resurrection (Acts 1:21,22).

Harald Riesenfeld, the respected Swedish New Testament scholar, concludes that for the disciples "the words and deeds of Jesus are a holy word, comparable with that of the Old Testament, and the handing down of this precious material is entrusted to special persons." (RiH.GT 19) J. P. Moreland adds:

> When one compares the synoptic gospels with one another, one finds that there is greater word-for-word agreement in the words of Jesus than in the incidental details of the surrounding historical narrative. This is what one would expect if the material was handled as holy tradition. (MoJP.S 144)

Thus, the disciples followed the practice of their Jewish communities in choosing special people, comparable in many respects to the rabbis, to be responsible for preserving and passing along the "holy" tradition. The task consumed enough time that these people were relieved of other household duties that they might devote time "to prayer and to the ministry of the word" (Acts 6:4).

The Jewish Milieu

The land of Palestine was multilingual. Evidence shows that Hebrew, Aramaic and Greek were all common, and scholars debate which had the greatest use in each region. At feast time, Jews from a wide variety of other nations, all with different languages, crowded into Jerusalem. The events of Pentecost, fifty days after Jesus' resurrection, indicate that very early in the life of the church the tradition about Jesus had to be translated into other languages. Even the single step of translating from Aramaic or Hebrew into Greek would account for some of the dissimilarities between the various gospel accounts.

Eventually, eyewitnesses to the life of Jesus began to die. At the same time, the church was growing by leaps and bounds especially among the Gentiles. Whereas Jewish believers may have been quite content to stick with an oral tradition, those in Greek-speaking communities apparently preferred a written report. Clement of Alexandria (c. AD 155–220) reports Mark's motivation for writing out his gospel account:

> When, at Rome, Peter had openly preached the word and by the spirit had proclaimed the gospel, the large audience urged Mark, who had followed him for a long time and remembered what had been said, to write it all down. This he did, making his gospel available to all who wanted it.[9]

Even after the gospel accounts were composed, evidence shows that the respect for oral tradition continued. You might wonder why, especially with the three synoptic gospels, the church didn't combine them all into one smooth-flowing account free of any apparent contradictions. Daniel-Rops answers:

> There were essays in this direction, one at least of which, that of the Assyrian Tatian, a pupil of Justin, was composed with very great skill and quickly became popular in the Syrian Churches. Perhaps she knew, with her marvelous sense of reality, that the small differences between the texts, so far from prejudicing their credibility, would strengthen it. And above all, with her profound respect for tradition, she knew she had not the right to make any alterations in documents which derived directly from the first witness. (AmF.SLC 39-40)

To further understand the *Sitz im Leben* (life situation) of the church and the preservation of the gospel story, it is helpful to know something about the Jewish culture at the time of the apostles.

> When Paul says in Galatians 4 that in the fullness of time God sent forth His Son, born of a woman and subject to the Law, he is speaking

dogmatically. But at the same time he is suggesting the existence of a fact which the historian cannot afford to neglect: that Jesus was born of a Jewish woman and brought up under the Torah. That means that he was familiar with, and subject to, the Torah.

One of the main tasks facing any scholar who would trace the origins, development and transmission of the gospel tradition must therefore be to determine, in general and in detail, its relation to the Torah. Few factors have been so important for the formation of the gospel tradition as the belief that the words and works of Christ were the fulfillment of the Law and the Prophets. If we modern scholars knew our Old Testament (the Hebrew text, the Aramaic targum and the Greek translations) off by heart, we would be able to see this in its correct perspective. (GeB.MM 324-25)

Thus the Swedish scholar, Birger Gerhardsson, challenged gospel scholars with the publication of his *Memory and Manuscript*. In the first half of the book, Gerhardsson explains the procedures Jewish authorities used to receive and transmit accurately their oral tradition. In the second half of the book he reveals the evidence for the early church's use of similar practices for passing on the oral tradition about Jesus.

Gerhardsson cites a number of rabbinic quotations to demonstrate how important it was in Jewish culture to receive and transmit its oral tradition accurately. For example, in the Babylonian Talmud, tractate Sotah 22*a* reveals that the Jews were intent to memorize even what they didn't understand: "The magician mumbles and does not understand what he is saying. In the same way the tanna recites and does not understand what he is saying." In the same Talmud, tractate Abodah Zarah 19*a* says, "One should always recite, (although one forgets and) although one does not understand what one is saying." In several different texts, a pupil is described as having learned a particular doctrine by the words, "He learned it from him 'forty times,' and it became for him as though it lay in his purse."[10]

In several places, the rabbis give their students mnemonic devices to help them memorize certain passages. In order to memorize:

> The loaves for the wave offering were seven (hand-breadths) long and four wide and their horns were four finger-breadths (high). The loaves of shewbread were ten (hand-breadths) long and five wide and their horns were seven finger-breadths (high)

Rabbi Judah (ben Ilai) advises, "so that you may not make a mistake (remember the mnemonic): ZaDaD YaHaZ."[11] These letters represent the numbers 7, 4, 4, 10, 5 and 7.

Those who have discovered the helpful technique of memorizing by repeating aloud will recognize the soundness of this advice: "Let your ears hear what you allow to cross your lips."[12] R. Akiba emphasized daily study of the Torah by saying, "Sing every day, sing every day."[13] Even today, Christians often find it easier to memorize Scripture by learning various Scripture songs and choruses. Gerhardsson also mentions "didactic facial expressions which were evidently used, as well as the use of gestures and bodily movements to impart dramatic shape to the doctrinal material." (GeB.MM 168)

Strong admonitions against forgetting included this one from H. Meir, "Every man who forgets a single word of his Mishnah (i.e., what he has learned), Scripture accounts it unto him as if he had forfeited his soul!"[14] If a teacher forgot what he once knew, for example because of bad health, he had to return to his own pupils to relearn what he had forgotten. (GeB.MM 169)

Is it any wonder that for hundreds of years the Jews were able to preserve volumes of oral tradition? They finally recorded the Mishnah in c. AD 200, the Jerusalem or Palestinian Talmud in AD 350–425, and the Babylonian Talmud in AD 500. When you think a moment that every one of the eyewitnesses to Jesus' life had at least some of the childhood training illustrated above, it is almost ludicrous to think that they would have allowed error to creep into the words of Jesus which they wanted to preserve. One almost wonders why Jesus needed to send the Holy Spirit to "bring to your remembrance all that I said to you" (John 14:26).

It is clear from the gospels that Jesus phrased his teaching in easy-to-remember segments. The parables are generally concise and easily recalled. Certain sayings such as Matthew 11:17 indicate Jesus' teaching skill within an oral culture: "We played the flute for you, and you did not dance; we sang a dirge, and you did not mourn." The story of the two who built their houses, one on sand and one upon the rock, contains parallels and contrasts in phraseology which stick with the listener (Matthew 7:24-27).

From the very beginning, though the disciples misunderstood what Jesus' messiahship meant, they did not doubt that he was the Messiah. John probably noticed that the other gospel writers failed to record some crucial events concerning the time prior to when they left their nets to follow Jesus. So he tells of Andrew finding Peter and announcing, "We have found the Messiah" (John 1:41).

When Philip told Nathanael about Jesus, he used clearly understood Jewish terms to refer to Jesus as the Messiah: "We have found Him of whom Moses in the Law and also the Prophets wrote" (John 1:45).

Using the Greek word for Messiah, Matthew's gospel recalls Jesus' teaching: "And do not be called leaders; for one is your Leader, that is, Christ."[15] Gerhardsson concludes:

> All historical probability is in favor of Jesus' disciples, and the whole of early Christianity, having accorded the sayings of the one whom they believed to be the Messiah at least the same degree of respect as the pupils of a rabbi accorded the words of their master!" (GeB.MM 332)

The Claims of Luke

Is it mere conjecture to suppose that the gospel writers used accurate oral traditions to compile their accounts of the life of Jesus? Probably the most valuable piece of information available to us to answer this question is the first four verses of Luke's account.

In this one sentence, Luke, Paul's traveling physician-companion, reveals how he, and in all probability the other gospel writers, compiled their accounts. He says:

> Inasmuch as many have undertaken to compile an account of the things accomplished among us, just as those who from the beginning were eyewitnesses and servants of the word have handed them down to us, it seemed fitting for me as well, having investigated everything carefully from the beginning, to write it out for you in consecutive order, most excellent Theophilus; so that you might know the exact truth about the things you have been taught (Luke 1:1-4).

Imagine for a moment that you are a late-first-century Christian reading this sentence. Neither the gospels nor the rest of the New Testament has yet been collected into what we call today the New Testament, but you are interested in knowing how Luke compiled his account. You would observe several interesting points, especially if you are reading this sentence in the Greek language in which it was written.

First, the account is clearly set forth as coming from a single individual. Any attempt to attribute this work to a group of redactors is blatantly inconsistent with its opening sentence. Since the writer of Acts also addresses Theophilus and mentions a previous account of Jesus' life, and because of all the stylistic and thematic similarities, it becomes obvious that both Acts and Luke were compiled by the same individual. The early church unanimously affirms Luke as that individual. The various "we" passages (e.g., Acts 16:10), as well as Acts 20:5–21:15 and 27:1–28:15, indicate Luke was most likely the author of the book of Acts and therefore is also the author of this Gospel According to Luke. Colossians 4:14, Philemon 24 and 2 Timothy 4:11 likewise all witness to Luke's identity as Paul's beloved companion and probable author of the two works, Luke and Acts.

Second, you will learn that Luke knew of many others who had already "undertaken" the writing of an account of the life of Jesus. Luke uses the verb *epicheireo,* meaning to undertake, attempt, set one's hand to, or try. In verse one, then, Luke is saying that, since many had attempted to draw up a narrative concerning Jesus' life, he felt he also should write an account as he had made a thorough investigation of the things that happened. He may have felt other attempts were not thorough enough, contained material he thought was unnecessary, or presented confusing arrangements of the content or the chronological sequence, at least for the audience he was addressing.

Third, you will learn from Luke's introduction that, while others are attempting to produce an account of Jesus' life, they are not necessarily compiling written accounts. The words "compile an account" literally read: "to repeat in proper order a narrative or account." These words, especially in a culture where the common mode of expression was oral rather than written, simply indicate that many of the early Christians were engaged in a process of recalling or retelling all that took place in the earthly life of Jesus and were concerned about preserving it in some kind of orderly fashion.

Fourth, you recognize that Luke has received his information from eyewitnesses. These eyewitnesses are known as being entrusted to faithfully pass on the things they have seen and heard. J. W. Wenham, a British scholar, has detailed some good evidence showing that even Luke himself may have been an eyewitness to at least part of Jesus' ministry. (WeJW.GO 118-27)

Mark also unconsciously reveals his acquaintance with reliable witnesses to the life of Jesus. For example, in Mark 15:21 he reports, "And they pressed into service a passerby coming from the country, Simon of Cyrene (the father of Alexander and Rufus), that he might bear his cross." There is no reason for Mark's parenthetical reference to Alexander and Rufus other than his expectation that his readers would know them. They had apparently become believers, possibly holding positions of leadership somewhere in the early church. Mark's casual reference to them indicates his personal acquaintance with firsthand eyewitnesses or earwitnesses who could confirm the accuracy of his report. Neither Matthew nor Luke, reporting the same event, mentioned Alexander and Rufus. They apparently didn't expect their readers to know them, or they may have felt it necessary not to reveal their identity in order to protect them from possible persecution.

Fifth, you anticipate seeing other gospel accounts in written form from other individuals. As you are reading Luke's account, you already may have seen others. Here, Luke's use of the word *kamoi*, "to me also," indicates Luke's awareness of other attempts to write down the things which happened, since he says, "It seemed good to me also to write." He would not have used the word "also" if he had not known of other writings being attempted, or possibly in circulation.

Sixth, you notice in verse three that Luke emphasizes the quality of his sources. The phrase, "having investigated everything carefully from the beginning," can also be rendered "having investigated or traced everything from its source."

Seventh, you appreciate Luke's efforts to be accurate with all that he reports. The word "carefully" in verse three literally means "accurately."

Eighth, you also appreciate Luke's efforts to conduct his investigation in an orderly manner and to arrange his account in the same orderly manner. In verse three, he uses the word *kathexes,* meaning "in order." It is difficult to tell whether this adverb is used to indicate a chronological progression in the account or logical methodology in his investigation. It seems to apply to both.

Ninth, you observe that Luke's purpose is to communicate to you the certainty and accuracy of all the events described. In verses three and four, he says to Theophilus (either a man named Theophilus or one who is a "lover of God" [the literal meaning of Theophilus]), "So that you might know the exact truth about the things you have been taught."

Tenth, you understand the words in verse 4, "the things you have been taught," as being those things you previously learned by oral instruction. Bible study as we understand it today was foreign to the first-century layman. As did the Jews, so the early Christians relied on oral instruction and memorization for their continued growth in the faith.

The Apostle Paul

When we come to the apostle Paul, we find what some would say is the greatest evidence for the truth of the Christian faith. Here is a man cut completely from the cloth of Jewish culture. Fashioned by it and steeped in it, he was probably one of the most intense protagonists of the day for rabbinic Judaism. In his own words, "I was advancing in Judaism beyond many of my contemporaries among my countrymen, being more extremely zealous for my ancestral traditions."[16] Paul's sudden conversion from persecutor of the church to its foremost early missionary is one of the most difficult challenges to a skeptic of biblical Christianity. Philip Schaff remarks that even "Dr. Baur, the master-spirit of skeptical criticism and the founder of the 'Tübingen School,'" felt constrained to admit that in "'the sudden transformation of Paul from the most violent adversary of Christianity into its most determined herald' he could see 'nothing short of a miracle.'" (ScP.HCC 315, quoting BaF.CH 1:47)

One of the main reasons the evidence from Paul is so strong is that he produced his letters so early. The chart on the next page compares the dates given by three recognized scholars in the field (representing both liberal and moderate views) and helps set the works of Paul in their historical time frame.

As you can see, even though different scholars vary on specific dates, it is usually not by more than two or three years. (Obviously Kümmel does not accept Pauline authorship on some of the New Testament books attributed to Paul.)[17]

Book	Kümmel[18]	Guthrie[19]	Robinson
1 Thessalonians	50	51	Early 50
2 Thessalonians	50-51	51	50-51
1 Corinthians	54-55	57	Spring 55
1 Timothy	100 +	61-64	Autumn 55
2 Corinthians	55-56	57	Early 56
Galatians	54-55	49-50	Late 56
Romans	55-56	57-58	Early 57

Book	Kümmel[18]	Guthrie[19]	Robinson
Titus	100 +	61-64	Late spring 57
Philippians	53-58	59-61	Spring 58
Philemon	56-60	59-61	Summer 58
Colossians	56-60	59-61	Late summer 58
Ephesians	80-100	59-61	Late summer 58
2 Timothy	100 +	61-64	Autumn 58

The dates of Paul's letters become particularly significant in view of objections critics raise against the gospel accounts. For example, critics are fond of dating the gospels fairly late because the gospels supposedly indicate a more sophisticated view of Christ ("high Christology") which would not have existed in earliest Christianity. But one of the chief indicators for a high Christology is the use of the word *Christ* as a name (as in "Jesus Christ") rather than as a title (as in "Jesus the Christ"). It is odd then that Paul, supposedly writing earlier than the gospel writers, exhibits this high Christology.

Matthew, Mark, Luke and John combined use the name "Jesus Christ" only five times. Paul uses it approximately 125 times. Whereas the gospel writers almost always refer to Jesus by the name "Jesus" alone, Paul almost always uses a term such as "Christ Jesus," "Lord Jesus," "Jesus Christ" or "our Lord Jesus Christ." The gospel writers only occasionally call Jesus "Christ" as though it were a name. Why?

There is only one good answer. The gospel accounts originated earlier than Paul's letters (early as they were) and preserved the wording of the earliest oral traditions through their formative stages to the completed written accounts. At the same time, however, the evidence demonstrates that the earliest Christians did refer to Jesus as the Messiah on a number of occasions.

Skeptics seem to delight in using Paul to claim that the church in his day knew little or nothing about an actual, historical Jesus; G. A. Wells, for example, writes:

> The eight Pauline letters I have accepted as genuine are so completely silent concerning the events that were later recorded in the gospels as to suggest that these events were not known to Paul, who, however, could not have been ignorant of them if they had really occurred. (WeG.HE 22)

Aside from the questionable arguments of Professor Wells to deny Paul of being the author of five of his letters, several other problems with the view expressed above occur. First, Paul had little desire, intention or motive to communicate in his letters factual, historical information about Jesus. Like his traveling companion, Luke, he would have been aware of attempts by certain other people to compile accounts concerning Jesus' life and they were certainly more qualified than himself. He openly admits, "I neither received it [the gospel] from man, nor was I taught it, but I received it through a revelation of Jesus Christ."[20] He was concerned enough about the accuracy of his gospel to visit with Peter and the others in Jerusalem, once three years after his conversion and again at least fourteen years after his conversion.

Peter, James, John and the rest confirmed Paul's faithfulness to the gospel message, but he was writing to Christians who already knew about Jesus' earthly life. Therefore, the focus of his letters was on the risen Jesus living his life out through Christians. Paul did not deny Jesus' life; he focused on applying the truth of Jesus' resurrection: "Christ in you, the hope of glory."[21] In 2 Corinthians 5:16, Paul makes clear that his concentration is on the risen Christ: "Even though we have known Christ according to the flesh, yet now we know Him thus no longer."

Paul did not initially receive the gospel through historical preservation, and his common touchstone with the historical gospels is mainly just that the risen Jesus whom he preached was the same historical Jesus who actually walked the earth.

A second problem with Professor Wells' view is that Paul does give a number of historical facts about the life of Jesus, and he even uses standard rabbinic vocabulary to explain how he had acquired this information. The fact that Paul's primary information about the gospel came by direct revelation from Jesus himself didn't prevent him from using his skills as a rabbi to receive and deliver the gospel. Simon Kistemaker explains:

> In the letters of Paul, the words, "receive" and "deliver" are technical terms referring to the transmission of a sacred trust. Hence, when Paul instructs the Christians at Corinth in the proper celebration of the Lord's Supper, he says: "For I received from the Lord what I also delivered to you, that the Lord Jesus on the night when he was betrayed took bread" (1 Corinthians 13:23). And in chapter 15 of that same epistle, he uses these terms again: "For I delivered to you as of first importance what I also received" (v. 3). (KiS.G 48-49)

This receiving and delivering of a sacred trust goes back to a foundational practice of the rabbis. According to Riesenfeld:

> As regards the nature of this Jewish tradition and its transmission, we are, as it happens, relatively well informed. But what justifies us in drawing from it a number of conclusions relating to primitive Christianity is the fact that the terminology used of the Jewish process of tradition reappears in the New Testament....
>
> *Paralambanein,* "take over," Heb. *qibbel,* denotes the imprinting of a tradition of doctrine with which one had been entrusted, while *paradidomi,* "hand over," Heb. *masar,* is used of its commitment to a particular pupil. The situation as here conceived is not the vague diffusion of narratives, sagas, or anecdotes, as we find it in folk-lore, but the rigidly controlled transmission of matter from one who has the mastery of it to another who has been specially chosen to learn it.... What was passed on in this way

> was, in the matter both of content and form, a fixed body of material....
> The ideal pupil was one who never lost one iota of the tradition. (RiH.GTB 17-18)

If ever there was an ideal pupil, it was Paul. For fourteen to seventeen years he studied and preached the gospel in the various regions surrounding his hometown of Tarsus. He finally went to Jerusalem to verify that the gospel revealed to him was the same as that of the first apostles, "for fear that I might be running, or had run, in vain."[22] That his message was the same as theirs is confirmed by his report:

> Seeing that I had been entrusted with the gospel to the uncircumcised, just
> as Peter had been to the circumcised...and recognizing the grace that had
> been given to me, James and Cephas and John, who were reputed to be pil-
> lars, gave to me and Barnabas the right hand of fellowship, that we might
> go to the Gentiles, and they to the circumcised.[23]

Was Paul really silent about Jesus' earthly life, as so many critics claim? Norman Anderson cites some of the most obvious historical references made by Paul:

> Jesus was a real man, "born of a woman, born under the Law" (Galatians
> 4:4)—and, as we have seen, of Davidic stock (Romans 1:3). His "meek-
> ness and gentleness" (2 Corinthians 10:1) were known and admired, yet
> he was "betrayed" (1 Corinthians 11:23) and crucified by the rulers of this
> world (1 Corinthians 2:8), the Jews themselves being basically responsible
> (1 Thessalonians 2:14, 15). The Last Supper is recounted in some length
> (1 Corinthians 11:23-25). There are also echoes of the teaching of Jesus—
> e.g., in the apostle's emphasis on love as fulfilling the law (Romans 13:10;
> Galatians 5:14), and on paying tribute to those to whom it is due (Mark
> 12:16,17; Romans 13:7). In regard to marriage, moreover, the apostle care-
> fully distinguishes between the commandment of the Lord and his own
> judgment (1 Corinthians 7:10-12,25,40). (AnN.JC 34)

Jesus also had brothers, one of whom was called James (1 Corinthians 9:5; Galatians 1:19). R. T. France adds:

> The principle that "the labourer deserves his wages" (Matthew 10:10; Luke
> 10:7) is quoted explicitly (and as the words of "Scripture"!) in 1 Timo-
> thy 5:18, and the same principle is given as what "the Lord directed" in
> 1 Corinthians 9:14. Here Paul again shows not only knowledge of what
> Jesus had taught, but also a special respect for it as on a different level of
> authority from his own views, simply because Jesus said it. (FrR.E 92)

In a number of instances, Paul conveys historical information which has been recognized by scholars as being even earlier than his writings. Moreland explains:

> Paul's letters contain a number of creeds and hymns (Romans 1:3,4;
> 1 Corinthians 11:23ff.; 15:3-8; Philippians 2:6-11; Colossians 1:15-18; 1 Tim-
> othy 3:16; 2 Timothy 2:8; see also John 1:1-18; 1 Peter 3:18-22; 1 John

4:2). Three things can be said about them. First, they are pre-Pauline and very early. They use language which is not characteristically Pauline, they often translate easily back into Aramaic, and they show features of Hebrew poetry and thought-forms. This means that they came into existence while the church was heavily Jewish and that they became standard, recognized creeds and hymns well before their incorporation into Paul's letters. Most scholars date them from [AD] 33 to 48. Some, like Hengel, date many of them in the first decade after Jesus' death.

Second, the content of these creeds and hymns centers on the death, resurrection, and deity of Christ. They consistently present a portrait of a miraculous and divine Jesus who rose from the dead. Third, they served as hymns of worship in the liturgy of the early assemblies and as didactic expressions for teaching the Christology of the church.

In sum, the idea of a fully divine, miracle-working Jesus who rose from the dead was present during the first decade of Christianity. Such a view was not a legend which arose several decades after the crucifixion. (MoJPS 148-49)

Other hymns or creeds include Romans 8:31-39 and 10:9,10.

Did Paul's gospel rest on historical events or was it merely a spiritual revelation? Paul answers that question in the clearest possible terms by using a creed which probably goes back to the very first years after the death and resurrection of Jesus. In 1 Corinthians 15:1-8, Paul declares:

> Now I make known to you, brethren, the gospel which I preached to you, which also you received, in which also you stand, by which also you are saved, if you hold fast the word which I preached to you, unless you believed in vain. For I delivered to you as of first importance what I also received, that Christ died for our sins according to the Scriptures, and that He was buried, and that He was raised on the third day according to the Scriptures, and that He appeared to Cephas, then to the twelve. After that He appeared to more than five hundred brethren at one time, most of whom remain until now, but some have fallen asleep; then He appeared to James, then to all the apostles; and last of all, as it were to one untimely born, He appeared to me also.

Whatever the form critic may say, one thing is obvious. The gospel message Paul received, believed and delivered to others rested on firm historical facts. Moreland notes that there are several indications that much of 1 Corinthians 15:1-8 was a pre-Pauline creed:

1. The words *delivered* and *received* are terms descriptive of rabbinic treatment of holy tradition, indicating that this is holy tradition received by Paul.

2. Several primitive early, pre-Pauline phrases are used ("the twelve," "the third day," "he was seen," "for our sins" [plural], "he was raised"). These phrases are very Jewish and early.

3. The poetic style is Hebraic.

4. The Aramaic *Cephas* is used; this was an early way of referring to Peter. (MoJP.S 150)

He notes further:

> 1 Corinthians was written in [AD] 55 and Paul first visited the Corinthians in 50, so the formula precedes that date. It was already a formalized statement before Paul shared it with the Corinthians. Most scholars date it from three to eight years after Jesus' death. This date fits well with the mention of James and Cephas, who were also mentioned in Galatians 1:18,19. It seems likely, therefore, that this formula was given to Paul at the meeting which took place three to four years after the crucifixion. A date of three to eight years also fits well with the heavily Semitic flavor of the formula. (MoJP.S 150)

Paul adds to the creed after the words "He appeared to more than five hundred brethren at one time," the words, "most of whom remain until now, but some have fallen asleep." These are hardly the words of someone trying to make up an alleged historical event which never took place. The German historian Hans von Campenhausen states concerning this passage, "This account meets all the demands of historical reliability that could possibly be made of such a text." (VoH.EE 44)

C. H. Dodd concludes:

> Thus Paul's preaching presents a special stream of Christian tradition which was derived from the mainstream at a point very near to its source.... Anyone who should maintain that the primitive Christian gospel was fundamentally different from that which we have found in Paul must bear the burden of proof. (DoC.AP 16)

CONCLUSION

In light of the formative period, the time it took to transfer the reports about Jesus from an oral to a written form, should we expect that the gospel writers could have given to us an accurate historical record of the things Jesus did and said? We first sought to view the question from within an oral rather than a literary culture. We next observed that the formative period was extremely short in comparison to what is required for myths and legends. We noted the problems inherent in depending on a theory of literary dependence of one gospel account upon another to explain the origin of the material. An accurate oral tradition surfaced as the best means of explaining the composition of the various gospel accounts. Finally, we looked at the confirming evidence of the true situation of the early church, the Jewish background of the first Christians, the report of Luke and the early ministry and writings of the apostle Paul.

The evidence available points to an affirmative answer. We certainly can trust that the gospel writers did pass on to us an accurate report of the life of Jesus.

9

HISTORY AND MYTH

I n view of the supernatural aspects the gospel writers attributed to the life of Jesus, can we sincerely believe that they gave us an accurate description of the Jesus who lived in history? One major argument against the historicity of the New Testament Jesus has been the similarity of mythological elements found in pagan religions during the same time the early Christian church was active. One source asks:

> If you Christians believe the stories of Jesus' miracles, if you believe the story of Jesus' miraculous birth, if you believe the story that Jesus was raised from the dead and ascended into Heaven, then how can you refuse to believe precisely the same stories when they are told of the other Savior Gods: Herakles, Asklepios, the Dioscuri, Dionysos, and a dozen others I could name? (CaDR.DSG 17)[1]

Christian college students are often devastated to hear of ancient religions which contained stories of resurrections, dying saviors, baptismal initiations, miraculous births and the like. The inference, of course, is that the early Christian writers borrowed these stories and attributed them to Jesus as they formulated the Christian religion. Jewish scholar Pinchas Lapide states:

> If we add to all these disturbing factors the statement that in the ancient world there were not less than a round dozen of nature deities, heroes, philosophers, and rulers who, all long before Jesus, suffered and died, and rose again on the third day, then the skepticism of most non-Christians can easily be understood.

> The Babylonian Tammuz, whose cult had spread to Jerusalem, the Syrian Adonis, the Phrygian Attis, the Egyptian Osiris, the Thracian Dionysos—to mention only the most important deities—all underwent suffering and martyrdom, some died on the cross. The death of some deities even had expiatory power. And in almost all cases their resurrection was connected with the hope for human immortality.

> The imprisonment of the savior of the world, his interrogation, the condemnation, the scourging, the execution in the midst of the criminals, the descent into hell—yes, even the heart blood of the dying gushing out of a spear wound, all these details were believed by millions of believers of the Bel-Marduk mystery religion whose central deity was called the savior sent by the Father, the one who raises the dead, the Lord and the Good Shepherd. (LaP.R 40-41)

Did the early Christians turn a human Jesus into a supernatural figure by borrowing supernatural elements from the mystery religions? In this chapter, we will attempt to answer that question by (1) observing some basic traits of mystery religions and comparing them to Christianity; (2) examining some specific alleged mythical roots of central Christian doctrine and practice; (3) identifying some fallacies committed by those who link Christianity with mystery religions; and (4) observing the uniqueness of the gospel description of Jesus when compared to the literature of the mystery religions.

BASIC TRAITS OF MYSTERY RELIGIONS: HOW SIMILAR ARE THEY TO THE GOSPELS?

Not all of the following traits will be found in all of the mystery religions. In general, however, you will notice most of the traits surfacing in each religion.

1. An attempt to explain the cycles of nature.

Dr. Ronald Nash, former head of the Department of Philosophy and Religion at Western Kentucky University, has authored or edited thirteen books on philosophy and religion. In his *Christianity and the Hellenistic World,* a work upon which we will rely heavily in this chapter, he explains:

> Central to the mysteries was their use of the annual vegetation cycle, in which life is renewed each spring and dies each fall. Followers of the mystery cults found deep symbolic significance in the natural process of growth, death, decay, and rebirth. (NaR.CHW 122)

E.M. Blaiklock calls this the etiological myth, "a story made up to account for an existing situation, fact, or phenomenon." (BlE.MM51) For example, the Eleusinian Mysteries explained the cycle of sowing and reaping through the story of Demeter (Ceres), goddess of grain. The story has Hades (Pluto or Pluton), god of the netherworld, carrying away Kore (Persephone), the daughter of Demeter (Ceres), to be a companion for his wife. Demeter, while searching for her daughter, refused to make the grain grow. Finally, Kore was allowed to come back to earth where she bore a son, Plutus, the symbol of a rich harvest. But because Kore had eaten a pomegranate seed, the symbol of death and birth, she was allowed to spend only two thirds of the year on earth; the other one third was to be spent with Hades. Blaiklock notes:

Obviously…there is nothing in the New Testament remotely resembling the etiological myth.…

To suggest that tales like that of the Last Supper were invented to account for a mysterious practice of the church, or that Peter's confession was forged to bolster a doctrine which had inexplicably evolved, is a type of literary criticism which would provoke only a smile in any other sphere of scholarship. The firm and undeniable dating of the records in the first century has cut much hothouse theory at the root. When liberal scholarship could postulate a second-century date for the documents, there was a somewhat wider field for the manoeuvering of fancy. Such open space has disappeared. (BIE.MM 54-55)

Even Ian Wilson, in his recent book undermining the reliability of the New Testament, admits:

Modern scholars have pointed out, the Christian story of death and resurrection is really quite different from the symbolism of the crop cycle which lies at the heart of the old fertility religions. On close inspection the parallels are unimpressive. (Wil.JTE 141)

2. An attempt to explain superior qualities of an outstanding individual.

Blaiklock calls this the accretion myth:

The fiction which, planted and fed by the imaginations of men, grows around some central core of historical truth. The apocryphal gospels, for example, contain a good deal of imaginative material, collected like forest moss around the trees of truth. (BIE.MM 55-56)

Another good example of this kind of myth is provided by Diogenes Laertius (third century AD) in his description of the birth of Plato (c. 429–347 BC):

Speusippos, in his writing "The Funeral Feast of Plato," and Klearchos, in his "Encomium on Plato," and Anaxilaides, in the second book "On the Philosophers," all say that there was at Athens a story that when Perikitione was ready (to bear children) Ariston was trying desperately but did not succeed (in making her pregnant). Then, after he had ceased his efforts, he saw a vision of Apollo. Therefore, he abstained from any further marital relations until she brought forth a child (from Apollo).

And Plato was born, as Apollodoros says in his "Chronology" in the 88th Olympiad, on the seventh day of Thargelion, which was the day the Delians say Apollo was born.[2]

Notice that Diogenes writes some 700 years after Plato, and that his description of Plato's alleged miraculous birth definitely does not claim it to be a virgin birth. Also,

Speusippus, Plato's nephew and good friend, was not willing to confirm the truth of the account as an eyewitness. He simply says that this was a story circulating around Athens.

The miraculous birth legend was fairly common in the Hellenistic world. Alexander the Great was allegedly conceived in Olympias, his mother, by the god Zeus-Ammon.[3] Diodorus Siculus describes the birth of Herakles as follows:

> They say that Perseus was the son of Danae, who was the daughter of Akrisios and Zeus. Andromeda, Kepheos' daughter, lay with him (Perseus) and bore Elektryon; then Euridike, daughter of Pelops, cohabited with him (Elektryon) and gave birth to Alkmene. Alkmene was taken by Zeus, through a deceit, and she bore Herakles. Thus, the root of his family tree, through both his parents, is said to go back to the greatest of the gods (i.e., Zeus), in the way we have shown.
>
> The excellence *(arete)* begotten in Herakles is not only seen in his great acts *(praxeis),* but was known before his birth. When Zeus lay with Alkmene, he tripled the length of the night, and, in the increased length of time spent in begetting the child, he foreshadowed the exceptional power of the child who was to be begotten.[4]

There are a number of differences between these stories and the account of the conception of Jesus. The cohabitation of a god with a woman is foreign to the New Testament. The mythical births were clearly not virgin births. There is nothing particularly outstanding about the morals of the mythical gods. The realism of actual life and the authority of eyewitness reports is absent to the point where the reader gets the feeling that the author does not really believe what he is writing. Cartlidge and Dungan write concerning the story of Pythagoras' unusual birth:

> It has been said that one hundred years after his death, around 497 B.C., hardly anyone at Athens still remembered anything of Pythagoras of Samos; seven hundred years later, his followers knew everything about him including the secret recipe of his favorite honey cakes. The author of this account of Pythagoras' ancestry and birth, the Neo-platonic, Syrian philosopher Iamblichus, was just such a follower. Living in the fourth century AD, he was a vigorous opponent of the newly emerging Christian religion, writing many books on Pythagoras and his teachings. (CaDR. DSG 134)

No wonder Origen would argue against Celsus as follows:

> But these stories are really fables (mythos). People just fabricate such things as this about a man whom they regard as having greater wisdom and power than most others. So they say he received at the beginning of the composition of his body a superior and more divine sperm, as if this were appropriate for those who surpass ordinary human nature.[5]

3. The use of secret ceremonies and procedures.

The ancient mystery cults shrouded many of their activities in secrecy. According to Nash, "The mystery rites tied the initiates together at the same time they separated them from outsiders." (NaR.CHW 123)

The initiate would receive a secret containing knowledge of how to be unified with the deity, usually at the time of his initiation. The lack of openness in these religions has made it somewhat difficult for modern researchers to discover more accurately how these cults operated and what they believed. In contrast, the New Testament does not speak of any such secret ceremonies. The early Christians boldly called all to openly give their lives to Christ and to be his eager witnesses. It is not until the creation of certain gnostic apocryphal works that religion once more becomes a matter of secrecy.

4. A lack of historical grounding.

As you read mystery religion texts, you notice that one phrase (with variations) appears a surprising number of times. It is the phrase, "It is said"; or "They say…"; Iamblichus, in his background material on Pythagoras begins, "It is said…".[6] When he speaks of Pythagoras mastering "the Daunian bear, which had severely harmed the inhabitants," again Iamblichus begins, "It is said that he mastered the Daunian bear."[7] Even when uncertain terms are not used, there is such a scarcity of convergence of historical sources that the reader gets the distinct impression that not many during or shortly after the individual's lifetime truly felt he was divine. It was just a fitting way to honor one supposedly so great to allow him to be called a god or a son of the gods. In addition, the Greek deities who were supposed to have walked among men are not described realistically, but rather as a character of fantasy would be. Norman Anderson contends:

> The basic difference between Christianity and the mysteries is the historical basis of the one and the mythological character of the others. The deities of the mysteries were no more than "nebulous figures of an imaginary past," while the Christ whom the apostolic kerygma [preaching of the gospel] proclaimed had lived and died only a few years before the first New Testament documents were written. Even when the apostle Paul wrote his first letter to the Corinthians the majority of some five hundred witnesses to the resurrection were still alive. (AnN.CWR 53)

5. An attempt to provide hope for life after death.

This need is universal, and we should not be surprised if various myths speak of supposed gods who die and subsequently resuscitate! What better way to provide a hope for the possibility of immortality. But, as Anderson states, "There is all the difference in the world between the rising or rebirth of a deity which symbolizes the coming of spring (and the reawakening of nature) and the resurrection 'on the third day' of a historical person." (AnN.CWR 53) We will return to the subject of the resurrection below.

6. An emphasis on emotional rather than doctrinal concerns.

Certainly there were cult followings of particular philosophers which were more concerned with ethics and correct belief. But, in general, true mystery religions were primarily concerned with the emotional state of their followers:

> The mysteries used many different means to affect the emotions and imaginations of their followers in order to quicken their union with the god: processions, fasting, a play, acts of purification, blazing lights, and esoteric liturgies. (NaR.CHW 124)

In both the early Dionysian and Cybelene cults there were strong emotional emphases. Dionysus was said to have been born from Zeus and a human mother. He then became the god of fruitfulness and vegetation (especially wine) and was thought to be embodied in certain animals. Festivals included drinking wine and indulging in sexual activity, and initiation seems to have been associated with the beginning of one's sexual life.

> After a torch-lit processional, the participants worked themselves into a drunken frenzy that led Dionysus' followers, mostly women, into an orgiastic revelry in which they attacked and dismembered an animal, ate its raw flesh and drank its blood. By eating their god, who was supposedly embodied in the animal they had torn apart, they thought they reached a state of divine possession that made them divine as well. (NaR.CHW 135)

Ah, the skeptic says, could this be where Paul and the early Christians got the Lord's Supper? Not a chance. As the great Princeton University New Testament professor J. Gresham Machen puts it:

> If Paul is dependent upon the pagan notion of eating the god, he must have deserted the religious practice which prevailed in his own day in order to have recourse to a savage custom which had long since been abandoned.... It is generally admitted that even where Christianity is dependent upon Hellenistic religion it represents a spiritualizing modification of the pagan practice. But at this point it would have to be supposed that the Christian modification proceeded in exactly the opposite direction; far from marking a greater spiritualization of pagan practice, it meant a return to a savage stage of religion which even paganism had abandoned. (MaJG.OPR 282-83)

Nash points out that both the meaning and symbolism of the Christian act are adapted from the Old Testament Passover. (NaR.CHW 152)

The emotionalism of the Cybelene cult went even further than that of the Dionysian cult. Cybele, "the Great Mother," was originally worshipped as the goddess of nature and later as the Mother of all gods and the mistress of all life. Emotionalism in the Cybelene cult

went beyond the sexual orgies that were part of the primitive Dionysiac

cult, as the frenzied male worshipers of Cybele were led to castrate themselves. Following their act of self-mutilation, these followers of Cybele
became "Galli," or eunuch-priests of the Cult. (NaR.CHW 139)

7. The provision of a mystical experience confirming union with their god and ultimate redemption or salvation and immortality.

Again, some scholars have tried to claim that the roots of the Christian message of
redemption are found in the mystery religions. But this position fails to explain the
many differences between Christian and pagan redemption.

1. The Christian method of redemption was not dependent upon a mystical
   experience; it was a matter of simple childlike acceptance of Jesus and his
   payment for sin on the cross.

2. Redemption in the mystery religions was concerned primarily with
   deliverance from burdens—such as fate, necessity, and death—
   that form the basic constraints of human life. On the other hand,
   Christian doctrine maintains that humans need to be saved from
   sin. (NaR.CHW 180)

   Christians also maintain that their faith does not offer fantasy deliverances;
   rather, it offers more realistic solutions to problems. It offers not necessarily
   freedom from hardship or death but instead strength through hardship and
   victory over death.

3. Not only did man need salvation from the power of sin, but also from the
   guilt of sin.

4. Christian redemption led to a change of moral character. The lack of
   moral influence within the mystery religions, says Nash, "is not really that
   surprising, given their origin in ancient fertility rites replete with sexual
   overtones." (NaR.CHW 181)

It is true, however, that both Christianity and the mystery religions were concerned
about redemption. Then again, redemption, salvation and fellowship with God have
all been almost universally recognized by the religions of the world as central needs of
man. And as Machen explains:

> There have been many religions of redemption, in many ages and among
> many peoples, which have been entirely independent of one another. It
> will probably not be maintained, for example, that early Buddhism stood
> in any fundamental causal relation to the piety of the Hellenistic age. Yet
> early Buddhism was a religion of redemption. (MaJG.OPR 274)

ALLEGED MYTHICAL ROOTS OF CHRISTIAN DOCTRINE AND PRACTICE

1. *The Taurobolium.*

The taurobolium was primarily associated with the cult of Cybele and Attis. It has been suggested as the source of inspiration for Revelation 7:14, "and they have washed their robes…in the blood of the lamb," and 1 Peter 1:2, "that you may obey Jesus Christ and be sprinkled with His blood." It also has been suggested as the inspiration for Christian baptism as explained in Romans chapter six. The rite, as described by the ancient writer Prudentius, called for the high priest being consecrated to be led down into a deep pit. The top of the pit is covered over by a wooden mesh grating. Then a huge bull, draped with flowers, has its breast pierced

> with a sacred spear; the gaping wound emits a wave of hot blood, and the smoking river flows into the woven structure beneath it and surges wide.
>
> …The falling shower rains down a foul dew, which the priest buried within catches, putting his shameful head under all the drops, defiled both in his clothing and in all his body.
>
> Yea, he throws back his face, he puts his cheeks in the way of the blood, he puts under it his ears and lips, he interposes his nostrils, he washes his very eyes with the fluid, nor does he even spare his throat but moistens his tongue, until he actually drinks the dark gore.
>
> …The pontiff, horrible in appearance, comes forth, and shows his wet head, his beard heavy with blood, his dripping fillets and sodden garments.
>
> This man, defiled with such contagions and foul with the gore of the recent sacrifice, all hail and worship at a distance, because profane blood and a dead ox have washed him while concealed in a filthy cave.[8]

There are several reasons the taurobolium cannot be the source for any Christian doctrine or practice.

- Most important, the taurobolium post-dates the New Testament writings by almost a hundred years. The German scholar Günter Wagner has written the definitive work on Christianity and the mystery religions. In it he explains:

  > The taurobolium in the Attis cult is first attested in the time of Antoninus Pius for AD 160. As far as we can see at present it only became a personal consecration at the beginning of the third century AD. The idea of a rebirth through the instrumentality of the taurobolium only emerges in isolated instances toward the end of the fourth century AD; it is not originally associated with this blood-bath. (WaG.PB 266)

Nash concludes his investigation by saying:

> It is clear, then, that the New Testament emphasis on the shedding of blood should not be traced to any pagan source. The New Testament teaching should be viewed in the context of its Old Testament background—the Passover and the temple sacrifices. (NaR.CHW 166)

In view of the late date of the taurobolium, if any borrowing was done, we suspect it was *from* the Christians, not *by* the Christians.

- There is no indication that the early Christians used actual blood in their rituals. Blood was simply a symbol of Jesus pouring his life out for his own, as can be seen when we fill in the words to Revelation 7:14 which we omitted in the first paragraph under this point: "and they have washed their robes *and made them white* in the blood of the Lamb."

- Christians (especially Jewish Christians) would have been repulsed by the practice. Prudentius was a Christian, and his words "foul dew," "shameful head," "defiled both in his clothing and in all his body," indicate that he considered the whole rite to be crude and blasphemous.

- The passage describes the consecration of a high priest, not a new convert.

2. Baptism.

Ceremonial washings have been observed as a means of purification by religions all over the world and from long before the time of Jesus. It has therefore been suggested that Christians copied their rite of baptism from pagan religions around them. But this is a gross oversimplification. Even to draw a strict parallel with Jewish baptism would be an oversimplification. For a thorough treatment of this subject, Günter Wagner's *Pauline Baptism and the Pagan Mysteries* should be consulted.

Christian baptism is a demonstration of the believer's identification with Jesus in his death, burial and resurrection. For the mystery cults it was different. Herman Ridderbos, professor of New Testament at Kampen Seminary in The Netherlands, states that "nowhere in the mystery religions is such a symbolism of death present in the 'baptism' ritual." (RiHN.POT 24)

More important, the chronology once again does not agree with a syncretistic view. Nash indicates:

> Ceremonial washings that antedate the New Testament have a different meaning from New Testament baptism, while pagan washings after AD 100 come too late to influence the New Testament and, indeed, might themselves have been influenced by Christianity. (NaR.CHW 151)

The evidence points to the practice of Christian baptism originating in Jewish baptism, having its meaning rooted in the historical events of the death, burial and resurrection of Jesus.

3. Resurrection.

An alleged example of resurrection in ancient myth is provided by the early Egyptian cult of Isis and Osiris. The myth has Osiris being murdered by his brother Seth, who then sinks the coffin containing Osiris' body in the Nile River. Osiris' wife, Isis, the goddess of heaven, earth, sea and the unseen world below, discovers her husband's body and returns it to Egypt. Seth, however, regains the body, cuts it into fourteen pieces, and scatters it abroad. Isis counters by recovering the pieces. Nash continues:

> It is at this point that the language used to describe what follows is crucial. Sometimes those telling the story are satisfied to say that Osiris came back to life. (As I shall point out later, even this statement claims too much.) But some writers go much too far and refer to Osiris's "resurrection." (NaR.CHW 137)

Nash's later discussion continues:

> Which mystery gods actually experienced a resurrection from the dead? Certainly no early texts refer to any resurrection of Attis. Attempts to link the worship of Adonis to a resurrection are equally weak. Nor is the case for a resurrection of Osiris any stronger. After Isis gathered together the pieces of Osiris's dismembered body, he became "Lord of the Underworld." As Metzger comments, "Whether this can be rightly called a resurrection is questionable, especially since, according to Plutarch, it was the pious desire of devotees to be buried in the same ground where, according to local tradition, the body of Osiris was still lying." One can speak then of a "resurrection" in the stories of Osiris, Attis, and Adonis only in the most extended of senses. And of course no claim can be made that Mithras was a dying and rising god. French scholar André Boulanger concludes: "The conception that the god dies and is resurrected in order to lead his faithful to eternal life is represented in no Hellenistic mystery religion." (NaR.CHW 172-73)[9]

If the "savior-gods" mentioned above can be spoken of as resurrected, then we need to differentiate Jesus' resurrection from theirs. Jesus was a person of history who rose from the dead never to die again. He appeared in the flesh several times before his ascension, and the story was told by eyewitnesses. James D. G. Dunn concludes:

> The parallel with visions of Isis and Asclepius...is hardly close. These were mythical figures from the dim past. In the sightings of Jesus we are talking about a man who had died only a few days or weeks earlier. (DuJ.E 71)

Another issue related to the resurrection has to do with the amount of time between the crucifixion and the resurrection. Attis is supposed to have come back to life four days after his death, one account has Osiris being reanimated two or three days after his death, and it is even suggested that Adonis may have been "resurrected" three days after his death. In the case of all three, there is no evidence earlier than the second century AD for the supposed "resurrection" of these mystery gods. Norman Anderson states that if borrowing there was by one religion from another, it seems clear which way it went. There is no evidence whatever, that I know of, that the mystery religions had any influence in Palestine in the early decades of the first century. And the difference between the mythological experiences of these nebulous figures and the crucifixion "under Pontius Pilate" of one of whom eyewitnesses bore testimony to both his death and resurrection is again obvious. (AnN.CWR 53-54)

4. Rebirth.

In 1925, Samuel Angus wrote:

> Every Mystery-Religion, being a religion of redemption, offered means of suppressing the old man and of imparting or vitalizing the spiritual principle. Every serious *mystes* (initiate) approached the solemn sacrament of Initiation believing that he thereby became "twice-born," a "new creature," and passed in a real sense from death unto life by being brought into a mysterious intimacy with the deity. (AnS.MRC 95-96)

Others also have claimed that the concept of rebirth is central to the mystery religions and that Christianity depended on them for its doctrine of the new birth. But the evidence for such claims is slim. The ceremonial washings of the Eleusinian cult were never attached to the idea of rebirth. There is only one reference attaching "rebirth" to the cult of Cybele and Attis. The reference is a fourth-century AD interpretation from Sallustius, whom one would expect was influenced by Christianity, not vice-versa. Only two debatable references, both from the second century AD, "use the imagery of rebirth." Nash continues:

> While there are several sources that suggest that Mithraism included a notion of rebirth, they are all post-Christian. The earliest…dates from the end of the second century AD…

> The most frequently discussed evidence alleged to prove the presence of rebirth in a mystery religion is an inscription on a Roman altar that appears to connect the taurobolium with a belief in rebirth. The Latin inscription *taurobolio criobolio que in aeternum renatus* can be translated "reborn for eternity in the taurobolium and criobolium."

> …But the problems connected with this hypothesis are enormous. For one thing, the Roman altar containing the inscription dates from AD 376. (NaR. CHW 174-76)

Before Nash, Machen had recounted this observation:

> It may come as a shock, therefore, to readers of recent discussions to be told that as a matter of fact the phrase does not appear until the fourth century, when Christianity was taking its place as the established religion of

the Roman world. If there is any dependence, it is certainly dependence of the taurobolium upon Christianity, and not of Christianity upon the taurobolium. (MaJG.OPR 240-41)

5. Sacrificial Death of the Deity.

From the earliest Greek mythologies all the way through Roman times, it was common to ascribe deity to outstanding individuals. Some of these were fictional mythological characters; others were elevated humans, usually Greek philosophers or Roman emperors. This practice was normal in polytheistic cultures.

The Jews were different. For them there was only one God. It is therefore remarkable that Palestinian Jews, and among them one of the most respected of their Pharisees, would begin proclaiming the deity of one who had walked among them. It would have been hard enough to begin proclaiming the message within the Roman world. But to start in Jerusalem, among the Jews—that was ridiculous! Still the evidence shows that the Christian gospel sprouted first among the Jews.

Is it possible that these Jews could have shaped their message from the mystery cults? Not likely. The claim to deity in the mystery religions did often spring from the stories concerning the so-called god's death and return to life again (at least spiritually). We have already seen that Jesus' resurrection is not paralleled in the mystery religions except where these religions tried to copy Christianity.

Nash gives six differences between the deaths of the so-called savior-gods and that of Jesus:

1. None of the so-called savior-gods died for someone else. The notion of the Son of God dying in place of his creatures is unique to Christianity.

2. Only Jesus died for sin. It is never claimed that any of the pagan deities died for sin. As Wagner observes, to none of the pagan gods "has the intention of helping men been attributed. The sort of death that they died is quite different (hunting accident, self-emasculation, etc.)"

3. Jesus died once and for all (Hebrews 7:27; 9:25-28; 10:10-14). In contrast, the mystery gods were vegetation deities whose repeated death and resuscitation depict the annual cycle of nature.

4. Jesus' death was an actual event in history. The death of the god described in the pagan cults is a mythical drama with no historical ties.

5. Unlike the mystery gods, Jesus died voluntarily. Nothing like the voluntary death of Jesus can be found in the mystery cults.

6. And finally, Jesus' death was not a defeat but a triumph. Christianity stands entirely apart from the pagan mysteries in that its report of Jesus' death is a message of triumph. (NaR.CHW 171-72)

Where then did Palestinian Jews get the message of a deified Messiah? The answer to that question will be given in chapter 15.

6. Miracles.

André Kole, one of the world's foremost illusionists, often tells his audiences that ever since there were people on earth to be deceived, there have been others around to deceive them. In view of the numerous debatable claims for the miraculous throughout history, it is understandable that critics would question the claims concerning Jesus' miracles in the gospel.

Claims to the miraculous are scattered throughout the literature of the mystery religions and other movements within the ancient Hellenistic world. Apollonius of Tyana, sometimes called "the pagan Christ," was alleged to have performed many of the same kinds of miracles that Jesus performed. How are we to judge these claims? Because of the breadth and importance of this subject, we will cover it in more detail in a later chapter. For now, we note only that there is a great difference between the miracles contained in ancient mythology and those in the Bible. C. S. Lewis, a noted literary scholar who spent most of his life studying mythological literature, wrote concerning the miracle stories of the myths, "The immoral and sometimes almost idiotic interferences attributed to gods in pagan stories, even if they had a trace of historical evidence, could be accepted only on the condition of our accepting a wholly meaningless universe." (LeC.M 133)

FALLACIES OF LINKING CHRISTIANITY WITH MYSTERY RELIGIONS

The first to plead his case seems just, until another comes and examines him.[10]

At first sight, some of the similarities between Christianity and various mystery religions are so striking that one feels compelled to believe Christianity borrowed certain phrases, stories, doctrines or practices from them. Skeptical critics, by ignoring or withholding certain facts, often give a distorted picture of Christianity's alleged relationship with the mystery religions. The following statement by Ian Wilson, for example, paints a distorted picture of the possible molding influences of early Christianity:

> It must be remembered that Galilee had been pagan until the second century B.C., and only became forcibly converted to the Jewish religion during the Hasmonean period that followed the Maccabean revolt. It is very probable that among ordinary people of Jesus' time there lingered superstitious hankerings for the old myth of the dying and resurrected god, just as in the West old superstitions and witch-cults persisted long after the introduction of Christianity. (WiI.JTE 141)

Obviously, there definitely were certain myths and superstitions existing in surrounding pagan lands. But the evidence shows that the early Christian spokesmen steadfastly refused to accept anything contrary to the gospel which had been revealed to them. Look at Paul and Barnabas in Lystra. No sooner had a lame man been healed at Paul's command than the whole city rushed out raising

> their voice, saying in the Lycaonian language, "The gods have become like men and have come down to us."
>
> And they began calling Barnabas, Zeus, and Paul, Hermes, because he was the chief speaker.
>
> And the priest of Zeus, whose temple was just outside the city, brought oxen and garlands to the gates, and wanted to offer sacrifice with the crowds.[11]

What an opportunity! If ever the early Christians had wanted to borrow from the mystery religions (even if just to attract more people to the faith), they could have made Christianity polytheistic right then and there! But no. It took Paul, formerly Saul the Pharisee, up to three years in Arabia and Damascus to reconcile the idea of a suffering, rising and divine Messiah with his Old Testament monotheistic convictions.[12] And so,

> when the apostles, Barnabas and Paul heard of it, they tore their robes and rushed out into the crowd, crying out and saying, "Men, why are you doing these things? We are also men of the same nature as you, and preach the gospel to you in order that you should turn from these vain things to a living God, WHO MADE THE HEAVEN AND THE EARTH AND THE SEA, AND ALL THAT IS IN THEM.... And even saying these things, they with difficulty restrained the crowds from offering sacrifice to them.[13]

The fickle multitude was so disappointed, the very next day they were persuaded to stone Paul and leave him for dead outside the gates of their city.

Having already observed some specific alleged mystery religion roots of Christianity, we now set forth six main fallacies of those who allege that mystery religions influenced Christianity.

Fallacy #1: Combinationalism or Universalism.

This is the error of first combining all the characteristics of all mystery religions from the fifteenth century BC all the way up to the fifth century AD, and then comparing this caricature to Christianity. Even Albert Schweitzer recognized this error years ago when he wrote:

> Almost all the popular writings fall into this kind of inaccuracy. They manufacture out of the various fragments of information a kind of universal mystery-religion which never actually existed, least of all in Paul's day. (ScA.PI)

Obviously, something true of one mystery religion in the fifteenth century BC but which ceased to be a part of it or any other religion by 1000 BC is probably not going to strongly influence Christianity. Or something true of a religion in another culture or area of the world may be thoroughly repulsed by the Jewish culture in Palestine. Again, elements from different religions when combined may look like something in Christianity even though the combined trait never really existed as such until practiced or believed by Christians.

Fallacy #2: Coloring the Evidence.

Nash attributes the cause of this error to careless language. He observes:

> One frequently encounters scholars who first use Christian terminology to describe pagan beliefs and practices and then marvel at the awesome parallels they think they have discovered. One can go a long way toward "proving" early Christian terminology. A good recent example of this can be found in Godwin's book *Mystery Religions in the Ancient World,* which describes the *criobolium* as a "blood baptism" in which the initiate is "washed in the blood of the lamb." An uninformed reader might be stunned by this remarkable similarity to Christianity (see Revelation 7:14), whereas a more knowledgeable reader will regard Godwin's description as the reflection of a strong, negative bias against Christianity. (NaR.CHW 126)

The criobolium was essentially the same as the taurobolium except that rams, instead of bulls, were used, probably for economic reasons. References to it likewise postdate Christian sources!

Fallacy #3: Oversimplification.

Critics also tend to use exaggeration and oversimplification in order to parallel Christianity and the mystery cults. Nash cautions:

> One will encounter exaggerated claims about alleged likenesses between baptism and the Lord's Supper and similar "sacraments" in certain mystery cults. Attempts to find analogies between the resurrection of Christ and the alleged "resurrections" of the mystery deities involve massive amounts of oversimplification and inattention to detail. Furthermore, claims about the centrality of a notion of rebirth in certain mysteries are greatly overstated. (NaR.CHW 126-27)

Fallacy #4: Who's Influencing Whom?

This error is probably the most serious methodological fallacy committed by those charging that Christianity borrowed its doctrine and practices from the mystery religions. The error here is to propose that Christianity adopted a particular feature of a mystery religion when there is no evidence that the feature existed in the particular religion until after Christianity had begun. What many fail to recognize is that the growth of the church was so explosive that other religions adopted Christian elements in order to attract Christians and to prevent the loss of their adherents to Christianity. Metzger attests, "In what T. R. Glover aptly called 'the conflict of religions in the Early Roman Empire,' it was to be expected that the hierophants of cults which were beginning to lose devotees to the growing Church should take steps to stem the tide." (MeB.MR 11)

The key here is dating. Most of the alleged parallels between Christianity and mystery religions, upon close scrutiny will show that Christian elements predate mythological elements. In cases where they do not, it is often Jewish elements which predate both Christianity and the myth, and which lent themselves to both religions.

There is a flip side to the coin. Following the first century AD, Christianity's chief rival was Mithraism. Mithras (earlier, Mithra), according to the Romans, was Sol Invictus (unconquered sun). The worship of Mithras therefore became associated with the sun, and, in AD 274, the date of its major festival was established as December 25, the date of the winter solstice. Apparently, "Sometime before 336 the church in Rome, unable to stamp out this pagan festival, spiritualized it as the Feast of the Nativity of the Sun of Righteousness."[14] The exact date of Jesus' birth has been a matter of debate for centuries, but it does seem clear that in this instance the date of the Christmas celebration was influenced by pragmatic rather than historical factors. In addition, after the third century there is increasing evidence of pagan and secular doctrines affecting changes in Christian belief. But these are later developments. There is no evidence that the *origin* of Christianity occurred by influence of the mystery religions. Its roots were too deeply sunk in Jewish soil.

Fallacy #5: False Attribution.

Scholars often fail to recognize that the real source for a Christian practice was an actual historical event or a Jewish practice or belief. Because something looks similar in a mystery religion, it gets attributed as the source for the Christian practice or belief. Critical discussions regarding the source of the Lord's Supper often fall into this error. Nash explains,

> Of all the mystery cults, only Mithraism had anything that resembled the Lord's Supper. A piece of bread and a cup of water were placed before initiates while the priest of Mithra spoke some ceremonial words.... Any quest for the historical antecedents of the Lord's Supper is more likely to succeed if it stays closer to the Jewish foundation of the Christian faith than if it wanders off into the practices of the pagan cults. As noted in the case of Christian baptism, the Lord's Supper looked back to a real, historical person and something he did in history during the Last Supper. And as every student of the New Testament knows, the occasion for Jesus' introduction of the Christian Lord's Supper was the Jewish Passover feast. Metzger is correct when he notes that "the Jewishness of the setting, character, and piety expressed in the [Christian] rite is overwhelmingly pervasive in all the accounts of the origin of the supper." (NaR.CHW 159; Metzger quote: MeB.MSM 17)

This conclusion is further confirmed by avoiding Fallacy #4 above. According to available evidences, Mithraism did not gain a foothold in the Roman Empire until after AD 100. M. J. Vermaseren, a specialist on the cult of Mithra, certifies, "No Mithraic monument can be dated earlier than the end of the first century AD, and even the more extensive investigations at Pompeii, buried beneath the ashes of Vesuvius in AD 79, have not so far produced a single image of the god." (VeM.MSG 29)

Likewise, historian Edwin Yamauchi concluded after several investigations, "Apart from the visit of the Armenian King, who was a worshiper of Mithra, to Nero, there is no evidence of the penetration of Mithra to the west until the end of the first century AD." (YaE.PCG 112)

No wonder Justin Martyr, as Nash notes, "referred to the Mithraic meal as a satanic imitation of the Lord's supper."[15] In view of the late date for the cult of Mithras in the Roman Empire, we can safely dismiss it as a possible influence on Christian origins.

Fallacy #6: Failing to Recognize the "Pedagogy of God."

Though Christianity teaches there is only one way to a relationship with God, it may be that God has actually used some of the pagan myths to carry out this teaching process within pagan cultures. In arguing for the actual occurrence of the resurrection of Jesus, the non-Christian Jewish scholar Pinchas Lapide reasoned:

> In view of this "pedagogy of God," would it not be possible that the Lord of the universe used the myth of the resurrection (which was well known to all pagans) in order "to eliminate idolatry in the pagan world" through the true resurrection of a just person and to carry "the knowledge of God" to the four corners of the earth by means of the Easter faith? (LaP.R 122)

Of course others had thought of a resurrection, but no one had yet actually accomplished it, not a true and complete bodily resurrection. God, in raising Jesus, was, among other things, directly challenging the false gods of the Greco-Romans.

One of the thrilling new discoveries in Christian missions confirms that God may have revealed, hundreds of years before it took place, the essential elements of the gospel story to various cultures which later mythologized these details through the centuries.

Don Richardson, recognized for his anthropological and linguistic work among the stone-age Sawi peoples of Irian Jaya, has documented the existence of gospel legends among remote tribes all over the world. As an example of how God has prepared various cultures for the acceptance of the gospel we quote here one of the many fascinating true stories found in Richardson's *Eternity in Their Hearts:**

> Deep in the hill country of south-central Ethiopia live several million coffee-growing people who, though divided into quite different tribes, share common belief in a benevolent being called *Magano*—omnipotent

---

* Excerpt quoted by permission of Regal Books, Ventura, CA.

Creator of all that is. One of these tribes is called variously the Darassa or—more accurately—the Gedeo people. Few of the Gedeo tribe's half-million members actually prayed to Magano. In fact, a casual observer would have found the people far more concerned to appease an evil being they called Sheit'an. One day Albert Brant asked a group of Gedeo, "How is it that you regard Magano with profound awe, yet sacrifice to Sheit'an?" He received the following reply: "We sacrifice to Sheit'an, not because we love him, but because we simply do not enjoy close enough ties with Magano to allow us to be done with Sheit'an!"

At least one Gedeo man, however, did pursue a personal response from Magano. His name—Warrasa Wange. His status—related to the Gedeo tribe's "royal family." His domicile—Dilla, a town located on an extreme edge of Gedeo tribal land. His method of approach to Magano—a simple prayer asking Magano to reveal Himself to the Gedeo people!

Warrasa Wange got a speedy response. Startling visions took his brain by storm. He saw two white-skinned strangers. "Caucasophobes"—people who dislike or fear "white men," commonly called Caucasians—will object, but what can I do? History must not have anticipated the modern trend toward caucasophobia!

Warrasa saw the two whites erect flimsy shelters for themselves under the shade of a large sycamore tree near Dilla, Warrasa's hometown. Later they built more permanent shiny-roofed structures. Eventually these structures dotted an entire hillside! Never had the dreamer seen anything even faintly resembling either the flimsy temporary structures or the shiny-roofed permanent ones. All dwellings in Gedeo land were grass-roofed.

Then Warrasa heard a voice. "These men," it said, "will bring you a message from Magano, the God you seek. Wait for them."

In a final scene of his vision, Warrasa saw himself remove the center pole from his own house. In Gedeo symbolism, the center pole of a man's house stands for his very life. He then carried that center pole out of town and set it in the ground next to one of the shiny-roofed dwellings of the strange men.

Warrasa understood the implication—his life must later stand in identification with those strange men, their message, and with Magano who would send them.

Warrasa waited. Eight years passed. During those eight years several other soothsayers among the Gedeo people prophesied that strangers would soon arrive with a message from Magano.

Then, one very hot day in December, 1948, blue-eyed Canadian Albert Brant and his colleague Glen Cain lurched over the horizon in a battered old International truck. Their mission—to begin missionary work for the glory of God among the Gedeo people. They had hoped to gain permission from Ethiopian officials to locate their new mission at the very center of the Gedeo region, but Ethiopians friendly to the mission advised that such a request would meet certain refusal due to the current political climate.

"Ask only to go as far as this town called Dilla," the advisors said with a wink. "It is quite distant from the center of the tribe. Those opposed to your mission will think you couldn't possibly influence the entire tribe from such a peripheral town!"

"There it is," Brant said to Cain. "It's only the very edge of the Gedeo population, but it will have to do."

With a sigh, he turned the old International toward Dilla. Glen Cain wiped sweat from his brow. "This is a hot one, Albert," he said. "I hope we can find a shady spot for our tents!"

"Look at that old sycamore tree!" Albert responded. "Just what the doctor ordered!"

Brant revved the International up a rise toward the sycamore. In the distance, Warrasa Wange heard the sound. He turned just in time to see Brant's old truck pull to a stop under the sycamore's spreading branches. Slowly Warrasa headed toward the truck, wondering...

Three decades later Warrasa (now a radiant believer in Jesus Christ, Son of Magano), together with Albert Brant and others, counted more than 200 churches among the Gedeo people—churches averaging more than 200 members each! With the help of Warrasa and other inhabitants of Dilla, almost the entire Gedeo tribe has been influenced by the gospel—in spite of Dilla's peripheral location! (RiD.ETH 56-58)

UNIQUENESS OF THE GOSPEL PORTRAYALS OF JESUS

Scholars and lay people alike have recognized for almost two millennia a clear distinction between the reports of the gospel writers and the creators of the myths of the mystery religions. For example, Walter Künneth, professor of systematic theology at Erlangen University in Germany, states concerning the exclusiveness of the gospel:

> The message of the resurrection did not appear to the contemporary world to be one of the customary cult legends, so that Jesus Christ would be a new cult hero standing harmoniously side by side with other cult heroes. But the message was in terms of strict exclusiveness: One alone is the Kyrios ("Lord"). Here every analogy fails. This witness, in contrast to the tolerance of the whole mythical world, comes with an intolerant claim to absoluteness which calls in question the validity and truth of all mythology. (KüW.TR 62)

Cartlidge and Dungan recognize the same:

If Christians utilized familiar concepts and terms in order to communicate their faith, they often gave them an exclusive significance. When they worshiped Jesus as their Savior, the effect was a powerful negation: "Neither Caesar, nor Asklepios, nor Herakles, nor Dionysos, nor Ptolemy, nor any other God is the Savior of the world—Jesus Christ is!" (CaDR.DSG 21)

Read through a number of the Greek myths and then read through the gospel accounts and you will notice a marked difference in the overall flavor of the material. Concerning the Gospel of John, often the most criticized of the gospel narratives, Blaiklock says:

I read him often in his simple Greek without translating and always gain an overwhelming impression of his directness, his intimacy with theme and reader. Simply read the story of the wedding at Cana (but correctly rendering, "Mother, what is that to do with me?") and feel the homely atmosphere, Mary's embarrassment, the best man's feeble joke (chapter 2). Follow on to the story of the rabbi (chapter 3) who came in the night and was annoyed at first because the answer to the question he was not allowed to ask was given by allusion to the books of Ezekiel and Numbers (Ezekiel 36:25-27; Numbers 21:4-9). And then read the story of the conversation at Sychar's well, with the Samaritan fighting her losing battle of words with the strangest Jew she had ever met (chapter 4). Read on to the poignant account of the Passion Week with its climax in the vivid resurrection stories, paralleled for simple reality only by the narrative in Luke. Simply read. These men were not writing fiction. This is not what myth sounds like. This is history and only thus set down because it was reporting. (BIE.MM 77-78)

New Testament translator and scholar J. B. Phillips describes his experience this way:

I have read, in Greek and Latin, scores of myths, but I did not find the slightest flavour of myth here. There is no hysteria, no careful working for effect, and no attempt at collusion.... One sensed again that understatement which we have been taught to think is more "British" than Oriental. There is an almost childlike candour and simplicity, and the total effect is tremendous. (PhJ.RT 77)

Blaiklock concludes:

There is only one ready explanation. Four men, under the dire compulsion of a truth which made them free, wrote of what they saw, or of what immediate and reliable eyewitnesses reported to them. It is as Rousseau said, men who could invent such a story would be greater and more astonishing than its central figure. (BIE.MM 77)

CONCLUSIONS

Though statements abound in popular literature that Christianity borrowed its gospel story from the myths of the pagan world, the tide of scholarly opinion has turned against this thesis. Moreland puts it:

> It cannot be emphasized enough that such influences are seen by current New Testament scholars to have little or no role in shaping the New Testament picture of Jesus in general or the resurrection narratives in particular. Both the general milieu of the gospels and specific features of the resurrection narratives give overwhelming evidence that the early church was rooted in Judaism. Jesus, the early church, and its writings were born in Jewish soil and Gentile influence was minimal. (MoJP.S 181)

Even when the hypothesis of syncretism was in its heyday, many of the top scholars were unconvinced. Probably the most influential German church historian and theologian of his day, Adolf von Harnack, shortly after the turn of the century, wrote:

> We must reject the comparative mythology which finds a causal connection between everything and everything else, which tears down solid barriers, bridges chasms as though it were child's play, and spins combinations from superficial similarities.... By such methods one can turn Christ into a sun god in the twinkling of an eye, or one can bring up the legends attending the birth of every conceivable god, or one can catch all sorts of mythological doves to keep company with the baptismal dove; and find any number of celebrated asses to follow the ass on which Jesus rode into Jerusalem; and thus, with the magic wand of "comparative religion," triumphantly eliminate every spontaneous trait in any religion.[16]

Why did the mystery religions competing with Christianity eventually perish, leaving Christianity as the primary religion of the Roman Empire? There are a number of answers, but a primary one is that Christians preached the resurrection of an actual, recent person of history. The mythological stories of the mystery religions just couldn't compete.

We have touched on a number of evidences to support the conclusion that the early Christians did not borrow from the mystery religions to form their story.

1. The amount of time between the subject of the myth and the sources which tell about the subject is very long, hundreds of years at the least. In many cases the subjects of the myth are not even located in history.

2. The sources which sound like precursors of Christianity were actually written after the New Testament canon was complete. If borrowing took place, it was the mystery religions which borrowed from Christianity. Not until later do we see language from the mystery religions penetrating the vocabulary of the church. Nash reports:

> It was in the third century, and not before, that the first real meeting took place between Christianity and the mystery religions. It was after

AD 300 that the terminology of the mystery cults first began to appear in the language of the church. (NaR.CHW 129)

It was most likely, then, that the mystery religions, faced with the loss of members to the expanding church, incorporated attractive elements of Christianity into their literature and practice.

3. The mystery religions were syncretistic while Christianity preached an exclusion of elements foreign to its revelation.

4. As Moreland states it:

> Differences far outweigh similarities. The mystery religions have a consort, a female deity who is central to the myth. They have no real resurrection, only a crude resuscitation. The mysteries have little or no moral context, fertility being what the mystery rites sought to induce. The mysteries are polytheistic, syncretistic legends unrelated to historical individuals. (MoJP.S 182)

5. The mystery religions were more concerned with the emotional state of their adherents than with correct doctrine.

6. Many alleged similarities between Christianity and the mystery religions appear only when Christian terminology is used to describe a mystery religion practice or myth.

There are certainly sincere individuals with genuine questions in this area of comparative religions. But the popularistic "lives of Jesus" which continue to roll off the presses today often appear to be nothing more than a grasping for excuses to avoid the issue of Jesus and his claims. As Blaiklock puts it:

> Could it be that there are always those irked under the thrust and pressure of Jesus Christ's commanding Person or searched and raked by His words who seek comfort in some hope that the records were falsified? In this hope of a delusion exposed, they turn the attack upon the historicity of Jesus. Christianity triumphed over its most serious opponent, the soldiers' worship of the soldierly Mithras, largely because Christianity could oppose to the legendary Mithras the historical reality of Christ. It is necessarily at Him that those aim their shafts, who indulge the strange deathwish that life is "all sound and fury, signifying nothing," and a hole in the damp turf the final escape. (BIE.MM 11)

10

EVIDENCE FROM
HISTORICAL GEOGRAPHY

Unlike the mythical accounts of various alleged gods which were discussed in the previous chapter, the gospel narratives describe Jesus as a man of flesh and blood who traveled to actual geographic locations and interacted with known historical persons. That he occupied a specific place in time and space becomes clearer as one studies the historical geography of Jesus' day. The details of history and geography in the gospel accounts yield clear evidence that the writers were not making up their story. This chapter will discuss some of that evidence and will also answer a few difficult questions which have been raised in these areas.

New evidence obtained from studying first-century Palestinian culture is beginning to shed light on the Jesus of the gospels. This new evidence is forcing many to turn away from their skepticism regarding what the New Testament teaches about Jesus.

Rudolf Bultmann, who viewed the New Testament as a historically flawed document, had never visited the sites in Israel and had never considered the influence of Jewish culture on Jesus. Martin Hengel of the University of Tübingen in West Germany said of the lack of considering the cultural element that it was a "bad old German tradition with dangerous results."[1]

HISTORICAL GEOGRAPHY

Historical geography seeks to relate events in history to geographic locations. Knowing what has happened in a certain location in the past reveals why Jesus would do something at that location when he was there. Since it would be practically impossible for a later Gentile writer to have knowledge of the historical-geographical context surrounding an event in Jesus' life, these incidents provide good evidence that what the gospel writers describe actually happened. A few examples:

In the city of Nain, Jesus raised the widow's dead son. Nain sits on the north side of a hill in southern Galilee. Just over the hill, on the south side, is the place where Elisha resuscitated the dead son of the Shunammite woman. Because the people of this locality were especially attuned to that miracle, Jesus was able to establish his authority by performing a similar miracle in the nearby town. The people of Nain responded, "A great prophet has arisen among us!" and, "God has visited His people!"

Mary and Joseph's flight to Egypt with the infant Jesus was not an odd move. Eighty-five percent of all Jews lived outside Israel, and Alexandria, Egypt, contained a large and old Jewish population. Joseph and Mary may have had friends or relatives there.

Jesus' home town of Nazareth is significant for several reasons. First, it was an obscure village "out in the sticks" with perhaps only twenty to thirty families living there. This is confirmed by the discovery of twenty-three tombs, believed to be the first-century cemetery for the entire town. Nazareth does not appear in any of the lists of cities found in Josephus, in the Old Testament, or in the Talmud. No wonder Nathanael, when Philip first told him about Jesus, responded, "Can any good thing come out of Nazareth?"[2]

Second, Nazareth sits on the side of a high ridge overlooking the Jezreel Valley. The geography fits well with Luke's description of the city when he reports, "They rose up and cast Him out of the city, and led Him to the brow of the hill on which their city had been built, in order to throw Him down the cliff."[3]

Third, the Jezreel valley, also called the Plain of Megiddo or Armageddon, was literally the front yard of Nazareth. More than 250 battles in history have been fought at this location, and the prophets predict the final battle will be waged here as well. Armies can enter the valley through seven major passes, making it an ideal battleground. As Jesus was growing up, he must have walked across this valley many times and perhaps here reflected often that "all those who take up the sword shall perish by the sword."[4] It is ironic and yet typical of the way God often works, that the one called "the Prince of Peace" should grow up looking out over "the battleground of history."

Also, Nazareth is in an area where the people frowned on the use of wood as an exploitation of the land. Houses were built primarily from the abundant supply of boulders. The Greek word for "carpenter" can be translated equally well as "stonemason," "smith," "craftsman," or "builder in wood, stone or metal." It is therefore possible that Joseph and Jesus did more stone construction than carpentry. As a result, Jesus may have been very strong and powerful in appearance. This, combined with his spiritual authority, undoubtedly enabled him to travel much on foot, speak to crowds of up to 5,000, drive merchants out of the Temple and pass through the midst of an angry mob attempting to throw him off a cliff.

THE QUESTION OF QUIRINIUS

Probably the most difficult apparent historical contradiction having to do with the gospels concerns Luke's report about a census taken while Quirinius governed Syria (Luke 2:2). Ian Wilson castigates Luke as follows:

> And after telling us that the announcement of the births of Jesus and John
> the Baptist took place in the reign of Herod the Great, who is known to

have died in 4 BC, the Luke author tries to offer a piece of impressive historical detail:

> Now at this time Caesar Augustus issued a decree for a census of the whole world to be taken. This census—the first—took place while Quirinius was governor of Syria, and everyone went to his home town to be registered (Luke 2:1-3).

Unfortunately, while the first-ever census among Jews did indeed take place during Quirinius' governorship, this did not and could not have happened until at least 6 AD, the first year that Judaea came under direct Roman rule, and it was reliably recorded by Josephus as an unprecedented event of that year. To put it bluntly, Luke has resorted to invention. (WiLJTE 55)

In actuality, we believe Wilson's book, *Jesus: The Evidence,* has distorted the evidence! Let's investigate. The census caused Joseph and Mary to travel to Bethlehem just prior to Jesus' birth. On some points Wilson is correct. Both Matthew and Luke agree that Jesus was born before the end of the reign of Herod the Great. It has been established with reasonable certainty that Herod's death took place in March or April of 4 BC. (See FiJ.BC 230ff.; and HoH.C 12-13) A census, not necessarily the first, was taken by Quirinius in AD 6. (FiJ.BC 234-36) But there is other evidence Wilson has ignored.

Fact #1. In Acts 5:37, Luke refers to the AD 6 census, indicating that he is conscious of where it fits in the chronology of the period. Luke calls this census *the* census, i.e., the well-known one of AD 6.

Fact #2. The Greek text of Luke 2:2 suggests a lesser known census prior to that of AD 6. The New American Standard Version translates Luke 2:2, "This was the first census taken while Quirinius was governor of Syria." It seems to us to be a faithful rendering of the sense of the Greek text which most literally reads: "This census, a first one, coming to pass when Quirinius is ruling, leading Syria." Since the Greek language often leaves out the word "is," it needs to be inserted and most naturally fits after the word "census." The sentence literally reads, "This census is a first one coming to pass when Quirinius is ruling Syria." If there had been only the one very well-known census of AD 6 under Quirinius, Luke would have said simply, "This is *the* census coming to pass when Quirinius..." We have no knowledge of any census taken after AD 6. Therefore, the grammar of Luke 2:2 seems most definitely to indicate that Luke wants his readers to disregard the AD 6 census and think of an earlier, lesser known census of approximately 5 BC.

Fact #3. Josephus confirms that the rebellion of AD 6 was a response to an enrollment (census) probably carried out rather heavy-handedly.[5] In contrast, the earlier Luke 2:2 census seems to have appealed to the custom of the Jews. At that time, about 5 BC, the Romans would have had two problems:

- Herod ruled Judea, not Quirinius.
- The people didn't like the Romans messing in their affairs.

From the standpoint of the Romans, the most diplomatic solution would be for Quirinius to negotiate a census carried out under Herod's auspices and according to the Jewish practice of registration by tribes. Thus Joseph and Mary traveled to Bethlehem, the city of David, and Joseph's "own city." The Romans' negotiating for this arrangement is indicated by the fact that they normally conducted censuses based on land ownership, not on hometowns. Occasionally, however, the Romans did make exceptions. An Egyptian papyrus of AD 104 indicates that the Egyptians were required to return to their home city for the Roman census in Egypt. (DeA.LAE 270-71)

But would Herod have been willing to acquiesce to such an arrangement? Most definitely, for Josephus records that he fell into disfavor with Caesar Augustus, being demoted from "friend" to "subject."[6] He would have needed to do whatever the Romans wanted him to do in order to regain Caesar's favor. Herod was close to death and having problems deciding on a successor. (He changed his will three times and killed three sons before deciding on Archelaus five days before his death.) The imminent death of Herod was further incentive for the Romans to have a census taken in preparation for a change of rulers.

Fact #4. In AD 6, Palestine was no longer under the rule of one king, but split up into several tetrarchies. Therefore, it would have been almost impossible for Joseph and Mary to be required to travel from Nazareth to Bethlehem as Luke reports unless it was prior to the death of Herod the Great. In order to travel from Nazareth to Bethlehem in AD 6, Joseph and Mary would have had to leave Galilee, governed by Herod Antipas and travel to Judea, now under direct control of the Roman government, which had just deposed Archelaus. But, as Wayne Brindle points out, the trip from Nazareth to Bethlehem "would have taken place only if there were one central authority over Palestine—such as only during the reign of Herod the Great." (BrW.CQ 27:51-52)

Fact #5. Luke 2:1 indicates that the census was in accordance with an empire-wide policy of registering all the people. This does not specify that all provinces were enrolled at the same time, only that Augustus was, as Hoehner states,

> the first one in history to order a census or tax assessment of the whole provincial empire. This is further substantiated by the fact that Luke uses the present tense indicating that Augustus ordered censuses to be taken regularly rather than only one time. (HoH.C 15)

The renowned archaeologist, Sir William Ramsay, affirmed:

> The first enrollment in Syria was made in the year 8-7 B.C., but a consideration of the situation in Syria and Palestine about that time will show

that the enrollment in Herod's kingdom was probably delayed for some time later. (RaW.WCB 174)

This would put the census of Luke 2:2 in about 6 or 5 BC, just before Herod's death.

Fact #6. Jesus was about thirty years old (Luke 3:23) when he began his ministry shortly after John the Baptist began his in "the fifteenth year of the reign of Tiberius Caesar" (Luke 3:1,2). Hoehner states:

> Since the fifteenth year of Tiberius can be dated c. A.D. 27 to 29, it would mean that if Christ were born in A.D. 6, He would only have been twenty-one to twenty-three years old, not about thirty years old. (HoH.C 19)

Some argue that if a census had occurred in 6 or 5 BC, Josephus would have said something about it. But this is an argument from silence which is invalidated by the fact that probably the only reason Josephus mentions the AD 6 census is that it was highlighted by the tumultuous events of the deposition of Archelaus, the Roman takeover of all his material goods, and the revolt of Judas of Galilee (also called "a Gaulanite").

Luke's Accuracy and Quirinius' Rulership of Syria

The mystery of the whole problem, which Luke seems to know and archaeologists haven't yet discovered, is how Quirinius could have been ruling Syria in or about 5 BC. The governors of Syria are all known from 12 BC until 4 BC. We do know that Quirinius was an effective military leader and administrator and that he held several positions of highest rank in and around Syria from as early as 12 BC until AD 7. Sometime between 12 BC and AD 1, Quirinius was in charge of the Homanadensian War, which was going on in a province neighboring Syria. Emil Schürer, the dominant scholar of the nineteenth century in this field, demonstrated that Syria was the most likely province from which Quirinius could have conducted the war and placed Quirinius as governor of Syria for a first term from 3 to 2 BC (ScE.HJP90 1:352) Ramsay, however, based on inscriptional evidence, believed that Quirinius was part of a cogovernorship about 8 to 6 BC. (RaW.BRD15 292-300) Finegan reasons:

> The resistance of the Homanadensians must have been broken by the time the net of Roman roads was laid out in the province of Galatia in 6 B.C.; therefore, at least the major part of this war must have been over by that date.... Quirinius could have been free to attend to other business in the East. (FiJ.BC 236-36)

English Canon E. C. Hudson has documented that Quirinius was highly successful in his mission against the Homanadensians. More than 4,000 prisoners were taken, Quirinius was awarded the distinction of a triumph, and those of the colony of Pisidian Antioch elected him honorary duumvir, or chief magistrate, with a prefect, M. Servilius, designated to act for him. (HuE.PF 15:106)

Quirinius' great ability contrasts vividly with the inexperience of Quinctilius Varus, official governor of Syria from 7 or 6 BC to 4 BC. Blaiklock, having investigated the evidence at length, shows that Varus

> was a man for whom Augustus may justifiably have entertained no great regard. Augustus, above all, was an able judge of men, and it was Quinctilius Varus, who, in AD 9, reprehensibly lost three legions in the Teutoburger forest in Germany, one of the most shocking disasters to Roman arms in the century. Assuming that Augustus had some misgivings over the ability of Varus to handle an explosive situation, it is easy to see a reason for a special intrusion, under other direction, in the affairs of Varus' province. A reasonable reconstruction might assume that Varus came to Syria in 7 B.C., an untried man. The census was due in Palestine in 8 or 7 B.C., and it could well be that Augustus ordered the man who had just successfully dealt with the problem of the Pisidian highlanders, to undertake the delicate task. Herod I had recently lost the favor of the emperor, and may have been temporizing about the taking of the census, a process which always enraged the difficult Jews. Quirinius' intervention, the requisite organization, and the preparation for the census, could easily have postponed the actual date of registration to the end of 5 B.C., a reasonable date.[7]

It is likely then that Quirinius held a ruling position over Syria by special commission. There is a key confirmation: Luke 2:2 allows for this leadership arrangement since the Greek term used does not specify that Quirinius was the official governor of Syria, only that he was in some way governing, ruling or leading Syria.

The dictum of Aristotle, commonly followed for all works of antiquity, is that the benefit of the doubt must be given to the author, not arrogated by the critic to himself.[8] The reason classical scholars follow this practice (and why New Testament critics ought to as well) is that the author of a classical work, being much closer to the events in question, has a decided advantage in knowing details of the situation which the critic, removed from the event by centuries of time, has no way of knowing. Therefore it is one thing to claim a historical contradiction but quite another to prove it.

Since the historical documentation of ancient times in general and of Syria at this time in particular is scanty, can we trust Luke for historical accuracy? Let's check his track record.[9]

During the first century, names of official government positions changed often. In spite of this fact, Luke has been found to precisely identify those he names with their correct titles. For example, when Cyprus switched from imperial province to senatorial province in 22 BC, the ruler's title changed as well. Still, Luke correctly identifies Sergios Paullus as "proconsul" of Cyprus rather than by his old title, "imperial legate." Luke also correctly designates the governors of Achaia and Asia as proconsuls since they were under the senate's jurisdiction rather than that of the emperor. Achaia was first under the senate from 27 BC to AD 15, then under the emperor until AD 44, and again under the senate from that time on. In Philippi, Luke's term "praetors" for the chief magistrates reflects a peculiar egotistical practice confirmed by Cicero: "Although they are called duumvirs in the other colonies, these men wished to be called praetors."[10] Concerning Luke's accuracy in Acts 17:6, an Australian scholar, David Hayles, has published a comprehensive review of the Quirinius issue. He asserts:

> It is relevant to note at this point that Luke is the only ancient author to have preserved the term *politarches* (Acts 17:6). Any doubts of his reliability in this respect have been shattered by the discovery of nineteen different inscriptions attesting the title in Thessalonica and Macedonia generally.
>
> (HaDJ.RS11 30)

In Acts 28:7, Luke calls Publius "the first man of the island," a title confirmed by Greek and Latin inscriptions as the correct reference to the ruler of Malta at that time. Though Matthew and Mark record the popular designation for Herod Antipas, "king," Luke refers to him by his official title of "tetrarch." As much as Antipas desired it, the Romans granted royal status only to his father, Herod the Great, and not to him. Critics used to charge Luke with an error in Luke 3:1, where he speaks of Lysanias as tetrarch of Abilene. The only Lysanias of Abilene known to modern historians until recently was a "king" by that name, one who was executed by Mark Antony in 34 BC. But once again Luke prevailed over modern critics when an inscription dated between AD 14 and 29 referred to, you guessed it, "Lysanias the tetrarch," a ruler during that time. (See RaW.BRD15 297ff.)

Luke's accuracy has been confirmed in other ways. Speaking of Luke's descriptions of local "color and atmosphere," Bruce relates:

> The accuracy which Luke shows in the details we have already examined extends also to the more general sphere of local color and atmosphere. He gets the atmosphere right every time. Jerusalem, with its excitable and intolerant crowds, is in marked contrast to the busy emporium of Syrian Antioch, where men of different creeds and nationalities rub shoulders and get their rough corners worn away, so that we are not surprised to find the first Gentile church established there, with Jews and non-Jews meeting in brotherly tolerance and fellowship. Then there is Philippi, the Roman colony with its self-important magistrates and its citizens so very proud of being Romans; and Athens, with its endless disputations in the market-place and its unquenchable thirst for the latest news—a thirst for which its statesmen had chided it three and four hundred years earlier. Then there is Ephesus, with its temple of Artemis, one of the seven wonders of the world, and so many of its citizens depending for their living on the cult of the great goddess; with its reputation for superstition and magic— a reputation so wide-spread in the ancient world that a common name for written charms or spells was *Ephesia grammata* ("Ephesian letters"). It was no doubt scrolls containing these spells that were publicly burnt as Paul

powerfully proclaimed a faith which set men free from superstitious fears (Acts 19:19). (Br.F.NTD 89)

In 1848, James Smith of Jordan Hill, an experienced yachtsman and well acquainted with the Mediterranean world where Paul's ship had sailed, published what became the standard work on Paul's shipwreck, *The Voyage and Shipwreck of St. Paul*. In it, he tells of Luke's remarkable accuracy and, by using details supplied by Luke, fixes the exact location of the shipwreck off the coast of Malta.

We must conclude that it is far safer to trust the eyewitness accuracy of Luke than the modern critic, removed by almost two millennia from the events and who has scant archaeological or textual evidence at his disposal. Bruce puts it:

> Now, all these evidences of accuracy are not accidental. A man whose accuracy can be demonstrated in matters where we are able to test it is likely to be accurate even where the means for testing him are not available. Accuracy is a habit of mind, and we know from happy (or unhappy) experience that some people are habitually accurate just as others can be depended upon to be inaccurate. Luke's record entitles him to be regarded as a writer of habitual accuracy. (Br.F.NTD 90)

GEOGRAPHY

The traveler to Israel almost immediately discovers the uniqueness of the land. Nowhere in the world is there a greater diversity of climate and geography in such a small area than in the land of Israel. It can be snowing in Jerusalem while only a few miles away it can be hot enough for sunbathing around the Dead Sea. The Dead Sea, at almost 1,300 feet below sea level, is the lowest spot on the surface of the earth. In the north, the Sea of Galilee, at almost 700 feet below sea level, contrasts markedly with the over 9,000-foot-high Mount Hermon just on the other side of Israel's northern border. But there are many obscure points of geography which only the native to the land could know or remember.

The gospel writers often casually refer to geographical features which indicate how familiar they are with the land. More important, Jesus seems to have done and said certain things in relationship to his surroundings with the purpose of leaving behind unforgettable messages vividly imprinted on the minds of the disciples. For example, at the base of the 9,000-foot-high "rock" of Mt. Hermon, Jesus says to Peter, "You are Peter [Gr. *Petros*, a stone], and upon this rock [Gr. *petra*, large rock, bedrock] I will build My church; and the gates of Hades shall not overpower it."[11] "Gates of Hades" was a rabbinic term referring to Gentile cities. Jesus was predicting that the mission entrusted to his apostles would one day overpower the Gentiles. Again, Jesus made his prediction in an appropriate place, as the base of Mount Hermon at Caesarea-Philippi contains numerous large niches carved into the cliff which housed statues of the Greco-Roman pantheon of gods.

Later, in Jerusalem, the disciples would be reminded again of Mount Hermon when Jesus cried out, "He who believes in Me, as the Scripture said, 'From his innermost being shall flow rivers of living water.'"[12] Most rivers begin with a trickle...but not the river Jordan. When the snows on Mount Hermon melt, the water seeps down through the mountain and then gushes full force from the base of the mountain. From personal observation, we can verify that some of these springs are more than ten feet across at the point where they flow out from under Mount Hermon.

The countryside around the Sea of Galilee made Jesus' teaching even more vivid by the way he incorporated the surroundings into that teaching. For example, from Capernaum on the northwest shore of the sea, one could see several cities on top of hills all around the sea. Directly opposite, on the southeast shore, lay Hippus, the largest city visible to those in Capernaum. Its primary location was not down by the water but high on a hill overlooking the sea. Several other cities and villages perched on hilltops around the Sea of Galilee. For example, Gamala was the zealot stronghold to the east. The lights of these cities would often remind the apostles of the time Jesus gestured toward them as he said, "You are the light of the world. A city set on a hill cannot be hidden."[13]

John states that Jesus "came to His own, and those who were His own did not receive Him."[14] This statement is certainly borne out by a list of towns Jesus did and did not visit. The towns he did visit consisted mainly of religious Jews: Capernaum, Chorazin, Bethsaida, Gennesaret, Cana and Nazareth. By curious contrast, there is no record of Jesus having entered the larger cities where Hellenized Jews mingled with Gentiles: Hippus, Gadara, Julias (next to Bethsaida), Sepphoris (less than five miles from Nazareth), Tiberias, Scythopolis and Caesarea Philippi (though he did visit the countryside around Caesarea Philippi). Jesus indicated on various occasions that his mission went beyond the Jews, yet he carried out his ministry almost exclusively among the religious or orthodox Jews.

Around the Sea of Galilee, in particular at Tiberias and Gadara, famous hot springs attracted those in need of healing. The hot springs of Gadara, also known as Emmatha, were the largest in the world other than those in Venice. Matthew's report fits naturally in this environment:

> And Jesus was going about in all Galilee, teaching in their synagogues, and proclaiming the gospel of the kingdom, and healing every kind of disease and every kind of sickness among the people. And the news about Him went out into all Syria; and they brought to Him all who were ill, taken with various diseases and pains, demoniacs, epileptics, paralytics; and He healed them. And great multitudes followed Him from Galilee and Decapolis and Jerusalem and Judea and from beyond the Jordan.[15]

Gadara was the largest city of Decapolis (Greek for "ten cities"); Tiberias, the largest of Galilee.

Even some of Jesus' strangest miracles are at home in this setting around the Sea of Galilee. One family of fish dwelling in this sea is called *Cichlidae*—or mouth-breeders. It is found only in Lake Victoria (Uganda), along the Nile River and in the Sea of Galilee. Cartographer Dr. Jim Fleming, who teaches classes in archaeology and historical geography at Hebrew University in Jerusalem, explains its significance:

> The female keeps the eggs in her mouth until they hatch. As the brood begins to grow she lets them out from time to time on an "outing," but quickly scoops them up when danger is near. The mother will fast until near starvation in order not to swallow her young. These strong instincts have given the Hebrew name of the fish "The Mother-Fish." After the young are off on their own the mother often keeps a substitute in her mouth. They are sometimes caught today with pebbles or Coke bottle caps in their mouths! The popular name for the fish is "St. Peter's fish" because of the gospel story in Matthew 17:24-27 about Peter catching a fish with a shekel coin in its mouth. (FiJ.JAS 6)

Galilee is a volcanic area. Volcanic rock is everywhere, and thorns grow there rapidly during the summer months. When Jesus told his parable of the four soils, his listeners would have related well to what he said. Later, his disciples would recall the parable easily whenever they visited the area.

The things Jesus did and said in and around Jerusalem likewise fit well with what is known of the local geography. The small town of Bethphage sits on the side of the Mount of Olives facing away from Jerusalem. It takes its name from a preseason fruit which grows on the fig trees of the area. The fruit is called *phage* (*fah*-gay) in Hebrew, and appears in the early spring with the first leaves. Did you ever wonder why Jesus was looking for figs on the fig tree when the text specifically says, "It was not the season for figs"? The answer is that even though it was not the season for figs (Gr. *sukon,* meaning ripe figs), the fact that the tree had leaves indicated that it also should have had the preseason figs *(phage),* which were edible. Since the tree contained no fruit, Jesus seems to have used it as an object lesson to warn against professing something by our appearance but having no fruit to back it up.[16]

From this same area one can look off to the south and see the Herodium with the Dead Sea shimmering in the distance behind it. Herod had this palatial fortress built between 24 and 15 BC. The small mountain on which it sits was heightened by using part of another nearby mountain. Immediately after cursing the fig tree at Bethphage, Jesus commented, "Truly I say to you, whoever says to this mountain, 'Be taken up and cast into the sea,' and does not doubt in his heart, but believes that what he says is going to happen; it shall be granted him."[17] Jesus was probably pointing at the Herodium and the Dead Sea as he spoke, indicating that not even the power of Herod (or other kings and authorities) could prevent the establishment of his kingdom.

Mustard trees still grow in Israel, and one can readily see that its minute seeds (hundreds can fit on the tip of a finger) and fifteen-foot height fit precisely with Jesus' parable:

> The kingdom of heaven is like a mustard seed…and this is smaller than all other seeds; but when it is full grown, it is larger than the garden plants, and becomes a tree, so that the birds of the air come and nest in its branches.[18]

In Jerusalem, from the steps on the southern side of the Temple where rabbis often addressed their pupils, the chalk-white tombstones that cover the Mount of Olives are clearly visible. Jesus probably gestured in that direction as he said:

> Woe to you, scribes and Pharisees, hypocrites! For you are like whitewashed tombs which on the outside appear beautiful, but inside they are full of dead men's bones and all uncleanness. Even so you too outwardly appear righteous to men, but inwardly you are full of hypocrisy and lawlessness.[19]

ALLEGED GEOGRAPHICAL CONTRADICTIONS

In *Jesus: The Evidence,* Ian Wilson charges:

> The Mark gospel exhibits a lamentable ignorance of Palestinian geography. In the seventh chapter, for instance, Jesus is reported as going through Sidon on his way [from] Tyre to the Sea of Galilee. Not only is Sidon in the opposite direction, but there was in fact no road from Sidon to the Sea of Galilee in the first century AD, only one from Tyre.[20]

Sidon most certainly does appear to be out of the way if Jesus were going directly back to the northwest shore of the Sea of Galilee from which he had come. But Mark 7:31 indicates that he looped around and approached the southeast shore of the Sea of Galilee through the region called Decapolis. If you view the Sea of Galilee as a clock, Decapolis was a region which bordered the sea from 3:00 to about 6:00.

Orthodox Jews did not normally travel in this area because the region was almost entirely inhabited by Gentiles and Hellenized Jews. Jesus, however, brought his disciples here immediately after their time in the regions of Tyre and Sidon. Now, an important question: What did these two regions have in common?

What they had in common was lots of Gentiles. Since Jesus is reported to have spent most of his ministry in Jewish territory, it is significant that these areas should be linked together. What Matthew and Mark are likely saying is that Jesus took his disciples on one last ministry tour through Gentile regions. This mission would set a precedent for the disciples' later concern regarding being his witnesses "even to the remotest part of the earth," even among the Gentiles.[21] Beginning on the northwest shore of the Sea of Galilee, they would have traveled northwest to Tyre, northeast to Sidon, southeast to the region of Decapolis and west to the Sea of Galilee. Far from showing a "lamentable ignorance" of the geography of Palestine, the passage helps explain why Jesus did not go directly back to the northwest shore of the Sea of Galilee, the location identified as his home.

Wilson's further contention that there was no road from Sidon to the Sea of Galilee is likewise immaterial. The gospels report numerous occasions where Jesus was going up mountains or into the wilderness to pray, and he consistently conducted his ministry in rural areas. There is therefore no reason why Jesus and the disciples could not have walked the less than twenty miles from Sidon to the Valley of Lebanon. Their route along the south side of Mount Lebanon would not have been too difficult. Only further north are the mountains of Lebanon imposing. This route would have allowed Jesus and his disciples a more direct path around to the southeast side of the Sea of Galilee.

Another alleged geographical contradiction treated unfairly by Wilson and others is the account of the demoniac(s) found in Matthew 8:28-34, Mark 5:1-20 and Luke 8:26-39. Wilson charges:

> Similarly the fifth chapter refers to the Sea of Galilee's eastern shore as the country of the Gerasenes, yet Gerasa, today Jerash, is more than thirty miles to the southeast, too far away for a story whose setting requires a nearby city with a steep slope down to the sea. (WilJTE 36)

Harper's Bible Dictionary likewise asserts:

> Gerasa…one of the three greatest cities of Roman Arabia…is thirty-three miles southeast of the Sea of Galilee in the mountains of Gilead. Hence Luke's identification of it with Jesus' healing of the demoniac (8:26) cannot be correct.

But neither Luke nor Mark say that the event happened *at* Gerasa. Matthew likewise does not say it happened *at* Gadara. All three writers use the expression "in the country of" followed by "the Gadarenes" in Matthew and "the Gerasenes" in Mark and Luke. In other words, all three writers chose to generally locate the event rather than specifically identify an exact location, and for good reason.

The best, possibly the only location along the east shore of the Sea of Galilee where this event could have occurred is a point approximately one mile north of the Decapolis city Hippus, and two miles south of the small first-century town of Gergesa. At this point the hillside drops steeply into the sea. The border between Gaulanitus in the north and Decapolis in the south intersected almost directly between the two cities, though there may have been confusion then, as now, over its exact location. It appears the site was just inside the border of the Decapolis. Since Gadara, approximately six miles southeast of the Sea of Galilee, was the chief city of the immediate area, Matthew apparently chose to call the area "the country of the Gadarenes. Decapolis generally may also have been known as 'the country of the Gerasenes' because of the greater prominence of Gerasa, 33 miles to the southeast."[22] Luke and Mark used this designation.

Some manuscripts behind all three accounts use the designation "country of the

Gergesenes," but the strongest evidence does not support this reading. It appears to be a later emendation or error which was introduced by a copyist who knew of the close proximity of Gergesa. The disciples, however, may have used the other designations because they knew they were in Decapolis, not Gaulanitus, which contained Gergesa. In any case, it is to their credit that they only used the general locator "in the country of" since they could not be sure of their exact location.

We believe that the origin of geographical, as well as other, apparent contradictions is simply ignorance or lack of information. Take Sir William Ramsay, who has been cited before concerning New Testament accuracy. He is regarded as one of the greatest archaeologists and geographers ever to have lived. He was a student of the German historical school of the mid-nineteenth century. As a result, he believed that the Book of Acts was a product of the mid-second century AD. He was firm in this belief. In his research to make a topographical study of Asia Minor he was compelled to consider the writings of Luke. As a result he was forced to do a complete reversal of his beliefs due to the overwhelming evidence uncovered in his research. Concerning Luke's ability as a historian, Ramsay concluded after thirty years of study that "Luke is a historian of the first rank; not merely are his statements of fact trustworthy...but also this author should be placed along with the very greatest of historians." (RaW.BRD53 222) He added, "Luke's history is unsurpassed in respect of its trustworthiness." (RaW.SPT 81)

VERIFYING THE NEW TESTAMENT?

Some skeptics love to use the argument, "How can you trust the gospel accounts? After all, there is so little there that is verified by unbiased historical record." This is a deceptive line of argument.

- It assumes, and let's be honest, that the Christians, being biased, wrote what was not true. We know from history that many have died for a philosophy that they believed to be true. The Jewish zealots of the first century are prime examples. Their courage and unflinching refusal to give in to their enemies in the face of the most cruel tortures speaks admirably for their commitment to their beliefs. But this is different from the charge being leveled against the writers of the New Testament, especially the writers of the gospels. These men are being charged with writing material they would have known to be false.

- It is inconceivable that such men would die martyrs' deaths for what they knew to be false. How much easier it would have been for Peter and Matthew and others of the early Christian martyrs to have simply gone back to their nets or other occupations which would not so gravely endanger their very lives. Yes, men and women will die for what they believe to be the truth, but only a severely deranged person will die for what he knows to be false.

- Though much information in the gospel records can be compared to historical reports from other sources, we must observe one preliminary caution: We should not fall into the trap of feeling that everything in the gospels needs to be "verified" or "confirmed" by something in a "non-Christian" source. For example, Josephus gives quite a bit of information which agrees with the gospel accounts, but historians have found plenty of errors in his work as well as in that of other writers of antiquity.

- There are also many statements in the Bible which contain information that does not exist in any other source of antiquity. Therefore, we can be encouraged by those pieces of historical information in the gospel record which are confirmed by other sources but we need not feel that everything in the gospel record must be verified by another source before it can be trusted.

The gospel narratives are literally covered with the fingerprints of history. If these writers conveyed historical information with such exactness on so many minute details, surely they can be trusted to convey an accurate picture of the words and works of their central figure, Jesus of Nazareth.

11

EVIDENCE FROM ARCHAEOLOGY

rchaeology is an exciting field of study, especially for the Christian. Christians and Jews both can approach this field with a great deal of confidence. Noted Jewish archaeologist Nelson Glueck has gone so far as to affirm, "It may be stated categorically that no archaeological discovery has ever controverted a biblical reference." (GlN.RD 31) Millar Burrows of Yale, not a conservative Christian, wrote:

> The Bible is supported by archaeological evidence again and again. On the whole, there can be no question that the results of excavation have increased the respect of scholars for the Bible as a collection of historical documents. The confirmation is both general and specific. The fact that the record can be so often explained or illustrated by archaeological data shows that it fits into the framework of history as only a genuine product of ancient life could do. In addition to this general authentication, however, we find the record verified repeatedly at specific points. Names of places and persons turn up at the right places in the right periods. (BuM.HAH 6)

H. M. Orlinsky, in *Ancient Israel,* discusses development of a new attitude regarding the negative results of previous radical criticism:

> More and more the older view that the biblical data were suspect and even likely to be false, unless corroborated by extrabiblical facts, is giving way to one which holds that, by and large, the biblical accounts are more likely to be true than false, unless clear-cut evidence from sources outside the Bible demonstrate the reverse. (OrH.AI 6)

While archaeology can be exciting, those who work in the field know that the work is often long, hot, dusty, tiring and tedious. Dramatically significant discoveries occur infrequently. Findings are often tentative, and the interpretations of discoveries in one generation are sometimes overturned by new discoveries in the next. One limitation of archaeology is the paucity of evidence. Edwin Yamauchi cautions:

> Historians of antiquity, in using the archaeological evidence, have very often failed to realize how slight is the evidence at our disposal. It would not be exaggerating to point out that what we have is but one fraction of a second fraction of a third fraction of a fourth fraction of a fifth fraction of the possible evidence. (YaE.SSS 13:9)

For this reason, it is imperative that both those supporting and denying the historical reliability of the gospel accounts not go beyond the evidence supplied by archaeology.

In considering historical reliability of the gospel accounts, archaeology can be very useful. First, it confirms places, names, times and events as being accurately reported in the gospel records. Joseph Free, in *Archaeology and Bible History,* states that "archaeology has confirmed countless passages which have been rejected by critics as unhistorical or contradictory to known facts." (FrJP.A I)

Second, archaeology can provide a feel for the cultural context of Jesus' day. Particular customs, places, even articles used in everyday life can shed light on things Jesus and his contemporaries are reported to have said or done.

Third, archaeology can provide linguistic and other information aiding in the accurate translation and interpretation of the gospel text. Again, Free states:

> Numerous passages of the Bible which long puzzled the commentators have readily yielded up their meaning when new light from archaeological discoveries has been focused on them. In other words, archaeology illuminates the text of the Scriptures and so makes valuable contributions to the fields of biblical interpretation and exegesis. (FrJP.A I)

In this chapter, we will see some of the specific ways archaeology has helped authenticate information given in the gospel accounts regarding: (1) the character or existence of particular people; (2) specific places; and (3) minute details mentioned in passing. We also will observe how archaeology has helped to resolve alleged historical contradictions in the accounts. Finally, we will discuss the momentous importance of the discovery of the Dead Sea Scrolls.

PEOPLE

Herod the Great

> And when Herod the king heard it, he was troubled, and all Jerusalem with him.... Then when Herod saw that he had been tricked by the magi, he became very enraged, and sent and slew all the male children who were in Bethlehem and in all its environs, from two years old and under, according to the time which he had ascertained from the magi (Matthew 2:3,16).

Radical (as well as not so radical) critics often attack the "nativity accounts" because so little extrabiblical evidence exists to "confirm" the reports as historical. As we have already noted, this attitude too confidently overestimates the quantity of sources available for this time period. What extrabiblical evidence is available suggests that we can be confident of the accuracy of the gospels. For example, the verses quoted above fit with what we know about Herod. An early coin, issued under Herod and showing palm branches bowing to a star atop a Macedonian helmet, illustrates his obsession that no one else usurp his throne. Professor Fleming explains that the coin was issued in 40 BC, the same year Herod received the title of "king" during his visit to Rome. That very year, the birth of a Messiah was expected in Rome according to the Fourth Eclogue of Virgil. Herod, therefore, upon his return, married Mariamne

> so as to become partaker in the blessing of the star of the Hasmoneans which was, like the star of the Macedonians, the symbol for messianic rulers born under a Jupiter/Saturn conjunction. He sent his sons to Rome to study in the house of Pollio, the family to which the coming of the messiah had been prophesied by Virgil. Herod did everything to become recipient of the messianic prophecy he had heard. The Macedonian helmet and Macedonian/Hasmonean star on his coin from the year 40 B.C. make it clear that his messianic aspirations go back to the very beginning of his career. (FIJ.LJ 13)

Josephus, in books 17 and 18 of his *Antiquities,* details how troubled all Jerusalem became as Herod neared the end of his life and had three of his own sons slain out of suspicion that they sought to usurp his kingdom. Matthew therefore accurately reflects the troubled state of Jerusalem's inhabitants at any report of a possible usurper of Herod's throne.

Pilate

When Pontius Pilate was governor of Judea... (Luke 3:1).

Until 1961 the only historical references to Pontius Pilate were secondary. That is, they referred to Pontius Pilate, it was thought, only because the gospels referred to him. Then two Italian archaeologists excavated the Mediterranean port city of Caesarea that served as the Roman capital of Palestine. During the dig they uncovered a two-by-three-foot inscription in Latin. Antonio Frova was able to reconstruct the inscription. To his surprise it read: "Pontius Pilate, Prefect of Judea, has presented the Tiberium to the Caesareans." This was the first archaeological discovery of a historical reference to the existence of Pilate.

The Common People

Archaeologists have uncovered many ossuaries (bone boxes) from the general time of Jesus. From inscriptions on the outside of the ossuaries, linguists have learned much about the language of the common people as opposed to that of the literary individuals who left works that survive to our day. The evidence shows that Greek, Aramaic and Hebrew were all spoken in Palestine at this time.

"These inscriptions," says R. T. France, "illustrate how common were many of the names found in the New Testament (Jesus, Joseph, Simon, Judas, Ananias, etc.); they even include, intriguingly, an 'Alexander, Son of Simon,' found in a tomb near Jerusalem probably belonging to a Cyrenian Jewish family, and described (in Hebrew) as QRNYT, which may mean 'Cyrenian'—could this be the man mentioned in Mark 15:21?" (FrR.E 145. Also see AvN.IJ 12:9-12)

PLACES

Nazareth

> And [Joseph] arose and took the child and His mother, and came into the land of Israel…and came and resided in a city called Nazareth.[1]

Joshua 19:10-15 lists the towns of the tribe of Zebulun. The city of Nazareth does not appear among them. Josephus gives the names of forty-five towns and villages in Galilee, but "Nazareth" is not among them. The Talmud names sixty-three towns and villages. Again, the name of Nazareth does not appear. You can understand why some critical scholars questioned the existence of a "city called Nazareth" in New Testament times.

In 1962, during Michael Avi-Yonah's excavations at Caesarea, the last two fragments of a three fragment inscription were found. It is known as the Nazareth inscription since it is the first known inscription citing the name "Nazareth." Inscribed on the marble slab is a list of the twenty-four priestly courses (1 Chronicles 25:7-18) with their surnames and the names of the Galilean towns or villages to which they had moved following the Roman destruction of Herod's Temple in AD 70. It provides incontestable evidence of the existence of the town of Nazareth in the first century AD.

Excavations at modern-day Nazareth show that it had been inhabited long before Roman times, but was, as we indicated earlier, an insignificant and very small village. Queen Helena, the mother of Constantine, had a church built over the site that had been indicated as the dwelling of Jesus' family. It was her practice to erect churches over sites mentioned in the gospels in order to preserve their memory. Through the ages, the Roman Catholic Church has continued the tradition whenever a church is destroyed by building a succeeding church where the previous one stood.

Excavations under the present Church of Annunciation gave further indication of the site's authenticity. A pedestal of the earliest church bore the words "Hail Mary," the greeting of Gabriel to Mary, the mother of Jesus. Remains of a ritual bath or *mikvah* indicate the early presence of orthodox Jews, possibly Jewish Christians who built their own synagogue. This should not be surprising as James 2:2 says, "If a man comes into your synagogue…," referring to a gathering of Christians.

It is a common rule of thumb that traditions from before Constantine's Edict of Milan (AD 313) are considered reliable since official nontoleration of Christians before 313 removed all material motivation for preservation of Christian sites. The findings at Nazareth definitely place the traditions associated with it in the "reliable" category. A mosaic inscription reading "Offering of Conon, Deacon of Jerusalem" preserves the memory of the famous martyr of Nazareth killed under Decius (249–251). Conon is reported to have claimed that he was a direct descendant of the family of Joseph and Mary. (MeE.AREC 131) A third-century plaster with an inscription petitioning "Christ Lord" indicates Christian veneration of the site prior to Queen Helena's visit to it. Though tourists to the present city of Nazareth may feel it has been commercialized, the archaeological evidence strongly supports the authenticity of the site.

Capernaum

> And leaving Nazareth, He came and settled in Capernaum, which is by the sea, in the region of Zebulun and Naphtali (Matthew 4:13).

Mark tells us that when Jesus "had come back to Capernaum several days afterward, it was heard that He was at home." Then Jesus healed the paralytic lowered through the roof. From Mark 1:29-34, it seems most likely that Jesus' "home" was the insula (a complex of many rooms, often used for extended families) of Peter's mother-in-law. We would expect it to be larger than normal by the inferences of Peter's prosperous fishing business and the number of people who apparently stayed there. Just such an insula has been preserved and excavated in Capernaum.

It was customary in the Byzantine period for Christians to build an octagon-shaped church over a *locus sanctus,* a holy place. The remains of such a church from the fourth and fifth century have been excavated at Capernaum. Directly beneath the church are the remains of an insula which revealed continuous occupation from the time of Jesus to the time the church was built. (Eleven levels of floors were revealed.) Additional walls and rooms were added to the first insula to form what apparently was a house-church. Excavation of the Byzantine church foundation revealed a reverence for the earliest structure in that its walls sometimes arched over those of the early insula so as not to destroy them. The careful scholars of archaeology, Drs. Eric Meyers and James Strange, report:

> The church in question was centered on one room of the block beneath. This room is 7.0 by 6.5 meters, large for an ancient house. (The synagogue at Magdala measures 8.17 by 7.25 meters.) The lowest floors of this room had early Roman pottery and coins sealed between them, which must mean that the founding and earliest use of this room, and therefore of the entire block of houses, was in the first century B.C.E. Either late in the first century or early in the second century C.E. this room received extensive interior remodeling: The floors were renewed several times and plastered, as were the walls. Sometime before the fourth century C.E. the pottery ceased to be simply domestic items. Ceramics discovered here dated after the first century tend to be storage jars and other "public" wares. (MeE.AREC 60)

They continue:

The excavators conclude that the house was founded c. 100 B.C.E. Sometime near the end of the first century C.E., someone plastered it three times, which may suggest conversion to a public building rather than merely the remodeling of a house...Furthermore, the absence of plain pottery correlates with a public rather than a private use for this part of the building. (MeE.AREC 129)

During the second and third centuries, Christian pilgrims incised graffiti into the plaster walls of the house-church. Writing, including the name of Peter and invocations to Jesus, was found on 134 fragments of plaster recovered from these walls. The expanded house church was apparently the one the pilgrim Egeria (or Aetheria) saw in approximately AD 380 when she reported, "At Capernaum the house of (the prince of the apostles) has been made into a church, with its original walls still standing." (FIJ.JAS 18)

Other insuli were uncovered at Capernaum, and R. T. France shows how their characteristics fit with details contained in the gospel accounts:

Other aspects of these Capernaum houses help to illuminate gospel stories. They are designed for communal rather than private living, and their crowded layout must have made privacy impossible, hence Jesus' need to go out of the town to be alone (Mark 1:35, etc.). Their floors of rough basalt blocks left large crevices, and the dark basalt walls and small windows explain the problem the woman in the parable had in finding her lost coin in such a crevice (Luke 15:8,9). (FrR.E 148)

The Pool of Bethesda

Now there is in Jerusalem by the sheep gate a pool, which is called in Hebrew Bethesda, having five porticoes. In these lay a multitude of those who were sick, blind, lame, withered (John 5:2,3).

The northeast quarter of the old city of Jerusalem was called Bezetha ("New Town") in the first century AD. Some significant excavations near St. Anne's Church in that quarter were conducted 100 years ago. These excavations uncovered the remains of an ancient church which marked the site of Bethesda.

F. F. Bruce describes later excavations which

identified the pool itself, or rather twin pools, lying north and south, with a rock partition between them. Porticoes evidently occupied the four sides and the partition. One of the first visitors to Jerusalem after it came under Christian control, the "Bordeaux pilgrim" (AD 333), saw and described the twin pools. The "Copper Scroll" from Qumran gives the name in the Hebrew dual number, Beth-esh-dathain, "the place of the two outpourings." There are few sites in Jerusalem, mentioned in the gospels, which can be identified so confidently. (BrF.NTD 94)

DETAILS

Millstones

The excavations at Capernaum also unearthed a significant number of first-century millstones. In fact, so many were recovered that it appears the inhabitants there took advantage of the plentiful volcanic rock to make and export mills to other areas. Hand mills could be turned by two women. Jesus referred to these smaller mills in Luke 17:35, "There will be two women grinding at the same place; one will be taken, and the other will be left." Earlier, while teaching in Capernaum, he said, "Whoever causes one of these little ones who believes in Me to stumble," and here he probably gestured toward a larger mill turned by a donkey when he warned, "it is better for him that a heavy millstone [literally, "millstone turned by a donkey"] be hung around his neck, and that he be drowned in the depth of the sea."[2]

Stone Waterpots

> Now there were six stone waterpots set there for the Jewish custom of purification, containing twenty or thirty gallons each (John 2:6).

During excavations of the Upper City in Jerusalem by Nahman Avigad, Professor Emeritus of Archaeology at the Hebrew University of Jerusalem, stone vessels continually surfaced within the stratums of the Second Temple Period (approximately 20 BC to AD 70). These stone vessels were previously regarded as isolated luxury items, but due to the discovery of them in almost every house it is known that their use was much more widespread. Avigad relates:

> The discovery of stone vessels became a routine matter in our work, for whenever we approached a stratum of the Second Temple period, and a building which was burnt during the destruction of the city in AD 70 began revealing itself, they invariably made their appearance as well. Thus, even in the absence of other specific chronological clues, we were often able to date a structure as Herodian solely on the basis of the presence of even a single stone vessel—or even mere fragments. Generally, these vessels are accompanied by traces of fire, obviously from the destruction of AD 70. (AvN.DJ 174)

Galilean Boat

> Now it came about on one of those days, that He and His disciples got into a boat, and He said to them, "Let us go over to the other side of the lake." And they launched out (Luke 8:22).

Moshe and Yuval Lufan, brothers from Kibbutz Ginosar, "lovers of archaeology" but not professional archaeologists, had a feel for the land that led them to some important discoveries. In January 1986, on the shores of the Sea of Galilee, between Kibbutz

Ginosar and Moshava Migdal, they discovered an early Galilean boat dating from the first century BC to the first century AD. It was apparently used for fishing, transporting goods and ferrying people.

The boat measures almost twenty-seven feet in length and about seven-and-a-half feet in width, certainly large enough for a crew of thirteen. Its discovery was made possible by the low level of the lake due to the lack of rain. For the next five to seven years the vessel underwent treatment in a special pool in which synthetic wax was added to the water to penetrate and strengthen the porous wood.

Phylacteries

Besides the Dead Sea Scrolls, also found in the archaeological dig at Qumran were small leather phylactery cases containing four small pouches into which minute rolls of very fine parchment had once been placed. Single compartment phylacteries also were found. Again, Jesus' words "they broaden their phylacteries" fit comfortably into the Jewish cultural context.[3]

Seat of Moses

> Then said Jesus to the crowds and to his disciples, "The scribes and the Pharisees sit on Moses' seat; so practice and observe whatever they tell you, but not what they do; for they preach, but do not practice" (Matthew 23:1-3 RSV).

The seat of Moses was not just a figurative term referring to the authority of Moses. At Chorazin, En-Gedi and Delos, carved stone seats of Moses have been found. The teacher in a synagogue would teach from this chair. The seat at Chorazin has an Aramaic inscription on its façade, indicating the most common language of the town during the second and third centuries AD.

The Temple

> And as He was going out of the temple, one of His disciples said to Him, "Teacher, behold what wonderful stones and what wonderful buildings!" (Mark 13:1)

Jesus' disciples were not the only ones who were in awe of the Temple. One rabbi, as recorded in the Talmud, remembered, "It used to be said: He who has not seen the temple of Herod has never seen a beautiful building."[4] The Temple Mount is the largest site of its kind in the ancient world, covering an area about the size of 25 to 30 football fields. The retaining walls rose approximately the height of a ten-story building above the outside street level. The smallest stone blocks used for constructing the walls weighed from two to five tons. Some of the largest stones are without equal anywhere in the ancient world. One measures 40 feet in length, 13 feet in width, 10 feet in height, and weighs close to 400 tons! Josephus speaks of the magnificence of the Temple in the fifteenth book of *Antiquities.* He tells, for example of 162 columns in four rows, each column 27 feet high and "the thickness of each pillar was such that three men might, with their arms extended, fathom it round."[5]

Luke's accuracy is attested by another discovery associated with the Temple. In Acts 21 he speaks of Paul going through the Temple purification process. When some Jews from Asia saw him there, they descended on him seeking to kill him and shouting out, "This is the man who preaches to all men everywhere against our people, and the Law, and this place; and besides he has even brought Greeks into the temple and has defiled this holy place." They had previously seen Paul with a Gentile, Trophimus, and "supposed that Paul had brought him into the temple." Speaking of the Jewish law prohibiting Gentiles from entering the inner courts of the Temple, Bruce relates the following discovery:

> That none might plead ignorance of the rule, notices in Greek and Latin were fastened to the barricade separating the outer from the inner courts, warning Gentiles that death was the penalty for trespass. One of these Greek inscriptions, found at Jerusalem in 1871 by C. S. Clermont-Ganneau, is now housed in Istanbul, and reads as follows:
>
> NO FOREIGNER MAY ENTER WITHIN THE BARRICADE WHICH SURROUNDS THE TEMPLE AND ENCLOSURE. ANYONE WHO IS CAUGHT DOING SO WILL HAVE HIM-SELF TO THANK FOR HIS ENSUING DEATH. (Br.F.NTD 93)

Tombs

The many first-century tombs which have been found confirm a number of details in the burial narratives concerning Jesus. The tombs often contain several short tunnels or ledges where bodies are laid for decomposition. Usually, after about a year, members of the family would return to place the bones in an ossuary. Jesus, however, was buried in a "new tomb" (Matthew 27:60), "in which no one had yet been laid" (John 19:41). The opening to a tomb was sealed either by a large boulder pushed up into it, or with a large round disc-shaped stone, called a *golel,* which was rolled in front of the entrance. The gospels indicate the second type of stone was used for Jesus' tomb. Sometimes the openings were no more than three feet high, as can be seen by tourists today. No wonder John says that he was "stooping and looking in."[6]

EVENTS

Sycamore Trees at Jericho

> And He entered and was passing through Jericho. And behold, there was a man called by the name of Zaccheus;…and he ran on ahead and climbed up into a sycamore tree in order to see Him, for He was about to pass through that way (Luke 19:1-4).

In 1904, Julius Wellhausen wrote that the statement in Luke's opening verse contradicted everything that followed because if Jesus had already entered the city, Zaccheus would simply have viewed him from a rooftop, not a sycamore tree. (WeJ.DE 103)

But Professor Jack Finegan, a highly regarded specialist in New Testament archaeology, demonstrated that Wellhausen's criticism was built upon the faulty supposition that Jericho was a city of tightly packed houses which would have been available to Zaccheus. Archaeological excavations have clearly distinguished two separate sites for Old Testament and New Testament Jericho. Finegan relates that Wellhausen's

> conception would fit with the tightly-packed buildings which were found when OT Jericho was excavated in Tell es-Sultan. But it does not accord with the findings at *Tulul Abu el-'Alayiq,* where the excavators draw their closest comparison with Roman cities such as Rome, Tivoli, and Pompeii. Like such cities, NT Jericho undoubtedly had its parks and villas, avenues and public squares, where fine trees grew. The sycamore tree, in particular, grows in Palestine mainly on the coast and in the Jordan Valley. That it was well known in ancient Jericho is shown by the finding of precisely this timber as bonding in one of the Hellenistic forts. (FiJ.ANT 85)

Crucifixion

> And when they came to the place called The Skull, there they crucified Him (Luke 23:33).

> The soldiers therefore came, and broke the legs of the first man, and of the other man who was crucified with Him (John 19:32).

According to ancient literary sources, tens of thousands of people died as victims to crucifixion throughout the Roman Empire, with thousands having been crucified in Palestine alone. Until 1968, however, no victim of crucifixion had ever been verified by remains discovered by archaeologists. In addition, many have questioned the historical accuracy of the nailing of the hands and feet. For example, J. W. Hewitt, in the *Harvard Theological Review* article entitled "The Use of Nails in the Crucifixion," said, "To sum up, there is astonishingly little evidence that the feet of a crucified person were ever pierced by nails." (HeJ.UN 25:29-45) He went on to say that the victim's hands and feet were bound by ropes to the cross.

For years Dr. Hewitt's statement was quoted as the final word. The conclusion was that the New Testament account of Jesus being nailed to the cross was false and misleading. Crucifixion by use of nails was considered legendary. It was believed that nails would rip the flesh and could not support a body on the cross.

Then, a revolutionary archaeological discovery was made in June of 1968. Archaeologist Vassilios Tzaferis, under the direction of the Israeli Department of Antiquities and Museums, found four cave-tombs at the site of *Giv'at ha-Mivtar* (*Ras el-Masaref*) just north of Jerusalem near Mount Scopus. These family tombs, hewn out of soft limestone, date from late second century BC to AD 70. Composed of forecourts which led to burial chambers, they housed fifteen limestone ossuaries that contained the bones of thirty-five individuals.

Tomb 1, dated back to the first century AD by its pottery, contained a number of ossuaries. In Ossuary 4, inscribed with the name Yohanan Ben Ha'galgol, were found the bones of an adult male and a child. The skeletal remains were examined by Dr. N. Haas of the department of anatomy of the Hebrew University and the Hadassah Medical School. Dr. Haas reported concerning the adult:

> Both the heel bones were found transfixed by a large iron nail. The shins were found intentionally broken. Death caused by crucifixion. (HaN.AO 20:42)

This discovery from the time of Jesus adds to the literary evidence solid archaeological evidence that the method of nailing individuals to a wooden cross as a means of execution, as mentioned in the New Testament, was unmistakably practiced by the Romans in Palestine.

Haas also concluded that Yohanan had the bones in both his legs broken by a *coup de grace,* and that "the percussion, passing the already crushed right calf bones, was a harsh and severing blow for the left one, attached as they were to the sharp edged wooden cross." (HaN.AO 20:57) When authorities wanted to hasten death or terminate the torture, the victim's legs were broken below the knees with a club. This prevented the victim from pushing himself up to relieve the tension on the pectoral or chest muscles. Either rapid suffocation or coronary insufficiency followed. In the case of Jesus, the legs of the two thieves crucified with him were broken, but those of Jesus were not because the executioners observed he was already dead.

The Empty Tomb

Matthew writes that some of the guards around Jesus' tomb came into the city to tell the chief priests all that had happened. After counseling together, the chief priests and the elders

> gave a large sum of money to the soldiers and said, "You are to say, 'His disciples came by night and stole Him away while we were asleep.' And if this should come to the governor's ears, we will win him over and keep you out of trouble." And they took the money and did as they had been instructed; and this story was widely spread among the Jews, and is to this day (Matthew 28:11-15).

Apparently word did reach the governor's ears, or by some other means, reached all the way to Rome. The emperor, probably Claudius (AD 41–54), sent word back to Palestine. His "decree," originally written in Latin and translated into Greek, was posted in, of all places, the obscure village of Nazareth, home of "the Nazarene." In 1878, a white marble slab, inscribed with the following words, was found in Nazareth:

Ordinance of Caesar. It is my pleasure that graves and tombs remain per-petually undisturbed for those who have made them for the cult of their ancestors or children or members of their house. If, however, anyone charges that another has either demolished them, or has in any other way extracted the buried, or has maliciously transferred them to other places in order to wrong them, or has displaced the sealing on other stones, against such a one I order that a trial be instituted, as in respect of the gods, so in regard to the cult of mortals. For it shall be much more obligatory to honor the buried. Let it be absolutely forbidden for anyone to disturb them. In case of violation I desire that the offender be sentenced to capital punish-ment on charge of violation of sepulchre. (MaP.FE 119)

Because the inscription contains lettering belonging to the first half of the first century, scholars place the date of its composition before AD 50. And since the cen-tral Roman government did not assume the administration of Galilee until after the death of Agrippa, the inscription must date from some time after AD 44. Claudius was emperor from AD 41–54 and is therefore the only candidate for the inscription's originator. In AD 49, Claudius expelled all Jews (and Jewish Christians) out of Rome. He appears to have studied the Jewish situation, at least to a certain degree, and found it displeasing. In one of his extant letters of AD 41, he

expressly forbids the Alexandrian Jews "to bring or invite other Jews to come by sea from Syria. If they do not abstain from this conduct," Claudius threatens, "I shall proceed against them for fomenting a malady common to the world." (BIE.A 81)

Many scholars believe Claudius' words "a malady common to the world" is a spe-cific reference to the growing Christian community across the empire.

The evidence, given in more detail by Blaiklock, therefore suggests that Claudius must have received a letter from the Procurator of Judea or Syria regarding the expan-sion of the Christian religion, which the Jewish authorities contended all began when the disciples stole the body of Jesus the Nazarene from its grave. Irritated, Claudius issued his directive with instructions that it be posted in the town of Nazareth. His irri-tation can especially be seen in the fact that this type of offense did not previously carry anything near the extreme penalty of capital punishment.

DEAD SEA SCROLLS

The noted American archaeologist William F. Albright called it "the greatest man-uscript discovery of all times." (AlW.BA 11:55) The French scholar André Dupont-Sommer declared, "It is not a single revolution in the study of biblical exegesis…[it is] a whole cascade of revolutions." (DuA.DSS 96, quoted in LaWS.DSS 13) Some claims are obviously sensational, but there is no doubt that the discovery of the Dead Sea Scrolls is probably the one most far-reaching archaeological discovery of the twentieth century.

There is also no doubt that it has generated one of the hottest controversies in a long time regarding scholarly integrity. For example, William Sanford LaSor, emeritus professor of Old Testament at Fuller Theological Seminary, charged:

> In the August, 1966, issue of *Harper's Magazine,* Allegro spun a story of falsifications, distortions, and innuendoes, the total effect of which was to belittle Jesus Christ, to discredit the New Testament, and to charge nearly all who have published anything on the Dead Sea Scrolls with being so biased that their works are not reliable. He said, "Scholars are afraid of what the scrolls reveal," and claimed that "the main message of the scrolls remains hidden nearly twenty years after their discovery." Echoing Edmund Wilson, he maintained that New Testament scholars boycotted the Scrolls, and complained that most of the scholars working on the scrolls had "taken Christian orders or been trained in the rabbinical tradition." In effect suggesting that he alone was capable of giving an unbiased report, since he had no religious commitment, he made a plea for money, so that "a new generation of uncommitted scholars" might have "the means of probing the significance [of the Scrolls] without fear or favor, undeterred by religious or academic pressure." (LaWS.DSS 20-21)[7]

John M. Allegro has proven ability as a scholar. He also has his own biases, as should be obvious from his close association with the secular humanist movement and his publishing of such works as *The Sacred Mushroom and the Cross: A Study of the Nature and Origins of Christianity Within the Fertility Cults of the Ancient Near East.* (AIJ.SM) In the following pages Allegro is quoted on a number of points. As a critic of the Christian faith his statements which substantiate Christian claims cannot be considered biased toward Christianity. Also, since Allegro is quoted by popularizers such as Ian Wilson (*Jesus: The Evidence*), it will help put Wilson's comments in the proper perspective. But first, some background:

In the 1948 printing of his book *Our Bible and the Ancient Manuscripts,* Sir Frederic Kenyon wrote:

> There is indeed no probability that we shall find manuscripts of the Hebrew text going back to a period before the formation of the text which we know as Massoretic. We can only arrive at an idea of it by a study of the earliest translations made from it.[8]

But even while Kenyon's book was being printed, discoveries were being made which would render similar statements false and outdated. On the northwest corner of the Dead Sea, Bedouin shepherds of the Ta'amirah tribe had begun to pull ancient scrolls from the caves of Qumran. Months and even years of intrigue gradually brought the documents to public light as archaeologists worked frantically to recover the scrolls intact before they could be broken up and the pieces sold as souvenirs. Many were lost, but those that survived were of major significance. Prior to the discovery of the Dead Sea Scrolls, the earliest known manuscript of the Hebrew Old Testament was from the late ninth or early tenth century AD. Now with one magnificent discovery, we possess manuscripts dating from as early as the third century BC.

Confirmation of Accuracy

What have we learned from the Dead Sea Scrolls? First, they confirm that between the first and ninth centuries AD, the Jewish scribal copying of the Old Testament Scriptures was accomplished with remarkably few errors. With the exception of minute copying errors here and there, the Dead Sea manuscripts exhibited virtually identical readings to their counterparts of the ninth century. What this means is that many scholars' doubts concerning the accuracy of the Massoretic (Masoretic) text (MT) as a reflection of the first-century text were unfounded. Allegro reports:

> Excitement had run high among scholars when it became known in 1948 that a cave near the Dead Sea had produced pre-Massoretic texts of the Bible. Was it possible that we were at last going to see traditions differing seriously from the standard text, which would throw some important light on this hazy period of variant traditions? In some quarters the question was raised with some apprehension, especially when news-hungry journalists began to talk about changing the whole Bible in view of the latest discoveries, but closer examination showed that, on the whole, the differences shown by the first Isaiah scroll were of *little* account, and could often be explained on the basis of scribal errors, or differing orthography, syntax, or grammatical form. (AIJ.DSS 65, emphasis ours)

Old Testament Quotes in the New Testament

Have you ever wondered why, when the New Testament quotes the Old Testament, the quote many times does not seem to match up exactly to its Old Testament counterpart? The Dead Sea Scrolls provide key information for answering that question.

Most Christians are familiar with the efforts of scholars to determine, through textual criticism, the most accurate rendering of what the original New Testament writings (called the autographs) said. In light of differing expressions in the various manuscripts which have come down to us from the first century, a central question which occupies the attention of New Testament scholars has obviously been, "What did the originals say?" Many Christians, however, take it for granted that the Old Testament text has been fairly well fixed. The MT has been accepted as the standard reliable rendering of the Old Testament originals, and, as stated above, the Dead Sea Scrolls confirm the MT of the ninth century as an accurate copy of the first-century AD text. But what the Dead Sea Scrolls also confirm is that the first-century text supporting the MT was not the only textual tradition of the Old Testament.

After the destruction of Jerusalem in AD 70, Jewish religious leaders recognized that the future of Judaism, with the Temple in Jerusalem now abolished, depended upon preserving the Old Testament Law in the hearts of the people. As Allegro states,

It was therefore essential for the unity of the Faith that the text of this work should be standardized and given the authority of the one favored recension, from which no serious variance would be allowed. A synod was convened at Jamnia, near Jaffa, between AD 90 and 100, at which certain disputed questions regarding the acceptability of some of the books were decided. At this time also, besides the text of the canon, the type of text to be used as standard must have been agreed upon, and perhaps even the type of script in which future copies of the law would be written.... Thus, from the end of the 1st century the standard text of the Bible was more or less fixed and has been preserved for us to the present time with remarkably few variations. (AIJ.DSS 60)

But since the Dead Sea Scrolls predate the council of Jamnia, they confirm that other textual traditions of the Old Testament books were widely circulated during the first-century period.

The Septuagint is a translation of the Hebrew Old Testament into Greek. There are also some additional books included. It is difficult to tell from tradition exactly how the Septuagint was prepared, but it is generally accepted that the Torah was translated by seventy-two Jewish elders in or around Alexandria during the reign of Ptolemy II Philadelphus in the middle of the third century BC. Various portions of the rest of the Old Testament were translated before and after this time. At least by 117 BC, the entire translation of the Hebrew Old Testament into Greek had been completed. (HaR.IOT 228ff.)

It is the Septuagint (LXX) version, rather than the MT, which appears to be quoted by most of the New Testament writers at several points. The Gospel According to Matthew may be the only book in the New Testament which does not have Old Testament quotes matching the LXX. The Gospel According to John and the book of Acts contain quotations which agree almost word for word with the LXX. Approximately half of Paul's Old Testament quotations agree fairly closely with the LXX. The question naturally arises: "Why did Jewish writers, steeped as they were in Hebrew culture, quote a Greek version of the Old Testament when a more accurate Hebrew version would have been more readily available?"

The Dead Sea Scrolls give evidence that the New Testament writers were not the only ones who considered the LXX version just as reliable as the MT version. While the scrolls do confirm that the MT is a faithful rendering of first-century Hebrew texts, they produce evidence that other Old Testament texts containing variants to those lying behind the MT were also in wide circulation among the Jews during the first century AD. In other words, the LXX is a Greek translation of another Hebrew version of the Old Testament used by many Jews.

The existence of several different textual traditions of the Hebrew Old Testament brought about several other Greek translations of the Old Testament. In the middle of the second century AD, Aquila brought out a translation agreeing more with the MT. Another version by Theodotion appeared at the dawn of the third century, and was followed a short time later with a version by Symmachus. Attempting to bring all these together, Origen, in the first half of the third century produced the *Hexapla*. This version contained six columns, the first for the Hebrew of the current standard text, the second for the Hebrew transliterated into Greek letters, the third for Aquila's version, the fourth for that of Symmachus, the fifth for the LXX with revisions by Origen himself and the sixth for the Greek version of Theodotion.

The Hebrew text of some of the scrolls found at Qumran, including one dated possibly as early as the end of the third century BC, clearly agrees with the LXX over the MT. There are also places in these documents where the Hebrew agrees with neither the text standing behind the LXX nor that standing behind the MT. In view of these findings, we may conclude that during the first century AD a number of different versions of the Old Testament were circulating within the Jewish and Jewish-Christian communities. Geza Vermes reports:

> The Qumran Scrolls of the Old Testament represent several textual or recensional traditions and not just a single one. Some biblical books testify to the *textus receptus* of the later Masoretic tradition; others, especially the books of Samuel and Jeremiah and the chronology of Kings, echo the Hebrew underlying the Greek Bible; others still correspond to the Samaritan version. (VeG.JWJ 104)

Just as in our day when different Christians quote from different versions of the Bible, Jews and Christians of the first century also quoted from different versions of the Old Testament Scriptures. It should not be surprising, then, that New Testament quotations of Old Testament Scriptures do not match up exactly. The differences do not indicate a deficiency in God's word, but rather our inability at this date to verify the original text of either the Old or New Testament. What this means for biblical scholarship is that not only must New Testament scholars work to recover the most faithful renderings of the original New Testament text, but Old Testament scholars also must pursue the discovery of the most reliable text reflecting the original Old Testament writings.

In these matters of textual criticism we must keep in mind that differences between various textual traditions are matters of detail with no bearing on major doctrines of Christian or Jewish faith.

Was John Influenced by Greek Gnosticism?

The gospel account most criticized as least reflective of the true historical Jesus has been the Gospel of John. Critics have often charged that the gospel and epistles of John draw heavily on Greek thought. A recent article in the *Atlantic Monthly*, for example, speaks of "its modest biographical content and its overlay of seemingly Hellenistic philosophy." (MuCu.W 42) The Dead Sea Scrolls, however, shed a different light on this issue. Allegro states:

It is a fact that the Qumran library has profoundly affected the study of the Johannine writings and many long-held conceptions have had to be radically revised. No longer can John be regarded as the most Hellenistic of the Evangelists; his "gnosticism" and the whole framework of his thought is seen now to spring directly from a Jewish sectarianism rooted in Palestinian soil, and his material recognized as founded in the earliest layers of gospel traditions. (AIJ.DSS 142-43)

This evidence from Qumran confirmed archaeological evidence from previous years. As Ian Wilson correctly points out:

The first shock to the nineteenth-century Germans, with their dismissive attitude toward the John gospel, came with the discovery and publication of the Rylands fragment. If a copy of the John gospel was in use in provincial Egypt c. 125 AD, its original, if it was composed at Ephesus (and at least no one has suggested it was written in Egypt), must have been written significantly earlier, probably at least a decade before 100 AD, as most scholars now recognize. A second shock was the discovery of the much-publicized Dead Sea Scrolls. Although generally thought to have been written by the Essenes, a Jewish sect contemporary with Jesus, they proved disappointingly to throw little new light on Jesus and early Christianity, at least in any direct way. The Scrolls contain no recognizable mention of Jesus, just as the Christian gospels, surprisingly, fail to refer to the Essenes. But the intriguing feature of the Scrolls is that their authors, undeniably full-blooded Jews, were using in Jesus' time precisely the type of language and imagery previously thought "Hellenistic" in John. As is well known, the John gospel prologue speaks of a conflict between light and darkness. The whole gospel is replete with phrases such as "the spirit of truth," "the light of life," "walking in the darkness," "children of light," and "eternal life." A welter of such phrases and imagery occur in the Dead Sea Scrolls' Manual of Discipline. (Wil.JTE 41)

Thus scholars were forced to recognize that John's imagery arose out of Jewish, not Greek (Hellenistic) or gnostic roots. In addition, scholars had to reckon with John's "detailed and accurate references to geographical features of Jerusalem and its environs before the city and its Temple were destroyed in 70 AD" (Wil.JTE 44) It is John, for example, who pinpoints the location of John the Baptist as being in Aenon (meaning "spring," the one near Salim), approximately a mile away (3:23). John distinguishes Cana as the one in Galilee as opposed to the Cana near Sidon (2:1). John not only says that Jesus took his disciples through Samaria, but also specifies the city of Sychar, and even more specifically, "the parcel of ground that Jacob gave his son Joseph; and Jacob's well was there," as it still is today (4:5,6). Only John mentions the Pool of Siloam (9:7) and the Pool of Bethesda with its five porches (5:2). Remains of both pools have been uncovered in Jerusalem. Also, only John distinguishes "Bethany beyond the Jordan" (1:28) from Bethany near Jerusalem, "about two miles off" (11:18). There is no doubt that John, like the other gospel writers, had definite theological purposes for his writing. Yet recognizing this point, the eminently qualified archaeologists, Myers and Strange, conclude:

> These examples could be multiplied many times and supplemented with examples of lore, customs, and other bits of information known to the author of this gospel. The point we wish to make, however, is simply that an unprejudiced reading of the Gospel of John seems to suggest that it is in fact based on a historical and geographical tradition, though not one that simply repeats information from the synoptics. In other words, this gospel, as well as Matthew, Mark and Luke, firmly anchors its tradition in the land, not in an ideal, heavenly Israel. (McE.AREC 161)

All of this evidence affirms what John himself claimed: "This is the disciple who bears witness of these things, and wrote these things; and we know that his witness is true."

SCHOLARLY CONCLUSIONS

Increasingly, archaeological evidence has continued to illuminate and confirm the reliability of the New Testament reports. Listen to the conclusions of several archaeologists and scholars of antiquity. William F. Albright wrote:

> The excessive skepticism shown toward the Bible by important historical schools of the eighteenth and nineteenth centuries, certain phases of which still appear periodically, has been progressively discredited. Discovery after discovery has established the accuracy of innumerable details, and has brought increased recognition to the value of the Bible as a source of history. (AIW.AP 127-28)

In another work he predicted what continues to be affirmed:

> As critical study of the Bible is more and more influenced by the rich new material from the ancient Near East we shall see a steady rise in respect for the historical significance of now neglected or despised passages and details in the Old and New Testament. (AIW.FSA 81)

Dr. Otto Betz of Tübingen concluded that "after the Dead Sea Scrolls were discovered, you could no longer say there was no historical Jesus."[10]

Some liberals of the higher critical approach have become "skeptical about skepticism."

Merrill Unger relates:

> The role which archaeology is performing in New Testament research (as well as that of the Old Testament) in expediting scientific study, balancing critical theory, illustrating, elucidating, supplementing and authenticating

historical and cultural backgrounds, constitutes the one bright spot in the future of criticism of the Sacred text. (UnM.AOT 25-26)

Millar Burrows, a scholar of exceptional stature, reveals concerning his attitude toward the Dead Sea Scrolls:

> It is quite true that as a liberal Protestant I do not share all the beliefs of my more conservative brethren. It is my considered conclusion, however, that if one will go through any of the historic statements of the Christian faith he will find nothing that has been or can be disproved by the Dead Sea Scrolls. (BuM.ML 39)

The Yale archaeologist further contends:

> Archaeological work has unquestionably strengthened confidence in the reliability of the Scripture record. More than one archaeologist has found his respect for the Bible increased by the experience of excavation in Palestine. (BuM.WM 1)

> On the whole such evidence as archaeology has afforded thus far, especially by providing additional and older manuscripts of the books of the Bible, strengthens our confidence in the accuracy with which the text has been transmitted through the centuries. (BuM.WM 42)

Though archaeology cannot answer all our questions about the past, it does provide one more source of confirmation that what the New Testament reports to us is reliable and accurate.

12

THE JEWISH FACTOR

J ust after World War II, a Scottish minister, R. A. Stewart, wrote: "A proper historical understanding of the New Testament is impossible without a detailed knowledge of Jewish literature and thought." (StRA.ERT 5)

His words proved almost prophetic—many Jewish scholars today are in the forefront of affirming the historicity of Jesus. Geza Vermes, David Flusser, Shmuel Safrai and Pinchas Lapide lead the way in reclaiming Jesus as a striking Jewish person of the first century. Vermes even asserts that "no objective and enlightened student of the gospels can help but be struck by the incomparable superiority of Jesus." (VeG.JTJ 224)

Professor Donald A. Hagner, Associate Professor of New Testament at Fuller Theological Seminary, has written a detailed analysis of the current reclamation of Jesus in Jewish scholarship. Concerning the contributions provided from the Hebrew perspective, he states:

> It will be obvious that Jewish scholars are in a particularly advantageous position to understand the teaching of Jesus. Familiar with the Bible (Old Testament), the development of early Judaism, the Jewish background of the gospels, and often learned in the difficult world of rabbinic literature, they are often able not only to place Jesus in historical context but also to enter the mental world of Jesus and to capture every Jewish nuance in his words. (HaDA.R 27)

The Jewishness of Jesus and the pervasive Hebraic quality of his surroundings repeatedly surface in the gospel accounts. Yet much of past New Testament scholarship has failed to deal with this critical aspect of the life of the historical Jesus. If one is to see Jesus of Nazareth as he actually was when he traversed the land of Palestine, then one cannot ignore the evidence of his Jewishness. In this chapter, then, we will focus on the Semitic flavor of the gospel accounts, Hebrew characterizations of Jesus and questions surrounding the Jewishness of Jesus.

SEMITIC FLAVOR OF THE GOSPEL ACCOUNTS

Linguistic Elements

There are good indications that Jesus, as well as some of the disciples, was trilingual. Though we will focus here on Aramaic and Hebrew as languages used by Jesus, there is evidence that he may well have conversed also in *Greek*. It needs to be emphasized that to speak Greek did not necessarily mean one had to be Greek or Hellenized. If for no other reason than to establish friendly trading relationships with those of other languages, we may expect that many first-century Jewish people learned to speak Greek. More to the point, there is good evidence within the gospel accounts themselves that Jesus could speak Greek. In Mark 7:24ff. Jesus says to the Greek-speaking Syrophoenician woman, "It is not good to take the children's bread and throw it to the dogs." The Greek word for "dogs" is a diminutive indicating household pets or puppies rather than wild dogs or filthy strays. Neither Hebrew nor Aramaic has a form corresponding to the diminutive. Therefore, if Jesus did not speak Greek, the Greek writer used an unnatural expression in translating his words. Again, in John 7:35, the Jews question Jesus' statement that he is going to a place where they won't be able to find him. They ask:

> Where does this man intend to go that we shall not find Him? He is not intending to go to the Dispersion among the Greeks, and teach the Greeks, is He?

In view of Jesus' common practice of dining with sinners and tax collectors, the Jews must have had no doubts about his ability to converse in the Greek language.

Thomas and Gundry reveal several other indications in the gospel narratives that Jesus and at least some of his disciples could speak Greek:

> John 12:20-23 strongly suggest that Philip, Andrew, and Jesus understood and spoke Greek...In the Greek text of John 21 Jesus uses two different Greek words for love and for tending the flock, and Peter uses two different words for know. However, none of these pairs can be reproduced in Hebrew or Aramaic; this was apparently a conversation originally carried on in Greek. Also, the play on the Greek words petra and petros in Matthew 16:18 cannot be reproduced in Hebrew or Aramaic and is best explained as occurring in a discussion originally carried on in Greek. In all likelihood, Jesus' conversations with the Syrophoenician woman, the Roman centurion, and Pilate were in Greek. Stephen (Acts 7) and James (Acts 15) quote from the Septuagint, thus giving evidence of their facility in the Greek language. (ThR.H 310-11)

Granting that Jesus probably spoke at least some Greek, one cannot fully appreciate him as a historical figure when viewed apart from what were probably his two primary languages: Aramaic and Hebrew.

Aramaic, a Semitic language very similar to Hebrew, is no longer spoken except in a considerably revised form in the three small Syrian villages of Malula, Bakha and Jubb Adin. But Aramaic used to be the *lingua franca* of the Persian Empire, and scholars have generally concluded that Jesus, like most of the inhabitants of Palestine, spoke Aramaic. The gospel accounts reflect this Semitic background in many ways:

- When the gospel sayings of Jesus and stories about him are translated from Greek back into Aramaic, "They are seen to be marked by regular poetical rhythm, and even, at times, rhyme." (BrF.NTD 39) This quality is an indication of the oral tradition behind the gospels.

- The gospel accounts contain several words that are definitely Aramaic and others thought to be. For example: *talitha cum,* "maid, arise"; *abba,* "father"; *ephphatha,* "be opened"; *kepha,* "rock"; *toma,* "Thomas"; *Kan'ana,* "the zealot"; *Bar* (for example, in Bartholomew), "son"; *rabbuni,* "rabboni"; *perisha* (meaning separated one), "Pharisee"; *golgolta* (meaning skull), "Golgotha"; *hakel dema* (meaning bloody ground), "Akelddama"; *shiloha,* "Siloam"; and *reka* (meaning silly fool), "raca." (DaG.JJ 11-14)

Hebrew, as a spoken language used by Jesus and other first-century Jews, is increasingly accepted by previously unbending scholars. Matthew Black, a staunch advocate of Aramaic as the primary language, now admits, "We must nevertheless allow possibly more than has been done before for the use of Hebrew in addition to (or instead of) Aramaic by Jesus Himself." (BlM.AA 47)

Some of the main arguments for the use of Hebrew include the following:

1. Harris Birkeland, a Scandinavian Semitic languages scholar, argues that the gospels preserve Aramaic words used by Jesus because he normally spoke Hebrew. When the Hebrew was translated to Greek, the Aramaic remained (though in a transliterated form). It would be similar to an English translation of a work written by a Russian who occasionally used French words. The French would remain in French. (BaJ.WL 15)

2. The Dead Sea Scroll discoveries "include both Hebrew and Aramaic material, but the quantitative predominance seems to be with the Hebrew (even excluding the actual biblical texts and counting only the fresh and original compositions)." (BaJ.WL 20) Hebrew was used for both religious and secular documents discovered, and appears to be a spoken vernacular of the first century.

3. Rabbinic statements attest the use of Hebrew as a spoken language. In the Mishnah, tractate Eduyoth 1.3 states: "A man must speak in the language of his teacher," and suggests that Hebrew would therefore naturally be preserved. More definite are statements like that of Rabbi Meir toward the

middle of the second century AD: "Everyone who is settled in the land of Israel, and speaks the sacred language...is assured that he is a son of the age to come."[1] Later in the second century, Rabbi Judah the Prince argued, "Why (use) the Syrian language [i.e., Aramaic] in the land of Israel? Either the sacred language or the Greek language."[2]

4. According to Luke 4:16-19, in light of the standard practice of synagogues, Jesus had to know Hebrew, and many in his audience in Nazareth probably understand what he read in Hebrew.

5. The fact that Hebrew was a language of daily communication among family members is strongly suggested by ossuary inscriptions from Dominus Flevit (on the Mount of Olives) and Mount Scopus. Some of the all-Hebrew inscriptions read: "Martha, our mother"; "Salome, the proselyte"; and, "Salome wife of Hannania, son of the Nazarite." (MeE.AREC 68)

   In addition, inscriptions on public buildings (i.e., meant to be read by the public) indicate Hebrew as a means of regular communication. A stone from the top southwest corner of the Temple enclosure (pinnacle of the Temple) was found inscribed in Hebrew: "Belonging to the place of trumpeting." (MeE.AREC 69)

   Archaeologists have also recovered vessels bearing the names of their owners in Hebrew. This evidence again speaks of the use of Hebrew on a daily personal level between family members. (MeE.AREC 70)

6. The compilation of the Mishnah, at the beginning of the third century AD, in a live Hebrew language (with the exception of about fifteen paragraphs and scattered words out of almost 800 pages) suggests strongly that the Jews continued to cling to their sacred language in spite of the disastrous wars with Rome in AD 70 and 135. James Barr, Professor of Semitic Languages and Literature in the University of Manchester, explains the declining use of Hebrew after AD 200 by noting that the blows to national pride in AD 70 and 135 were enough to erode the desire of most Jews to cling to the Hebrew language in spite of other languages being used all around them. (BaJ.WL 28)

7. In the gospel accounts themselves, even more Hebrew words than Aramaic words appear. For example: *levonah*, "frankincense"; *mammon; wai*, "Woe!"; *rabbi; Beelzebub; corban; Satan; common*, "cummin"; *raca* (yes, it was listed as Aramaic too!); *moreh*, "rebel"; *bath* (a wet measure); *kor* (a dry measure); *zuneem*, "tares"; *mor* (myrrh); *sheekmah*, "sycamore"; and *amen* (used approximately 100 times in the gospel accounts).

8. The word order in much of the Greek manuscripts of the gospels is actually more Hebrew than Greek. (LiRL.HT 9-10)

It is important to note that both Hebrew and Aramaic are Semitic languages and they have many similarities. These distinctly Semitic features show up often in the gospel accounts. For example, the repeated use of *and* has led many scholars to the conclusion that a Hebrew or Aramaic original stands behind at least some of our present Greek text. Luke 2:7 illustrates the point well. It reads:

> *And* it came about that while they were there, the days were completed for her to give birth. *And* she gave birth to her firstborn son; *and* she wrapped Him in cloths, *and* laid Him in a manger, because there was no room for them in the inn. *And* in the same region there were some shepherds staying out in the fields, *and* keeping watch over their flock by night. *And* an angel of the Lord suddenly stood before them, *and* the glory of the Lord shone around them; *and* they were terribly frightened. *And* the angel said to them…

Had the original report been composed in Greek, the text would have read something like,

> Then it came about that while they were there, the days were completed for her to give birth. When she gave birth to their firstborn son, wrapping Him in cloths she laid Him in a manger, because there was no room for them in the inn. In the same region there were some shepherds staying out in the fields where they were keeping watch over their flocks by night. Suddenly, an angel of the Lord stood before them, the glory of the Lord shining around them. They were terribly frightened, but the angel said to them…

Taking all the evidence of Aramaic and Hebrew together, the gospel reports and those they describe become undeniably Semitic.

Whether Jesus spoke Hebrew, Aramaic or a mixture of both, the arguments above attest to the faithfulness of the gospel texts as reliable eyewitness reports of the things Jesus said.

Pedagogical Elements

Jewish scholarship has helped most to identify Jesus' Jewishness by showing the parallels between his teaching and rabbinic teaching. When you compare these teachings, you can begin to see how far-fetched the idea is that the life of Jesus was made up by zealous churchmen of the second and third centuries. As the leadership of the church shifted from Jerusalem to Antioch to Rome between the first and fourth centuries, there also was a predominant shift from a Jewish Christianity to a Gentile Christianity. In fact, the history of the first two centuries of the church confirms that it was primarily Gentile in character by the beginning of the second century AD. It would therefore be highly unlikely for a Gentile of the second century or later to mold an account of the life of Jesus which so thoroughly reflected the first-century Hebrew culture.

The Jews of Jesus' day were meticulous educators, as they have been throughout most of their history. A passage from the Mishnah (Aboth 5.15) demonstrates their active concern about what their students absorbed:

> There are four types of people who sit in front of the sages: The sponge, the funnel, the strainer and the sifter. The sponge—it soaks up everything; the funnel—it takes in at one end and lets out at the other; the strainer—it lets out the wine and retains the dregs; and the sifter—it lets out the bran dust and retains the fine flour.

In order to stimulate the student not to just "memorize the right answers," the teacher, or rabbi, would ask questions of his students. Not only were the students expected to be able to answer the questions, but they also were expected to answer them by phrasing equally good questions, showing they had thought through the original questions thoroughly. Perhaps this is why Rabbi Hillel said, "A timid student does not learn." (Aboth 2.6) David Bivin, the director of the Jerusalem School of Synoptic Studies, writes:

> This pattern of answering questions with questions was so common that in the Hebrew of Jesus' day the word for "question" came to be a synonym for "answer." (BiD.Q 5)

Bivin gives several examples which illustrate the deep Jewish roots of Jesus' learning and teaching styles:

> Twelve-year-old Jesus was lost and finally discovered by his parents, "sitting in the Temple among the rabbis, listening to them and asking them questions" (Luke 2:46). The gospel writer comments in the following verse, "And all those listening to him were amazed at his wise answers." If Jesus was only asking questions, how is it that the listeners were impressed by his answers? This would seem very strange indeed if one did not know that in the rabbinic world in which Jesus lived, a student's answers were given in the form of questions....

Jesus answered a question with a question on other occasions as well. When he was asked by the Temple authorities what right he had to do "these things" (cleansing the Temple), he answered by saying, "I will also ask you something. Now tell me, was John's baptism of God or of men?" (Luke 20:3-4)...

The best example in the teaching of Jesus of the kind of question a rabbi commonly would ask his students is found in Luke 20:41-44, in which he asked:

> How can one say that the Messiah is the descendant (literally "son") of David? David himself says in the book of Psalms, "the Lord said to my lord, 'Sit here at my right hand until I make your enemies your footstool.'" David calls him lord, so how can he be his descendant?
>
> This is a typical rabbinic riddle based on a seeming contradiction in a passage of Scripture. (BiD.Q 5)

The first of Hillel's rules of interpretation was called *kal vachomer* (simple and complex). (BiD.PRI 1) This principle has to do with deducing something that is not very apparent from something that is apparent or already known. It often uses the words how much more as in "Silence becomes a scholar; how much more a fool" (Tosefta: Pesachim 9:2). Mishnah: Sanhedrin 6.5 is another example:

> Rabbi Meir said, "While the man is in agony, what does the Tongue say? 'My head is hurting! My arm is hurting!' If the Scripture has thus spoken: 'I agonize over the blood of the wicked,' *how much more* over the blood of the righteous that is shed?"

Jesus used this same rabbinic device in his teaching. One example is found in Matthew 7:9-11 where he says:

> Or what man is there among you, when his son shall ask him for a loaf, will give him a stone? Or if he shall ask for a fish, he will not give him a snake, will he? If you then, being evil, know how to give good gifts to your children, *how much more* shall your Father who is in heaven give what is good to those who ask Him!

In Matthew 6:28-30, Jesus says:

> But if God so arrays the grass of the field, which is alive today and tomorrow is thrown into the furnace, will He not *much more* do so for you, O men of little faith?

Jesus, being Jewish and thoroughly acquainted with the teachings of the rabbis, makes a number of statements which have close parallels in the rabbinic literature. Professor Gustaf Dalman, founder of the Institute for the Study of Antiquity in the Holy Land, gives the following among many others (DaG.JJ 225-29):

- "And by your standard of measure, it shall be measured to you" (Matthew 7:2; Mark 4:24; Luke 6:38).

  vs.

  "With the measure with which one measures, it will be measured unto him" (Sot. 1.7; Tos. Sot. 3.1,2; Siphre, 28*b*).

- "Therefore whatever you want others to do for you, do so for them; for this is the Law and the Prophets" (Matthew 7:12; Luke 6:31).

  vs.

  "What is hateful to thee, do it not unto thy neighbour. This is the whole Law and the rest is the interpretation thereof" (Hillel. b. Sab. 31a). [The "Golden Rule" has been taught in many different forms. Jesus' version is unique in that it is a positive rather than negative approach. He does not say "Don't do what you don't want others to do to you," like Hillel. This approach only keeps one from doing harmful actions. Rather, Jesus says, "Do what you would like others to do for you." This approach, while eliminating harmful actions, also adds the responsibility to do acts of kindness, benevolence, etc. to others.]

- "Blessed are the merciful, for they shall receive mercy" (Matthew 5:7).

  vs.

  "Whenever thou art merciful, God is merciful to thee" (p. Bab. k. 6c).

- "For everyone who exalts himself shall be humbled, and he who humbles himself shall be exalted" (Luke 14:11).

  vs.

  "My humiliation is my exaltation, and my exaltation is my humiliation" (Hillel. Lev. R. I. (2b).

While the similarities of Jesus' teaching to that of the rabbis provide substantial evidence for the historicity of Jesus as a first-century teacher, some may wonder if there was anything at all unique about Jesus. Rabbi H. G. Enelow has observed the following tension between Jewish and Christian writers:

> Jewish writers have tried to prove that anything taught by Jesus may be found in Jewish literature, and that therefore he could not be called original; while Christians have deemed it necessary to defend Jesus against the charge of borrowing or reproducing from Jewish sources, lest his originality be impugned. (EnH.JV 14)

Traditionally, Jewish people have been taught that anything good in the gospels is nothing new; anything new is nothing good. The truth is that there is much that flows out of the teaching of the rabbis, and there is much that is unique to Jesus. A good example is in Jesus' use of parables as a teaching device.

The two standard authoritative reference works on the parables of Jesus are *The Parables of the Kingdom* by C. H. Dodd and *The Parables of Jesus* by Göttingen professor of New Testament and late Jewish religion Joachim Jeremias. Both affirm that readers must interpret Jesus' parables within their original life setting. They defend the parables as being authentically from Jesus, for the content of the parables emerges from the historical Jewish situation of Jesus as opposed to the situation of the early church.

Christians and non-Christians alike have almost universally appreciated the parables of Jesus as a supreme teaching device. But it is important to realize that this mode of instruction was not unique to Jesus. Jewish literature preserves more than four thousand rabbinic parables. Here is an example of one such parable:

A person in whom there are good deeds and who has studied the Torah extensively, what is he like? A man who builds first [of] stones and then afterwards [of] mud bricks. Even if a large quantity of water were to collect beside the stones, it would not destroy them. But a person in whom there are not good deeds, though he has studied Torah, what is he like? A man who builds first [of] mud bricks and then afterwards [of] stones. Even if only a little water collects, it immediately undermines them. (BiD.L 6)

Now, compare the above parable with the parable which Jesus gives in Matthew 7:24-27:

Therefore everyone who hears these words of Mine, and acts upon them, may be compared to a wise man, who built his house upon the rock. And the rain descended, and the floods came, and the winds blew, and burst against that house; and yet it did not fall, for it had been founded upon the rock. And everyone who hears these words of Mine, and does not act upon them, will be like a foolish man, who built his house upon the sand. And the rain descended, and the floods came, and the winds blew, and burst against that house; and it fell, and great was its fall.

So what makes Jesus so different? What was it that Jesus said that seems to have caught the attention of the world for the last 2000 years? Why was he any different than the rabbis who preceded him? Synoptic studies scholar David Bivin answers that question here:

It was not the way he taught or even the general content of his teaching that made Jesus unique among the rabbis. What *was* unique about Jesus was who he claimed to be, and he rarely ever taught without claiming to be not only God's Messiah, but more startlingly, *Immanuel,* "God with us."

It is just this claim that marks a difference between Jesus' parable of the house built on bedrock and all the other rabbinic parables which deal with the same theme. All the other rabbis spoke of knowing and doing the words of Torah, but Jesus introduced his parable with the words, "A person who hears *these words of mine* and does them...." No other rabbi is recorded as ever having spoken like that or having made the claims inherent in Jesus' words. He was clearly speaking as only God would speak, and none of his contemporaries could have missed or ignored that fact. (BiD.L 5)

The rabbinic parallels to sayings of Jesus confirm again that the gospel accounts give us a reliable picture of the historical Jesus. The Jesus of the gospels was not a Jesus made up by the early church, but a thoroughly Jewish teacher from within the Jewish culture, yet one who spoke out in a uniquely prophetic fashion.

One final Semitic element we will observe in Jesus' teaching style is his use of hyperbole. Hyperbole is a common Middle Eastern means of communication in which the speaker uses exaggeration for effect. The hearers understand that the expression is not to be taken literally, only the intent behind the expression.

George Lamsa, translator, commentator and author of more than twenty books, was raised speaking Aramaic. In his *A Key to the Original Gospel*, he gives many examples of Semitic use of hyperbole. Among them:

> "If you can build that house in two months, I will kill myself." This means, "The task can never be accomplished."

> "If you can buy this pair of shoes for less than two dollars, I will change myself into a donkey." This means that the shoes cannot be bought for less.

> "If you marry that woman, I will cut off my right arm." This means, "It is an impossibility."

> "If I don't tell the truth, you can pluck out my eye." This means, "What I say is true."

> "If I married that beautiful girl, I would never die." This means, "The happiness of the marriage eliminates the thought of the death." (LaG.IBE 79)

Hyperbole in the gospels is sometimes subtle unless one understands the culture. For example, in the parable of the prodigal son, nothing could be more distasteful to a Jew than to be the servant of a Gentile and taking care of his swine.

At other times, hyperbole is more direct. In Luke 14:26, Jesus says:

> If anyone comes to Me, and does not hate his own father and mother and wife and children and brothers and sisters, yes, and even his own life, he cannot be My disciple.

Obviously Jesus does not mean literal hatred toward one's parents, for he commanded his followers to love even their enemies.[3] He is using hyperbole to communicate the depth of love a disciple must have for him if he is truly committed to him. That the early Christians understood this is seen in Paul's words to Timothy: "But if anyone does not provide for his own, and especially for those of his household, he has denied the faith, and is worse than an unbeliever."[4] Matthew 10:37,38 more clearly communicates to the modern reader what Luke reports Jesus saying by the use of hyperbole: "He who loves father or mother more than Me is not worthy of Me; and he who loves son or daughter more than Me is not worthy of Me."

Robert Stein, Professor of New Testament at Bethel Theological Seminary, expresses one reason why exaggeration or hyperbole was especially important to Jesus:

> At times exaggeration serves a most useful function in speech and literature. It frequently has great mnemonic value since it creates a picture that is unforgettable. Who can forget the figures of a speck in one eye and a log in another, a camel going through the eye of a needle, straining gnats and swallowing camels? Such pictures are long remembered. No doubt Jesus

intended such language to aid his hearers in remembering what he taught, for without access to pencil and paper or cassette recorders the vast majority of his audience had no means of preserving what he taught other than to memorize his words. The use of exaggeration made the task of remembering easier. (StR.DS 94)

Cultural Elements

The setting of all four gospel accounts is unmistakably first-century Hebrew. Some events seem strange to us but are perfectly natural in the Jewish culture of Jesus' day. For example, Luke 7:38 speaks of a woman weeping and wetting Jesus' feet with her tears. Weeping was an important part of Jewish culture. Professional mourners were hired for funerals, and many Jews had "tear vases" where they collected the tears of their grief. The woman described by Luke may literally have been pouring out the tears from her tear vase to indicate to Jesus her sorrow for her sins. The present day visitor to Israel may observe many of these ancient tear vases in museums there.

Luke 2:24 speaks of another of many cultural practices mentioned in the gospel narratives. In obedience to Leviticus 12:2,6,8 Joseph and Mary brought the sacrifice required after the birth of a child. Their offering of two turtledoves or pigeons indicates that they were among the poor of the land.

Hebrew marriage customs help to explain what otherwise appears to be a contradiction in Matthew 1:18,19. In verse 18, Mary is only betrothed to Joseph, whereas in verse 19, Joseph is called her "husband." The Reverend James Freeman, who compiled a vast collection of Bible customs, explains:

> Espousal among the Hebrews was something more than what a mere marriage engagement is with us. It was considered the beginning of marriage, was as legally binding as marriage itself, and could not be broken off save by a bill of divorce. Hence we find that Joseph is called the "husband" of Mary. (FrJM.M 330)

Jesus' confrontation with the Sadducees in Mark 12 accords with what we know about the attitude of the Sadducees regarding levirate marriage. In Yebamoth 4.6*b* of the Palestinian Talmud, the Sadducees again use levirate marriage, this time to mock the Pharisees. There they pose the hypothetical problem of one of thirteen brothers who is required to be joined in levirate marriage with the widows of his twelve deceased brothers.

The account of the woman with the hemorrhage becomes much more meaningful and realistic in light of the Jewish laws of purity.[5] The woman's condition meant that she had been continuously ceremonially impure for twelve years, and that by the law, touching Jesus' garments would defile him. She is understandably frightened when she learns that Jesus detected her act. And can you imagine the rare sense of compassion she must have felt when Jesus said to her, "Daughter, your faith has made you well; go in peace."[6]

The synoptic gospels speak of Jesus cleansing the Temple at the beginning of his last

week in Jerusalem. John indicates that he had previously performed the same operation at the beginning of his ministry. It was not that Jesus objected to the exchanging of
money. Roman coins, which most of the people carried and which were stamped with
the image of Caesar, could not be used in the Temple under the Mosaic prescription
against graven images. Therefore there was a legitimate need for moneychangers—the
people needed the Jewish coins because they contained only geometric, floral or ceremonial decorations. But Jewish sources tell us that some of the priestly families made
personal profits on the dealings there. (FIJ.JJ 13)[7] What incensed Jesus was the corruption
and commotion going on in a place that was supposed to represent God's majesty and
purity, a place that was supposed to be used for prayer.

One striking feature of the gospel narratives is that they speak of Jesus going almost
exclusively to Jewish towns in order to carry out his ministry. The accounts record that
Jesus entered only two cities which were not primarily orthodox Jewish: the Gentile city
of Sidon and the Samaritan city of Sychar. Since we are told of no incident occurring in
Sidon, we have no report of any ministry performed by Jesus inside a Gentile city. It is
striking that the gospels report Jesus going into Bethsaida, but not Julius, probably 100
yards away. He goes into obscure Nazareth, but not the major city of Sepphoris approximately three miles away. He goes into the country or regions of Decapolis, Caesarea
Philippi and Tyre, but not into the Gentile cities themselves. Everything in the historical geographical situation is thoroughly Jewish—orthodox Jewish.

The gospels make comments in a number of places which show that Jesus was very
pro-Semitic; some even sound strongly anti-Gentile. In Matthew 15:26 and Mark 7:27,
Jesus refers to Gentiles as "dogs" after stating, "I was sent only to the lost sheep of the
house of Israel." In Matthew 10:5,6, Jesus instructs his disciples not to go "in the way of
the Gentiles, and do not enter any city of the Samaritans." In John 4:22, Jesus, speaking as a Jew to a Samaritan, says, "You worship that which you do not know; we worship that which we know; for salvation is of the Jews."

Not only does the Hebrew culture reflected in the gospel accounts help to confirm
their authenticity, but it also helps establish the significance of the events described. A
good example is the descriptions given concerning the Last Supper. Pinchas Lapide
observes the event through Hebrew eyes:

> Jesus as a Jew, faithful to the Scriptures, celebrated the seder in the Passover
> night in Jerusalem, spoke the prescribed blessing over the "bread of afflic-
> tion" vicariously for all table companions, broke it, ate of it, and distrib-
> uted the remainder unto his disciples who consumed it "inclined," as it is
> fitting for freed slaves. (LaP.R 76)

Notice that the Passover meal was eaten in a reclining position. This was how the
wealthy and free ate. All in Israel, rich and poor, were to eat this meal in this position as
a remembrance of their deliverance from bondage in Egypt. Everything about the meal
was designed to cause the participants to remember the angel of death passing over the

homes marked with the blood of the lamb on the night of their deliverance. But what did Jesus tell his disciples to remember? "Do this in remembrance of Me."[8] From that point on, the memorial meal was for the purpose of remembering him. According to the chronology of John's gospel account, Jesus was dying on the cross the next day at the same time that the Passover lambs were being sacrificed in the Temple. The people called John the Baptist a prophet. It was he who said of Jesus some three years previously, "Behold the Lamb of God who takes away the sin of the world!"[9]

HEBREW CHARACTERIZATIONS OF JESUS

In view of the Jewishness of Jesus, there have been a number of attempts to identify the historical Jesus with particular Jewish factions. We briefly examine the chief suggested possibilities here:

Was Jesus an Essene?

With the comparatively recent discovery of the Dead Sea Scrolls, some writers have tried to identify Jesus with the Essenes, and even further with the Essene Teacher of Righteousness. (Scholars almost unanimously agree that Qumran was an Essene community.)[10] Even long before the scrolls were discovered, Renan is credited with calling Christianity "a sort of successful Essenism." (MiA.TBT 167) Another Frenchman, André Dupont-Sommer, following in Renan's footsteps, evaluated the information in the scrolls this way:

> Everything in the Jewish New Covenant (as found in the Scrolls) heralds and prepares the way for the Christian New Covenant. The Master from Galilee, as the New Testament writings present him to us, appears as an astonishing reincarnation of the Master of Justice (the Teacher of Righteousness) in many respects.... Like him, he was condemned and put to death. Like him, he ascended to heaven, near to God.... Like him, he will be the supreme judge at the end of time. Like him, he founded a church whose members eagerly awaited his glorious return. (MiA.TBT 167)

Scholars have reacted strongly against this kind of identification of Christianity with the Qumran community, and for good reason. First, there is no indication that Jesus ever visited Qumran. Second, any similarities between the two are most easily explained by their respective roots in the Old Testament, not by borrowing from each other. Third, Dupont-Sommer's interpretation of the Teacher of Righteousness being "condemned, and put to death" is *not* found in the scrolls. As the translator of one scroll, a commentary on the book of Habakkuk, Dupont-Sommer himself filled in a gap in the text with the words, "He persecuted the Teacher of Righteousness." Dr. William Sanford LaSor, professor emeritus of Old Testament at Fuller Theological Seminary, criticizes the way in which some have attempted to identify Jesus with Qumran:

> Let me give an example, chosen because it is much more obvious than

some of the subtle ones of the same nature. Powell Davies, speaking of the meals of the Qumran sects, says (with no textual basis whatever) that the priest may have said, when blessing the bread, "This is my body." Then Davies says that the members of the sect may have thought of the wine as the blood of the Messiah. Then he concludes, "This, then, was the Essenic sacred meal, so close as to be almost identical with the sacred meal of the early Christians." But notice that he first read into Qumran what he found in the New Testament, and then he found that the Qumran document resembled the New Testament. This is circular logic of the most flagrant sort. (LaWS.DSS 25)

There are similarities between Christianity and the Essenes, and Jesus probably had some contact with them. (See ChJ.R 104) Both spoke strongly against divorce. Both taught concerning the end times. Both demanded complete surrender to the one true living God. Both practiced baptism, although the Essenes often repeated theirs while Christians did not. Both had communal meals—the Essenes looked forward to a future banquet with the Messiah, while the Christians looked back in remembrance of their Messiah until he would come again. There were some organizational similarities between the Essene and Christian communities, too, although parallels can be drawn between local churches and local synagogues as well.

It is conceivable that Jesus had friends among the Essenes. Josephus indicates the presence of an Essene community in Jerusalem, which may have maintained a monastery-like dwelling for its adherents. The gospel accounts relate one interesting piece of evidence that Jesus may have arranged for the Last Supper to take place at such a location. A knowledge of first-century Hebrew customs is especially helpful here. Professor Jim Fleming, a lecturer at Hebrew University in Jerusalem, explains:

> Remember the disciples are following a *man* with a water jug? Normally women and donkeys, I'm afraid in that order, hauled water. But the Essenes did not marry, so you would expect to see women, donkeys and Essene monks at any water source. (FIJ.JJ)

Wherever the disciples ate the Last Supper, the dwelling was large and contained two stories. Many of these types of dwellings were located in first-century Jerusalem in the "upper city" and have been uncovered by archaeologists.

Finally, Jesus' instruction to his disciples, "Carry no purse, no bag, no shoes.... And whatever house you enter, first say, 'Peace be to this house'" (Luke 10:4,5), is similar to Josephus' description of the Essenes:

> They have no certain city, but many of them dwell in every city; and if any of their sect come from other places, what they have lies open for them, just as if it were their own; and they go into such as they never knew before, as if they had been ever so long acquainted with them. For which reason they carry nothing with them when they travel into remote parts, though still

they take their weapons with them, for fear of thieves. Accordingly there is, in every city where they live, one appointed particularly to take care of strangers, and provide garments and other necessaries for them. [11]

"Must we then conclude," asks another French scholar, Jean Danielou, "that he [Jesus] was an Essene, at least at some period of his life? Here historians are unanimous in affirming the contrary." (AmESLC 28) There are just too many differences, and the similarities are also found among other devout Jews. Some of the differences were:

1. The Qumran community evidenced a very strict seating arrangement by rank, whereas Jesus taught his disciples to seek the lower seats.

2. While the Essenes were legalistic in fulfilling their scriptural duties, Jesus, and the Christians after him, practiced and preached a freedom to follow the spirit of the law rather than the letter of the law. The *Damascus Document* of the Essenes, for example, states: "If a beast fall into a well, let no man draw it out on the Sabbath" (11,13). By contrast, in Luke 14:5, Jesus agreed with the Pharisees when he said, "Which one of you shall have a son or an ox fall into a well, and will not immediately pull him out on a Sabbath day?"

3. Whereas the Essenes strictly adhered to the laws governing ritual purity, Jesus taught, "Not what enters into the mouth defiles the man, but what proceeds out of the mouth, this defiles the man." He often touched lepers and sick people, technically making himself ritually unclean.

4. The Teacher of Righteousness revealed a profound awareness of his own sin, yet there existed no such awareness on the part of Jesus.

5. The Essenes withdrew from society and condemned sinners, but Jesus exhibited compassion toward sinners and taught his disciples to love their enemies. Professor James Charlesworth comments:

> It is conceivable that Jesus may have been thinking about and rejecting the [Essene] exhortation to hate the sons of darkness, when he stated, "You have heard that it was said, 'You shall love your neighbor and hate your enemy'" (Matthew 5:43). The best, and possibly only, real Jewish parallel to the rule to hate others is found in the Dead Sea Scrolls. In fact, according to the Rule of the Community at the time of the yearly renewal, Essenes chanted curses on all the sons of darkness, specifically those who are not Essenes, including Jews who masquerade as Essenes. (ChJ.R 105)

Because of some marked similarities as well as other differences between Jesus and the Qumran community, it is easy for writers to make wrong inferences. As LaSor states:

> If, for example, I wish to demonstrate a close similarity between the Dead Sea Scrolls and the New Testament, I can go through both bodies of

literature and select the statements that are most similar. The results will be impressive.

On the other hand, if I wish to demonstrate that there is really no similarity between these two religious writings, then I can list all of the striking differences. Again the results will be impressive. (LaWS.DSS 22)

We conclude, then, that Jesus definitely was not an Essene, and surely was not the Dead Sea sect's Teacher of Righteousness, even though he did have some teachings similar to theirs, and may have had contact with some of the sect's members.

Was Jesus a Zealot?

H. S. Reimarus, Robert Eisler and more recently University of Manchester professor of comparative religion, S. G. F. Brandon, have been among those scholars describing Jesus in Zealot terms.[12] Since much of the Zealot (or possibly pre-Zealot rebel) activity centered in Galilee, and not far from Jesus' headquarters in Capernaum, Jesus had to confront the issue and probably on several occasions. France cautions:

> What we cannot do is imagine a Jesus who operated in a purely pietistic world antiseptically isolated from the violent currents of Jewish nationalism deriving from Judas the Galilean and his like. Their passionate longing for the independence of Israel, and their willingness to take violent action to achieve it, is an essential part of the background against which a "real" Jesus must be understood. (FrR.E 54-55)

Unless one plans to use the extreme higher critical approach of throwing out all the relevant passages in the gospels, the evidence from these sources indicates that Jesus did not see the Zealot methodology as his means of successfully accomplishing his mission. In John 6:15, when he perceives that the people are proclaiming him *the* Prophet, i.e., the Messiah, and are about to take him by force and make him their king, he takes off for the mountains.

In Matthew 5:41, Jesus says, "And whoever shall force you to go one mile, go with him two." This is hardly the statement of a Zealot, for it refers to the law of the Romans which permitted a soldier to compel a Jewish citizen to carry his pack up to a distance of one mile. Zealots vehemently hated this practice.

France explains other non-Zealot teachings of Jesus:

> He also preached a message not of liberation for the Jews and their capital, but rather of destruction. His repeated threats of judgment to fall on "this evil generation" were balanced by his prediction that people "from east and west" would come into the messianic banquet, while Jews (who assumed they would be there by right) would find themselves excluded (Matthew 8:11, 12). Several of his parables focus on the rejection of those who regarded themselves as the people of God, and their replacement by those

they despised (especially the striking sequence of three parables directed against the official Jewish leadership in Matthew 21:28–22:14). (FrR.E 162)

In Mark 12:13-17, some Pharisees and Herodians come to Jesus to check out his Zealot tendencies. They tried to put him on the spot by asking him whether it was lawful to pay a poll-tax to Caesar. If he said yes, they figured the people would desert him. If he said no, they would have all the evidence they would need against him for inciting rebellion among the people. It was plain to see what they were doing. Jesus replied, "Why are you testing me [setting a trap for me]?" His classic answer, "Render to Caesar the things that are Caesar's, and to God the things that are God's," boosted his esteem in the eyes of the people all the more. But it was hardly the answer of a Zealot.

As we have seen earlier, Peter and the other disciples, especially Simon the Zealot, probably did have strong Zealot tendencies or at least sympathies. But to class Jesus among the Zealots just doesn't stand up under the evidence.

Was Jesus a Pharisee?

In view of the many confrontations of Jesus with the Pharisees the question may at first seem ridiculous. But in addition to the psychological observation that an individual's most heated arguments may often occur with those closest to him, there is quite a bit of evidence which has led some scholars to declare that Jesus was a Pharisee. Joseph Klausner, Abraham Geiger, Daniel Chwolson, Martin Buber, Paul Winter, Shalom Ben-Chorin and Hyam Maccoby all see Jesus as a Pharisee, though some with qualifications. (See HaDA.R 230-32) Others like Abrahams, Montefiore, Rabbi Samuel Umen and Asher Finkel, while not regarding Jesus as a Pharisee, do put him on common ground with many of the Pharisees.

Much of the impetus for seeing Jesus as a Pharisee or close to the Pharisees comes from comparative studies showing that a good part of Jesus' teachings are paralleled in the rabbis. Jewish scholar Hyam Maccoby asserts:

> Jesus was not only educated as a Pharisee; he remained a Pharisee all his life…. As a rabbi, Jesus was a typical Pharisee teacher. Both in style and content, his religious teachings show an unmistakable affinity to Pharisaism, and especially to the teachings of the great apostle of Pharisaism, Hillel. (MaH.RJ 106-7)

Once again, however, the only way scholars are able to make Jesus a Pharisee is by using the higher critical approach to the verses in the gospels which demonstrate he was not a Pharisee. The Jewish higher critical scholars hold that these verses (usually containing sayings of Jesus) were later written into the gospel material by an allegedly anti-Semitic early church. The evidence does show a closeness of some of Jesus' teachings to that of some of the Pharisees, particularly those of the school of Hillel. (Hillel was the teacher of Gamaliel, the teacher of Saul of Tarsus.) But when Jesus differed with the Pharisees, the concerns were major foundational issues underlying the Pharisees' entire approach and behavior. Jesus' repeated clashes with the Pharisees on the issue of the Sabbath are a prime example.

Of even more importance was the issue of his own identity and that of the Messiah to come. For example, it would not be difficult for a Pharisee to agree with Jesus that the most important commandment was to love God with all of one's heart, soul and mind (Matthew 22:37). But immediately following this teaching, Jesus asks the Pharisees a question for the purpose of clarifying the identity of the Messiah: "What do you think about the Christ, whose son is He?" (Matthew 22:42). When they answer "The son of David," Jesus engages them in some deductive reasoning often used by the rabbis: "Then how does David in the Spirit call Him 'Lord,' saying, 'The LORD said to my Lord, "Sit at My right hand, until I put Thine enemies beneath Thy feet"'?" In other words, was the Messiah just to be an earthly figure born from the lineage of David? According to verse 46, the Pharisees neither answered him nor ever asked him a question again.

Immediately following this dialogue, probably as the scribes and Pharisees walk away, Jesus turns to his disciples and the people gathered there. He directs them first to obey the Pharisees in what they tell them to do, but second, not to copy their behavior. Every time Jesus says "the scribes and the Pharisees" do such and such, or "woe to you scribes and Pharisees," he clearly declares himself to be not one of them.

The gospel accounts reveal other marked differences between the Pharisees and Jesus. In the Sermon on the Mount, Jesus states several times: "You have heard that it was said…" He is referring to the rabbinical practice of citing the opinions of earlier rabbis as a basis for their teaching. When Jesus continues by saying, "But I say to you…" the logical question in the minds of his hearers was, "So who are you?" Everything Jesus did and said pointed to the authority given him from above, not from other men. Geza Vermes recognizes:

> All three synoptic evangelists assert at the outset of his preaching career that his style differed from that of the scribes. Their prime concern was to invest all religious doctrine with the sanction of tradition as being part of a strictly defined chain of transmission originating—in fact, or by means of exegetical ingenuity—in Scripture, and preferably in the Pentateuch. Jesus, by contrast, is said to have taught with *exousia*, with authority, without feeling the need for a formal justification of his words. (VeG.JWJ 31)

Matthew records: "The result was that when Jesus had finished these words, the multitudes were amazed at His teaching; for He was teaching them as one having authority, and not as their scribes" (Matthew 7:28-29).

The gospel accounts contain 89 references to Pharisees, most of which are negative. Unless one is prepared to throw them all out by means of an extreme higher critical approach, it is impossible to accept Jesus as a Pharisee.

Was Jesus a Galilean Hasid?

Galilee was a land apart. To its west and north lay the Gentile lands of the Syrophoenecians. To the northeast lay the Gentile territory of Gaulanitis, to the southeast, the Gentile lands of the Hellenized cities called Decapolis, and last but not least, to the south lay Samaria, land of the half-Jews, although they might just as well have been fully Gentile for all the Jews cared. Galilee, then, was isolated geographically from Judea, and the isolation carried over into the social order. Judea, with Jerusalem leading the way, was more sophisticated, better educated and more prone to city life. Its only sea contained no life and much of the land was arid, forcing the people into the cities. Galilee was fertile, and its sea teemed with fish. It was largely a rural area, and the people in Jerusalem seem to have thought of it as being out in the sticks. No wonder Jesus' parables contain so many allusions to agriculture and the countryside. As Vermes puts it, he was "at home among the simple people of rural Galilee." (VeG.JTJ 49) In regard to language, the dialect in Galilee was different from that down south in Jerusalem, as can be seen by the bystanders' charge to Simon Peter: "Y'all don't talk like us down here" (Matthew 26:73, slightly revised).

Not only were the dialects different, but the Judaism of the north differed from that of the south as well. Though the Sadducees ruled in Jerusalem, the Pharisees had the people's hearts. Therefore, in the south the Pharisaic emphasis on the traditions of the elders was most pervasive. In the north, prior to AD 70, the Pharisees had not yet established themselves as the primary spiritual leadership. Vermes informs us:

> Fragments from rabbinic literature point towards a sporadic Pharisee presence in Galilee and an absence of impact during the first century AD. Yohanan ben Zakkai, the leader of Jewish restoration after the destruction of Jerusalem, spent some time in the town of Arab, possibly before AD 50; two of his legal rulings concerning the observance of the Sabbath were enacted there. Yet according to a third-century AD tradition, on realizing that despite eighteen years of effort he had failed to make any mark, he exclaimed: "Galilee, Galilee, you hate the Torah!" (VeG.JTJ 49)

Josephus, on the other hand, presents the people of Galilee as deeply devoted to the law both in theory and in practice. (MeE.AREC K7) If we remember that the prophet Elijah was from this area and held in great esteem, the picture begins to emerge of a down-to-earth Galilean people, devoted to the law but especially to the prophets, not highly concerned with the sophisticated Pharisaic reasoning practiced down south in Jerusalem, but intensely committed to practically applying the law to their lives in the spirit of the prophets' injunctions.[13] Jesus was reared in this environment, and here he carried out the longest portion of his ministry.

The roots of the Pharisees and Essenes are vague, but most scholars believe that both groups emerged from the Hasidim (pious ones) who helped the Maccabeans recapture the Temple in the second century BC. They apparently later broke away from the

Maccabeans because of the worldliness of the Maccabeans. During the first centuries BC and AD, the Hasidim, independent of the Pharisees and Essenes, became known for their piety and for their ability to effect change through answered prayer and the performance of miracles. Before the turn of the millennium, Honi the Circle-Drawer (Josephus calls him Onias the Righteous) became known for ending a drought through his prayers. In the first century AD, the Galilean Hanina ben Dosa gained a reputation for his ability to work miracles. Jewish scholars recognize the tension that existed between the Hasidim and the Pharisees, and Vermes sums it up this way:

> S. Safrai, for example, is prepared to admit that the religious practice taught by the Hasidim was "highly individual and sometimes, indeed, opposed to that generally prevailing," and that, although revered by the rabbis, the Hasidim were not identical with them. D. Flusser, in a slightly different context, also speaks of the "inevitable tension between charismatic miracles...and institutional Judaism." (VeG.JTJ 80)

> It is hardly surprising that the stories concerning Honi and Hanina— not to mention Jesus—often contain an element of open or veiled disapproval when it is remembered that the entire rabbinic tradition has passed through the channel of "orthodoxy." (VeG.JTJ 80)

He continues:

> The charismatics' informal familiarity with God and confidence in the efficacy of their words was also deeply disliked by those whose authority derived from established channels. Simeon ben Shetah, the leader of the Pharisees in the first century B.C., would have wished to excommunicate Honi, but dared not. Similarly, the jibe, "Are you a prophet?" addressed to Hanina, as well as the assertion that the "prince" Yohanan ben Zakkai was superior to him the "servant," were all aimed at neutralizing and eliminating a power and authority apparently, but unascertainably, of divine origin. (VeG.JTJ 81)

Was Jesus a Galilean Hasid? Because these "holy ones" were so individualistic, apparently not organized into a company of any sort, and fairly unknown in surviving literature, there seems to be no reason Jesus could not be called a Galilean Hasid. However, there is one other designation which also has been acceptably applied to him by some Jewish scholars.

Was Jesus a Prophet?

> A prophet is not without honor except in his home town, and in his own household (Matthew 13:57).

> Nevertheless I must journey on today and tomorrow and the next day; for it cannot be that a prophet should perish outside Jerusalem (Luke 13:33).

There is no doubt that Jesus regarded himself as a prophet.[14] The multitudes also recognized him as a prophet[15] just as they held John the Baptist to be a prophet.[16] Among Jewish scholars, Montefiore held Jesus to be "one of the greatest and most original of our Jewish prophets." (MoC.WJT 33:516) Another Jewish scholar, L. J. Edgar wrote: "Not only was Jesus a prophet but there is good ground for believing that he was a prophet true to the essentials of Judaism." (EdL.JVJ 6) Vermes declares, "That Jesus was a charismatic prophet rings so authentic, especially in the light of the Honi-Hanina cycle of traditions…" (VeG.JTJ 90)

Again, if we do not excise all the relevant material in the gospels by means of a higher critical approach, Jesus certainly qualifies as "a prophet in Israel." Geza Vermes demonstrates that even the higher critic cannot logically deny that Jesus' contemporaries saw him as a prophet:

> The common assumption held by New Testament interpreters appears to be that the prophetic image of Jesus was conceived by friendly outsiders, but that, not being good enough, not sufficiently suitable within the circle of his closer companions, it was replaced by more fitting titles. That this was not, in fact, the case is shown by the obituary attributed to one of the Emmaus disciples two days after Jesus' death. He was, Cleopas says, "a prophet mighty in deed and word before God and all the people." (VeG.JTJ 88, quoting Luke 24:19)

It is therefore reasonable to accept Jesus as at least a prophet.

QUESTIONS SURROUNDING THE JEWISHNESS OF JESUS

Was Jesus' Acceptance of Gentiles Manufactured by the Writers?

There is a Jewish tour guide in Israel who likes to remind his groups of a popular ditty: "How odd of God to choose the Jews," to which he responds, with a twinkle in his eye, "Not so, for the Goyim annoy Him!" (*Goyim* means "Gentiles.") Another cord of evidence for the reliability of the gospel narratives is that they accurately communicate the racial tension known to have existed between Jews and Gentiles in the first century.

On at least one occasion, this racial tension seems to be the only reason Jewish people turned against Jesus. As a miracle-working Galilean Hasid and prophet, Jesus returns to preach in his hometown of Nazareth and is welcomed with open arms. After all, this was Galilee, the breeding ground of charismatic Hasidim. Luke 4:15 says that as Jesus began teaching in the synagogues of Galilee he was being praised by all. In Nazareth, he brings a rather controversial Sabbath morning reading in that he stops reading right in the middle of a verse proclaiming the arrival of the favorable year of the Lord in definite messianic terms. Even after saying, "Today this scripture has been fulfilled in your hearing," the text states, "And all were speaking well of Him" (Luke 4:22). Jesus continues preaching up to the point where he speaks of Elijah being sent to a Gentile town and a Gentile widow. The murmuring in the congregation begins. In his next sentence he speaks of Elisha healing none of the lepers in Israel but only Naaman the Syrian—a Goy! The text continues:

> And all in the synagogue were filled with rage as they heard these things; and they rose up and cast Him out of the city, and led Him to the brow of the hill on which their city had been built, in order to throw Him down the cliff.[17]

What a change in attitude. God's favorable attitude toward the Goyim didn't annoy Jesus, but it sure got to the congregation in his hometown!

John tells us that even before beginning his ministry in Galilee Jesus took his disciples through Samaria (John 4). Normally, orthodox Jews took a route going north by way of the Jordan River Valley, bypassing the Samaritans. For Peter and some of the others, this trip was probably morally offensive! Did you ever wonder why Jesus sent *all* his disciples into the city to buy food (verse 8)? Can you imagine what an imposing bunch they would have been toward the "contemptible" Samaritan woman? But Jesus seems to have had, from the very beginning of his ministry, the one missing ingredient most of Judaism had overlooked for more than 2,000 years—Genesis 12:3: "And in you [the future nation of Israel] all the families of the earth shall be blessed." Jesus knew that God's plan for Israel was that they should be a blessing and not a curse to the Gentiles. As a result of his conversation with the woman, many of the Samaritans from her home town put their faith in Jesus. What a way to begin a ministry among orthodox Jews. Apparently, not even the half-Goyim annoyed Jesus.

When Jesus came into Capernaum, a Gentile centurion sent Jewish elders to Jesus (Luke 7:3). The centurion seemed to have been a compassionate man, possibly even a convert to Judaism. He built the Jews their synagogue and exhibited great concern for the life of his slave. His humility and great faith are evident in his message to Jesus:

> Lord, do not trouble Yourself further, for I am not fit for You to come under my roof; for this reason I did not even consider myself worthy to come to You, but just say the word, and my servant will be healed. For indeed, I am a man under authority, with soldiers under me; and I say to this one, "Go!" and he goes; and to another, "Come!" and he comes; and to my slave, "Do this!" and he does it.[18]

Not only did this Goy not annoy Jesus, but Jesus marveled at him. Making a showcase of faith out of the man, Jesus said to all those around him, "Not even in Israel have I found such great faith." Ouch! That must have stung the ears of Jesus' orthodox friends just a little bit. There is only one other record of Jesus marveling at something: Mark 6:6, speaking of the attitude of his Jewish neighbors in his own hometown, it says simply: "And He wondered at their *unbelief*."

In Luke 17:11-19, Jesus healed ten lepers and only one came back to give thanks. Jesus questioned, "Were none found who turned back to give glory to God, except this foreigner?" His favorable attitude toward the Samaritan reminds one of his parable of the good Samaritan.

The higher critic's favorite ploy for dealing with all these passages is simply to assert that the later, mostly Gentile church inserted them into the accounts in order to make Jesus more favorable to the Gentiles. But if they were going to do that, why didn't they also remove those verses where Jesus says things like, "I was sent only to the lost sheep of the house of Israel"; or, "Salvation is of the Jews"?[19] Look especially at the first of the two passages. Piecing Matthew 15 together with Mark 7, you can see that the Syrophoenician woman cried out to Jesus as he was inside a house. But he seemed to ignore her. His statement, "I was sent only to the lost sheep of the house of Israel" seems out of place in light of his normal compassion for people. Some scholars think he was testing his disciples or questioning them, "Was I sent only to…?" But then his next statement again sounds unusually harsh: "It is not good to take the children's bread and throw it to the dogs." If Gentile redactors were in the habit of embellishing and extracting passages in the Gospels, it is surely a major miracle that they didn't attack this one first. In fact, the different details in the two accounts show that the writers followed two separate traditions. Thus the redactors would have been doubly negligent in their censorship.

The evidence from a Hebraic perspective is compelling. The Gospels are a reliable record of a historical Jesus who was thoroughly Jewish and carried out his ministry to "his own." But he also maintained a wider perspective: The Goyim were to be included among God's chosen. How odd of God!

Was Jesus Married? Was It Required?

Jewish society stressed the importance of the commandment to "be fruitful and multiply" (Genesis 1:28), and some popularizers have exploited this fact. In *Holy Blood, Holy Grail,* the authors state:

> If Jesus were indeed as celibate as later tradition claims, it is extraordinary that there is no reference to any such celibacy. The absence of any such reference strongly suggests that Jesus, as far as the question of celibacy was concerned, conformed to the conventions of his time and culture—suggests, in short, that he was married. (BaM.HB 331)

The authors go on to quote the Mishnah as saying, "An unmarried man may not be a teacher," but they fail to give the reference in the Mishnah or to inform their readers that statements in the Mishnah are made by rabbis mostly living in the time period after AD 70. In fact, one unmarried rabbi in the generation following that time explains his celibacy in Tosefta: Yebamoth 8.7: "What shall I do? I am in love with Torah. Others can enable the world to continue to exist." Shmuel Safrai, a professor at Hebrew University and, a specialist in Jewish literature and history of the Second Temple period, gives a more accurate picture of the times. According to Professor Safrai, rabbis of this time period often waited until age thirty or forty to marry since they had to spend many years away from home as students and itinerant teachers. [20]

On What Day Was the Last Supper?

The synoptic gospels indicate that the Last Supper was a Passover meal, apparently on Thursday night, the night of Jesus' arrest. But John, speaking of the events on Friday morning, says that the Jewish leaders "led Jesus therefore from Caiaphas into the Praetorium; and it was early; and they themselves did not enter into the Praetorium in order that they might not be defiled, but might eat the Passover." [21] Why then did the disciples, according to the synoptics, eat the Passover meal on Thursday night when the Jewish leaders (and the rest of the Jews) celebrated Passover on Friday night?

Hoehner gives probably the most thorough yet concise review of the evidence on the question. He proposes, and we agree, that the best solution is to recognize that the synoptic gospels reflect a Galilean calendar which was apparently followed by Jesus and the Pharisees. By this method

> the Galileans, and with them Jesus and His disciples, had the Paschal lamb slaughtered in the late afternoon of Thursday, Nisan 14, and later that evening they ate the Passover with the unleavened bread. On the other hand, the Judean Jews who reckoned from sunset to sunset would slay the lamb on Friday afternoon which marked the end of Nisan 14 and would eat the Passover lamb with the unleavened bread that night which had become Nisan 15. Thus, Jesus had eaten the Passover meal when His enemies, who had not as yet had the Passover, arrested Him. (HoH.C 87)

This solution seems to satisfy not only the gospel accounts, but also evidence from the Mishnah, the Babylonian Talmud and Josephus, all of which Hoehner cites. The main point here is that the historical situation of first-century Jerusalem was more complex than what many authors paint it to be. Bits and pieces of information are often helpful in piecing together evidence matter-of-factly reported to us in the gospels.

Are Accounts of the Trial of Jesus Anti-Semitic?

The charge is repeatedly made that the gospel accounts represent the anti-Semitic attitude of later Gentile Christians who redacted the writings. Maurice Goguel, for example, believes that the Romans collaborated with the Jews in order to arrest Jesus, and concludes: "The Gospel narrative which attributes this initiative wholly to the Jews is a biased perversion of the primitive tradition." (GoM.LJ 469)

It is important, whenever someone claims a particular statement is anti-Semitic, to know whether the person making the statement is Jewish or non-Jewish. In teaching his class on New Testament to Jewish students at Hebrew University in Jerusalem, Professor Fleming says he begins by saying "I don't know why some Jews are so sensitive about the *supposed* anti-Semitism of the New Testament. How can anyone say, 'I will vomit you out of the land' is anti-Semitic? How can anyone say, 'Your prayers are a stench to the nostrils of God' is anti-Semitic?" And of course they all get upset. "How could you say that isn't anti-Semitic?" Then I remind them it's Isaiah and Jeremiah that I am quoting.[22]

If the gospel writers wanted to whitewash the Romans and defame the Jews, it is impossible to explain many statements in their narratives. Why would they have Pontius Pilate scourging Jesus? Why wouldn't they have Pilate taking responsibility and putting an end to the whole thing? Certainly he had the authority to do so.

And what about all the pro-Jewish statements in the gospel accounts? John, for example, supposedly the most anti-Semitic of the gospel writers, has Jesus saying, "Salvation is of the Jews."[23] Or why does Luke have Jesus saying regarding those who crucified him. "Father, forgive them; for they do not know what they are doing."[24] That doesn't sound like someone trying to heap condemnation on the Jews.

When the gospel writers (remember, they are Jewish too) say negative things about the Jewish leaders, they are saying nothing that other Jews were not already saying. Excavations in the upper city of old Jerusalem, which uncovered the large homes of the more wealthy and aristocratic Jews, also uncovered dishes with the family name "Kathros" on them. The name also appears in a Baraitha which reveals the character of the ruling priestly families of Jesus' day:

> Woe to me because of the house of Hannan [Annas] because of their whispers! Woe to me because of the house of Kathros, because of their pens! [a probable reference to the forging of illegal documents]…For they are high priests and their sons are treasurers, and their sons-in-law [Caiaphas was the son-in-law of Annas] are overseers, and their servants beat the people with rods.[25]

Are the gospel reports anti-Semitic? Judging by the rabbinic reflection above, it appears that more than just the gospel writers were concerned about corruption in the high court. It is known that Sanhedrin members in the Herodian period were appointed for political favors, and it is not likely that such a Sanhedrin would act in the most just and pious manner. The gospel writers were not anti-Semitic. They simply reported what others of their fellow Jews had already observed.

New Testament writers often use the term "the Jews." It is a general term referring to a group of Jewish people, most often Jewish leaders and their employees or servants, who are involved in a particular action. When a New Testament writer states that "the Jews" did such and such, he does not mean the entire race of Jews. He means simply the Jews who were there. Was it, for example, all the Jews in Jerusalem who called for Jesus to be crucified? Of course not. Jesus' own disciples were Jews. It was simply the crowd of Jews who were there. And as Ian Wilson brings out, "With twenty thousand

Temple servants and eighteen thousand workmen on their payroll, the Temple's controllers would scarcely have had any difficulty in finding a mob to perform to whatever tune they called." (WiI.JTE 126) In fact, the gospel writers never once say "the Jews" crucified Jesus. They refer to the mob simply as "they." Further, Luke, writing in Acts 4:24-28, demonstrates conclusively that the very earliest church did not see the Jews as "Christ-killers." When Peter and John return to their friends after being jailed and interrogated, they all agree in prayer:

> O Lord, it is Thou who didst make the heaven and the earth and the sea, and all that is in them, who by the Holy Spirit, through the mouth of our father David Thy servant, didst say,

> Why did the Gentiles rage, and the peoples devise futile things? The kings of the earth took their stand, and the rulers were gathered together, against the Lord, and against His Christ.

> For truly in this city there were gathered together against Thy holy Servant Jesus, whom Thou didst anoint, both Herod and Pontius Pilate, along with the Gentiles and the peoples of Israel, to do whatever Thy hand and Thy purpose predestined to occur.

The point of the gospel accounts is not to assign blame. The message the New Testament wants its readers to get is simply: "It was people like me who killed Jesus; it was my sin that put him on the cross." Thus Paul would write, "For I delivered to you as of first importance what I also received, that Christ died for *our* sins."[26] Likewise, Peter recorded, "And He Himself bore *our* sins in His body on the cross."[27]

CONCLUSION

As one learns more about the first-century Jewish milieu, it becomes apparent that the gospel accounts reflect the viewpoints of those living within the Hebrew culture, not those observing it, or manufacturing it, from without. A deeper knowledge of this Jewish factor provides increased assurance that the gospel writers recorded accurately the events of Jesus' life which actually took place. It also helps us to see beyond our preconceived ideas of what Jesus was like. As France puts it:

> The increased study of Judaism of the Roman period has led to some important clarification of much of our understanding of Jesus. Traditional ways of envisaging the gospel scenes have been altered, and Jesus has increasingly come into clearer light as a man of his times. As we learn more to see him as a contemporary Jew would have seen him, we may expect to come closer to the real Jesus. If in the process we lose some of the stereotypes which have made Jesus for many a blue-eyed Caucasian with the values and attitudes of a middle-class Englishman, this is not something to be regretted. (FrR.E 15)

13

JESUS AND MIRACLES

From the beginning of this book we have said that the primary question regarding the historicity of Jesus is not whether he existed. Rather, the question is whether or not Jesus lived the kind of life the gospel writers portray him as having lived. These writers blatantly report that Jesus performed miracles.

Because many people today believe miracles are impossible, they naturally doubt the authenticity of the gospel accounts. Historian Michael Grant, for example, speaking of the virgin birth of Jesus, asserts, "The historian, who can take no cognizance of his miraculous birth to the Virgin Mary, has to conclude that his father was Joseph, the son of Jacob (or Heli)." (GraM.JHR 171)

F. F. Bruce observes, "For many readers it is precisely these miracle-stories which are the chief difficulty in the way of accepting the New Testament documents as reliable." (BrF.NTD 62)

France adds:

> Undoubtedly the most powerful motive for questioning the historical reliability of the gospels has been the fact that they record ideas and events which are foreign to most modern Western scholars' conception of what may be accepted as "historical." At the narrative level we find angels, miracles, the raising of the dead, a visionary experience of Jesus speaking with men who died centuries earlier, and Jesus' own bodily resurrection. At the level of thought, the gospels envisage a God who controls events, to whom man is accountable, with a future prospect of heaven or hell, and Jesus as the one who determines a man's destiny. Here is a total world view with which modern secular culture cannot be comfortable, and which in the view of many scholars has forfeited any claim to be regarded as "historical." (FrR.G 86)

The term *miracle* is somewhat elusive. Even in the rather concise *Webster's New World Dictionary*, there are two definitions given: "1. an event or action that apparently contradicts known scientific laws; 2. a remarkable thing." Anyone familiar with the philosophical debates regarding miracles can easily see that the definition chosen will send the arguments in entirely different directions.

The Greek New Testament and other Greek works of antiquity use two different Greek words for the one English word *miracle*. The first is *dunamis*, literally meaning "a work of power." The second, which is rarely used by other Greek writers but is often used by the gospel writers, is *semeion*, meaning "sign." A general New Testament definition of *miracle*, then, would be: "a work of rare or unusual power which signifies or points to a significant fact."

The miracles recorded of Jesus in the gospels were not intended to provide 100 percent objective certainty to hostile inquirers. On the contrary, Isaiah 45:15 says: "Truly, Thou art a God who hides Himself, O God of Israel, Savior!" Jesus often refused to perform miracles for those who demanded signs of him, but performed miracles for the humble, downtrodden and those who generally would be more sincere in their approach to God. This was in keeping with the character of God expressed in Jeremiah 29:13: "And you will seek Me and find Me, when you search for Me with all your heart."

ARE MIRACLES POSSIBLE?

We find that one particular attitude surfaces repeatedly in historical studies. It is what we call the "Hume hangover." It is the argument by the eighteenth-century skeptic, David Hume, that belief can only be justified by probability and that probability is based upon the uniformity or consistency of nature. In other words, we are right in only believing experiences that are normal to ordinary human experience. Anything that is unique so far as normal human experience is concerned—such as a miracle—should be rejected, according to Hume and his followers.

Another way of expressing this view of history is that we live in a closed universe in which no element of the supernatural can intervene. Therefore, every event (past, present and future) must have a natural explanation. No matter what happens or how strong the evidence, this attitude dictates that the supernatural or miraculous must be rejected.

A detailed analysis of Hume's argument reveals an abundance of logical inconsistencies. For example, he states, "But it is a miracle that a man should come to life, because that has never been observed in any age or country." (HuD.IC 10. 1). It hasn't? There are several reports of such in both the Old and New Testaments. Isn't it more the case that Hume has adopted an omniscient attitude of a priori excluding all reports of miracles from possibly being valid? And what if, for example, the raising of Lazarus is conclusively proven to be authentic? Then, by Hume's definition, the raising of Jesus is no longer a miracle. No wonder the Bible simply describes these events as "works of power" and "attesting signs." It avoids all philosophical quibbling and takes one back to the historical evidence.

Hume argues, "And as a uniform experience amounts to a proof, there is here a direct and full proof, from the nature of the fact, against the existence of any miracle." (HuD.IC10.1) But does a uniform experience amount to a full proof against miracles? If there is a God, then the first time in history that he performs a particular miracle is preceded by a uniform experience against such a miracle. But such a uniform experience does not preclude an all-powerful God from performing such a work.

The flaw of the "uniform experience" argument is that it does not hold up under all circumstances. For example, when explorers returned from Australia with reports of a semi-aquatic, egg-laying mammal with a broad, flat tail, webbed feet and a snout resembling a duck's bill, their reports defied all previous uniform experience classified under the laws of taxonomy. Hume would have had to say that "uniform experience amounts to a proof…a direct and full proof, from the nature of the fact, against the existence of any" duck-billed platypus! But his disbelief in such an animal would not preclude its existence.

In part II of his argument, Hume speaks of the requirements needed to yield "full assurance." (HuD.IC10.2) But if a fact must have 100 percent certainty in order to be credible, then we must rule out almost all facts of history and science as being credible.

Hume continues in the next paragraph of part II:

> The passion of surprise and wonder, arising from miracles, being an agreeable emotion, gives a sensible tendency toward the belief of those events from which it is derived. And this goes so far that even those who cannot enjoy this pleasure immediately, nor can believe those miraculous events of which they are informed, yet love to partake the satisfaction at second hand, or by rebound, and place a pride and delight in exciting the admiration of others. (HuD.IC10.2)

This argument may fit with Hume's society of the eighteenth century, but it is nonsense when applied to the Christians of the first century AD. These men and women gained insults, rebukes, persecutions and death for spreading the "rumor" of the resurrection and other miracle reports about Jesus.

In a later paragraph Hume states: "The many instances of forged miracles and prophecies and supernatural events…ought reasonably to beget a suspicion against all relations of this kind." (HuD.IC10.2) But does a forged $100 bill mean that we ought to suspect every $100 bill of being a forgery?

> To simply say that, because some reported supernatural events are ridiculous and untrue, therefore any reported supernatural occurrence or miracle is untrue denotes faulty reasoning. It is "guilt" by association, or a case of throwing the baby out with the bath water. (McJ.A74)

Hume argues against the possibility of miracles by asserting that "it forms a strong presumption against all supernatural and miraculous relations that they are observed chiefly to abound among ignorant and barbarous nations." (HuD.IC 10. 2) But here Hume simply fails to recognize the differences between superstition and magical effects, and supernatural events which carry the marks of authenticity. Colin Brown, Professor of Systematic Theology at Fuller Theological Seminary, asserts:

> It would be equally naive for modern man to think that miracles were somehow much easier to accept in the ancient world than they are today. If miracles were as commonplace in antiquity as we popularly assume, they would hardly have counted as miracles at all and would have been indistinguishable from the normal course of events. As a matter of fact, miracles in the Old Testament are very few and far between. In those that are mentioned, stress is frequently laid on Yahweh's control of nature (as in the plagues on Egypt and the crossing of the Red Sea) rather than on violations of nature. If there was a difference between ancient and modern attitudes toward miracles, it did not turn on actual testimony to the miraculous. Despite the vast difference between modern man's understanding of nature and science and that of his ancient counterpart, the miraculous was still miraculous for ancient man. (BrC.M 281)

Hume's argument sounds persuasive as a whole primarily because of his effectiveness as a writer. Yet the logical inconsistencies within his argument demand that his conclusion be rejected.

Dr. Lawrence Burkholder, former chairman of the Department of the Church at the Harvard Divinity School, admits that his approach to history had been greatly influenced by Hume's argument that for something to be true it must conform to the uniformity of nature. After realizing that every historical event is, to some extent, or in some way unique, he confessed, "I'm beginning to feel the limitations of Hume." (BuL.DCR 12:6)

Dr. Burkholder says that Hume's argument against miracles

> is limiting the possibility of accepting what in later times and events I find to have been a fact. He is telling me I really can't believe anything unless it corresponds to past experience. But I find myself increasingly refusing to predict the future. I find myself becoming much more modest when it comes to saying what is possible and what is not possible, what may happen in the future and what may not happen. And this same modesty is beginning to take the form of a reluctance on my part to say what could have happened in the past and what would not have happened. (BuL.DCR 12:6)

Burkholder adds, "It seems to me I have some right at least to be open to the possibility that something may have happened which by analogy we call the resurrection." (BuL.DCR 12:7)

Professor Clark Pinnock, speaking of a confidence in Hume's methodology and the need to naturalize all historical events, points out that the experience against miracles is uniform only if we know that all the reports about miracles are false, and this we do not know. No one has an infallible knowledge of "natural laws," so that he can exclude from the outset the very possibility of unique events. Science can tell us what *has* happened, but it cannot tell us what *may* or *may not* happen. It observes events; it does not create them. The historian does not dictate what history can contain; he is open to whatever the witnesses report. An appeal to Hume bespeaks ignorance of history. (PiC.TT 12:8)

Dr. Wolfhart Pannenberg of the University of Munich adds, "The question... whether something happened or not at a given time some thousand years ago can be settled only by historical argument." (PaW.DC 12:10)

Dr. John Warwick Montgomery, writing about those individuals who still adhere to a closed system (all events have to have a natural explanation), exclaims:

Since Einstein, no modern has had the right to rule out the possibility of events because of prior knowledge of "natural law." The only way we can know whether an event *can* occur is to see whether in fact it *has* occurred. The problem of miracles, then, must be solved in the realm of historical investigation, not in the realm of philosophical speculation. (MoJW.WHG 71)

With the passing of the Newtonian epoch we need to leave room for the unpredictable, the unexpected and the incalculable element in the universe. (NeW.RB 33)

Dr. Vincent Taylor, a prominent New Testament critic, warns against too great a dogmatism. Concerning the limitations of science in evaluating the miraculous he writes:

In the last 50 years we have been staggered too often by discoveries which at one time were pronounced impossible. We have lived to hear of the breaking up of the atom, and to find scientists themselves speaking of the universe as "more like a great thought than like a great machine." This change of view does not, of course, accredit the miraculous; but it does mean that, given the right conditions, miracles are not impossible; no scientific or philosophic dogma stands in the way. (TaV.FGT 135)

Frenchman Ernest Renan denounced the resurrection of Jesus. He admitted to starting his research of Jesus' life assuming "there is no such thing as a miracle. Therefore the resurrection did not take place." Such an attitude would never be tolerated in a court of law. Renan's conclusion about the resurrection of Jesus was *not* based upon historical inquiry but rather upon philosophical speculation.

This mind-set resembles that of the man who says, "I have made up my mind—don't confuse me with the facts."

EVALUATING MIRACLE CLAIMS

Hellenistic Miracle Claims

> There is an old theater and shrine of Dionysos between the market place and the Menius. The statue of the god is the work of Praxiteles. Of the gods, the Eleans worship especially Dionysos; indeed they say their god invades the Thyia [a temple of Dionysos] during the annual feast…The priests carry three kettles into the building and set them down empty, when the town citizens and strangers, if they happen to be there, are present. The priests, and any others who wish, put a seal on the doors of the building. In the morning they come to read the signs and when they go into the building they find the kettles filled with wine. These things most trustworthy men of Elis, and strangers with them, swear to have happened. This is by word of mouth; I myself did not arrive at festival time.[1]

If one believes that miracles are at least possible, then the next step is to evaluate the evidence for miracle claims which are made. David Hume was correct in maintaining that both the gullibility of man and the desire of some to deceive others have been extensively revealed throughout history.

The account above is typical of miracle claims within Greek culture. It is also suspect on a number of points. First, Pausanias (a second-century writer) admits he never observed the event firsthand, and his words "by word of mouth" suggest that the reports are probably on the level of gossip. Second, the purported miracle is so similar to that of Jesus at the wedding in Cana that one wonders if the priests of Dionysos have invented something to persuade their adherents not to adopt the fast-growing Christian faith. Third, the incident has too much the feel of a magician's act. It is not spontaneous and could have been accomplished easily by someone who had remained in the temple in a hidden compartment and poured wine into the kettles during the night. By contrast, the spontaneous works of Jesus acted as signs and met immediate needs of people. Jesus at the wedding in Cana had apparently been put on the spot and was rendering assistance to an embarrassed host whose wine had run out. The Dionysos "miracle" thus appears to be a staged production.

Of somewhat greater credibility is the life of Apollonius (or Apollonios) of Tyana, a Neo-Pythagorean who flourished during the second half of the first century AD. All we know of him comes from "The Life of Apollonios of Tyana," a biography by Flavius Philostratus written no earlier than AD 217. Philostratus was born on the island of Lemnos c. AD 172, studied rhetoric in Athens, moved to Rome where he acquired a reputation as a sophist and was drawn into the "salon" of the literary and philosophic empress Julia Domna, wife of Septimius Severus and mother of the emperor Caracalla. Caracalla donated funds to build a temple to Apollonius in Tyana, and Julia commissioned Philostratus to write a fitting account of Apollonius' life. It is important to note that Philostratus was being paid to write of one held to be a god by those who commissioned him. Cartlidge and Dungan describe the outcome:

In other words, just as Caracalla's architects built a shrine for Apollonios out of marble, one of his court rhetoricians built a temple out of words—for the same purpose, i.e., to celebrate Apollonios' god-like nature and inspire reverence for him. Thus, Philostratus' narrative is a virtual catalogue of every rhetorical device known to the professional sophistic writers of that time: sudden supernatural omens, mini-dialogues on the favorite topics of the day, colorful bits of archeological lore, plenty of magic, rapid action scenes, amazing descriptions of fabled, far-off lands, occasional touches of naughty eroticism, and a whole series of favorite "philosophical" scenes: the Philosopher lectures his disciples on being willing to die for truth; the Philosopher is abandoned by his cowardly disciples; the Philosopher confronts the tyrant; the fearless Philosopher is alone in prison unafraid; the Philosopher victoriously defends himself in the court, and so on. On the other hand, Philostratus included enough accurate historical details to give his writing the ring of genuine truth. But mixed in with the real people and places are all sorts of imaginary "official" letters, inscriptions, decrees, and edicts, the whole bound together by an "eyewitness" diary. Finally, to give it the proper supernatural flavor, he has included a number of miraculous, supernatural occurrences: dreams, pre-vision, teleportation, exorcism and finally, vanishing from earth only to reappear later from heaven to convince a doubting disciple of the soul's immortality. (CaDR.DSG 205-6)

The resemblance of so many of the alleged miracles of Apollonius to those of Jesus makes the reader suspect that among the sources used by Philostratus were the various gospel accounts and the book of Acts. Philostratus' work might best be described as one of semi-historical fiction. It is hardly the type of evidence necessary to sustain a serious belief in the miracles it describes. One Greek myth scholar, Elizabeth Haight, concluded that Philostratus wrote

with full knowledge of Xenophon's romantic biography of Cyrus the Great as the ideal ruler, of the Greek novels of war and adventure, of the Greek love romances…and of the Christian Acts with a saint for a hero. [In view of all these possibilities] Philostratus chose to present a *theios aner*, a divine sage, a Pythagorean philosopher, as the center of his story. To make the life of his hero interesting and to promulgate his philosophy, he used every device of the Greek and Latin novels of the second and third centuries. And the credulity, the discourses, the aspirations of his characters belong as much to the whole first three centuries of the Empire as [just] to the age of the Severi [when he wrote]. Philostratus has written out of the restless cravings of that time another romance to help men escape from the burden of their fears to life's fairer possibilities. (HaE.ME 111ff.)

Before leaving this section we need to emphasize that most reports of supernatural activity can be evaluated based on the evidence supporting (1) whether or not the event occurred; and (2) whether the effect was produced by some trick or deception of the alleged miracle worker. At the same time, it is important to recognize that if a supernatural event does occur, it does not necessarily mean that God is behind it. In recent years, a heightened interest and participation in witchcraft and the occult has confirmed to many the reality of a supernatural source described in the Bible as "Satan," "the devil" and other such terms. If the biblical worldview is accurate, we can expect that there are supernatural effects which have happened throughout history and whose source is satanic.[2]

Miracles Within the Jewish Context

> Once they said to Honi the Circle-Drawer: "Pray that it may rain."...He prayed but it did not rain. Then what did he do? He drew a circle, and stood in it, and said before God: "Lord of the world, thy children have turned to me because I am as a son of the house before thee. I swear by thy great name that I will not move hence until thou be merciful towards thy children." It then began to drizzle. "I have not asked for this," he said, "but for rain to fill cisterns, pits and rock-cavities." There came a cloud-burst. "I have not asked for this, but for a rain of grace, blessing and gift." It then rained normally.[3]

Honi the Circle-Drawer, called Onias the Righteous by Josephus, was one of the Hasidim of the first century BC. Like others of the charismatic holy men, he did not endear himself to all Jews of his day. In fact, Josephus reports that he was stoned to death by a mob of wicked Jews. Following the above account, further comments show that the religious leaders tolerated Honi more than they liked him. They thought he was like a spoiled child before God; nevertheless they knew God answered his prayers.

In view of what we covered earlier regarding oral tradition among the Jews, this account of Honi seems historically credible. It was reported by eyewitnesses who were less than friendly admirers and it was reliably transmitted. The event does not appear to have been staged or to have been the work of a magician. Rather, it appears that Honi stands in the line of prophets such as Elijah who also prayed for rain to cease and begin. There seems to be no reason to deny that the God of Israel could have performed this miracle.

Another figure even closer to Jesus in time and geographic location is Hanina ben Dosa. Hanina was a Galilean of the first century, from a town about ten miles north of Nazareth. All of his recorded activity occurred before AD 70. He would have been a contemporary of the apostle Paul, although there is no evidence that they ever met. He is said to have once healed the son of Gamaliel (or Gamliel), very likely the same Gamaliel Paul claimed as his former teacher. The account runs as follows:

> Our rabbis say, once upon a time Rabban Gamliel's son got sick. He sent two men of learning to Rabbi Chanina ben Dosa to beg him mercy from

God concerning him. He saw them coming and went to a room upstairs and asked mercy from God concerning him. When he had come back down he said to them, "Go, the fever has left him." They said to him, "What? Are you a prophet?" He said, "I am not a prophet nor am I the son of a prophet. But this I have received from tradition: if my prayer of intercession flows unhesitatingly from my mouth, I know it will be answered, and if not, I know it will be rejected." They sat down and wrote and determined exactly the moment he said this, and when they came back to Rabban Gamliel he said to them, "By the Temple service! You are neither too early nor too late but this is what happened: in that moment the fever left him and he asked for water!"[4]

Hanina, like other charismatic Hasidim, ignored some or many of the traditions of the oral law. Again, he seems to stand in the tradition of the prophets and to have exhibited the marks of having a true relationship with the God of Israel. Vermes says of him:

Tradition represents Hanina as one who, to his wife's great displeasure, lived in total poverty. A younger contemporary of his, Rabbi Eleazar of Modiin, saw Hanina and those like him as the incarnation of "men of truth hating evil gain": those, that is to say, who "hated their money, and all the more, the mammon of other people." The same lack of acquisitiveness, indeed the same positive embrace of poverty inspired by absolute reliance on God, is fundamental to Jesus' outlook and practice. (VeG.JTJ 77)

We see no need to deny that the God of Israel may well have worked through Hanina's life with supernatural answers to prayer such as the one cited above. The account has the marks of realism and seems to have been transmitted accurately. There are, within rabbinic literature, accounts which seem obviously to have been constructed more for the purpose of making a point than for reporting historical information. But Hanina's healing episode seems more clearly to be the reporting of an actual historical incident.

In contrast to the Hellenistic miracles, many of the Jewish miracles, such as those cited above, have several marks of credibility. One mark concerns the issue of motive. In the Hellenistic world miracles were looked upon as a proof of divine authority. The Hellenistic world also believed in many gods, and that great people, such as emperors or empresses, could become gods or goddesses. These two factors worked as motivating forces for admirers of certain individuals or for the individuals themselves to embellish their lives with stories of the miraculous. Not so in the Jewish world. For the Jew, miracles were signs pointing toward particular truths God desired to reveal. In addition, the Jewish people understood that not all miracles were from God. It was required of them to test the prophets:

If a prophet or a dreamer of dreams arises among you and gives you a sign or a wonder and the sign or the wonder comes true, concerning which he spoke to you, saying, "Let us go after other gods (whom you have not known) and let us serve them," you shall not listen to the words of that prophet or that dreamer of dreams; for the LORD your God is testing you to find out if you love the LORD your God with all your heart and your soul. You shall follow the LORD your God and fear Him; and you shall keep His commandments, listen to His voice, serve Him, and cling to Him. But the prophet or that dreamer of dreams shall be put to death, because he has counseled rebellion against the LORD your God who brought you from the land of Egypt and redeemed you from the house of slavery, to seduce you from the way in which the LORD your God commanded you to walk. So you shall purge the evil from among you.[5]

As a result of the Jewish attitude toward miracles, there was no motivation for them to attribute to any individual a supernatural feat unless such an incident had actually come to pass.

The Jewish attitude toward miracles also helps to explain why the religious authorities of Jesus' day were not greatly impressed by Jesus' miracles. Even in the Talmud, as we noted in part I, the rabbis seem totally accepting of the fact that Jesus and his disciples were able to perform healing. Likewise, as noted earlier, the reliable portion of Josephus' mention of Jesus attributes to Jesus "marvelous works," an expression otherwise used for miracles. The gospel accounts as well indicate that the concern of the Pharisees was not whether Jesus had performed the miracles, but rather what the source of his power was.[6] Since they concluded that the source of Jesus' power was not God, it was incumbent upon them to obey Deuteronomy 13:1-5 and have Jesus slain. Though both Jewish and gospel sources indicate that aristocratic members of the Sanhedrin had selfish reasons for wanting Jesus killed, Christians should recognize also that there were likely devout Jews within the Sanhedrin who sincerely believed Jesus was guilty of a capital offense. Colin Brown emphasizes:

> To the official Judaism of Jesus' day, Jesus was a blasphemer who dealt in the occult and who was thus rightly put to death, especially if his activities might prompt an unfortunate clash with the Roman authorities. Perhaps the Christian church has never fully appreciated the importance of Deuteronomy 13 for the official Jewish understanding of Jesus. It provides the all-important clue to the attitude of Jewish leaders. The decision to get rid of Jesus was not prompted simply by envy and malice. In their eyes Jesus was a messianic pretender and false prophet who sought to justify his deviant teaching and practices by signs and wonders. To the Jewish leaders, signs and wonders were proof of guilt, providing clear-cut evidence (if only they could get competent witnesses to testify) that would justify the purging of evil from the midst of the people of God. (BrC.M 288)

Finally, the Jewish attitude toward miracles is profoundly significant for an accurate study of the gospel texts. All four gospel writers reflect a Jewish, not a Hellenistic perspective. As such, the miracles which appear in their texts are not there for embellishments or even as proofs of the veracity of their accounts. They are there because, like it or not, the gospel writers *had* to include them if they were to reflect what really took place in the earthly life of Jesus.

Naturalistic Attempts to Explain the Gospel Miracles

It is when Ian Wilson, in his popular book *Jesus: The Evidence,* comes to the chapters on the miracles and resurrection of Jesus that he is at his most desperate. We agree with him when he says, "That Jesus performed deeds that men called 'miracles' is therefore one of the best attested items of information about him." (Wil.JTE 99) It is in his attempted explanation of how Jesus performed these miracles that we cannot agree.

Wilson theorizes that Jesus was a master hypnotist who accomplished his miracles through hypnotism. Wilson primarily focuses on the healing miracles but does try to apply the hypnosis theory to the transfiguration and the turning of water into wine at Cana. He suggests that the inebriated guests at the wedding feast made good subjects for a mass hypnosis. As for the other nature miracles such as Jesus' walking on the water, stilling the storm and withering of the fig tree, these are not mentioned. Perhaps he thought it was going too far to suggest that Jesus hypnotized the fig tree!

Wilson first introduces hysteria as the cause of many different kinds of diseases including "disfiguring skin conditions, blindness, apparent inability to hear or speak, and all manner of symptoms of mental illness." (Wil.JTE 102) As support for this point he refers his readers to one chapter of Gordon Ambrose's and George Newbold's *Handbook of Medical Hypnosis.* (AmG.HMH) It is certainly not enough to convince an objective reader that Jesus traveled throughout a Palestinian countryside filled with hysterical people. What Wilson does not say, but what must be true for his theory to work, is that every person Jesus cured had to be hysterical. Not very likely, to say the least!

Then Wilson's next step is to suggest hypnosis as the *cure* Jesus used for his miracles. Of course one immediate problem with this thesis is the people, such as the centurion's servant and the Syrophoenecian woman's daughter, who Jesus healed at long distance. Wilson gives no evidence that hypnosis can be accomplished on a subject not present or previously put under a post-hypnotic trance.

Wilson does give examples of healing accomplished through hypnosis, but even his most celebrated example (an individual with ichthyosis, a rare skin disease) claimed only a 50 to 95 percent success rate depending on the area of this particular individual's body that was targeted by the hypnotist. The whole scenario just doesn't fit the information given in the gospel accounts. Jesus' healings were sudden (with one exception) and complete, and there is no evidence whatsoever of Jesus using hypnotic techniques.

The really big problem with this whole hypnosis theory is that there is such a huge disconnect between Jesus' teaching of his disciples to be truthful, honest and full of faith, and his practice of deception which he would have used to perform the healings by hypnosis yet claim that it really was the power of God residing in him. And where did Jesus pick up this knowledge of hypnosis?

On page 106, Wilson makes a weak attempt to suggest that Jesus may have gained his knowledge of hypnotism from the Egyptians, the mystery religions, or both. The evidence for the use of hypnotism in the ancient world is so scant that Wilson apparently felt compelled to hurry on to another topic. That hypnotism is used to effect the kinds of healing Jesus performed is nowhere attested. Then comes one of Wilson's most inaccurate statements:

> That whatever Jesus was using for his miracles was not an exclusive appurtenance of divinity, but was well within the powers of ordinary men, is quite evident from the gospels themselves, which describe him sending out his disciples to do the same healing work that he undertook himself: "He summoned his twelve disciples, and gave them authority over unclean spirits with power to cast them out, and to cure all kinds of diseases and sickness" (Matthew 10:1).

The quote completely misses the intent of the passage in Matthew's account. First, the writer's intent was to say that this authority was not "within the powers of ordinary men"; thus they had to receive it from Jesus. Second, as we have already said, Jesus' miracles were not intended, nor would they have been interpreted by Jews, as proof positive of Jesus' divinity. Third, if Jesus could heal at long distance, then he certainly could give to his disciples the authority to heal in his name. To suggest that Jesus simply taught his disciples hypnosis not only misses the point of the passage but also makes the evangelists liars even though they were willing to die for their lies, and for no gain. This point relates as well to Wilson's comment on page 113:

> Morton Smith would interpret in this way the "trip" Lazarus was sent on, his four days in the tomb being spent not in real death but in a death-like trance, all too easy to induce in hypnosis. It can even be done from a distance via post-hypnotic suggestion.

If Jesus put Lazarus in a deathlike, post-hypnotic trance, then Jesus is not one of the greatest figures in history; he is one of history's most despicable deceivers.

On page 109, Wilson misinterprets another passage:

> Jesus was not, therefore, in any way unique in possessing the power to exorcise. That such practices were relatively common, and not always successful, is well illustrated by an Acts account of a bungled attempt at exorcism by the sons of the Jewish chief priest Sceva: "The man with the evil spirit hurled himself at them and handled them so violently that they fled from the house naked and badly mauled" (Acts 19:13-16).

The point of this passage is that Sceva's sons (who, by the way, were attempting to use Jesus' name to accomplish exorcism) did not have the unique authority that Jesus had to perform the exorcism.

The objective reader of the passage could never draw the conclusion from it that "such practices were relatively common."

On page 143, in his chapter on the resurrection of Jesus, Wilson states:

> It is possible, if Dr. Morton Smith's theories are valid, that Stephen received one of the special hypnotic initiations, for he is certainly spoken of as a worker of "miracles and great signs" (Acts 6:8). One notable feature of hypnosis is a striking change in facial expression on the part of the subject while in the "trance" state, a phenomenon which may explain the information in Acts that, when he was before the Sanhedrin, Stephen's "face appeared to them like the face of an angel" (Acts 6:15).

Does anything more need to be said? Will not the sensible reader recognize that the evidence is being stretched to accommodate an unworkable theory?

On page 144, speaking of Paul's conversion experience, Wilson states that "Paul's reference to the event clearly indicates that he had been turned in his tracks by something of considerable hypnotic force." How did Paul receive this hypnotic force? He was completely unwilling (the subject's willingness is a key prerequisite for successful hypnosis), and he never sat under any of the so-called initiates in order to receive it. We must conclude that it takes more faith to believe Wilson's theory than to believe the gospel reports that God accomplished all these things by his power.

The Marks of Authenticity on the Gospel Miracles

The context of the gospel miracle narratives is the Jewish culture and its Old Testament background. Riesenfeld emphasizes:

> If we analyze the motives which form the content of the miracle narratives—and we must interpret the miracles as actions with a symbolic purpose which have their clear counterparts in the analogous symbolic acts of the Old Testament prophets—we find that the symbolism of all the miracles which occur and are described in the gospels rests on a genuine Old Testament and Jewish basis. It certainly did not arise in a Hellenistic milieu. (RiH.GTB 9)

We already have quoted hostile witnesses to the gospel who indicate that Jesus was, in fact, a worker of miracles. These references included: (1) the reliable portion of the Testimonium Flavianum;[7] (2) a reference from Rabbi Eliezer ben Hyrcanus c. AD 95;[8] (3) a rabbinic discussion c. AD 110 as to whether it was permissible to be healed in Jesus' name;[9] (4) a Talmudic statement that "Jesus practiced magic [a Jewish reference to satanic miracles] and led Israel astray";[10] and (5) the attribution of Jesus' miracles to sorcery by the second-century critic Celsus."[11]

The early Christians did not need to prove that Jesus had performed miracles. They simply appealed to the knowledge of their listeners. Less than two months after Jesus' crucifixion, on the day of Pentecost, Simon Peter told a large gathering, "Jesus the Nazarene, a man attested to you by God with miracles and wonders and signs which God performed through Him in your midst, just as you yourselves know…"[12] Peter therefore appeals to the knowledge of hostile witnesses, that they themselves were aware of the miracles of Jesus. That he wasn't immediately shouted down demonstrates that the wonders Jesus performed were well known. It is significant that this kind of firsthand testimony to the miraculous does not occur either in other religions or in Greek or Roman mythology.

Charles Anderson notes the following marks of authenticity on the gospel accounts:

> For the most part, the miracles were not performed in private. In a great many instances, there were unbelievers present when a miracle was performed. The miracles of Jesus were diverse in character and were performed in a variety of places and over a period of time. The acknowledgment of the cured should also be noticed. (AnC.CQ 130)

In addition, the words and works of Jesus are so inextricably meshed together that much of the gospel would make little or no sense if the miracles were removed.

Another mark of authenticity on the miracles of Jesus is that they were obviously performed not to inspire awe but to verify a message. Bruce notes:

> Our Lord did not esteem very highly the kind of belief that arose simply from witnessing miracles.[13] His desire was that men should realize what these things signified. They were signs of the messianic age, such as had been foretold by the prophets of old. (BrF.NTD 69)

The miracles of Jesus are in keeping with reality. They do not appear as the fantasies of imagination. Rather, they are presented as serious historical events which we might expect to occur if a supernatural God were attempting to verify a truth by breaking into the natural order. Again, Bruce observes:

> In literature there are many different kinds of miracle-stories; but the gospels do not ask us to believe that Jesus made the sun travel from west to east one day, or anything like that; they do not even attribute to Him such monstrosities as we find in the apocryphal gospels of the second century. In general, they are "in character"—that is to say, they are the kind of works that might be expected from such a person as the gospels represent Jesus to be. As we have seen, not even in the earliest gospel strata can we find a non-supernatural Jesus, and we need not be surprised if supernatural works are attributed to Him. (BrF.NTD 62)

Anderson affirms, "We have here no exhibition, no deception, no attempt at ego inflation that so completely underlies the miracles of other religious founders." (AnC.CQ

127) The gospel miracles also do not reflect the superstitious elements which are depicted in later Christian literature, especially that of the Middle Ages.

In view of these marks of authenticity on the gospel miracles, it is reasonable to conclude, as does Anthony Harvey, a leading Anglican scholar:

> In general, one can say that the miracle stories in the gospels are unlike anything else in ancient literature.... They do not exaggerate the miracle or add sensational details, like the authors of early Christian hagiography [lives of the saints]; but nor do they show the kind of detachment, amounting at times to scepticism, which is found in Herodotus or Lucian.... To a degree that is rare in the writings of antiquity, we can say, to use a modern phrase, that they tell the story straight. (HaA.J 110)

14

THE RELIABILITY OF THE
RESURRECTION REPORTS

The resurrection of Jesus of Nazareth is one of the most wicked, vicious, heartless hoaxes ever foisted upon the minds of humanity…OR…it is the most important fact of history. Further, the gospel writers who report the actual bodily resurrection of Jesus are viciously deceptive, hopelessly deceived…or boldly honest.

How can one believe in the historicity of the Jesus of the gospels when the gospel accounts of his life contain such an incredible story of his literal, bodily resurrection from the dead? If we are to accept the historicity of Jesus, we must have good reasons for believing that the gospel writers spoke accurately of Jesus' resurrection. If they did not, we have little hope of their having conveyed to us an accurate description of the rest of his life.

A previous volume, *The Resurrection Factor,* has dealt with the evidence for the resurrection of Jesus. (See MCJ.RF) In this chapter, we will narrow our focus to investigate only the evidence for the reliability of the resurrection reports. We will look at three main areas of evidence: (1) the early origination of the reports; (2) the historical nature of the reports; and (3) early Christian belief in the resurrection of Jesus.

EARLY ORIGINATION

The Letters of Paul

We have spoken primarily in this book about the gospel accounts of Jesus' life. However, scholars are virtually unanimous in agreeing that Paul's first letter to the Corinthians, as well as other letters he wrote, predate the finished form of the gospel accounts. Both Galatians (written probably in AD 48 or 49 from Syrian Antioch) and 1 Thessalonians (most likely written in AD 50 or 51 from Corinth) contain clear statements that God raised Jesus from the dead. Thus Paul is writing within 15 to 21 years of the resurrection that it actually occurred. Paul's earliest testimony to the resurrection, however, goes all the way back to within approximately three years of its occurrence. Let us explain. In 1 Corinthians 15:3-8 (written c. AD 55) he says:

> For I delivered to you as of first importance what I also received, that Christ died for our sins according to the Scriptures, and that He was buried, and that He was raised on the third day according to the Scriptures, and that He appeared to Cephas, then to the twelve. After that He appeared to more than five hundred brethren at one time, most of whom remain until now, but some have fallen asleep; then He appeared to James, then to all the apostles; and last of all, as it were to one untimely born, He appeared to me also.

Scholars have seen in this passage, not the words of Paul, but a very early report or creed which was in fact "received" from the first witnesses and which Paul then "delivers" just as it was delivered to him. The Jewish scholar Pinchas Lapide relates eight linguistic factors which give evidence for the fact that Paul is passing on a very early report concerning the resurrection:

1. Vocabulary, sentence structure, and diction are clearly not Pauline.

2. The parallelism of the three individual statements is biblically formulated.

3. The threefold "and that" characterizes the Aramaic and Mishnaic Hebrew way of narration.

4. The "divine passive" of "being raised" paraphrases God's action of salvation in order not to mention God, in accordance with the Jewish fear of the name.

5. The Aramaic form of the name "Cephas," not Simon, as Luke gives it in the parallel passage 24:32, sounds more original.

6. The double reference "in accordance with the Scriptures" supports twice in three lines both the death and the resurrection of Jesus—as it probably corresponds with the faithfulness of the early church to the Hebrew Bible.

7. "The twelve" [signifies]...a closed group of the first witnesses....

8. Finally, the statement, which in its basic features is repeated in almost all later reports of the resurrection, narrates the course of four events which were understood as salvation bearing: He died for our sins...was buried... was raised...and appeared... (LaP.R 98-99)

The British scholar James D. G. Dunn affirms concerning 1 Corinthians 15:3-8:

> Paul was converted within two or three years of Jesus' death, perhaps as little as eighteen months after the first reports of Jesus being seen alive after his death. And almost certainly he received this basic outline of the gospel very soon after his conversion, as part of his initial instruction. In other words, the testimony of 1 Corinthians 15:3-8 goes back to within two or three years of the events described. (DuJ.E 70)

Within five years after the crucifixion, Paul was in Jerusalem having opportunity to confirm this creedal statement with Peter and James.[1] Even more compelling is Paul's challenge underlying the phrase, "He appeared to more than 500 brethren at one time, most of whom remain until now." As Sir Norman Anderson puts it:

> In these words he put his whole credibility at stake; for what he wrote was, in effect, an implicit invitation to any who doubted his statement to put it to the test, since the majority of five hundred witnesses were still available to be questioned. And in the ancient world it would not have been a terribly difficult task to contact some of them. (AnN.JC 121)

In view of Paul's early testimony regarding the resurrection of Jesus, any contention that this event was simply legend is unthinkable. Legends develop through many generations and centuries, not within a couple of years.

Paul also makes sure his readers understand that he is speaking of a physical resurrection. Professor Robert Gundry, who teaches Greek language and literature and New Testament studies at Westmont College, shows that "Paul's juxtaposing Jesus' burial and resurrection, which literally means 'raising,' entails that his resurrection means the raising of his buried body." (GuR.PR 4) Gundry continues:

> In the further part of 1 Corinthians 15 Paul writes about the future resurrection of believers after the pattern and on the ground of Jesus' resurrection. His use of the Greek word *soma* in this discussion therefore says something about the nature of Jesus' resurrection. If the future resurrection of believers will be somatic [bodily], so also was Jesus' resurrection, as is only natural to deduce from the aforementioned juxtaposition of burial and raising. Now *soma* means the physical body. Even as a metaphor it means the physical body, only the physical body as an analogy for something else. Right here in 1 Corinthians, for example, Paul's famous metaphor of the body for the church goes down to the physical details of different bodily parts— head, eyes, ears, nose, hands, feet, genitals (12:12-27). (GuR.PR 5)

The Gospel According to Mark

Though Paul's letters were probably written before the gospel accounts were completed, there is again compelling evidence that Mark's narrative is based on a very early tradition which goes back to the actual eyewitnesses.[2] The evidence includes:

1. Each part of the passion narrative makes little sense when separated from the rest. Therefore scholars have accepted it as a unified whole which existed before Mark wrote his gospel.

2. Joseph of Arimathea is specifically mentioned by name. Since, as a member of the Sanhedrin, his name would have been well known, someone inventing the story would probably not have used it. Moreland states, "No

one could have invented a person who did not exist and say he was on the Sanhedrin if such were not the case." (MoJPS 167) Anyone in Jerusalem could very easily walk over to his house and check out the story firsthand.

3. The tomb of Jesus accords with what archaeology has revealed about first-century Jewish burial sites.

4. The naming of specific women as the first witnesses to the empty tomb was highly embarrassing for the first-century Jews. A woman's testimony was considered as practically worthless in a court of law and was hardly ever allowed. No invented account would have named any women as the first witnesses if it wanted to gain credibility. Moreland notes, "This probably explains why the women are not mentioned in 1 Corinthians 15 and the speeches of Acts, since these speeches were evangelistic." (MoJPS 168) Further, that Mary Magdalene (one previously possessed by demons) is named would have further eroded confidence in the report. The only possible reason for a writer including this information is that he was compelled to tell the truth, the whole truth and nothing but the truth.

5. The narrative is restrained and devoid of theological reflection and mythological embellishment which abounds in the apocryphal gospels. For example, in "The Gospel of Peter," Jesus leaves the tomb supported by two men descended from heaven. Their heads stretch up to heaven, but Jesus' head stretches past the clouds. A cross trails behind all three. It answers yes to a voice which asks, "Hast thou preached to them that sleep?"

6. The difficulty of harmonizing all the details in the four gospel accounts attests to the writers calling it as they (or their sources) saw it.

7. The presence of Semitic forms of speech negates any possible thought of later Hellenistic mythological influence.

This kind of evidence indicates that the resurrection reports are so early that they must have originated, just as they claim, from the very events which they describe.

HISTORICAL NATURE

In addition to the evidence indicating a very early origination of the resurrection reports, other evidence demonstrates that they are historical, not mythological, legendary or fictitious in nature.

Lack of Window Dressing

The credibility of the accounts of the resurrection, both those of the gospel writers and that of Paul, is increased by the lack of window dressing which one would normally expect to accompany an event of this magnitude. As the Jewish scholar Pinchas Lapide, writing from a Jewish perspective, states:

Nowhere is the event designated as a "miracle," as an event of salvation, or as a deed of God, a fact which tends to support the plausibility of the report for the disinterested reader. We do not read in the first testimonies of an apocalyptic spectacle, exorbitant sensations, or of the transforming impact of a cosmic event. (LaP.R 100)

According to all New Testament reports, no human eye saw the resurrection itself, no human being was present, and none of the disciples asserted to have apprehended, let alone understood, its manner and nature. How easy it would have been for them or their immediate successors to supplement this scandalous hole in the concatenation of events by fanciful embellishments! But precisely because none of the evangelists dared to "improve upon" or embellish this unseen resurrection, the total picture of the gospels also gains in trustworthiness. (LaP.R 97)

This is a remarkable statement by one who has no Christian axe to grind. Continuing along the same lines, Sir Norman Anderson asks:

What legend-monger would ascribe the first interview with the risen Christ to Mary Magdalene, a woman of no great standing in the Christian church? Would he not have ascribed such an honour to Peter, the leading apostle; or to John, the "disciple whom Jesus loved"; or—more likely still, perhaps—to Mary the mother of our Lord? And who can read the story of the appearance to Mary Magdalene, or the incident in which the risen Christ appeared to two disciples on Easter Day on an afternoon walk to Emmaus, or the episode in which Peter and John raced each other to the tomb, and seriously conclude that these are legends? They are far too dignified and restrained; far too true to life and psychology. The difference between them and the sort of stories recorded in the apocryphal gospels of a century or two later is both striking and significant. (AnN.JC 123)

The idea that the resurrection story was derived from pagan mystery religions and Greek myths is no longer taken seriously. William Craig, Professor of Philosophy at Westmont College, having completed two earned doctorates in studies related to this area, is well acquainted with the Hellenistic myth theory and those who have propagated it. In a recent lecture in Peoria, Illinois, he stated, "I know of no reputable New Testament scholar or historian today who would any longer defend the view that the Christian ideas of the resurrection were derived from parallels of pagan religions."

Honesty Regarding Disciples' Failures

The accounts of the resurrection obtain even greater credibility because of their honesty in informing the reader of the disciples' failure to grasp the significance of the resurrection or to believe in Jesus following the resurrection. The women, on their way to the tomb, give no hint of an expectation that Jesus had accomplished a bodily resurrection, indicating their misunderstanding of his predictions to rise again from the dead. Mary Magdalene says more than once, "They have taken away the Lord out of the tomb, and we do not know where they have laid Him" (John 20:2, cf. John 20:15).

Luke 24:11 says that the words of the women appeared to the disciples as nonsense. Only that "other disciple" (probably John), who ran to the tomb with Peter, is credited with having "believed." Mark 16:11 states that when the disciples heard the women's report, "They refused to believe it." And why should they? Mary Magdalene had previously suffered from mental instability, a condition which had been cured only after Jesus cast out seven demons from her. For all the disciples knew she may have had a relapse.

After Cleopas and another disciple met the risen Jesus on the road to Emmaus, they returned to the other disciples to report what they had seen. "They did not believe them either," says Mark 16:13.

Then Jesus came to stand in their midst and reproached them "for their unbelief and hardness of heart, because they had not believed those who had seen Him after He had risen" (Mark 16:14). Luke 24:38-46 describes Jesus' attempts to overcome their unbelief. John 20:20 says simply, "He showed them both His hands and His side."

And then there is Thomas. Since he missed this first meeting of Jesus with all the disciples gathered together, he responds to the other disciples' report, "Unless I shall see in His hands the imprint of the nails, and put my finger into the place of the nails and put my hand into His side, I will not believe" (John 20:25). Jesus therefore appears to all of the disciples with Thomas included eight days later.

But even all of this is not enough for the disciples. If our chronology is correct, it is only after the events described above that the disciples, in obedience to the original instructions of Jesus, proceed to Galilee "to the mountain which Jesus had designated" (Matthew 28:16). Can't you just see the disciples waiting for Jesus to appear? Days go by and no Jesus. This mountain probably overlooked the Sea of Galilee, and no doubt the fishermen among the bunch looked down on those waters thinking how good it would be to haul in a big catch. Finally Peter says bluntly what others are also thinking, "I am going fishing." Thomas, Nathanael, John, James and two other disciples go with him.

While they are fishing, Jesus makes his appearance, telling them where to cast the net in order to obtain a large catch of fish. Then after conversing over breakfast with Peter and the others who had been fishing, it seems Jesus also must have gone with them back to the others still waiting on the mountain. But Matthew 28:17 states, "And when they saw Him, they worshiped Him; but some were doubtful."

The honesty of the gospel writers to report all of these doubts of the disciples speaks loud and clear that these reports are of a historical nature, very unlike the popular mythologies of surrounding pagan religions.

CONTRAST WITH JEWISH LEGENDS

Pinchas Lapide, strongly committed to the Jewish faith, nevertheless is careful to distinguish between the historical nature of the resurrection in the gospels and the embellished narratives which he finds in the Jewish Targums and Midrash. He explains:

> The Targums are translations of the biblical text into the Aramaic popular language which were made before the time of Jesus. They embellished this translation by paraphrastic statements, enlargements, and explanations. Another example is the Midrash—that "investigation of the Scriptures" which frequently takes the biblical text only as the starting point for a plethora of moral teachings, homilies, legends, and tales, in order to deepen the Holy Scriptures and "to bring heaven closer to the community." (LaP.R 101)

> To blame the rabbis and evangelists for deception or to accuse them of lying would have been as foreign to the Jews and Jewish Christians of that time as an accusation of "embellishment" against Shakespeare's *Macbeth* would be to us. The best proof for the solid faith in the resurrection is probably the realistic way in which the two oldest gospels describe the painful death and Jesus' cry of despair on the cross: "And Jesus uttered a loud cry, and breathed His last" (Mark 15:37). (LaP.R 109-10)

Other Evidence

Other evidence for the historical nature of the resurrection reports includes:

- There is no mention of Jesus' tomb ever being venerated as were those of at least fifty other prophets, later including Hanina ben Dosa. The only good explanation is that Jesus' bones were no longer there. (YaE.EMH 4:4-16)

- Matthew records that the only Jewish response to the preaching of the resurrection was the accusation that the disciples stole the body. This is an implicit acknowledgment that the tomb was empty as the resurrection accounts report.

- Similarly, it would have been impossible to preach the resurrection in Jerusalem if the tomb still contained Jesus' body. The big question therefore is, "Who's got the body?" That question is discussed in *The Resurrection Factor*. For now, it is enough to see that the reports of the empty tomb are confirmed by the historical situations.

- If someone invented the resurrection story, one would think the disciples would be out on the streets proclaiming it the very next day. But the gospel writers include a seven-week delay during which time the disciples are gathering for prayer and seeing occasional appearances of Jesus. During this period they still seem to be generally confused and impotent regarding their mission. Not until the filling of the Holy Spirit at Pentecost do they become bold witnesses. The narratives therefore lack signs of being contrived. Their descriptions of the abnormal attest their veracity.

But What About the Contradictions?

Although Lapide argues for the actual bodily resurrection of Jesus, he nevertheless follows the lead of other critical scholars when he says of the resurrection in the gospels:

> In no other area of the New Testament narrative are the contradictions so glaring. Nowhere else are the opposites so obvious and the contrasting descriptions so questionable as in the realm of the resurrection of Jesus.
> (LaP.R 34-36)

Ian Wilson accuses, "The various accounts of the scene at the empty tomb on the first Easter morning are so full of inconsistencies that it is easy to deride them." In actuality, those who see contradictions in the resurrection accounts often betray that they have only superficially studied the accounts. Ian Wilson, for example, charges, "The writer of the John gospel describes Mary Magdalene arriving at the tomb alone.... The Matthew author relates that Mary Magdalene was accompanied by 'Mary the mother of James and Joseph.'" (WiI.JTE 138) There is in fact no contradiction here. One could resolve the problem just by saying that John focused on Mary Magdalene alone, while Matthew focused on the group.

In actuality, the apparent contradiction is one of a series of clues which help answer such questions as where the different women stayed on the Sabbath and what routes they took to the tomb on Sunday morning. The whole scenario is impressively revealed by the outstanding British New Testament scholar John Wenham, in his book *Easter Enigma*. (WeJW.EE) In it he pieces together the available evidence to demonstrate that the resurrection reports contain, not contradictions, but clues to the many individual and group activities of the key witnesses to the events of the crucifixion and resurrection of Jesus.

Any attorney who has faced the task of piecing together apparently conflicting courtroom testimony can understand how difficult it is to reconcile a contradiction between two witnesses. For many years, until his retirement, Sir Norman Anderson was the Director of the Institute of Advanced Legal Studies at the University of London. As one thoroughly acquainted with apparent conflicts in the testimony of different witnesses, he states:

> I must confess that I am appalled by the way in which some people—biblical scholars among them—are prepared to make the most categorical statements that this story cannot possibly be reconciled with that, or that such and such statements are wholly irreconcilable, when a little gentle questioning of the witnesses, were this possible, might well have cleared up the whole problem. Sometimes, indeed, a tentative solution may not be very far to seek even without such questioning, although the suggested

reconciliation cannot, of course, be proved; and in others there may well be a perfectly satisfactory solution which evades us. (AnN.JC 139)

Solutions to apparent Bible contradictions provide confidence that other alleged conflicts also have solutions. Often, the solutions reveal just how precisely God has communicated to us in the Bible. Apparent contradictions become assuring confirmations of the Bible's minute accuracy and trustworthiness.[3]

EARLY CHRISTIAN BELIEF

Virtually all biblical scholars today agree that, whether or not Jesus rose from the dead, at the very least the first disciples sincerely believed that he had. The question, then, is where did the early Christians get this belief in the resurrection? Craig states:

> Without belief in the resurrection of Jesus, Christianity could never have come into being. The crucifixion would have remained the final tragedy in the hopeless life of Jesus. The origin of Christianity hinges on the belief of these earliest disciples that Jesus had risen from the dead. The question now inevitably arises: How does one explain the origin of that belief? As R. H. Fuller urges, even the most skeptical critic must posit some mysterious *X* to get the movement going but the question is, what was that *X*? (CrW.RO 93)

Scholars, especially in Germany, have tried and found wanting the theory that Christianity borrowed its resurrection story from the Greek myths and pagan mystery religions. Increasingly, therefore, scholars today are looking for Jewish roots of the resurrection accounts.

There is no doubt that religious Jews did believe in a bodily resurrection. Craig summarizes some of the main evidence:

> The Jewish doctrine of resurrection is attested three times in the Old Testament (Ezekiel 37; Isaiah 26–29; Daniel 12:2) and flowered during the intertestamental period (2 Maccabees 7:9-42; 12:43-5; 1 Enoch 5:7; 22:1-14; 51:1; 61:5; 90:33; 91:9-10; 100:4-5; Testament of the Twelve Patriarchs [Judah] 25:1,4: [Zebulun] 10:2; [Benjamin] 10:16-18; 2 Baruch 30:2-5; 50:1; 4 Esdras 7:26-44). It was probably not the result of Iranian influences, but rather the logical outworking of Yahweh's power over death and the future (Psalm 16:10; 49:16; Isaiah 25:8; 49:16). The deaths of the Jewish martyrs provided a powerful stimulus to the development of this doctrine. During Jesus' day the belief in bodily resurrection had become a widespread hope, being championed by the Pharisees, with whom Jesus sided on this score against the Sadducees (Matthew 22:23-33; cf. Acts 23:8). (CrW.RO 4)

There are two significant differences, however, between the Jewish belief in bodily resurrection and the Christian belief in Jesus' resurrection. First, though Jewish biblical history contained accounts of resuscitation, the Jewish people believed that true bodily resurrection would only occur at the end of time or history, not within history as a historical event. Every "resurrected" person eventually died again. Second, the Jewish view of resurrection conceived it as general, not just of a single individual. These two aspects, that the resurrection would be (1) general, and (2) at the end of history, are always in view in the Jewish perception of resurrection. Craig states:

> Thus, when Jesus assures Martha that her brother Lazarus will rise again, she responds, "I know that he will rise again in the resurrection at the last day" (John 11:24). She has no idea that Jesus is about to bring him back to life. Similarly, when Jesus tells his disciples he will rise from the dead, they think he means at the end of the world (Mark 9:9-13). (CrW.CS 93)

Dunn emphasizes:

> The resurrection the Pharisees looked for was the resurrection of the dead at the end of history, the "general resurrection"—the resurrection of which Daniel speaks: "Many of those who sleep in the dust of the earth shall awake, some to everlasting life, and some to shame and everlasting contempt" (Daniel 12.2). The unusual feature about the Christian claim was their belief that Jesus alone had been raised before the end. (DuJ.E 73)

There is therefore no reason, according to Jewish belief, that the early Christians should have developed a belief in the bodily resurrection (1) within history, or (2) of a single individual, namely Jesus. In Craig's words, "The mysterious X is still missing." (CrW.RO 6) We are therefore driven back to the resurrection accounts for an explanation.

In addition, though the first Christians, almost all Jewish, continued to worship in the synagogue and observe the Sabbath as a day of rest, they also began to gather on the first day of the week (Acts 20:7) to "break bread," most likely in celebration of the resurrection of Jesus. (See CaDA.FS 280-302) This practice points once again to the resurrection narratives as the only explanation left.

Finally, the dramatically changed lives of the early Christians call for an equally dramatic explanation as a believable cause. In this regard, the testimony of the non-Christian Jewish scholar Pinchas Lapide is a powerful one. We use the word "non-Christian," not in a disparaging sense, but rather in the sense that Lapide does not believe in Jesus as the Messiah. Yet in a strong gesture of reconciliation with those he believes to be his brothers in the faith of the one true living God of Abraham, Isaac and Jacob, Lapide expresses his firm conviction in the historical actuality of the bodily resurrection of Jesus:

> How can it be explained that, against all plausibility, his adherents did *not* finally scatter, were *not* forgotten, and that the cause of Jesus did *not* reach its infamous end on the cross?
>
> How could a proclaimer of salvation, three times disappointed, three times disappointing, become the starting point of the greatest and most influential world religion?

How was it possible that his disciples, who by no means excelled in intelligence, eloquence, or strength of faith, were able to begin their victorious march of conversion only *after* the shattering fiasco on Golgotha—a march which put all their successes before Easter completely into the shadow?

In other words: How did it nevertheless come about that the adherents of Jesus were able to conquer this most horrible of all disappointments, that Jesus despite everything, became the Savior of the church, although his predictions were not fulfilled and his longed-for parousia did not take place? (LaP.R 69)

Lapide answers these questions by reviewing his own struggle and the conclusions to which his study led him:

In regard to the future resurrection of the dead, I am and remain a Pharisee. [The Pharisees believed in a bodily resurrection.] Concerning the resurrection of Jesus on Easter Sunday, I was for decades a Sadducee. [The Sadducees did not believe in a bodily resurrection.] I am no longer a Sadducee since the following deliberation has caused me to think this through anew. In none of the cases where rabbinic literature speaks of such visions did it result in an essential change in the life of the resuscitated or of those who had experienced the visions. Only the vision remains which was retold in believing wonderment and sometimes also embellished, but it did not have any noticeable consequences.

It is different with the disciples of Jesus on that Easter Sunday…. When this scared, frightened band of the apostles which was just about to throw away everything in order to flee in despair to Galilee, when these peasants, shepherds, and fishermen, who betrayed and denied their master and then failed him miserably, suddenly could be changed overnight into a confident mission society, convinced of salvation and able to work with much more success after Easter than before Easter, then no vision or hallucination is sufficient to explain such a revolutionary transformation. For a sect or school or an order, perhaps a single vision would have been sufficient— but not for a world religion which was able to conquer the Occident thanks to the Easter faith. (LaP.R 125-26)

On the same point, the British scholar C. F. D. Moule states:

If the coming into existence of the Nazarenes, a phenomenon undeniably attested by the New Testament, rips a great hole in history, a hole the size and shape of the resurrection, what does the secular historian propose to stop it up with?…The birth and rapid rise of the Christian Church… *remain an unsolved enigma for any historian who refuses to take seriously the only explanation offered by the Church itself.* (MoCF.PNT 3,13)

CONCLUSION

The evidence available points to a very early origination of the reports of Jesus' resurrection. The reports are so early, in fact, that they had to originate with the disciples themselves telling their experiences of that first Sunday morning when they found the tomb empty. The reports they gave were of a historical, not a mythological or legendary, nature. These reports tell of Jesus' resurrection in such a way that the story could not have been borrowed from either Hellenistic or Jewish expectations. It is therefore most logical to accept the reports as those of men and women simply passing on the things they had observed. In other words, the reports of Jesus' resurrection are reliable historical sources to what actually took place.

MESSIAH AND SON OF GOD?

All four gospel writers repeatedly refer to Jesus as "Christ," the Greek translation for the Hebrew "Messiah," meaning "anointed one." Even more alarming to the Hebrew mind, the gospel writers all repeatedly refer to Jesus as the Son of God. Putting the two together, Mark opens his account: "The beginning of the gospel of Jesus Christ, the Son of God." According to Matthew 16:16, Peter did the same when he answered Jesus, "Thou art the Christ, the Son of the living God."

These statements in the gospel narratives (as well as the early teaching of Paul and others) raise a critical question to the issue of Jesus' historicity: If the gospel writers wrongfully wrote of Jesus as Messiah, Son of God, even God himself, how can they be trusted to give us an accurate description of the historical Jesus? We must discuss, therefore, whether or not the gospel writers were wrong in attributing messiahship and deity to Jesus.

The thought that Jewish writers might ascribe deity to another human being has brought much criticism to the gospel accounts. Ian Wilson, in his book *Jesus: The Evidence,* has one chapter called "How He Became God." In it he even claims that "no gospel regarded Jesus as God, and not even Paul had done so." (WiLJTE 168) According to Wilson, the deifying of Jesus was primarily a product of the fourth-century Council of Nicaea, not the belief of early Christians.

In this chapter, therefore, it is necessary to sort out the historical details related to Jesus' alleged messiahship and deity. Did he think of himself as Messiah and Son of God? What did he mean by the terms "Son of God" and "Son of Man"? What did the people understand him to mean? In order to answer these questions, we first must understand what the people expected Messiah to be like.

MESSIANIC EXPECTATIONS

For about a hundred years, beginning in 164 BC, the Jewish people tasted independence. Professor Jim Fleming, reflecting on the final loss of Jewish national sovereignty, states:

Although this period had found its abrupt termination with the campaign of the Romans and General Pompey (63 B.C.), hope for its restoration had never been given up completely. Jesus was born into a time when the people anticipated the coming of the Messiah (cf. Psalm of Solomon 17) and freedom from the Roman yoke. (FIJ.LJ 5)

One of the best analyses of first-century messianic expectations has been done by Geza Vermes. He observes that at this time there was both a widespread popular belief about what Messiah would be like and a number of minority splinter opinions: "It would seem more appropriate to bear in mind the difference between general messianic expectations of Palestinian Jewry, and peculiar messianic speculations characteristic of certain learned and/or esoterical minorities." (VeG.JTJ 130)

In order to determine what kind of Messiah the Jewish masses generally expected, Vermes advises, "A reliable answer is to be found in the least academic, and at the same time most normative literary form: prayer."

Therefore, one of the best surviving sources regarding messianic expectation during this time is the Psalms of Solomon, probably written just after the Roman conquest of Judaea in 63 BC. These psalms (obviously not written by Solomon) reflect the common view of a righteous, reigning Messiah who would militarily reestablish Israel's sovereignty and restore a just government over the nation:

> Behold, O Lord, and raise up unto them their king, the son of David…
> And gird him with strength, that he may shatter unrighteous rulers…With
> a rod of iron he shall break in pieces all their substance, He shall destroy the
> godless nations with the word of his mouth…And he shall gather together
> a holy people…He shall have the heathen nations to serve him under his
> yoke…And he shall be a righteous king, taught by God…And there shall
> be no unrighteousness in his days in their midst, For all shall be holy and
> their king the Anointed (of) the Lord.[1]

Psalm of Solomon 18 speaks of God's Anointed, who will "use his 'rod' to instill the 'fear of the Lord' into every man and direct them to 'the works of righteousness.'" (VeG.JTJ 181)

Fleming notes:

> A popular "paperback," written perhaps a generation or two before Jesus,
> reflects the thoughts of many who flocked to Jesus along the plain of Gen-
> nesaret…"A holy king will come and reign over all the world—and then
> his wrath will fall on the people of Latium, and Rome will be destroyed to
> the ground…O poor and desolate me! When will the day come, the judg-
> ment day of the eternal God, of the great king?" (Sibylline Oracles). (FIJ.JAS 21)

Both the Zealots and the Sicarii (a group with aims similar to those of the Zealots) found in this commonly held expectation fertile soil for the cultivation of their military cause. Others, like the Pharisees, were content to wait for one fashioned more clearly in the mold of King David. "Son of David" was the popular term, taken from the Old Testament, for the expected Messiah. Philo's description of the expected Messiah probably best expresses the military prowess of the coming one. In his book *Rewards and Punishment,* he interprets Balaam's prophecy in Numbers 24:7 in this way: "'For there shall come forth a man,' says the oracle, 'and leading his host to war he will subdue great and populous nations, because God has sent to his aid the reinforcement which befits the godly, and that is dauntless courage of soul and all-powerful strength of body, either of which strikes fear into the enemy and the two, if united, are quite irresistible.'"[2] Vermes concludes:

> Ancient Jewish prayer and Bible interpretation demonstrate unequivocally that if in the intertestamental era a man claimed, or was proclaimed, to be "the Messiah," his listeners would as a matter of course have assumed that he was referring to the Davidic Redeemer and would have expected to find before them a person endowed with the combined talents of soldierly prowess, righteousness and holiness. (VeG.JTJ 134)

It is therefore understandable why, especially in view of the Roman occupation of Israel's land, most Jewish people would not see in Jesus what they expected of the Messiah.

Millar Burrows of Yale wrote, "Jesus was so unlike what all Jews expected the son of David to be that his own disciples found it almost impossible to connect the idea of Messiah with him." (BuM.ML[V] 68) And finally, as the Jewish scholar Samuel Sandmel puts it, "Any claims made, during the lifetime of Jesus, that he was the Messiah whom the Jews had awaited, were rendered poorly defensible by his crucifixion and by the collapse of any political aspect of his movement, and by the sad actuality that Palestine was still not liberated from Roman dominion." (SaS.JU/56 33)

The popular concept of Messiah as a reigning military deliverer, then, was a natural deterrent for most Jewish people to consider Jesus as Messiah. The question is: Was the popular conception of the coming Messiah the correct one?

It is clear that not all Jewish people of Jesus' day held the majority opinion. Vermes observes, "In addition to the royal concept, messianic speculation in ancient Judaism included notions of a priestly and prophetic Messiah, and in some cases, of a messianic figure who would perform all these functions in one." (VeG.JTJ 135) The Testament of Levi, for example, said:

> Then shall the Lord raise up a new priest…And he shall execute a righteous judgment upon the earth…And his star shall arise in heaven as of a king… And there shall be peace in all the earth…And the knowledge of the Lord shall be poured forth…as the water of the seas…And the spirit of understanding and sanctification shall rest upon him.[3]

The Qumran community seems to have looked forward to three messianic figures. One of their documents predicts, "Until there shall come the Prophet and the Messiahs of Aaron and Israel." (VeM.DSS 87) Second Baruch 30:1 speaks of the Messiah returning "in glory" from earth presumably to heaven, and 4 Ezra 14:9 speaks of a Messiah ("my Son") dwelling apparently in heaven. Fourth Ezra 7:29 speaks of the death of Messiah, as do other references, some of which may be later than AD 135 and therefore alluding to the death of Simon bar Kosiba (Kokhba), whom Rabbi Akiba held to be the Messiah.

The important point is that not everyone held to the popular concept of the long-awaited Messiah. There was enough obscurity in what Messiah was to be that a number of the especially religious Jews found the charisma of Jesus to fit with their picture of the Messiah. The fact that they also expected him to deliver Israel from Roman oppression made Jesus' primary mission more complicated. Fleming explains:

> The crowds along "our side" [of the Sea of Galilee] so constantly pressed upon Jesus that he had difficulty teaching the people. His reputation as a healing rabbi preceded his desire to be known as a teacher. When Jesus is on "our side" he often tells people he heals to keep it quiet so that multitudes wouldn't assemble for healing, signs, and wonders. Many Jews associated Jesus' healing gifts with that of a Messiah who might lead the country in revolt against Rome. Many in the crowds were probably curious to see what position he would take concerning Roman oppression. (FiJ.JAS 21)

Whether or not Jesus primarily wanted to be known as a teacher may be questioned. What is clear is that the popular concept of Messiah did not fit his concept of Messiah.

Coupled with one other factor, it becomes abundantly clear why Jesus did not go around publicly announcing, "I am the Messiah; follow me." The big problem was the Romans. They were completely aware of the popular messianic expectations of the Jewish people. Tacitus (writing at the beginning of the second century AD) reports, "There was a firm persuasion...that at this very time the East was to grow powerful, and rulers coming from Judea were to acquire a universal empire."[4] At about the same time, writing about the decade following the destruction of the Temple in AD 70, Suetonius wrote, "There had spread over all the Orient an old and established belief, that it was fated at that time for men coming from Judea to rule the world."[5] It is obvious that the Romans were ready at a minute's notice to crush any messianic uprising. No wonder Jesus did not go around blurting out, "I am the Messiah." As we will see, he had much more effective ways of making that announcement.

The gospels reveal often the messianic expectations of the people. From the beginning of Jesus' earthly life, when Simeon in the Temple identifies Jesus as the long-awaited Messiah, to the end, when many honor him as Messiah at the triumphal entry into Jerusalem, the gospel accounts accurately reflect these expectations.

The messianic expectations of the Jewish people provide one of the strongest reasons for trusting the accuracy of the gospel accounts as they describe Jesus' activities. Skeptics often claim that the life of Jesus described in the gospel is too supernatural to be believed. What is often forgotten is that the great cause of the disciples died on the cross. Jesus certainly did not fulfill the messianic expectations of his disciples. Something had to happen, something no less powerful than what the gospel accounts record, in order to motivate Jewish men and women to risk their lives to propagate this message which was so diametrically opposed to the prevailing messianic opinion of the day.

DID JESUS THINK HE WAS MESSIAH?

> In fact, since the figure of the Messiah appears not to have been central to the teaching of Jesus, and since no record has survived of any hostile challenge concerning his messianic status before his last days in Jerusalem; since, moreover, he deliberately withheld his approval of Peter's confession and, in general, failed to declare himself to be the Christ, there is every reason to wonder if he really thought of himself as such. (VeG.JTJ 149)

In this statement, Geza Vermes raises the following four objections to the proposition that Jesus believed himself to be the Messiah:

1. that the figure of the Messiah was not central to Jesus' teaching;
2. that there is no record of any hostile challenge, prior to his last days in Jerusalem, to Jesus' messianic status;
3. that Jesus deliberately withheld his approval of Peter's confession that Jesus was the Christ;
4. that, in general, Jesus failed to declare himself to be the Christ.

Let's evaluate each point separately.

Objection #1. "The figure of the Messiah appears not to have been central to the teaching of Jesus."

Put yourself in Jesus' sandals. If you were the Messiah, would you have focused all your teaching on the correct conceptualization of the Messiah? Consider these points:

First, your ministry is one of traveling and you know that every time you use the word *Messiah* everyone out there is going to misinterpret what you are saying. It's a loaded word.

Second, from your vantage point (as Messiah) you know that the people's concept of the Messiah is not the only thing askew. More important, their whole picture of the kingdom of God has become distorted. A casual reading through the red print in a red print edition of the book of Matthew will reveal how much Jesus needed to teach the people in addition to a correct view of Messiah.

Third, actions speak louder than words. If you really were the Messiah, wouldn't it be more effective to demonstrate it rather than just teach about it?

Fourth, Jesus did, in an indirect but more effective way, clarify the true meaning and purpose of Messiah's role through what he said. Looking again only at Matthew's gospel, he showed that

- Messiah must fulfill all righteousness (3:15);
- Messiah is the revealer of the Kingdom of heaven (4:17);
- Messiah makes men fishers of men (4:19);
- Messiah teaches with supreme authority, e.g., "You have heard that it was said…but I say to you…"(chapters 5–7);
- Messiah came to fulfill the Law and the Prophets (5:17).

We could go on, but you get the point. Everything Jesus said pointed to a correct view of the kingdom of God being established by himself as Messiah.

But more directly, Jesus did attempt to clarify through his teaching the identity of the Messiah. All three synoptic gospels record his question to a group of rabbis: "What do you think about the Messiah, whose son is He?"[6]

When they respond, "The Son of David," he asks, "Then how does David in the Spirit call Him 'Lord,' saying 'The LORD said to my Lord, "Sit at my right hand, until I put Your enemies beneath Your feet"'? If David calls Him 'Lord,' how is He his son?" No one gave him an answer. Jesus was driving at something which was outside the Pharisees' categories of possibility. Could the Messiah possibly be Lord over David, in other words, from eternity? The answer: "No comment!" It's kind of like the man who walks up to a famous actor, say Jack Nicholson, and says, "Has anyone ever told you that you look a lot like Jack Nicholson?"

When Nicholson responds, "Maybe that's because I *am* Jack Nicholson," the man answers, "No, you couldn't be. Jack Nicholson has more hair than you do."

What can you say? The man already has his categories and you don't fit.

Jesus was driving at the same point immediately afterward when he spoke to the crowd standing around him. In the middle of his teaching he stated, "And do not be called leaders; for one is your leader, that is, Christ."[7] Later, he spoke to his disciples about how to recognize false messiahs and even identifies the Son of Man, his favorite term of self-reference, as the Messiah.[8] The clear indication of his words is that the Messiah is more than an earthly figure. In John 7:25-29, Jesus seeks to clarify the nature of the Messiah. This time the response is an order for soldiers to take him into custody.[9]

In John 17, as Jesus prays in front of his disciples, he makes a number of startling claims. Clearly referring to himself, he claims among other things:

1. that God gave him authority over all mankind (verse 2);
2. that he, Jesus, is the giver of eternal life (verse 3);
3. that eternal life consists in knowing him in the same way one knows God (verse 3);

4. that Jesus was in glory with God the Father in eternity past (verse 5);

5. that Jesus came forth from God the Father (verse 8);

6. that Jesus is one with God the Father (verse 8);

7. that Jesus is going back to God the Father (verse 13); and

8. that God the Father is in Jesus.

In view of these claims the purely human Messiah of popular belief is an awfully puny figure. Therefore, when Vermes says that Jesus did not make the figure of Messiah central to his teaching, we must disagree. He did not make a purely human Messiah figure central to his teaching, but as we develop below, he makes his identity as more than the purely human Messiah central to his teaching.

Objection #2. "No record has survived of any hostile challenge concerning [Jesus'] messianic status before his last days in Jerusalem."

If Jesus specifically avoids using the term *Messiah* because of its misleading connotation, and in view of the Roman occupation, then why should we expect any record of confrontation over the messianic issue? In view of Jesus' works and claims, the hostile witnesses were concerned about a much more serious matter—blasphemy! As a result, the record does show that the confrontations almost always focused on the issue of Jesus' authority to teach and do the things he said and did.

Objection #3. "[Jesus] deliberately withheld his approval of Peter's confession."

How anyone can say that Jesus did not express approval of Peter's confession "You are the Christ, the Son of the living God" is beyond us. Matthew, an eyewitness, records that Jesus commended Peter in at least four specific ways:[10]

1. He specifically states that Peter is blessed for recognizing that Jesus is the Messiah. Would Jesus have called Peter blessed for making a false confession?

2. The challenge of Jesus' entire ministry among the Jewish people was to help them get their eyes off of an earthly kingdom where they would reign supreme over the Goyim and onto a spiritual kingdom fulfilling God's promise to Abram, "In you all the families of the earth shall be blessed" (Genesis 12:3). When Peter recognizes Jesus as the Messiah, despite his nonmilitary approach, Jesus commends him, "Flesh and blood did not reveal this to you, but My Father who is in heaven." (By the way, notice the "My Father." That was definitely unconventional. Traditional Jews said only, "Our Father.")

3. Jesus commended Peter, "And I say to you that you are Peter [meaning 'a stone'], and upon this rock [probably referring either to Jesus himself or the statement Peter has made] I will build My church; and the gates of Hades shall not overpower it." That is quite a commendation.

4. Jesus states he will give to Peter the keys of the kingdom of heaven and authority to "bind" and "loose" on earth what has been bound and loosed in heaven. Again, that is quite a nice commendation; in fact, a reward for getting his eyes properly focused on God's interests. Lest the reader think Jesus is incapable of rebuking a false statement, look down just four verses further to see an example of Jesus' non-commendation of Peter when he gets his eyes back on a man-centered kingdom. When Peter says that Jesus shouldn't be talking about going to Jerusalem to suffer and die, Jesus responds to Peter:

> Get behind Me, Satan! You are a stumbling-block to Me; for you are not setting your mind on God's interests, but man's (Matthew 16:23).

If Peter had wrongly called Jesus the Messiah, Jesus was certainly ready and willing to soundly rebuke Peter for it! We must therefore conclude that Jesus most definitely did not withhold his approval of Peter's confession.

Objection #4. "In general, [Jesus] failed to declare himself to be the Christ [Messiah]."

Again, the evidence of the firsthand accounts of Jesus' earthly life is solidly against this proposition. We already have stated important reasons Jesus usually avoided overtly claiming to be the Messiah and why he "warned the disciples that they should tell no one that He was the Christ" (Matthew 16:20). But this is different from not declaring himself the Messiah. In often more subtle but much more powerful ways, Jesus declares himself to be Messiah on almost every page of the gospel accounts.

Even as early as age twelve, Jesus refers to God as "My Father."[11] He continues to use the term throughout the gospel accounts—a total of forty times! Jerusalem scholar Dr. Robert Lindsey explains the significance of this expression:

> Synagogue prayers contain the expression, "Our Father [Avinu] who is in heaven," many times, and Jesus taught his disciples to pray a prayer which also begins, "Our Father who is in heaven." The expression, "My Father [avi]" however, almost certainly must have seemed improper to the Jews of that period. Only once in the Hebrew Scripture is God referred to as "my Father," and that is in Psalm 89, which speaks of the coming Messiah. Verse 26 reads, "He will call to me, 'Avi ata'—'You are my Father,'" The Messiah has the right to call God "my Father." I am quite sure that the rabbis of Jesus' day taught the people to say "Our Father who is in heaven," because to say "my Father" was reserved for the Messiah alone.
>
> Second Samuel 7:14 also contains a prophecy about the Messiah: "I will be to him a father, and he will be to me a son." This verse marks the beginning of a coming Messiah who is the son of God.
>
> It was known from Psalm 89:26, 2 Samuel 7:14, and Psalm 2:7 that the Messiah would be the son of God, but these verses do not contain the

expression "son of God." What is used is, "He will call to me, 'You are my Father'"; "I will be a father to him, he will be a son to me"; and, "You are my son, this day I have brought you forth." This is the Hebraic way of expressing messiahship—it is the way the Holy Spirit spoke and the way Jesus spoke. (LiR.MC 11)

Jesus also declared himself Messiah by the things he did. Look at John the Baptist in John 11. John is sitting in Herod's prison and has some free time on his hands. He begins to review the events of his life and especially reflects on whether or not he should have been referring his disciples to Jesus several months back.[12] Having some doubts, he sends a question to Jesus by way of his disciples: "Are you the coming one, or shall we look for someone else?"[13] Jesus tells John's disciples:

> Go and report to John the things which you hear and see: the blind receive sight and the lame walk, the lepers are cleansed and the deaf hear, and the dead are raised up, and the poor have the gospel preached to them.[14]

Jesus drew these words from two verses found in Isaiah. The first, 35:5, occurs in the midst of a passage speaking of the arrival of the kingdom of God in Zion. The second, 61:1, is found in a context announcing the favorable year of the Lord. John, therefore, would have understood Jesus as saying not only "Yes, I am the Messiah," but also, "Here, I'm willing to give you proof that no one else can bring that my claims are true." In this sense, then, every time Jesus healed someone or performed some attesting sign, he was declaring himself to be Messiah.

We have mentioned earlier how Jesus declared himself Messiah in the triumphal entry. A verse in the Babylonian Talmud, Menahoth 78b, has Rabbi Yohanan explaining that "outside the wall" of Jerusalem means not further than the wall of Bethphage. When Jesus mounts the donkey foal in Bethphage and rides into Jerusalem, he is making a very definite statement that he understands himself to be Messiah. He clearly intends to fulfill Zechariah 9:9:

> Rejoice greatly, O daughter of Zion!
> Shout in triumph, O daughter of Jerusalem!
> Behold, your King is coming to you;
> He is just and endowed with salvation,
> Humble, and mounted on a donkey,
> Even on a colt, the foal of a donkey.

The people clearly understood Jesus' intentions. Fleming states:

> The palm became a symbol of Jewish nationalism. But on Palm Sunday the poor population of Jerusalem was feeling the heavy arm of Rome over them. There was a popular understanding by Jews of Jesus' day that Messiah would come during the Passover season. (Do you remember in John's Gospel that after Jesus fed the 5,000 the people "wanted to make him

king because it was Passover"?) The role Messiah would play in the hopes
of the populace was that he would deliver the people from oppression…
as in the days of the exodus from Egypt. By bringing the palm branches
the people were in a way saying, "Jesus, we are all with you…you see you
have enough of a following to do something about the Roman garrison in
Jerusalem." (FIJ.JJ 7)

There are five incidents reported in the gospel accounts cited by Vermes as the most
prominent, which might be used to show that Jesus declared himself to be the Messiah.
(SeeVeG.JTJ 140-43) The first and only one Vermes accepts as authentically from Jesus is the
occasion of Jesus' question regarding David's reference to "his son" as "lord."[15] This he
dismisses as simply "an *ad hominem* exegetical argument," i.e., one in which he simply
wanted to show that the Pharisees used incorrect methods of interpreting the Scriptures, not that he necessarily agreed that David's son was some kind of superhuman
lord. But Jesus most definitely is pressing the point of the nature of the Messiah for he
opens the conversation by asking them, "What do you think about the Christ? Whose
son is He?" The logical conclusion is, if he is David's son, and if you are still waiting for
him, and if David calls him "Lord," then the Messiah must be existing already prior
to coming into human history. Jesus is most definitely making a point which he states
more directly to his own disciples when he prayed, "I came forth from Thee [God]."[16]

The other four passages Vermes dismisses as inauthentic without any reason except
that he does not believe Jesus said what the gospel writers have him saying. This is a
favorite ploy of the higher critics when the evidence most runs against their beliefs. The
passages are: (1) Jesus' announcement of his second coming;[17] (2) Jesus' promise, "For
whoever gives you a cup of water to drink because of your name as followers of Christ,
truly I say to you, he shall not lose his reward";[18] (3) and (4) Jesus teaching the two disciples on the Emmaus road, "Was it not necessary for the Christ to suffer these things
and to enter into His glory?"[19] and, "Thus it is written, that the Christ should suffer
and rise again from the dead the third day."[20] At the very most, Vermes could have discounted the last two as not within the earthly life of Jesus. But all four references, seen
in context, are definite declarations of Jesus that he considered himself the Messiah.

In John 4, Jesus spoke with a Samaritan woman outside the city of Sychar. In the
course of their conversation, the woman said to Jesus, "I know that Messiah is coming
(He who is called Christ); when that One comes, He will declare all things to us." Jesus
probably felt more freedom in Samaria about disclosing his identity. Messianic expectations were quite subdued since the Samaritans believed only in the Pentateuch. Jesus
therefore revealed to the woman, "I who speak to you am He."[21] There was no question
about it. Jesus clearly declared himself to be the Messiah.

Another declaration of Jesus that he was the Messiah occurred at his trial before the
high priest Caiaphas, the chief priests and the elders and scribes.[22] In Mark's account,
when the high priest finally asked Jesus directly, "Are you the Christ, the Son of the
Blessed One?," Jesus responded "I am; and you shall see the Son of Man sitting at the

right hand of Power, and coming with the clouds of heaven." Notice that Jesus clearly spoke of himself. The term "Son of Man" was the way he usually referred to himself.[23] Notice also that Jesus clearly identified himself as the one about whom Daniel prophesied when he revealed,

> I kept looking in the night visions, and behold, with the clouds of heaven one like a Son of Man was coming, and he came up to the Ancient of Days and was presented before Him. And to Him was given dominion, glory and a kingdom, that all the peoples, nations, and men of every language might serve Him. His dominion is an everlasting dominion which will not pass away; and His kingdom is one which will not be destroyed.[24]

In this passage Daniel reveals this coming one, and Jesus claims for himself: (1) that he will come with or on the clouds of heaven; and (2) he will be given supreme authority over all mankind for all eternity. For the Sadducees, who controlled the Sanhedrin at this time and for whom "the Messianic hope played no role,"[25] this claim was tantamount to blasphemy. (Blasphemy meant not just a claim to be God, but also slander against God or even against other persons.) Though the concept of Messiah would have been interpreted differently by Jesus, the scribes (Pharisees) present and the Sadducees, there can be no doubt that Jesus clearly claimed he was that Son of Man to come, the Messiah.

That Jesus claimed to be Messiah is confirmed by the report which the Sanhedrin must have delivered to Pilate in view of that claim. Norman Anderson explains:

> The crucifixion, however, does seem to provide convincing proof of one point about which New Testament scholars have been much divided—and to which passing reference has already been made: namely, that Jesus himself did believe that he was the Messiah. It is true that he did not make any such claim explicitly in his public preaching—partly, no doubt, for political reasons, but largely because of the mistaken expectations this would have aroused among his hearers. But it was clearly as a potential threat to Rome that Pilate and his minions delivered him to a death largely reserved for "the armed robber and the political insurgent" (Betz, p. 84). This is explicit in the inscription on the cross: "JESUS OF NAZARETH, THE KING OF THE JEWS" (John 19:19), which would seem to echo the Evangelists' report that part of the conversation between Pilate and Jesus had been about this very point (Matthew 27:11; Mark 15:2; Luke 23:3; John 18:33-37). And this, in its turn, must have been prompted by the fact that the "blasphemy" for which the Sanhedrin had condemned him was his reply to the question (put to him on oath by the high priest), "Are you the Christ, the Son of the Blessed One?" with the words: "I am...And you will see the Son of Man sitting at the right hand of the Mighty one and coming on the clouds of heaven" (Mark 14:61-64)—an affirmation that had naturally been reported by the chief priests to Pilate in explicitly political terms. (AnN.JC 82-83)

Though a number of Jewish scholars in the past have attempted to deny that Jesus thought of himself as the Messiah, others now support his messianic consciousness. One is Samuel Sandmel, recognized as the leading U. S. Jewish authority on the New Testament and early Christianity. He was a professor at Yale, then at Hebrew Union College in Cincinnati up to his death in 1979. Sandmel concluded, "I believe that he believed himself to be the Messiah, and that those scholars who deny this are incorrect." (SaS.WJ 65,109)

David Flusser, professor of comparative religion at Hebrew University in Jerusalem, like other Jewish scholars, sees "inauthentic" passages in the gospel texts. Still he maintains that "other apparently authentic sayings of Jesus can be understood only if it is assumed that Jesus thought himself to be the Son of Man."[26] For Flusser, Jesus' concept of "Son of Man" was both messianic and divine. (HaDA.R 254)

While we're on the subject, let's pause for a minute to consider the meaning of the term *Son of Man.*

SON OF MAN—WHO IS HE?

With the term *Son of Man,* we have a simple but profound concept made terribly confusing by modern scholars. Vermes writes:

> Contemporary New Testament scholarship has expended much effort, erudition and ink to agree in the end on almost nothing except that the Son of Man is a vitally important title. (VeG.JTJ 186)

But Vermes himself goes on to further confuse the issue by claiming that the phrase does not retain a "titular use" as used by Jesus.

Let's propose a simple definition and see if it fits with all the biblical uses of the term. At its lowest common denominator, a son of man is simply one born of humanity. He is one born from the human race. In the Old Testament it is used almost always in this manner. For example, Psalm 144:3 says: "O LORD, what is man, that Thou dost take knowledge of him? Or the son of man, that Thou dost think of him?" Often the term occurs in the parallelism we see in this verse, i.e., son of man = man. "Son of man" in the Old Testament always carries the general meaning of one born from humanity or a representative of humanity. Most often it refers to a specific individual. Of its 106 occurrences, 91 refer to Ezekiel and one refers to Daniel.

In only one of its occurrences is it used to describe someone of apparently more than mere human proportions. That's right; the text is Daniel 7:13, quoted above. This one was described as being *like* a son of man, i.e., having the form of a man. But this personage comes "with the clouds of heaven," is given dominion, glory and a kingdom in which "all the people, nations, and men of every language might serve him"; and, "His dominion is an everlasting dominion which will not pass away; and his kingdom is one which will not be destroyed." He is given this dominion as its ruler. In verses 18, 22 and 27 we learn that "the saints of the Highest One will receive the kingdom," obviously as its subjects. No wonder this occurrence was commonly accepted as referring to the Messiah to come.

Of the more than eighty Son-of-Man references in the New Testament, all but one refer to Jesus. Only three are found outside the gospels.[27] Hebrews 2:6 quotes Psalm 8:4 referring to one born of humanity. All the rest refer to Jesus in one way or another. Some reflect him only in his humanness, such as having nowhere to lay his head (Matthew 8:20; Luke 9:58), or eating and drinking with tax collectors and sinners (Matthew 11:19; Luke 7:34). Here, the Son of Man clearly is identified with humanity.

In most of the gospel texts, however, the Son of Man takes on more than mere human dimensions. He has the authority to forgive sins, he is called Lord of the Sabbath, his resurrection is predicted often, he has authority to execute judgment, he gives imperishable food and he is to be glorified.

The most remarkable observation, however, is that at least twenty-seven of the Son-of-Man references in the gospel accounts in some way allude to Daniel 7:13-14. The attempts of higher critics to dismiss these passages are almost comical. For Jesus and the disciples, the Son of Man was a fully human figure, but one who took on a messianic dimension far beyond the popular messianic expectations of their day.

WAS JESUS THE MESSIAH?

In the Old Testament, there are hundreds of prophecies about and allusions to the coming Messiah. The brilliant nineteenth-century Oxford professor Canon Henry Liddon found 332 "distinct predictions which were literally fulfilled in [Jesus]."[28]

For example, Daniel 9:25-26 indicates that the Messiah had to come before the second Temple was destroyed (AD 70). Micah 5:2 speaks of the Messiah's birthplace as Bethlehem Ephrathah, the town where Jesus was born. Isaiah 35:5-6 speaks of the blind, deaf, lame and dumb being healed. Isaiah 42:6 and 49:6 speak of the Messiah as a light to the Gentiles. Zechariah 9:9 predicts that the Messiah would come humbly, "mounted on a donkey, even on a colt, the foal of a donkey." Psalm 22 provides a graphic description of one undergoing crucifixion (even though crucifixion was unknown to the psalmist), and Jesus quoted its opening verse as he hung on the cross. Zechariah 12:9-10 even mentions in one passage the two separate comings of the Messiah:

> And it will come about in that day that I will set about to destroy all the nations that come against Jerusalem [second coming]. And I will pour out on the house of David and on the inhabitants of Jerusalem, the Spirit of grace and of supplication, so that they will look on Me whom they have pierced [occurred at first coming]; and they will mourn for Him, as one mourns for an only son, and they will weep bitterly over Him, like the bitter weeping over a first-born.

But the Christian must be careful not to overstate the case. There are hundreds of additional messianic prophecies in the Old Testament which have not yet found their fulfillment in Jesus. This is by necessity, for if it is prophesied that the Messiah had to suffer and die and yet is also to subsequently reign over an eternal kingdom (at least part of which is established on earth) then it follows that Messiah must somehow rise from the dead and come again. The most important and overlooked question is: Does the Old Testament predict that the Messiah must first suffer and die?

Christians and critics alike today are often so focused on the issue of Jesus' resurrection that they forget the other half of the apostles' preaching. Peter preached in the Temple, "But the things which God announced beforehand by the mouth of all the prophets, that His Christ *should suffer*, He has thus fulfilled."[29]

Paul reasoned with the Thessalonians in their synagogue "explaining and giving evidence that the Christ *had to suffer* and rise again from the dead, and saying, 'This Jesus whom I am proclaiming to you is the Christ.'"[30] Before King Agrippa Paul reported:

> And so, having obtained help from God, I stand to this day testifying both
> to small and great, stating nothing but what the Prophets and Moses said
> was going to take place; that the Christ *was to suffer*, and that by reason
> of His resurrection from the dead He should be the first to proclaim light
> both to the Jewish people and to the Gentiles.[31]

The apostles were saying nothing new. Jesus himself repeatedly stated that he had to go to Jerusalem to suffer, die and be raised from the dead.[32] But where in the Old Testament was this prophesied?

Many Jewish people today are surprised to find the following passage in the Jewish Bible, what Christians call the Old Testament:

> See, my servant will act wisely; he will be raised and lifted up and highly
> exalted. Just as there were many who were appalled at him—his appear-
> ance was so disfigured beyond that of any man and his form marred
> beyond human likeness—so will he sprinkle many nations, and kings will
> shut their mouths because of him. For what they were not told, they will
> see, and what they have not heard, they will understand.
>
> Who has believed our message and to whom has the arm of the LORD been
> revealed? He grew up before him like a tender shoot, and like a root out of
> dry ground. He had no beauty or majesty to attract us to him, nothing in
> his appearance that we should desire him. He was despised and rejected by
> men, a man of sorrows, and familiar with suffering. Like one from whom
> men hide their faces he was despised, and we esteemed him not.
>
> Surely he took up our infirmities and carried our sorrows, yet we con-
> sidered him stricken by God, smitten by him, and afflicted. But he was
> pierced for our transgressions, he was crushed for our iniquities; the pun-
> ishment that brought us peace was upon him, and by his wounds we are
> healed. We all, like sheep, have gone astray, each of us has turned to his own
> way; and the LORD has laid on him the iniquity of us all.

He was oppressed and afflicted, yet he did not open his mouth; he was led like a lamb to the slaughter, and as a sheep before her shearers is silent, so he did not open his mouth. By oppression and judgment he was taken away. And who can speak of his descendants? For he was cut off from the land of the living; for the transgression of my people he was stricken. He was assigned a grave with the wicked, and with the rich in his death, though he had done no violence, nor was any deceit in his mouth.

Yet it was the LORD's will to crush him and cause him to suffer, and though the LORD makes his life a guilt offering, he will see his offspring and prolong his days, and the will of the LORD will prosper in his hand. After the suffering of his soul, he will see the light of life and be satisfied; by his knowledge my righteous servant will justify many, and he will bear their iniquities. Therefore I will give him a portion among the great, and he will divide the spoils with the strong, because he poured out his life unto death, and was numbered with the transgressors. For he bore the sin of many, and made intercession for the transgressors. [33]

For more than 1700 years, the Jewish rabbis interpreted this passage almost unanimously as referring to the Messiah. This fact is thoroughly documented in S. R. Driver and Adolf Neubauer's *The Fifty-Third Chapter of Isaiah According to the Jewish Interpreters*. (DrS.F 37-39) They quote numerous rabbis during this period who equated the servant of Isaiah 53 with the Messiah.

Not until the twelfth century AD, no doubt under the suffering of Jews at the hands of the Crusaders, did any Jewish interpreter say that Isaiah 52:13–53:12 refers to the whole nation of Israel, the most common interpretation today among Jewish scholars. Even after Rashi (Rabbi Solomon Yitzhaki) first proposed this interpretation; however, many other Jewish interpreters have held, even to the present, the traditional Talmudic view that Isaiah 53 speaks of the Messiah. [34] One of the most respected Jewish intellectuals of all history, Moses Maimonides (AD 1135–1204), rejected Rashi's interpretation, and he taught that the passage was messianic. (MoS.LM 25:364-66)

Rashi and other Jewish interpreters are not necessarily grasping at straws to suggest that the servant is the nation of Israel. Isaiah 43:10 says to the people of Israel: "'You are My witnesses,' declares the LORD, 'and My servant whom I have chosen.'" Surely then, they would say, the servant must be Israel.

That this interpretation is in error can first be seen in Isaiah 52:14 where the nation of Israel is compared to the servant: "Just as many were astonished at you, My people, so His appearance was marred more than any man." In 53:8, the servant bears punishment that should have been born by "my people" (obviously Israel). It makes no sense for the nation of Israel to bear substitutionary punishment for the nation of Israel. Therefore Israel cannot be the servant of Isaiah 52:13–53:12.

But what about Isaiah 49:3, "And He said to Me, 'You are My Servant, Israel, in Whom I will show My glory'"? Good question!—because it leads to a clearer understanding of why the Messiah had to come on Israel's behalf. The key to identifying the servant in Isaiah 52:13–53:12 is to see who he is in the three previous "servant songs" of Isaiah: 42:1-9; 49:1-12; and 50:4-9. Since these passages spoke of the servant, for example, establishing justice in the earth (Isaiah 42:4) and regathering the Jewish people from worldwide exile (Isaiah 49:8-13), Jewish interpreters have traditionally held the servant songs to be speaking of the Messiah, not the nation of Israel. Even in Isaiah 49:3, it is not saying that Israel is the servant; rather it is saying that the servant (Messiah) is the true Israel! In verses 5 and 6 we see: "Now says the LORD, who formed Me from the womb to be His Servant…'to *raise up the tribes of Jacob, and to restore the preserved ones of Israel.*'" The point is that Jacob (Israel) had gone astray, especially from the commission God gave to him: "In you and in your descendants shall all the families of the earth be blessed" (Genesis 28:14). The Servant (Messiah) was now to stand in Israel's place to do two things: (1) to bring the nation of Israel back to God (Isaiah 49:5); and (2) to be a light to the nations, as seen in verse 6:

> It is too small a thing that You should be My Servant…I will also make You
> a light of the nations so that My salvation may reach to the end of the earth.

If you caught what is going on here in Isaiah, you probably are realizing right now why Jesus so often appealed or alluded to this prophet. The Servant is the Messiah. The Messiah had to suffer and die for many. He also had to be raised from the dead (Psalm 16:10). When the monumental event of the resurrection did occur and the disciples were filled at Pentecost with the Spirit of God, they preached everywhere the message "that Messiah died for our sins according to the Scriptures, and that He was buried, and that He was raised on the third day according to the Scriptures."[35] To judge from the earliest surviving Christian literature, 1 Thessalonians, they also preached that the Messiah would come again.

Was Jesus the Messiah? If not, then there is to be no Messiah. No one prior to AD 70 had his credentials. All the prophecies which could be fulfilled in his first coming were fulfilled in Jesus. And he sealed it all with his own resurrection from the dead. It is therefore fitting to refer to Jesus as the Christ, if one uses Greek terminology, or as the Messiah if one uses Hebrew terminology.

SON OF GOD

As a rule, Christians quickly interpret this term as meaning deity. But there are a number of occurrences of "Son of God" or "God's Son" in the gospels, and in the rest of the Bible, where the term either probably or definitely does not mean "deity" to the one using it or at least to others hearing it. Colin Brown states that the gospel evidence alone suggests that "Son of God" had a range of connotations that were not necessarily divine. It is an oversimplification to say that the title "Son of God" expresses Jesus' divinity and "Son of Man" his humanity. (BrC.M 296)

In fact, we may have to go even further and say that almost no one within the Jewish world of Jesus' day who heard or used the term "Son of God" thought of it in the sense of deity. After reviewing the Old Testament and intertestament literature, Geza Vermes concluded, and we believe fairly accurately: "All in all, it would appear that a first-century AD Palestinian Jew, hearing the phrase *son of God,* would have thought first of all of an angelic or celestial being; and secondly, when the human connection was clear, of a just and saintly man." (VeG.JTJ 200)

Even within the gospel accounts, Vermes' conclusion is fairly accurate. Luke calls Adam "the son of God," but no one would think of Adam in a divine sense.[36] When the centurion at the foot of the cross exclaimed "Truly this was the Son of God" (Matthew 27:54; Mark 15:39), he probably meant it in the sense which Luke reports, "Certainly this man was innocent" [literally "righteous"] (Luke 23:47). Even Peter, when he answered Jesus, "Thou art the Christ, the Son of the living God (Matthew 16:16)," may not, at least at that time, have understood the term in a divine sense, for a few verses later he demonstrated that he still thought in terms of an earthly messianic kingdom. Peter used the term in the sense of God's message to David regarding his son, Solomon: "I will be a father to him and he will be a son to Me" (2 Samuel 7:14).

That same verse, 2 Samuel 7:14, also predicts Solomon's fall into iniquity and the resulting chastisement which occurred through the divided kingdom. But the two verses immediately preceding it speak of an eternal kingdom being established through David's seed. Thus, even though Peter likely thought of Jesus as Messiah of an earthly kingdom, there must have been some question in his mind as to how the Messiah would continue to rule "forever." There are hints such as this one all through the Old Testament that the Messiah would be more than just a mortal man. For example, Isaiah 9:6, a clear messianic passage, must have caused at least a few Jewish heads to be scratched:

> For a child will be born to us, a son will be given to us; and the government
> will rest on His shoulders; and His name will be called Wonderful, Coun-
> selor, Mighty God, Eternal Father, Prince of Peace.

Dr. Norman Geisler, former Professor of Philosophy of Religion at Dallas Theological Seminary, states concerning the Old Testament that

> the Messiah is identified with Yahweh or Deity in many passages. He is
> called "mighty God" in Isaiah 9:6 and Yahweh in Zechariah 12:10 and
> again in 14:3-9. The Messiah is labeled "Lord" (Adonai) in Psalm 110:1
> and "God" (Elohim) in Psalm 45:6 (cf. Hebrews 1:8). According to Micah
> 5:2 He pre-existed before Bethlehem. And He is identifiable with the Old
> Testament angel of Yahweh (Isaiah 63:7-10) who is the I Am of Exodus
> 3:14 (cf. vss. 3-5). (GeN.IC 6)

Undoubtedly, the firm monotheism of Jewish rabbis moved them to seek other interpretations of these passages rather than wrestle with the question of how to attribute deity to the Messiah while maintaining the clear Old Testament teaching that there is only one God. For most Jews of Jesus' day, then, Messiah meant king—but certainly not God.

Because of messianic passages such as 2 Samuel 7:14 and Psalm 2:7 ("Thou art My Son, today I have begotten Thee") the term *Son of God* became naturally associated with the Messiah. Thus Caiaphas demanded of Jesus, "I adjure You by the living God, that You tell us whether You are the Christ, the Son of God."[37] He was not asking if Jesus was deity, only if he was the Messiah. But Jesus gave him and the rest of the Sanhedrin more than they could wish. Breaking his silence to previous questions, Jesus summarized the most important aspects of his teaching and belief about his own identity. He replied, according to Mark, "I am [Heb., *Ani hu*] and you shall see the Son of Man sitting at the right hand of Power, and coming with the clouds of heaven."[38]

Remember that just a few days earlier Jesus had completely disrupted the operations of the Temple. Now, the Sanhedrin members hear this Galilean rabble-rouser claiming

- that Messiah, Son of God (Son of the Blessed One), and Son of Man are all the same and refer to him;

- that he would sit at God's right hand of power ruling over all his enemies (Psalm 110:1-2);

- that he was "a priest forever according to the order of Melchizedek" (Psalm 110:4);

- that he did what he did by God's authority and power (Psalm 110:5-7);

- that he would be seen coming with the clouds of heaven; and most important,

- that he in fact was Yahweh God.

Lecturer Jon A. Buell and his co-author O. Quentin Hyder explain:

> Jesus' words, though quiet, are stunning in their audacity. *Ani hu* in this passage is rendered simply "I am" in many translations, as if it were a simple reply to the "Are you...?" of Caiaphas. However, it is the same phrase, used in the same way, that we have seen elsewhere translated "I am He." Surely Jesus realizes that his audience, intense in their quest for evidence against him, will interpret his words in the full sense of their theophanic meaning. It is a deliberate claim to deity, and, if not quite what Caiaphas has expected, an even greater blasphemy to his ears. (BuJ. 34)

DID JESUS REALLY BELIEVE HE WAS GOD?

Those who wrote the historical accounts of Jesus' life were thoroughly Jewish. The accounts themselves clearly bear witness that the witnesses' natural tendency was to see Jesus in a conquering messianic, not a divine messianic, posture. Even on the night of Jesus' arrest, the disciples brought swords to Jesus.[39] As devoted worshippers of Yahweh, it must have been quite difficult for them to report some of the things Jesus said and did which attributed deity to himself. Vermes states concerning the alleged deity of Jesus, "The identification of a contemporary historical figure with God would have been inconceivable to a first-century AD Palestinian Jew." (VeG.JTJ 212) The thrust of Vermes' conclusions is that Jesus himself never would have imagined that he was God. Let's look at the evidence.

In Matthew 12:6, Jesus says to the Pharisees, "I say to you, that something greater than the Temple is here." How much greater? Look at verse 8. Referring to himself, Jesus asserts, "The Son of Man is Lord of the Sabbath." How can anyone be Lord of the Sabbath except God who instituted it? This is a direct claim to deity.

In Matthew 23:37, Jesus speaks as though he has personally observed the whole history of Jerusalem:

> O Jerusalem, Jerusalem, who kills the prophets and stones those who are
> sent to her! How often I wanted to gather your children together, the way
> a hen gathers her chicks under her wings, and you were unwilling.

In Mark 2:1-12, Jesus tells a paralyzed man, "My son, your sins are forgiven." Some scribes sitting there caught the obvious intent of Jesus' words and reasoned:

> Why does this man speak this way? He is blaspheming; who can forgive
> sins but God alone?

Jesus challenged them:

> Which is easier, to say to the paralytic, "Your sins are forgiven"; or to say,
> "Arise, and take up your pallet and walk"? But in order that you may know
> that the Son of Man has authority on earth to forgive sins...

And then Jesus healed the paralytic. The implication was obvious. No one forgives sin but God. Anyone could say he is able to forgive sin; but Jesus proved he had the authority to forgive sin when he healed the paralytic. Jesus was clearly claiming deity for himself. Jon Buell and Quentin Hyder state that

> there isn't a single verse in the Old Testament (or other Jewish literature)
> that clearly designates for the Messiah the power to forgive sins, although
> the same literature does ascribe this power to Jehovah! In pardoning sin,
> then, Jesus was asserting the ascribed power of deity, not that of messiah-
> ship. (BuJ. 23)

Back again in Matthew, at the end of the Sermon on the Mount (7:21-23), Jesus speaks of himself as the ultimate judge who will have authority to deny entrance into the kingdom of heaven.

In the next paragraph, rather than say "Everyone who hears the words of God or

Torah will lay a strong foundation for their lives," Jesus states, "Everyone who hears these words of Mine…"

David Bivin, a researcher of the Hebraic background of the gospel accounts, concludes:

> It was not the way he taught or even the general content of his teaching that made Jesus unique among the rabbis. What *was* unique about Jesus was who he claimed to be, and he rarely ever taught without claiming to be not only God's Messiah, but more startlingly, *Immanuel,* "God with us." (BiD.L 5)

It is surprising how critics try to reject Jesus' constant references to himself as deity. Ian Wilson, for example, writes:

> In the Mark gospel, the most consistent in conveying Jesus' humanity, a man is represented as running up to Jesus and addressing him with the words "Good Master." Jesus' response is a firm rebuke: "Why do you call me good? No one is good but God alone" (Mark 10:18). (WiI.JTE 176)

Wilson's interpretation is 180 degrees in the wrong direction. Seen within the context of the situation, Jesus obviously is using irony. In essence, he is arguing logically: (1) If no one is good but God alone, and (2) if I am good, then (3) I must be God.

Often Jesus receives worship and does nothing to discourage it (see Matthew 14:33; John 9:38). You would think one who severely rebukes Peter for trying to keep him from God's will of being crucified would also severely rebuke someone offering worship to him which rightly ought to be given only to the one true living God. Paul severely reacted against being deified at Lystra (Acts 14:8-18). How much more should Jesus have reacted if he were only a mere man? Did he not quote Deuteronomy 6:13 to Satan during his temptation, "You shall worship the Lord your God, and serve Him only"? Yet Jesus clearly accepted worship of himself.

One notable occurrence of Jesus accepting worship is in Matthew 21:15-16. Children cry out in praise to Jesus, "Hosanna to the Son of David." Some commentators interpret "Hosanna" in a stiffly literal sense, rendering the statement "Save us, Son of David." But this cannot be, for (1) it would actually read: "Save us to the Son of David," which makes little or no sense; (2) the chief priests and scribes who saw Jesus receiving the praise "became indignant and said to Him, 'Do you hear what these are saying?'" as though Jesus should have silenced them; and most important, (3) Jesus replied by attributing to himself something which was meant for God alone. He replies, "Have you never read, 'Out of the mouth of infants and nursing babes Thou [God] hast prepared praise for Thyself [God]'?" Did you catch what Jesus said? Basically it was, "When those children praise me, they are praising God!"

Of all the gospel writers, John most clearly perceived the cues Jesus gave about his identity. For his effort to report those cues, he has been the most criticized gospel writer of all, allegedly falling under Hellenistic influence. Scholars today, however, have begun to realize the inaccuracy of this charge. In John 8:58, when Jesus proclaimed to a Jewish crowd, "Truly, truly, I say to you, before Abraham was born, I Am," he was claiming two aspects of deity for himself:

- the eternal existence of God; and
- the name of God.

Jesus was referring his listeners to Exodus 3:13-14 where Moses tells God:

> Behold, I am going to the sons of Israel, and I shall say to them, "The God of your fathers has sent me to you." Now they may say to me, "What is His name?" What shall I say to them?

God answered Moses,

> I AM WHO I AM... Thus you shall say to the sons of Israel, "I AM has sent me to you."

Any Jewish person would have heard Jesus' claim to deity loud and clear. That is why the very next verse in John's account says, "Therefore they picked up stones to throw at Him."

In all, Jesus uses the term *I am* (Gr. *Ego eimi)* more than nineteen times in reference to himself in the gospel according to John.[40] Often it is used to make claims about himself that would normally only be thought appropriate for God. For example, "I am the bread of life, he who comes to Me shall not hunger, and he who believes in Me shall never thirst" (6:35); "I am the light of the world; he who follows Me shall not walk in the darkness, but shall have the light of life" (8:12); "Unless you believe that I am He, you shall die in your sins" (8:24); "I am the good shepherd" (10:11-14) [cf. Psalm 23:1: "The LORD is my shepherd"]; "I am the resurrection, and the life; he who believes in Me shall live even if he dies" (11:25).

Earlier, in John 5:17, Jesus claimed to be continuing the work of the Father. He also called God "My Father." In John 10:28-30 Jesus again called God "My Father." He also claimed to be the giver of eternal life and to be one with the Father. On both occasions, the Jewish crowds picked up stones to stone him because, as they put it, "You, being a man, make Yourself out to be God" (John 10:33; cf. 5:18).

In John 14:6, Jesus did not just claim to be teaching mankind the truth; he claimed that he was the truth. In John 14:9, Jesus admonished Philip, "He who has seen Me has seen the Father." In Isaiah 42:8, God said, "I am the LORD, that is My name; I will not give My glory to another." But in John 17:5, Jesus prayed, "And now, glorify Thou Me together with Thyself, Father, with the glory which I ever had with Thee before the world was."

In John 5:19ff., Jesus gives a long monologue in which he makes repeated claims to be on the same level of authority as God the Father.

"Even in his parables," says Norman Geisler, "Jesus claimed functions reserved only for *Yahweh* in the Old Testament, such as being Shepherd (Luke 15), Rock (Matthew 7:24-27), and Sower (Matthew 13:24-30)." (GeN.IC 14)

C. S. Lewis puts all these claims in the right perspective when he reminds his readers that Jesus was a Jew among Jews:

> Among these Jews there suddenly turns up a man who goes about talking as if He was God. He claims to forgive sins. He says He has always existed. He says He is coming to judge the world at the end of time. Now let us get this clear. Among pantheists, like the Indians, anyone might say that he was a part of God, or one with God: there would be nothing very odd about it. But this man, since He was a Jew, could not mean that kind of God. God, in their language, meant the Being outside the world Who had made it and was infinitely different from anything else. And when you have grasped that, you will see that what this man said was, quite simply, the most shocking thing that has ever been uttered by human lips. (LeC.M 54-55)

WAS JESUS THE GOD HE THOUGHT HE WAS?

The question, Is Jesus God? is fundamentally different from the question, Is God Jesus? In the latter, God is limited to earth during the earthly life of Jesus. In the former, God simply manifests himself in human flesh. Of course this does mean that a trinitarian theology (or at least a dual-personality theology) must be adopted in order to keep God from vacating his sovereign rule over the universe during the life of Jesus.

Many Jewish scholars today no longer criticize Christians as being tritheists. Though these scholars almost universally reject the doctrine of the trinity, they do not generally deny the logical possibility of a single God manifesting himself in more than one personality.

This is not the place to demonstrate the doctrine of the trinity, but it is necessary to see that such a concept is not ruled out by the Old Testament Scriptures. If the Old Testament does rule out such a doctrine, then it is ridiculous to think of Jesus possibly being God.

In fact, the Old Testament actually suggests a plurality of personalities in one God from the very beginning. Genesis 1:26 states: "Then God said, 'Let Us make man in Our image, according to Our likeness.'" Old Testament scholars Keil and Delitzsch have reviewed the arguments proposed against this verse and found them wanting. (KeC. COT 1:61-62) It is enough to say that if the passage doesn't demand the multiple person view, it certainly allows for it, and the most natural reading of the passage supports it.

One of the greatest objections to the trinity usually comes from the most often recited verse among the Jewish people, Deuteronomy 6:4: "Hear, O Israel! The LORD is our God, the LORD is one!" The Hebrew word used here for "one" is *echod,* meaning a *composite* unity. It is the same word used in Genesis 2:24 where the husband and the wife are commanded to become *one* flesh. Had the writer of Deuteronomy 6:4 wished to express an *absolute* unity, he could have used the Hebrew word, *yachid.*

Then there are a number of passages which either suggest or require that the Messiah be seen as deity. Psalm 45, for example, begins as a song celebrating "the King's marriage." Yet in verse 3 it seems to move to a Messiah-type figure and in verses 6 and 7 it reads:

> Thy throne, O God, is forever and ever; a scepter of uprightness is the scepter of Thy kingdom. Thou hast loved righteousness, and hated wickedness; Therefore God, Thy God, has anointed Thee with the oil of joy above Thy fellows.

Sir Norman Anderson reviews a number of other passages concerning the Messiah:

> His sway was to be not only universal (Psalm 2:8) but [also] eternal (Isaiah 9:7), and even divine (Psalm 45:6-7). The prophet Micah speaks of his pre-existence (Micah 5:2); Jeremiah describes him as "The Lord our Righteousness" (Jeremiah 23:6); and Isaiah speaks of him as "Wonderful Counselor, Mighty God, Eternal Father, Prince of Peace" (Isaiah 9:6)... And it is interesting in this context to note that the statement in Hebrews 1:6 ("And when He again brings the first-born into the world, He says, 'And let all the angels of God worship him'") almost certainly represents a quotation taken from the "Septuagint" Greek version of the Old Testament of words omitted from the end of Deuteronomy 32:43 in the now official Hebrew or "Massoretic" text, but present in that of the Dead Sea Scrolls. (AnN.JC 73-74)

Some have tried to render "Mighty God" of Isaiah 9:6 as "Mighty Warrior." It is not the most natural translation and would seem to conflict with "Prince of Peace." The 1917 Jewish Publication Society translation of Isaiah 9:6 (9:5 in Jewish versions) reads, "For a child is born unto us, a son is given unto us; and the government is upon his shoulder; and his name is called wonderful in counsel, is God the Mighty, the everlasting Father, the ruler of peace" (the latter half of this verse is found in their footnote). The "is" found between "counsel" and "God" is purely arbitrary and breaks the continuity of the sentence. The Hebrew text gives no indication it should be there. Further, the "in" between "wonderful" and "counsel" is not found in the Hebrew text. The sheer force of the verse cannot be undermined.

Psalm 2:12 commands that the Messiah should be worshipped:

> Do homage to the Son, lest He become angry, and you perish in the way, for his wrath may soon be kindled. How blessed are all who take refuge in Him!

Some Jewish translations have attempted to substitute the adverb "purely" or "in purity" for the noun "son" in this verse. But this cannot be supported, for in the six other places in Scripture where the Hebrew *bar* is translated as "pure," it is an adjective, not an adverb. The Septuagint (250 BC) translated the word into the Greek for "child."

In Zechariah 12:10, God says, "They will look on Me whom they have pierced." How can one pierce God unless he manifests himself in the flesh? Of the ten other places where "pierce" is used, at least nine times a person is either thrust through or pierced to death; the remaining occurrence refers to wounded soldiers.

In Daniel 7:14, the Messiah is given an everlasting kingdom, "that all the peoples, nations, and men of every language might serve Him." But if everyone is serving the Messiah, then no one would be left to serve the Lord unless the Lord and the Messiah are somehow united.

We can say then that the Old Testament, in some places at least, allowed for and in other places required that the Messiah to come should be identified as God eternal. Thus, if Jesus was Messiah, and if Messiah was God, then Jesus had to be God.

Returning to the first disciples, E. M. Blaiklock observes:

> One of the sources of youth's disillusionment is the fading halo around the head of some human hero it has hastily sought to worship. Not so with Christ and His disciples. For three years they trod together the lanes and byways of Galilee and Judea. They climbed together the rough roads up to Jerusalem, sat together in the lush grass above Tabgha. Together they bore the heat of Jericho and the cold winds of the Galilean lake. They shared His chill rest beneath the stars, His breakfast on the beach. Together they bore the storms and tensions in the holy city, together they enjoyed Bethany's hospitable home. Surely, this was test enough if shrewd men were to know Him. What happened? Far from detecting the hidden flaw, the human burst of annoyance at the end of a weary day, personal ambition betrayed by a chance word or unwise confidence, far from finding in Him disappointing blemishes, they found that their sense of wonder and reverence grew. (BIE.MM 85)

It is an amazing fact that the message of Jesus, including his deity, was spread abroad by these Jewish men and women. As James D. G. Dunn, Professor of Divinity at the University of Durham in England, states:

> The testimony comes not from Gentiles to whom the deification of an emperor was more like a promotion to "the upper chamber." It comes from Jews. And Jews were the most fiercely monotheistic race of that age. For a Jew to speak of a man, Jesus, in terms which showed him as sharing in the deity of God, was a quite astonishing feature of earliest Christianity. (DuJ.E 61-62)

It is remarkable enough that a Jew like Thomas would come to the point of calling Jesus "My Lord and my God!"[41] But then there is Paul. It is unbelievable how critics tend to forget he was a Jew *par excellence*. He was trained in Judaism by none other than Rabbi Gamaliel. He was so zealous for his monotheistic faith that he began persecuting the Christians. His goal in life was to help bring to pass Isaiah 45:22-23 where God says through the prophet, "I am God, and there is no other...*to me every knee will bow,* every tongue will swear allegiance" [emphasis ours]. And then Paul discovered that this one had stepped out of eternity and into time. Now Paul writes of him:

He existed in the form of God…but emptied Himself…being made in the likeness of men…He humbled Himself by becoming obedient to the point of death, even death on a cross…*that at the name of Jesus every knee should bow…and that every tongue should confess that Jesus Christ is Lord* [emphasis ours].[42]

That Paul meant "God" by the term *Lord* is clear from Romans 10:13 where he quotes Joel 2:32: "Whoever calls on the name of the LORD will be delivered." In Joel 2:32, the LORD is clearly God.

These first-century Jewish men and women came to accept Jesus as the God of their monotheistic faith. Why? Certainly they had been attracted to him by his teaching and attesting miracles. At some point they obviously put two and two together to see that Jesus, the Son of Man, was also Messiah, that Messiah was God and therefore that Jesus must also be God. But it was the resurrection that solidified their conviction. Norman Anderson summarizes:

> He frequently made claims which would have sounded outrageous and blasphemous to Jewish ears, even from the lips of the greatest of prophets. He said that he was in existence before Abraham and that he was "lord" of the sabbath; he claimed to forgive sins; he frequently identified himself (in his work, his person and his glory) with the one he termed his heavenly Father; he accepted men's worship; and he said that he was to be the judge of men at the last day, when their eternal destiny would depend on their attitude to him. Then he died. It seems inescapable, therefore, that his resurrection must be interpreted as God's decisive vindication of these claims, while the alternative—the finality of the cross—would necessarily have implied the repudiation of his presumptuous and even blasphemous assertions. (AnN.JC 113-14)

It seems therefore only fitting that in speaking of Jesus we should now refer to Him with a capital *H.*

PART III

APPLICATIONS *and* CONCLUSIONS

16

JESUS AND THE POPULAR PRESS

T here is nothing wrong with making something popular. The erudite arguments of the scholars many times need to be translated into everyday language and concepts.

SO WHAT'S WRONG WITH POPULAR?

But often the "popularizer" selects only that information or those scholars that support his own bias without dealing with the arguments raised by scholars on the other side. To some extent, all popularizers are guilty of this tendency. Therefore, the layman must be careful that the source he reads gives an accurate description of both sides of an issue and sound reasons for its agreement with one rather than the other.

Another problem with many popularistic approaches, whether it be to Jesus, science or whatever other subject, is that the writer may make statements or promote positions which long since have been rejected by knowledgeable scholars. He is able to "get away with it" only because of the public's lack of knowledge on the subject. Thus a need arises for other books equally popular which can "set the record straight."

Our desire has been to compile enough information to allow the average student or layman to accurately evaluate books, lectures, films and articles about the historical Jesus. For, as Louis Cassels wrote in the *Detroit News*:

> You can count on it. Every few years, some "scholar" will stir up a short-lived sensation by publishing a book that says something outlandish about Jesus. (CaL.DJ 7A)

With that in mind, let's look at a few common fallacies which surface again and again in popular (as well as not-so-popular) books about Jesus.

PITFALLS OF THE POPULARIZERS

1. The Cafeteria-Line Approach

The method by which the writer or critic simply picks out of the gospel material whatever suits his tastes, as if proceeding along the food line in a cafeteria, is all too commonly found. Again, Cassels comments:

> The amazing thing about all these debunk-Jesus books is that they accept as much of the recorded gospels as they find convenient, then ignore or repudiate other parts of the same document which contradict their notions.
>
> (CaL.DJ 7A)

This approach is especially noticeable in those who hold a naturalistic view toward the gospel accounts. Liberal theology of the nineteenth century, for example, tended to accept everything in the gospel narratives except the supernatural elements and any statements supporting the deity of Christ. In the twentieth century, Rudolf Bultmann, buttressed by the arguments against miracles which were also used by nineteenth-century liberals, concluded: "We can know almost nothing concerning the life and personality of Jesus." (BuR.JW 8) At least he was consistent. For if you remove the supernatural from the gospel accounts, virtually nothing else in the gospel makes sense. Jesus' teachings on faith, the kingdom of heaven and many other subjects become sheer nonsense. The church becomes little more than a social club, rather than a fellowship of people who observe God as alive and active in their midst.

Those who study form and redaction criticism will also observe the cafeteria-line approach in operation. The choices made as to what is "authentic" and what is "unauthentic" in the gospel accounts often are quite arbitrary, based on a preconceived bias, and supported by previous arbitrary conclusions. The "assured results of higher criticism" are not so assured as many have thought.

Sometimes popular writers and journalists pick up "scholarly conclusions," which are primarily opinions supported by cafeteria-line evidence, and they report as fact those conclusions which suit their own tastes and preconceived conclusions. One influential journalist, for example, recently reported Jesus' question, "Who do you say that I am?" in the following manner:

> It is the question, it seems, of a man who wishes to disturb but who is also himself disturbed; of a man who has somehow found himself in deeper waters than anticipated; of a man at once baffled and intrigued by a destiny that he may have begun to glimpse but of which he is not fully aware. And thus, seeking guidance, seeking perhaps to ken the range of possibilities, Jesus puts the question to his followers. (MuCu.W 37)

If one reads the three gospel accounts describing the incident, it is difficult to see how this writer can reach his conclusion. As we have seen, in Matthew, Jesus successively commends Peter for his answer and rebukes him for his attempt to persuade Jesus not to go to Jerusalem. Especially in light of the messianic expectations of the people, Jesus comes across as thoroughly in command of His senses, completely knowledgeable of what lies ahead, clear in His convictions, needing no guidance Himself but seeking to prepare His flock for what He knew awaited all of them in Jerusalem.

2. A Reliance on the Questionable Results of Higher Criticism

Undoubtedly the most common fallacy of most popular, scholarly and semischolarly depictions of Jesus is building conclusions on higher critical opinions. When the writer wishes to distort, or ignores as unauthentic, certain material in the gospel narratives, the method he invariably uses is to make it sound as though all modern scholars are thoroughly agreed with the conclusions of higher criticism. Montgomery observes:

> Moreover, the modern "authorities"…are consistently of a particular kind: They represent a radical tradition of New Testament criticism which reflects nineteenth-century rationalistic presuppositions (e.g., A. Schweitzer), and which issues in the form criticism school *(formgeschichtliche Methode)* of Dibelius and Bultmann, an approach regarded as misleading and outmoded by much of recent biblical scholarship. (MoJW.HC 18)

Particularly galling are the attempts to classify all gospel-believing scholars as uninformed "fundamentalists," completely ignoring sound arguments and reasoning from conservative, highly qualified scholars. In 1985, for example, at a symposium of mainly "free thought" advocates and secular humanist scholars, gospel believers were constantly tagged "fundamentalists" with demeaning adjectives and innuendos.[1] It was amusing at one point when a speaker was asked a question which he said he could not answer since one would have to know a host of ancient languages in order to reply. He, and most of the others in the room, laughed this off as impossible and proceeded with further questions.

What they overlooked or didn't know, however, was that some of the most determined defenders of the Christian faith in the last century have been those who have learned well the multitude of ancient languages relating to biblical times. For example, the late Dr. Gleason Archer, former professor of Old Testament at Trinity Evangelical Divinity School, was fluent in at least twenty ancient and Indo-European languages. Before him, Dr. Robert Dick Wilson, the late nineteenth- and early twentieth-century Princeton professor, mastered forty-five languages and dialects in order to study and defend the Old Testament reliability. As a student in seminary, he would read the New Testament in nine different languages, including a Hebrew translation which he had memorized syllable for syllable! Whereas many students went to Germany to take in higher critical theories of the day, Wilson stated that he studied in Germany so that there would be no professor on earth who could lay down the law for him. If Robert Wilson and Gleason Archer are examples of "uninformed fundamentalists," may their tribe increase!

3. A Rejection or Ignoring of Historical Evidence

Also commonly seen in various approaches to Jesus is a disregard for the evidence of history. One good example is the attitude of many scholars and popularizers toward the apostle Paul. The charge is made repeatedly that the real founder of Christianity was Paul, not Jesus, and that Paul was so Hellenized that all the writings of the New Testament reflect his non-Jewish theology rather than actual history. But as we have seen, claims for a deified Messiah originate in the Old Testament, not in Paul. Paul's theology was derived from his rabbinically trained reflection on Jesus' life as a fulfillment of Old Testament predictions and allusions to the Messiah. We would expect both Paul and the gospels to reflect similar theology as brothers in a common faith, but there are too many historical fingerprints on the gospel accounts to attribute them to an unreliable origin.

Bultmann, relying almost solely on literary criticism and a philosophical predisposition against the supernatural, ignores virtually everything historical about Jesus' resurrection. Gary Habermas, Professor of Apologetics and Philosophy at Liberty University, states:

> Bultmann's treatment of the resurrection of Jesus is accomplished without a historical investigation of any sort. He concludes at the outset, "Is it not a mythical event pure and simple? Obviously it is not an event of past history." (HaG.AE 37, quoting BuR.KM 38)

John Macquarrie, a noted commentator on the theology of Rudolf Bultmann, states:

> And here we must take Bultmann to task for what appears to be an entirely arbitrary dismissal of the possibility of understanding the resurrection as an objective-historical event...The fallacy of such reasoning is obvious. The one valid way in which we can ascertain whether a certain event took place or not is not by bringing some sweeping assumption to show that it could not have taken place, but to consider the historical evidence available, and decide on that. (MacJ.ET 185-86)

In the remainder of this chapter we will look at some major fallacies found in various treatments of Jesus' life today.

FALSE PORTRAYALS OF THE LIFE OF JESUS

Ian Wilson and Jesus: The Evidence

The book *Jesus: The Evidence* is not all bad. Wilson obviously had to read widely in order to gather such an impressive range of material. In places he provides good information such as the phrases from the Dead Sea Scrolls' Manual of Discipline showing that John was not as Hellenistically influenced as was previously thought (p. 41). There are also good refutations of positions such as that of G. A. Wells (that Jesus never existed at all).

The tone of his book, however, often betrays what seems to be a deliberate attempt to undermine the integrity of the New Testament and the early Christians. Wilson often uses the clever device of describing someone else's position using the evidence against the gospel which that person produced, but in the end, while not necessarily agreeing with the person's position, he leaves the reader hanging with doubts produced by the evidence. He does not say whether there is any counterevidence, nor does he produce it. Describing Bultmann's position, for example, he says:

> Jesus' famous saying, "Always treat others as you would like them to treat you; that is the meaning of the Law and the Prophets" (Matthew 7:12) may be found mirrored almost exactly in a saying of the great Jewish Rabbi Hillel, from less than a century before Jesus: "Whatever is hateful to you, do not do to your fellow-man. This is the whole law" [Torah]. We cannot therefore be sure that this was ever said by Jesus. (Wil.JTE 38)

He at least could have told his readers (1) that the statement by Hillel actually confirms the historicity of Jesus' statement by showing His Jewishness; and (2) that Jesus' statement differs from all other known similar teaching in that it is stated in the positive rather than the negative.

One of the main problems with the book is that Wilson is excessively influenced by the arguments of higher criticism. Speaking of the Gospel of Mark, for example, he states:

> It displays one overwhelming characteristic, a denigration of Jews and a whitewashing of Romans. Whoever wrote Mark portrays Jesus' Jewish disciples as a dull, quarrelsome lot, always jockeying for position, failing to understand Jesus. The entire Jewish establishment, Pharisees, Sadducees, chief priests and scribes, is represented as being out to kill Jesus.... By contrast Pilate, the Roman, is portrayed as positively pleading for Jesus' life: "What harm has he done?" (Mark 15:14). (Wil.JTE 46)

The intent of this argument, of course, is to show that Mark, writing his gospel in Rome, did not report accurate history but distorted propaganda designed to gain favor with the Romans. But while it is true that the gospel writers undoubtedly tried to relate the gospel within different cultural contexts, here we have Mark reporting exactly the same question Pilate was asking as reported by Matthew (27:23), and Matthew wrote his gospel to a primarily Jewish audience.

Further, the other gospels also report the faults of the disciples and the desires of the Pharisees, Sadducees, chief priests and scribes to put Jesus to death. Mark also has Pilate capitulating to the crowd, hardly honorable for a Roman leader, and Mark has Roman soldiers beating, mocking, spitting on and crucifying Jesus. In other words, they were just as guilty as the Jewish leaders. You get the feeling that no matter what the gospel writers would have written, the higher critics would try to rip them to shreds—unless, of course, they would have dropped the supernatural and the deity of Christ.

Wilson uses terminology such as, "To soften the blow a little Mark felt obliged to add…" and "Matthew altered the last phrase to…" and "Luke took the none-too-creditable step of replacing the whole account…apparently trying to explain away the incident." (Wil.JTE 109) He, along with the higher critics, is basically saying that the gospel writers are dishonest, but he, like the critics, rarely comes right out and says it.

The gospel writers had a problem that Wilson and other critics fail to perceive: the problem of telling an unbelievable but true story. Whenever they report something the least bit abnormal, you can bet they will be criticized for it. Wilson writes in another place:

> According to Mark and the other synoptic writers, the trial was conducted by "the chief priests and the elders and the scribes…the whole Sanhedrin" (Mark 14:53-55). However, as has been pointed out very convincingly by most Jewish scholars, the historical authenticity of an overnight meeting on this occasion of the full Sanhedrin, the supreme Jewish council, is extremely doubtful. No normal Sanhedrin meeting ever took place at night, and the difficulties of summoning appropriate representatives from their beds at festival time would have been far greater than simply holding Jesus overnight, or indeed over several nights had there been any legitimate trial. (Wil.JTE 121)

But that is the whole point. This was not a normal Sanhedrin meeting. We have already seen from Jewish sources that the house of the chief priests was no bastion of integrity. In fact, knowing of Judas' plot, they probably planned the meeting in advance. Notice Matthew 26:57: "And those who had seized Jesus led Him away to Caiaphas, the high priest, where the scribes and the elders *were gathered* together" (emphasis ours).

Finally, Wilson draws some very far-fetched conclusions, especially when he states:

> In view of Jesus' powers of hypnosis, discussed in chapter six, it is possible that he prepared his disciples for his resurrection using the technique that modern hypnotists call post-hypnotic suggestion. By this means he could have effectively conditioned them to hallucinate his appearances in response to certain prearranged cues (the breaking of bread?), for a predetermined period after his death. (Wil.JTE 141)

Aside from the fact that an honest reading of the gospel accounts shows such a stunt to be completely contrary to the character of Jesus, it also ignores the evidence. As soon as the disciples in the upper room, or on the Emmaus road, or at the Sea of Galilee looked down to see the fish bones lying on the platter Jesus used, they would have realized that they had not been hallucinating.

"Jesus: The Evidence"—Take Two

In 1984, London Weekend Television aired a three-part series designed to be a companion to Ian Wilson's book. Their conclusions were so different from his, though, that he disassociated himself from the TV version's position. Said Peter Foster, a senior tutor at Durham University, "Every page of the script is full of challengeable assumptions or blatant errors."[2]

Here are a few examples from its third program: It asserts that resurrection was common in ancient religions. But as we have seen, these resurrections were entirely different from that of Jesus (they were more like recurring resuscitations with the changing of the seasons) and were not reported as historical events by firsthand witnesses. There is the usual claim of contradictions between the resurrection accounts, completely ignoring John Wenham's explanations in *Easter Enigma*. It attempts to explain the empty tomb in terms of either the Jews or the Christians stealing the body, theories long since discounted as untenable. And it suggests that the apocryphal "Gospel of Thomas" is more reliable than the canonical gospels. Very few scholars would support this conclusion.

G. A. Wells and The Existence of Jesus

With virtually no scholarly support anywhere in the world, Professor Wells continues to vigorously assert that there is no evidence that Jesus ever existed at all. He seems to have a corner on the market for that position, having now written three books on it to not more than one for anyone else. (WeG.JEC, WeG.DJE, 75 and WeG.HE) Prometheus Books, a secular humanist publisher, seems to supply a sufficient number of readers for Wells to keep putting out his material. Yet, as Professor Habermas reflects:

> Comparatively few recent scholars postulate that Jesus never lived. Such positions are usually viewed as blatant misuses of the available historical data. (HaG.AE 31)

In order to hold his position, Wells has to late-date the gospels to c. AD 100. His views are about a hundred years out of date, as even the most radical scholars today generally date the synoptics between AD 65 and 80, and some recent scholars (not necessarily conservatives, either) are pushing for dates in the 50s. Concerning Wells' methodology, R. T. France writes:

> Wells' books are written with a painstaking attention to detail and a calmly rational tone, but his method is that of a man who knows where he is going, and who therefore always selects from the range of New Testament studies those extreme positions which best suit his thesis, and then weaves them together into a total account with which none of those from whom he has quoted would agree. (FrR.E 12)

Professor James Dunn responds to one of Wells' central arguments:

> G. A. Wells, Professor of German in the University of London, has concluded from Paul's virtual silence regarding Jesus' own ministry and teaching that the Jesus of the gospels never existed...Suffice it to underline the fact that the relative silence of Paul regarding "the historical Jesus" is well

known to all scholars working in this area. None that I know of shares Professor Wells' opinion. Other explanations are much more plausible. For example, that Paul was so absorbed by his faith in the risen and exalted Christ that he had little need or occasion to refer back to Jesus' earthly ministry apart from the central episode of his death and resurrection. Or, that the traditions about Jesus were sufficiently familiar to his congregations and noncontroversial, so that he need do no more than allude to them, as he quite often does.

The alternative thesis that within thirty years there had evolved such a coherent and consistent complex of traditions about a nonexistent figure such as we have in the sources of the gospels is just too implausible. (DuJ.E 29)

Bizarre Interpretations

There are four unrelated depictions of Jesus that we group together because of their bizarre conclusions.

Topping the list is J. M. Allegro's *The Sacred Mushroom and the Cross.* (AIJ.SM) Allegro argues here that "Jesus" was originally a code name for an ancient hallucinogenic mushroom used by the people who became the first Christians. Though Allegro has shown himself to be a competent linguistic scholar, his efforts on this book received the distinction of the following public rebuke from other scholars (most of whom are not evangelical Christians), published in some of the leading newspapers of Great Britain:

> From Professor Sir Godfrey Driver, F.B.A., and others:
>
> Sir,
>
> A good deal of publicity has recently been given to a book (*The Sacred Mushroom and the Cross*) by Mr. J. M. Allegro, formerly a lecturer at Manchester University.
>
> This is a work upon which scholars would not normally wish to comment. But the undersigned, specialists in a number of relevant disciplines and men of several faiths and none, feel it their duty to let it be known that the book is not based on any philological or other evidence which they can regard as scholarly.
>
> In their view this work is an essay in fantasy rather than philology.
>
> [Signed] G. R. Driver, Professor Emeritus of Semitic Philology, Oxford University; P. R. Ackroyd, Professor of Old Testament Studies, London University; G. W. Anderson, Professor of Old Testament, Edinburgh University; J. N. D. Anderson, Professor of Oriental Laws, London University; James Barr, Professor of Semitic Languages, Manchester University; C. F. Beckingham, Professor of Islamic Studies, London University; Henry Chadwick, Dean of Christ Church, Oxford University; John Emerton,

Regius Professor of Hebrew, Cambridge University; O. R. Gurney, Professor of Assyriology, Oxford University; E. G. Parrinder, Reader in Comparative Study of Religions, London University; D. Winton Thomas, Emeritus Professor of Hebrew, Cambridge University; Edward Ullendorff, Professor of Ethiopian Studies, London University; G. Vermes, Reader in Jewish Studies, Oxford University; and D. J. Wiseman, Professor of Assyriology, London University. (BIE.MM 8-9)

The Passover Plot by **Hugh Schonfield** gained rapid popularity when it was released. (ScH.TPP) The historical evidence in support of this approach is nonexistent. (See McJ.RF) The author simply invents an unknown young man to conveniently appear whenever an explanation is needed for a reburial or an appearance of Jesus. That the lives of the disciples would be so irreversibly transformed by such a hoax would make them gullible beyond belief.

In *Holy Blood, Holy Grail,* the authors blatantly admit to using the cafeteria-line approach. They state:

> It was not our intention to discredit the gospels. We sought only to sift through them—to locate certain fragments of possible or probable truth and extract them from the matrix of embroidery surrounding them. We were seeking fragments, moreover, of a very precise character—fragments that might attest to a marriage between Jesus and the woman known as the Magdalen. Such attestations, needless to say, would not be explicit. In order to find them, we realized, we would be obliged to read between lines, fill in certain gaps, account for certain caesuras and ellipses. We would have to deal with omissions, with innuendos, with references that were, at best, oblique. And we would not only have to look for evidence of a marriage. We would also have to look for evidence of circumstances that might have been conducive to a marriage. (BaM.HB 330)

It would be difficult to find a more thorough explanation of the cardinal sin of biblical interpretation: *eisegesis*, or reading into the text. The authors obviously are not approaching the text with an objective willingness to discover the real intent of the original writers. Professor Habermas describes the result:

> It is held that since Jesus and his mother are called to a wedding in John 2:1-11 and since they play a major role, it must therefore automatically be Jesus' own wedding. Apparently no one can play a major role at anyone else's wedding, even if he is able to do miracles! In the account of the raising of Lazarus in John 11:1-46, it is asserted that, since Martha ran out to greet Jesus upon his arrival while Mary waited in the house until Jesus asked for her (vss. 20,28), Mary must be Jesus' wife! The authors even admit a non sequitur argument by such reasoning.

It is obvious that, oftentimes in such theses, conclusions are arrived at only by taking out of the gospels and even adding to them what one would like to find. In this case, the authors even admit this procedure. (HaG.AE 77)

The Lost Years of Jesus. A fourth bizarre approach to the life of Jesus has Him as an international traveler to India, Tibet and even Japan. One book we have seen along these lines is *The Lost Years of Jesus* by Elizabeth Clare Prophet. (PrE.LY) We highly recommend this book for all form critics. It is an excellent opportunity to observe firsthand what myth and legend really look like! The main problem with this book is that the reader is led along for over 350 pages and every time some concrete evidence is about to be revealed, it vanishes into thin air. There is none. The book is basically a come-on for a pseudo-Christian Eastern mystical religion retreat ground. It completely ignores the Jewishness of Jesus, having Him in the Orient from age thirteen to age twenty-nine. This "historical breakthrough that will shake the foundations of modern Christendom" is in actuality long on conjecture and short on history. Very short!

"The Last Temptation of Christ"

A disclaimer at the beginning of the 1988 film "The Last Temptation of Christ" states that it is based not on the gospels but upon the 1955 novel of the same name by Nikos Kazantzakis. The knowledgeable viewer quickly discovers that the film is almost void of accurate historical detail. Three examples are:

- The geography and customs of the people are more African than first-century Semitic.

- Though there is a definite attempt made at realism, the result can be described only as ineffective. How anyone could be persuaded by the ravings of the film's John the Baptist, or Jesus' pathetically passive sermons or the neo-orthodox preaching of Paul ("It's not important what Jesus was really like, only what people believe about him"), is the real mystery of this film.

- John the Baptist, known from the gospels to be about six months older than Jesus, is portrayed as being about forty years older than Jesus.

The filmmakers generally seem to have ignored good historical sources such as Josephus, to say nothing of the gospels.

If the gospel writers did reveal an accurate portrait of the Jesus who lived in history, then "Temptation" is not just fictional—it is anti-Christian. For example, the Jesus of history taught that "everyone who looks on a woman to lust for her has committed adultery with her already in his heart." The Jesus of "Temptation" often commits adultery in his heart and states that the only reason he doesn't commit the physical act is that he is afraid.

Other fallacies abound as well. For example:

> Jesus...announces that his death will pay for his own sins rather than for
> the sins of mankind. And he picks up dirt and stones and says, "This is my
> body, too," which apparently makes him a founder of pantheism as well
> as Christianity. (LeJ.HF 36)

Jesus is portrayed as mentally deranged and so confused that no one in his right
mind actually would have followed Him, much less died for Him.

Probably the only substantial question raised by the film is whether or not filmmakers and authors have a right to destroy the reputation of a famous historical figure for
the sake of their own creative interests. As columnist Patrick Buchanan put it, could one

> defend a film titled "The Secret Life of Martin Luther King," that depicted
> the assassinated civil rights leader as a relentless womanizer...[or] a film
> portraying Anne Frank as an oversexed teenager fantasizing at Auschwitz
> on romancing some SS guards? Of course not. (BuP.CB A-9)

Jesus the Semi-Zealot

S. G. F. Brandon's *Jesus and the Zealots* is written on a more scholarly level than typical popularized approaches to the life of Jesus. The curious thing about the book is
that all the way through, Brandon seems to be arguing to identify Jesus as a Zealot but
in the end stops short of doing so.

Despite the scholarly level of this work, it is riddled with speculation and with
faulty reasoning. For example, Brandon, in typical form-critical ridicule of the Gospel
According to Mark, states:

> The Jewish historian Josephus records a number of instances, which we
> must note in greater detail later, of messianic pretenders who roused the
> people with promises of deliverance and were destroyed by the Romans. In
> none of these cases did the Jewish authorities arrest them, condemn them
> for blasphemy and hand them over to the Romans. Why they should have
> acted so with Jesus, as Mark describes them as doing, is, therefore, the more
> remarkable. (BrS.JZ 7)

Actually, it is not so very remarkable, for there are some profound differences
between Jesus and the typical Zealot-styled messianic pretender. For one, they didn't
go around claiming to be God and decisively refuting the religious teaching of the Jewish religious leaders. For another, they directed their attacks at the Romans. But Jesus,
on two separate occasions, directed the only physical antagonism recorded of Him
toward the Temple, the main revenue collection center of the Jewish establishment.

Brandon builds much of his case on details such as: "Luke similarly records an incident that Mark might well have deemed it politic to suppress, namely, that Jesus took
the precaution of seeing that His disciples were armed before going to Gethsemane."

(BrS.JZ 16,324) Come on! When the disciples said, "Lord, look, here are two swords," Jesus answered, "It is enough" (Luke 22:38). Is Brandon trying to tell us that with two swords Jesus' disciples were sufficiently armed to take on the whole Roman army, the greatest fighting machine in the world?

Another fact upon which Brandon builds his case is that Jesus "had among his disciples a professed Zealot." (BrS.JZ 78) But Jesus also had among His disciples a tax gatherer. Should we then make Jesus out to be an agent of the Roman Internal Revenue Service?

Other scholars have not been convinced that Jesus was anything like the Zealots. Dr. Vermes states:

> There is no evidence, in my reading of the gospels, that would point to any particular involvement by Jesus in the revolutionary affairs of the Zealots, though it is likely that some of his followers may have been committed to them and have longed to proclaim him as King Messiah destined to liberate his oppressed nation. (VeG.JWJ 12)

Even Ian Wilson agrees when he summarizes:

> Had he been involved in politics, we might at least have expected his utterances to be peppered with references to past historical events, such as Jerusalem's capture by Pompey, or Herod the Great's collaboration with the Romans, even if he avoided anything seditious on current affairs. But such subjects are simply not part of his vocabulary. (WiI.JTE U4)

Aside from the fact that the book is riddled with speculation, its main problem is that it makes no sense whatever out of statements of Jesus such as His declaration to Pilate:

> My kingdom is not of this world. If My kingdom were of this world, then My servants would be fighting, that I might not be delivered up to the Jews; but as it is My kingdom is not of this realm.[3]

And what about Jesus' rebuke of Peter on the night Jesus was arrested? "Put your sword back into its place; for all those who take up the sword shall perish by the sword."[4] These statements, when compared to others given by Jesus (e.g., the Sermon on the Mount) are undeniably authentic to a fair inquirer.

On final analysis, *Jesus and the Zealots* is a good example of speculative reconstructions of Jesus' life and how the authors of those works attempt to build their case. They inevitably employ the following steps:

1. Relying upon the "assured results of higher criticism," they attempt to destroy the overall historical reliability of the gospel narratives by attributing their development to successive layers of early Church beliefs, myths and legends.

2. Step one leaves the door open for the cafeteria-line approach of picking and

choosing what parts of the gospel narratives will be convenient for their particular thesis. The texts selected are held to be "the kernel" of historically reliable material in the gospel accounts.

3. Finally, various non–New Testament "evidence" is elevated and applied. Brandon at least uses fairly reliable sources of Roman and Jewish culture; others use much more questionable material from "secret" gospels and the like.

To set the record straight, Brandon repudiated any claim that Jesus was a Zealot in his later journal article "'Jesus and the Zealots': A Correction." (BrS.JZC 17:453)

The Book Jesus the Magician

Probably the most irritating thing about Morton Smith's *Jesus the Magician* is the matter-of-fact arrogance with which the author states theories as conclusions. "In the first place," Smith charges, "the gospels repeatedly contradict each other, even as to the course of events." (SmM.JTM 3)

By the examples he cites, it is clear he means "appear to contradict each other," for in no way does he demonstrate an identifiable contradiction, only different emphases or reporting methods used by different gospel writers.

"In the second place, the gospels were written, not merely to record events, but also to produce and confirm faith in Jesus the Messiah (that is, 'the Christ'), the Son of God—not a historical figure, but a mythological one." (SmM.JTM 3) Again, this is presented as a statement of fact, but it is one with which many scholars would disagree, as we have seen throughout our study.

Concerning questions regarding Jesus' resurrection, His claim to be Messiah and His teachings, Smith asserts, "On these and similar questions the evidence of the gospels is always suspect and often self-contradictory." (SmM.JTM 17) It is evident that Smith, finishing his book at the University of Tübingen where Strauss completed his *Life of Jesus* more than a hundred years ago, has not taken into account much of the scholarship disagreeing with Strauss in the interim. Smith makes the same old charges, for example: "There is no likelihood that the Christians had reliable reports of what was said in the Sanhedrin." (SmM.JTM 20) Really? There was at least one, maybe two, Christian sympathizers at that meeting. The texts say that the "whole" council was gathered. This would have included Joseph of Arimathea and probably Nicodemus as well. They could easily have given eyewitness testimony to what happened.

As would be expected, Smith relies on the most radical critical ideas in order to do away with evidence from the gospel accounts. He relies on especially late dates for the gospels: "Written c. AD 75, Mark was used in the 80s and 90s by both Matthew and Luke." (SmM.JTM) As we have seen, most scholars would no longer accept such dates of origin.

The distortions of evidence which seem to occur in almost every paragraph make

Smith appear as one who is bent on proving his theory no matter what the evidence says. For example, speaking of Jesus turning the water into wine, Smith asserts, "The Cana story is probably also a fiction; it has been shown to have been modeled on a Dionysiac myth." (SmM.JTM 26) But as we saw earlier, the Dionysiac myth was likely modeled on the Cana story, for the origin of this myth is certainly later than the reports of Jesus' miracle. The reader should understand that the myth is almost certainly from the second century and probably a deliberate attempt to keep the Dionysiac worshippers from becoming Christians.

Another distortion is evident in Smith's comparison of Jesus with Apollonius of Tyana. (SmM.JTM 84ff.) We have already examined some of the problems associated with the report of the life of Apollonius. The evidence of reliability is extremely suspect and falls pitifully short of that for the reliability of the gospel accounts.

Even Smith's handling of the New Testament should cause readers to be cautious. Citing Acts 19:19, he states: "Lots of magic was practiced in the early churches." But the text proves exactly the opposite. The context of the passage indicates that magic was practiced among the people of Ephesus, probably both Jews and Greeks, that some Jewish exorcists even tried unsuccessfully to use Jesus' name to accomplish exorcisms, and that as the people sincerely believed in Jesus, they were confessing their sins and bringing their magic books to be burned. The church did not condone magic, it condemned it!

Smith produces much "evidence" to which most readers have no access, texts of ancient magic practice in Egypt and Hellenistic cultures around Palestine. Rarely does Smith discuss the dates of origin for those sources or give objective arguments both for and against the points he makes. Even the endnoting system used (and followed also by Ian Wilson) is obscure as there is no indication in the text when Smith has put further information in a footnote. *Jesus the Magician* is more confusing than clarifying, more distortion than accurate assessment of the evidence.

One final weakness of the book is that Smith approaches the gospel evidence with a clear Hellenistic bias. He almost completely ignores the Jewishness of the gospel writers, the works they produced, and the Person of Jesus.

CONCLUSION

There are many other depictions of Jesus' life which could be reviewed here. But then this chapter would be endless. Our desire is that with this book, you will have enough information at your fingertips to evaluate any approaches to the life of Jesus which confront you. After evaluating the evidence for the Jesus who really lived in history, it is our firm conviction that the gospel writers accurately described the life He lived on earth. We hope that is your conviction as well.

A NEW BEGINNING

To know Jesus from history is to know Him from afar. It is only to know *about* Him rather than to actually *know* Him. Yet the historical record of His life reveals that He intensely desired that "all mankind" might know Him personally. On the eve of His crucifixion, when He knew death was imminent and the most important thoughts filled His mind, we find Him praying before His disciples:

> Father, the hour has come; glorify Your Son, that the Son may glorify You, even as You gave Him authority over all mankind, that to all whom You have given Him, He may give eternal life. And this is eternal life, that they may know You the only true God, and Jesus Christ whom You have sent.[1]

Either Jesus was supremely egotistical or He was revealing the whole purpose of His life within human history: that anyone from all mankind might come to know Him. Not just know about Him, but actually know Him in a personal way.

One of the most powerful evidences that Jesus lived, died and rose from the dead is the changed lives of His disciples, from those of the first century down to those in the present time. Hundreds of millions of people throughout history have been able to say that they have come to know Him and that He has changed their lives.

During the nineteenth century, critical scholars put a dividing line between the Jesus of history and the Christ of faith. Our experience, along with that of Christians throughout history, is that no such barrier exists. Because of the resurrection, the historical Jesus continues to live in history. As the apostle Paul wrote, "Jesus Christ is the same yesterday and today, yes and forever."[2]

We can understand why Paul did not devote much space in his writings to the earthly life of Jesus. Knowing Jesus in the present is too exciting. And discovering the historical Jesus in one's everyday experience is without a doubt the greatest discovery one can make!

NOTES
BIBLIOGRAPHY
INDEX

NOTES

I n regard to the codes used, please see "Explanation of the Reference Codes" immediately preceding the introduction. For the key to these codes, please see the bibliography.

INTRODUCTION

1. See TaV.FGT, BaW.GA and McE.WFC for good surveys on form criticism.

2. Karl Ludwig Schmidt, *Der Rahmen der Geschichte Jesu* (Berlin: Trowitsch and Son, 1919). It has not been published in English.

3. The respective English translations are Martin Dibelius, *From Tradition to Gospel*, translated by Bertram Lee Woolf (New York: Charles Scribner's Sons, 1935), and R. Bultmann, *The History of the Synoptic Tradition*, translated by John Marsh (New York: Harper and Row, 1963).

4. The books referred to here include *Jesus* by M. Dibelius, *The Founder of Christianity* by C. H. Dodd, *The Servant-Messiah* by T. W. Manson, *Jesus the Messiah* by W. Manson and *The Formation of the Gospel Tradition* and *The Life and Ministry of Jesus*, both by Vincent Taylor.

5. *Free Inquiry* (Buffalo, NY: Spring 1985), 5:23.

CHAPTER 1—THE UNUSUAL NATURE OF EXTRABIBLICAL REFERENCES TO JESUS

1. Justin Martyr, *First Apology* 35. 7-9, in RoA.ANF.

2. Ibid., 48. 3.

3. See Justin Martyr, *First Apology* 34.2; Tertullian, *Against Marcion* 4. 7, 19, in RoA.ANF. [AS]

4. See Harold W. Hoehner, *Chronological Aspects of the Life of Christ* (Grand Rapids: Zondervan Publishing House, 1977), especially chapter 2, but practically all of the book applies as he fits together the chronological details. Excellent documentation. Luke 3:1-3 says John the Baptist began his ministry in the fifteenth year of Tiberius, which is known to be AD 29. Jesus began his ministry a short time later.

5. Josephus, *Antiquities* 18. 1. 1 (4-10). [AS]

6. Ibid., 18. 1. 6 (23).

7. E.g., Matthew 8:4; 9:30; Mark 5:43.

8. Mark 5:19.

9. E. M. Blaiklock, *Jesus Christ: Man or Myth?* p. 10. His reference in Cicero is *De Bello Gallico* 4. 20-36; 5. 8-23. [AS]

CHAPTER 2—REFERENCES TO JESUS BY ANCIENT SECULAR WRITERS

1. Julius Africanus, *Chronography* 18. 1, in RoA.ANF. [AS]

2. Ibid.

3. For the date AD 29 being the commencement of Jesus' ministry, see the options and arguments summarized in Harold W. Hoehner's *Chronological Aspects of the Life of Christ*.

4. Africanus, *Chronography* 18. 1 in RoA.ANF. [AS]

5. Origen, *Against Celsus* 2. 33, in RoA.ANF. [AS]

6. Ibid., 2. 14.

7. Ibid., 2. 59.

8. The reference commonly cited by scholars who deal with the Greek text, e.g., in the Loeb edition, is XVIII, 63-64, and refers to the 63rd and 64th sections of book 18 in the Greek text of *Antiquities*. We will give both references in all following quotes, citing the reference used by the Greek text in parentheses. This passage, then, is 18. 3. 3 (63-64).

9. Josephus, *Antiquities*, Loeb edition, vol. IX, p. 496.

   Nathaniel Lardner (see LaN.W) was one of the few who thought the mention of James and Jesus in this passage was written in by Christian copyists sometime before AD 200. He felt that the account Josephus gave of James' death did not match up with that of Hegesippus, which is found in Eusebius' *The History of the Church* 2. 23. [AS]

   But this is clearly not the case, for Josephus' account is chiefly concerned with the activities of Ananias and his subsequent removal from the priesthood. The stoning of James is a one-sentence detail in that account. Hegesippus, on the other hand, focuses on the person of James and develops the context quite extensively. He confirms everything that Josephus has said, namely that James was handed over to be stoned, but adds additional detail such as the fact that certain of the Sanhedrin wanted to use James to persuade the multitudes to turn away from Christ; that prior to James' stoning he was thrown off of the parapet of the city wall; that, surviving the fall, he was stoned while praying forgiveness for his executioners; and that, still continuing to live, his death was completed by a blow on the head with a fuller's club. The accounts are completely compatible. They only contradict each other when one forces them to say what they do not necessarily say. In addition, if a later Christian interpolator did insert the mention of James into Josephus at this point, one would think that he would have made stronger efforts to make Josephus' account of James' death parallel more closely the account given by Hegesippus. As the two accounts now stand, each relating different details but in no way definitely contradicting each other, the evidence is as conclusive as one might expect that neither account has been tampered with and that both may be accepted as we now have them.

10. Origen (as well as Eusebius a century later) also quotes Josephus as saying, "These things happened to the Jews in requital for James the Righteous, who was a brother of Jesus known as Christ, for though he was the most righteous of men, the Jews put him to death" *(Against Celsus* 1. 47, in RoA.ANF [AS]).

11. Paul Winter, "Excursus II—Josephus on Jesus and James." This article is a valuable bibliographic resource. Winter lists 47 of the most important reference works on this question: 9 defending the authenticity of the Testimonium, 17 against authenticity and 21 maintaining that the passage was originally in Josephus but that it was only modified, not inserted, by a later copyist.

12. Josephus, *Antiquities*, Loeb edition. Since this passage is much disputed, we have used the translation considered most authoritative.

13. Eusebius, *The History of the Church* 1.11. 7; *Demonstration of the Gospel* 3. 5.105. [AS]

14. Origen, *Against Celsus* 1.47 and *Commentary on Matthew* 10.17, in RoA.ANF. [AS]

15. It is important to note that the apologetic value for these early Christians was not to the historicity of Jesus, but that someone in a respected position in the Roman Empire would look favorably on the person and teaching of Jesus. The historicity of Jesus did not become an issue until recent centuries.

16. It seems that those who want to reject the entire passage are in the habit of writing as though virtually all other scholars support them. This is not the case. Most scholars who have studied this issue opt for this third alternative. For an excellent and respected bibliography of scholars supporting the various positions, see WiP.J in ScE.HJP/73 428-30.

17. Pliny, *Epistles* 10. 96.

18. Ibid., 10. 97.

19. Tacitus, *Annals,* Loeb edition 15. 44.

20. Justin Martyr, *First Apology* 34. 2; 48. 3. (Found in RoA.ANF. [AS])

21. Tertullian, *Against Marcion* 4. 7, 19. (Also found in RoA.ANF. [AS])

22. Consider his statements about the fire in Rome as compared to Suetonius' *Life of Nero* 38 and Pliny's *Natural Histories* 17. 5. [AS]

23. See *Annals of Tacitus* 15. 15,20,45,54,64,73 (WaB.AT). [AS]

24. See *Annals* 15. 10 and 16 (WaB.AT). [AS]

25. Eusebius, *The History of the Church* 4. 9. [AS]

26. Suetonius, *Life of Claudius* 25. 4. [AS]

27. E.g., Josephus does not mention any Jew called Chrestus.

28. Suetonius, *Life of Nero* 16. [AS]

29. Lucian, *The Death of Peregrine* 11-13. [AS]

30. British Museum Syriac MS. Addition 14,658. The date of the *manuscript* is in the seventh century but the letter itself is from the second or third century.

CHAPTER 3—REFERENCES FROM THE RABBIS

1. E.g., Matthew 15:2; Mark 7:5.

2. Mark 7:9.

3. Luke 11:46.

4. Ezra 7:10, emphasis added.

5. Five tractates are called orphan tractates since they don't strictly fit under the seder where they are located.

6. Josephus, *Antiquities* 20. 8. 6 (169-72). [AS]

7. *Yalkut Shimeon:* (Salonica) Section 725 on *wayissa mishalo* (Num. 23. 7), according to Midrash Y'lamm'denue. [RS]

8. Babylonian Talmud: Gittin 56*b*-57*a*. [RS]

9. KIJ.JN 31 gives references as follows: Tractate Kallah, ed. Koronel, p. 18*b* (Hamishshah Kuntresim, Vienna, 1864, p. 3*b*); Kallah, Talmud, ed. Ram., p. 51a; Bote Midrashoth, ed. S. A. Wertheimer, Jerusalem, 1895; III, 23; Dalman, appendix to Laible, pp. 7-8. [RS]

10. Babylonian Talmud: Sanhedrin 43*a*. [RS]

11. Tosefta: Hullin 2.22. Also in the Jerusalem Talmud: Shabbath 14*d* and Abodah Zarah 27*d*, 41*aj* and the Babylonian Talmud: Abodah Zarah 27*b*. R-Rabbi. (RS)

12. Origen, *Against Celsus* 1. 32, in RoA.ANF. [AS]

13. Babylonian Talmud: Yebamoth 62*b*. [RS]

14. Baraitha—Babylonian Talmud: Abodah Zarah 16*b*,17*a*. Also in Tosefta: Hullin 2.24. Words in braces (curly brackets) are from the Munich manuscript [RS]

15. Tosefta: Yebamoth 3.3. [RS]

16. Babylonian Talmud: Yebamoth 4. 49*a* [RS]

17. John 8:41.

CHAPTER 4—MARTYRS, CONFESSORS AND EARLY CHURCH LEADERS

1. See Origen, *Against Celsus* 1. 47, and Eusebius, *The History of the Church* 2. 23, respectively, in RoA.ANF. [AS]

2. See quote from Josephus, *Antiquities* 18. 5. 2 (116-19), which appears in chapter 2 above.

3. Origen, *Against Celsus,* Preface. 1, in RoA.ANF. [AS]

4. Tertullian, *Apology* 50. [AS]

5. Origen, *De Principiis* 2. 3. 6, in RoA.ANF. [AS]

6. All quotes and references are from J. B. Lightfoot's translation unless otherwise noted. (LiJ. AF)

7. Clement, *Corinthians,* 46, in RoA.ANF. [AS]

8. Ignatius, *Ephesians,* 17, in RoA.ANF. [AS]

9. Ignatius, *Ephesians,* 67, in RoA.ANF. [AS]

10. Ignatius, *Magnesians,* 1, in RoA.ANF. [AS]

11. Ignatius, *Trallians,* 9, in RoA.ANF. [AS]

12. Ignatius, *Smyrnaeans,* 1 in RoA.ANF. [AS]

13. Ignatius, *Smyrnaeans,* 2, in RoA.ANF. [AS]

14. Ignatius, *Smyrnaeans,* 3, in RoA.ANF. [AS]

15. Ignatius, *Smyrnaeans,* 4, in RoA.ANF. [AS]

16. Eusebius, *The History of the Church* 3. 39. [AS]

17. Ibid.

18. Ibid.

19. Ibid. Refers to Papias' reproduction of this story.

20. *Letter of [from] the Smyrnaeans* 9-11, in RoA.ANF. [AS]

21. Polycarp, *Philippians* 8. [AS]

22. Eusebius, *The History of the Church* 4. 3. [AS]

23. *New International Dictionary of the Christian Church,* J. D. Douglas, "Aristides." [R]

24. Justin Martyr, *Dialogue with Trypho,* 9, in RoA.ANF. [AS]

25. Justin Martyr, *First Apology,* 34, in RoA.ANF. [AS]

26. Ibid., 35.

27. Eusebius, *The History of the Church* 9. 22. 2. [AS]

28. Irenaeus, *Against Heresies* 3. 1. 1, in RoA.ANF. [AS]

29. Ibid., 3. 2. 2.

30. Tertullian, *Apology* 5, in RoA.ANF. [AS]

31. *New International Dictionary of the Christian Church,* J. D. Douglas, "Origen." [R]

CHAPTER 5—AGRAPHA, APOCRYPHA AND PSEUDEPIGRAPHA

1. The books are the same but are numbered differently in different collections.

2. Cf. Colossians 4:16; 2 Peter 3:15-16.

3. *New International Dictionary of the Christian Church,* Donald Guthrie, "Canon of Scripture." [H]

4. *Zondervan Pictorial Encyclopedia,* Donald Guthrie, "Canon of the New Testament." [R]

5. Ibid.

6. Ibid.

7. *International Standard Bible Encyclopedia,* E. M. Yamauchi, "Agrapha." [R]

8. Eusebius, *The History of the Church* 4. 22. 8. [AS]

9. Jerome, *Against the Pelagians* 3. 2, in RoA.ANF. [AS]

10. John 21:25.

11. *Zondervan Pictorial Encyclopedia,* William White, "Agrapha." [R]

12. Ibid.

13. The heading of the letter reads: "From Letters of Clement, author of the Stromateis [Miscellanies], to Theodore." See BrF.JCO 184.

14. DuJ.E 52. Quoting Chadwick's comments on a TV follow-up program to the British TV series "Jesus: The Evidence."

CHAPTER 6—ARE THE BIBLICAL RECORDS RELIABLE?

1. William F. Albright, "Toward a More Conservative View," *Christianity Today* 7 (January 18, 1963): 3.

2. Reported by Michael P. Harris, Marlin Levin and James Willwerth in "Who Was Jesus?" *Time* (August 15, 1988), p. 41.

3. Ibid.

4. MoJW.HC 29, summarizing Aristotle, *Art of Poetry (De Arte Poetica),* 1460*b*-61*b*.

5. Ibid.

6. Eusebius, *The History of the Church,* 3. 39. [AS]

7. Irenaeus, *Against Heresies* 3. 1. 1. [AS]

8. *Encyclopedia International* 4:407. [R]

9. *The Jewish Encyclopedia* 8:508. [R]

CHAPTER 7—HIGHER CRITICISM: HOW "ASSURED" ARE THE RESULTS?

1. *Harper's Bible Dictionary,* Paul Achtemeier, ed. "Biblical Criticism." [R]

2. See Josh McDowell, *More Evidence,* pp. 185-326, for more information on form and redaction criticism, the two more prominent disciplines of higher criticism through the middle of the twentieth century.

3. Robert Mounce, personal interview, July 2, 1974.

4. Mounce interview.

5. McGinley's last sentence is quoted from Léonce de Grandmaison, *Jesus Christ* (1935), I:115.

6. Response by Harold W. Hoehner at end of NaR.CF, 159.

7. For a concise yet authoritative description of the origin and development of redaction criticism, see the Introduction to William L. Lane's commentary, *The Gospel According to Mark* (LaW.GAM).

8. Harold W. Hoehner, "Jesus, the Source or Product of Christianity?" lecture at the University of California at San Diego, La Jolla, California, January 22, 1976.

CHAPTER 8—THE GOSPEL BEFORE THE GOSPELS

1. Matthew, Mark and Luke are called "synoptic" gospels because their parallel texts yield a synopsis [Gr., *sunopsis,* meaning "seen together"] which "discloses their similarities and differences."

2. William F. Albright, "Toward a More Conservative View," *Christianity Today* 7 (January 18, 1963): 3.

3. Robinson is not a conservative Christian but is known as a scholar who tries to weigh the evidence accurately. Many scholars have therefore been cautious about criticizing his conclusions.

4. Acts 1:1.

5. Luke 1:1-3.

6. J. G. Herder, *Christliche Schriften* (Riga, 1796), 2:191-93, quoted in ReB.RSG 10-11.

7. J. K. L. Gieseler, *Historisch-kritischer Versuch über die Entstehung und die frühesten Schicksale der schriftlichen Evangelien* (Leipzig: Engelmann, 1818), p. 90, quoted in ReB.RSG 11.

8. StB.TFG. (Streeter's arguments are found in this work.)

9. Eusebius, *The History of the Church*, 6. 14. [AS]

10. Babylonian Talmud: Megillah 7*b*, Ketuboth 50*a*, Berakhoth 28*a*, and elsewhere. [RS]

11. Mishnah: Menahoth 11. 4. [RS]

12. Babylonian Talmud: Berakhoth 13a. [RS]

13. Babylonian Talmud: Sanhedrin 99*b*. [RS]

14. Mishnah: Aboth 3. 9. [RS]

15. Matthew 23:10.

16. Galatians 1:14.

17. Chart from Harold W. Hoehner class notes.

18. Werner Georg Kümmel, *Introduction to the New Testament*, rev. ed., Howard Clark Lee, trans. (Nashville: Abingdon Press, 1875).

19. Donald Guthrie, *New Testament Introduction*, 3rd ed. (Downers Grove, IL: InterVarsity Press, 1970).

20. Galatians 1:12.

21. Colossians 1:27.

22. Galatians 2:2.

23. Galatians 2:7-9.

CHAPTER 9—HISTORY AND MYTH

1. The authors attribute the quote to the second-century philosopher Celsus. In reality, it appears nowhere in the only extant source of Celsus' writings, Origen's *Against Celsus*. At best it is a paraphrased summary of similar arguments which Celsus raised against the Christians of his day.

2. Diogenes Laertius, *Lives of Eminent Philosophers* 3. 1-2 [AS], quoted in CaDR.DSG 129.

3. See Plutarch, *Parallel Lives*, Alexander 2. 1–3. 2. [AS]

4. Diodorus Siculus, *Library of History*, 4. 9. 1-10 [AS], quoted in CaDR.DSG 136.

5. Origen, *Against Celsus* 1. 37, in RoA.ANF. [AS]

6. Iamblichos, *The Life of Pythagoras* 3. [AS]

7. Ibid., 60-61.

8. Prudentius, *Peristephanon* 10. 1011-50. [AS]

9. Nash quotes from André Boulanger, *Orphee: Rapports de l'orphisme et du christianisme* (Paris, 1925), p. 102.

10. Proverbs 18:17.

11. Acts 14:11-13.

12. Galatians 1:17-18.

13. Acts 14:14-15,18.

14. *New International Dictionary of the Christian Church*, s.v. "Christmas" by James Taylor. The term *Sun of Righteousness* is from Malachi 4:2. [R]

15. Justin Martyr, *First Apology* 66, in RoA.ANF. [AS]

16. Adolf von Harnack, *Wissenchaft und Leben* (Giessen, 1911), 2:191, quoted in NaR.CHW 118-19.

CHAPTER 10—EVIDENCE FROM HISTORICAL GEOGRAPHY

1. Reported by Michael P. Harris, Marlin Levin and James Willwerth in "Who Was Jesus?" *Time* (August 16, 1988), p. 38.

2. John 1:46.

3. Luke 4:29.

4. Matthew 26:25.

5. Josephus, *Antiquities* 18. 1. 1 (1-8). [AS]

6. Ibid., 16. 9. 3 (286-90). [AS]

7. *Zondervan Pictorial Encyclopedia*, E. M. Blaiklock, "Quirinius." [R]

8. Aristotle, *Art of Poetry (De Arte Poetica)*, 14606-16. [AS]

9. For more details on the examples given in the text, see BrF.NTD 82-91.

10. Cicero, *De Lege Agraria*.

11. Matthew 16:18.

12. John 7:38.

13. Matthew 5:14.

14. John 1:11.

15. Matthew 4:23-25.

16. See Mark 11:12-14 and Matthew 21:18-19.

17. Mark 11:23.

18. Matthew 13:31-32.

19. Matthew 23:27-28.

20. The bracketed word "from" replaces Wilson's word "to," an obvious typographical or inadvertent error. The corrected sentence is a common alleged contradiction cited by critics.

21. Acts 1:8.

22. *Zondervan Pictorial Encyclopedia*, J. C. DeYoung, "Gadara, Gadarenes." [R]

CHAPTER 11—EVIDENCE FROM ARCHAEOLOGY

1. Matthew 2:21,23.

2. Matthew 18:6; Mark 9:42; Luke 17:2.

3. Matthew 23:5.

4. Babylonian Talmud: Baba Bathra 4a [RS]

5. Josephus, *Antiquities* 15.11. 6 (413). [AS]

6. John 20:6.

7. This book is one of the best basic resources on the subject.

8. The quote also appears in earlier printings of the book. See, for example, Frederic Kenyon, *Our Bible and the Ancient Manuscripts* (New York: Harper & Brothers Publishers, 1941), p. 48.

9. John 1:24.

10. Reported by Michael P. Harris, Marlin Levin and James Willwerth in "Who Was Jesus?" *Time* (August 15,1988), p. 39.

CHAPTER 12—THE JEWISH FACTOR

1. Palestinian Talmud: Shekalim 3. 3. [RS]

2. Babylonian Talmud; Baba Kamma 82*b*-83*a*, Sotah 49*b*. [RS]

3. Matthew 6:43-44.

4. 1 Timothy 6:8.

5. Matthew 9:20-22; Mark 5:25-34; Luke 8:43-48.

6. Luke 8:48.

7. See under "Are Accounts of the Trial of Jesus Anti-Semitic?" on page 249 for one early Jewish comment on this.

8. Luke 2:19.

9. John 1:29.

10. See VeG.JWJ 123, 128 for a concise evaluation of the issues.

11. Josephus, *Wars of the Jews* 2. 8. 4 (124-25). [AS]

12. Throughout this work the author tries to identify Jesus with the Zealot cause but stops just short of calling him a full-fledged Zealot.

13. When we speak of Jerusalem as being down south we're being more American than Jewish. For the Jews, one went up to Jerusalem, because of its topographical elevation.

14. See also Mark 6:4; Luke 4:24; John 4:44.

15. See Matthew 4:19; 21:11,46; Mark 6:15; Luke 7:16; 24:19; John 4:19; 6:14; 7:40; 9:17.

16. Matthew 14:5; 21:26; Mark 11:32; Luke 1:76; 20:6.

17. Luke 4:28-29.

18. Luke 7:6-8.

19. Matthew 15:24 and John 4:22.

20. Shmuel Safrai, "A Jewish Bachelor," *Jerusalem Perspective* 1 (October, 1987): 4.

21. John 18:28.

22. Jim Fleming, in a lecture at the Jerusalem Center for Biblical Studies, Jerusalem, Israel, January, 1987.

23. John 4:22.

24. Luke 23:34.

25. Babylonian Talmud: Pesahim 57*a*.

26. 1 Corinthians 1:3 (emphasis ours).

27. 1 Peter 2:24 (emphasis ours).

CHAPTER 13—JESUS AND MIRACLES

1. Pausanius, *Description of Greece* 6. 26. 1ff. [AS]

2. See Josh McDowell, *Understanding the Occult,* for more information on that subject.

3. Mishnah: Taanith 3. 8. [RS]

4. Babylonian Talmud: Berakhoth 346 [RS]; Gamliel is another spelling of Gamaliel.

5. Deuteronomy 13:1-5.

6. See Matthew 9:34; 12:24; Mark 3:22; Luke 11:15.

7. Josephus, *Antiquities:* 18. 3. 8 (63-64). [AS]

8. Babylonian Talmud: Shabbath 104*b*, Tosefta: Shabbath 11.15. [RS]

9. Babylonian Talmud: Abodah Zarah 27*b*; Tosefta: Hullin 2.22ff. [RS]

10. Babylonian Talmud: Sanhedrin 43*a*, 107*b*. [RS]

11. Origen, *Against Celsus* 1. 38; 2. 48, in RoA.ANF. [AS]

12. Acts 2:22.

13. Cf. John 2:23-25; 6:26.

CHAPTER 14—THE RELIABILITY OF THE RESURRECTION REPORTS

1. Galatians 1:18-19.

2. The following points are given in more detail in MoJP.S 166-70, and more originally in BoE.FE.

3. The following resources can be very helpful in resolving apparent Bible contradictions:

- Gleason L. Archer, *Encyclopedia of Bible Difficulties.* Especially helpful for discrepancies caused by language peculiarities.

- W. F. Arndt, *Bible Difficulties.*

- W. F. Arndt, *Does the Bible Contradict Itself?*

- Johnston M. Cheney, *The Life of Christ in Stereo.* (Currently available under the title *Jesus Christ, the Greatest Life.*)

- Jack Finegan, *Handbook of Biblical Chronology.* This book has a wealth of information on dates of biblical events and historical happenings surrounding these events. It is the standard work on Bible chronology and has never been surpassed.

- John W. Haley, *Alleged Discrepancies of the Bible.* This book has been around for a long time and contains good information on the causes of apparent discrepancies as well as proposed solutions to most alleged contradictions in the Bible.

- *Zondervan Pictorial Encyclopedia,* Merrill C. Tenney, ed., 6 vols. [R] One of the best Bible encyclopedias around.

- Robert L. Thomas and Stanley N. Gundry, *A Harmony of the Gospels.* Additional material at the end of the *Harmony* is excellent. For example see their essay, "The Genealogies in Matthew and Luke," for four possible solutions to this apparent contradiction.

- In addition to the above works, we recommend that you read widely in good commentaries on particular books of the Bible. Scholars who have the time and ability to focus their attention on single Bible books and issues within them can provide insights which can solve most alleged contradictions in the Bible.

CHAPTER 15—MESSIAH AND SON OF GOD?

1. Psalm of Solomon 17:23-36 (21-32), as quoted in VeG.JTJ 251.

2. Philo, *De praemiis* 95. [AS]

3. *Testament of Levi* 18:2-7, as cited in VeG.JTJ 136

4. Tacitus, *Histories* 5. 13. [AS]

5. Suetonius, *Life of Vespasian* 4. 5. [AS]

6. Matthew 22:41-48; Mark 12:35-37; Luke 20:41-44.

7. Matthew 23:10.

8. Matthew 24:5,23-27 (and cross references).

9. John 7:32.

10. See Matthew 16:13-20.

11. Luke 2:49.

12. John 1:35-37.

13. Matthew 11:3.

14. Matthew 11:5.

15. Matthew 22:41-46; Mark 12:36-37; Luke 20:41-44.

16. John 17:9.

17. Matthew 24:3-5,23-27 (and cross references).

18. Mark 9:41.

19. Luke 24:26.

20. Luke 24:46.

21. John 4:26. The historicity of this passage is strengthened by the woman's statement, "Our fathers worshipped

in this mountain; and you people say that Jerusalem is the place where men ought to worship." Historically, the central theological difference between the Jews and the Samaritans was that the former claimed Jerusalem for the proper center of worship, while the latter claimed Mount Gerizim just on the western side of Sychar.

22. Matthew 26:57-68; Mark 14:53-65.

23. "Son of Man" occurs 81 times in the gospel accounts.

24. Daniel 7:13-14.

25. *Zondervan Pictorial Encyclopedia,* D. A. Hagner, "Sadducees." [R]

26. *Encyclopedia Judaica,* David Flusser, "Jesus," 10:14. [R]

27. Acts 7:56; Hebrews 2:6; Revelation 1:13.

28. HaF.B 160. See Josh McDowell, *Evidence That Demands a Verdict,* pp. 145-75, for specific prophecies.

29. Acts 3:8.

30. Acts 17:3.

31. Acts 26:22,23.

32. Matthew 16:21; 17:12; Mark 8:31; 9:12; Luke 9:22; 17:25; 22:15; 24:26,47.

33. From the Prophet Isaiah 52:13–53:12 (NIV), written c. 700 BC.

34. Prior to Rashi, there were some rabbis who interpreted the passage as referring to someone else, for example Moses or Hezekiah. This was by far a minority view.

35. 1 Corinthians 15:3,4.

36. Luke 3:38.

37. Matthew 26:63—cf. Mark 14:61; Luke 22:67.

38. Mark 14:62—cf. Matthew 26:64; Luke 22:69,70.

39. Luke 22:38.

40. John 4:26; 6:35,41,48,51; 8:12,18,24,28,58; 10:7,9,11,14; 11:25; 13:19; 14:6; 15:1.

41. John 20:28.

42. Philippians 2:6-11.

CHAPTER 16—JESUS AND THE POPULAR PRESS

1. "Jesus in History and Myth" conference held at the University of Michigan under the auspices of the Biblical Criticism Research Project of the Committee for Scientific Examination of Religion, April 19–20, 1985.

2. Peter Foster is quoted in a newspaper article entitled, "TV Series Is Ridiculed," which appeared in the *Universe* on April 6, 1984, with no by-line.

3. John 18:36.

4. Matthew 26:52; John 18:10 identifies Peter as the sword-wielder.

AFTERWORD—A NEW BEGINNING

1. John 17:1-3 with Old English "Thy," "Thee," "Thou," "gavest" and "hast" modernized to "Your," "You," "gave" and "have."

2. Hebrews 13:8.

BIBLIOGRAPHY
CODE KEY EXPLANATION

After many of the quotes listed in this book a reference code appears, such as: (GreM.MA 23-24). For the rationale of the codes please see "Explanation of the Reference Codes" immediately preceding the introduction. The code for each of the works in this bibliographical list that has been quoted in the book is shown in the column in front of the listing of that work.

MODERN SOURCES:

AlW.AP   Albright, W. F. *The Archaeology of Palestine*. Revised edition. Harmondsworth, Middlesex: Pelican Books, 1960.

AlW.BA   Albright, W. F. *Biblical Archaeologist* 11 (1948).

AlW.FSA   Albright, W. F. *From the Stone Age to Christianity*. Baltimore: Johns Hopkins Press, 1946.

AlW.RD   Albright, W. F. *Recent Discoveries in Bible Lands*. New York: Funk and Wagnalls, 1965.

AlW.CT   Albright, W. F. "Toward a More Conservative View." *Christianity Today* 7 (January 18, 1963).

AlJ.SM   Allegro, John M. *The Sacred Mushroom and the Cross: A Study of the Nature and Origins of Christianity Within the Fertility Cults of the Ancient Near East*. London: Hodder & Stoughton, 1970.

AlJ.DSS   Allegro, John. *The Dead Sea Scrolls: A Reappraisal*. New York: Penguin Books, 1964.

AmG.HMH   Ambrose, Gordon, and Newbold, George. *Handbook of Medical Hypnosis*. London: Bailliere Tindall & Cassell, 1968.

AmF.SLC   Amiot, François; Brunot, Amédée; Danielou, Jean; and Daniel-Rops, Henri. *The Sources for the Life of Christ*. Translated by P. J. Hepbume-Scott. New York: Hawthorn Books, 1962.

AnC.CQ   Anderson, Charles C. *The Historical Jesus: A Continuing Quest*. Grand Rapids: William B. Eerdmans Publishing Co., 1972.

    Anderson, Hugh, ed. *Jesus*. Englewood Cliffs: Prentice Hall, 1967.

AnJ.CTW   Anderson, J. N. D. *Christianity: The Witness of History*. Downers Grove: InterVarsity Press, 1970.

AnN.CWR   Anderson, Norman. *Christianity and World Religions*. Downers Grove, IL: InterVarsity Press, 1984.

AnN.JC   Anderson, Norman. *Jesus Christ: The Witness of History*. Downers Grove, IL: InterVarsity Press, 1986.

AnS.MRC   Angus, Samuel. *Mystery-Religions and Christianity*. London: J. Murray, 1925. Reprint, New Hyde Park, NY: University Books, 1967.

ArG.EBD   Archer, Gleason L. *Encyclopedia of Bible Difficulties.* Grand Rapids: Zondervan Publishing House, 1982.

ArG.LF   Archer, Gleason L. "Linguistic Factors in the New Testament Witness to Jesus Christ." A paper read at the "Jesus Christ: God and Man" conference, an international colloquium of scholars in Dallas, November 13–16, 1986.

           Archer, Gleason L. *A Survey of Old Testament Introduction.* Chicago: Moody Press, 1964.

ArA.G   Argyle, A. W. "Greek Among the Jews of Palestine in New Testament Times." *New Testament Studies* 20 (October 1973): 87-89.

ArW.BD   Arndt, W. F. *Bible Difficulties.* St. Louis: Concordia Press, 1971.

ArW.DBC   Arndt, W. F. *Does the Bible Contradict Itself?* Fifth edition. Revised. St. Louis: Concordia Press, 1955.

           Arnold, Thomas. *Christian Life—Its Hopes, Its Fears, and Its Close.* London: T. Fellowes, 1859. Sixth edition.

AvN.IJ   Avigad, Nahman. *Israel Exploration Journal* 12 (1962).

AvN.DJ   Avigad, Nahman. *Discovering Jerusalem.* Nashville: Thomas Nelson Publishers, 1983.

BaM.HB   Baigent, Michael; Leigh, Richard; and Lincoln, Henry. *Holy Blood, Holy Grail.* New York: Dell Publishing Co., 1983.

           Barbet, Pierre. A *Doctor at Calvary.* New York: P. S. Kennedy and Sons, 1953. BaW.GA Barclay, W. *The Gospels and Acts.* London, 1976.

BaWE.GC   Barnes, W. E. *Gospel Criticism and Form Criticism.* Edinburgh: T. & T. Clark, 1936.

BaJ.WL   Barr, James. "Which Language Did Jesus Speak?" *Bulletin of the John Rylands Library* 53 (Autumn 1970).

BaCK.NTB   Barrett, C. K. *The New Testament Background.* New York: Harper & Row Publishers, 1961.

BaH.KM   Bartsch, Hans-Werner, ed. *Kerygma and Myth.* Translated by Reginald H. Fuller. London: SPCK, 1962.

BaF.CH   Baur, Ferdinand C. *Church History of the First Three Centuries.* Second edition. Tübingen. English translation by Allan Menzies. London, 1878.

BeH.FU   Bell, H. I., and Skeat, T. C., eds. *Fragments of an Unknown Gospel and Other Early Christian Papyri.* Published by Trustees of the British Museum, 1936.

           Bender, A P. "Beliefs, Rites, and Customs of the Jews, Connected With Death, Burial, and Mourning." *The Jewish Quarterly Review* 7 (1895).

BeP.JG   Benoit, Pierre. *Jesus and the Gospels,* vol. 1. Translated by Benet Weatherhead. New York: Herder and Herder, 1973.

           Bergsma, Stuart. "Did Jesus Die of a Broken Heart?" *The Calvin Forum.* March 1948.

BeE.TI   Best, Ernest, and Wilson, R. McL., ed. *Text and Interpretation.* Cambridge, England: Cambridge University Press, 1979.

BiD.L   Bivin, David. "Looking Behind Rabbinic Parables." *Through Their Eyes* 1 (November, 1986): 5.

BiD.PRI   Bivin, David. "Principles of Rabbinic Interpretation." *Through Their Eyes* 2 (April 1987).

BiD.Q   Bivin, David. "Question for Question." *Through Their Eyes* 2 (January, 1987): 5.

BiD.UDW   Bivin, David, and Blizzard, Roy Jr. *Understanding the Difficult Words of Jesus: New Insights From a Hebraic Perspective.* Austin: Center for Judaic-Christian Studies, 1983.

BlM. AA   Black, Matthew. An *Aramaic Approach to the Gospels and Acts.* Third edition. Oxford: Clarendon Press, 1967.

BlE.A   Blaiklock, E. M. *The Archaeology of the New Testament.* Grand Rapids: Zondervan Publishing House, 1970.

BlE.CSU   Blaiklock, E. M. "The Christmas Story Unearthed." *Eternity* (December 1976), pp. 16-17.

BlE.MM   Blaiklock, E. M. *Jesus Christ: Man or Myth?* Nashville: Thomas Nelson Publishers, 1984.

B1R.JR   Blizzard, Roy, and Bivin, David. "Study Shows Jesus as Rabbi." *Through Their Eyes* 1 (September 1986): 1,6.

BoE.FE   Bode, Edward L. *The First Easter Morning.* Rome: Biblical Institute Press, 1970.

BoE.WV   Bode, Edward L. "The First Easter Morning: Women Visit the Empty Tomb of Jesus." A paper read at the "Jesus Christ: God and Man" conference, an international colloquium of scholars in Dallas, November 13–16, 1986.

BrS.JZ   Brandon, S. G. F. *Jesus and the Zealots.* Manchester: Manchester University Press, 1967.

BrS.JZC   Brandon, S. G. F. "'Jesus and the Zealots': A Correction." *New Testament Studies* 17 (July 1971).

BrW.CQ   Brindle, Wayne. "The Census and Quirinius: Luke 2:2." *Journal of the Evangelical Theological Society* 27 (March 1984): 43-52.

BrC.M   Brown, Colin. *Miracles and the Critical Mind.* Grand Rapids: William B. Eerdmans Publishing Co., 1984.

BrA.TT   Bruce, A. B. *The Training of the Twelve.* Reprint edition of 1894 original. Grand Rapids: Kregel Publications, 1971.

BrF.AC   Bruce, F. F. "Archaeological Confirmation of the New Testament." In *Revelation and the Bible.* Edited by Carl Henry. Grand Rapids: Baker Book House, 1969.

BrF.BP   Bruce, F. F. *The Books and the Parchments.* Revised edition. Westwood: Fleming H. Revell Co., 1963.

BrF.DG   Bruce, F. F. *The Defense of the Gospel in the New Testament.* Grand Rapids: William B. Eerdmans Publishing Co., 1977.

BrF.HS   Bruce, F. F. *The Hard Sayings of Jesus.* Downers Grove, IL: InterVarsity Press, 1983.

BrF.JCO   Bruce, F. F. *Jesus and Christian Origins Outside the New Testament.* Grand Rapids: William B. Eerdmans Publishing Co., 1974.

BrF.NTD   Bruce, F. F. *The New Testament Documents: Are They Reliable?* Fifth revised edition. Grand Rapids: William B. Eerdmans Publishing Co., 1985.

BrF.NTH   Bruce, F. F. *New Testament History.* London: Hodder & Stoughton, 1980.

BrF.T   Bruce, F. F. *Tradition Old and New.* Grand Rapids: Zondervan Publishing House, 1970.

BuP.CB   Buchanan, Patrick J. "Christian-bashing a popular sport in Hollywood." *Glendale News Press* (July 27, 1988).

BuJ.J   Buell, Jon A., and Hyder, O. Quentin. *Jesus: God, Ghost or Guru?* Grand Rapids: Zondervan Publishing House, 1978.

BuR.EF   Bultmann, Rudolf. *Existence and Faith: Shorter Writings of Rudolf Bultmann.* Selected, translated and introduced by Schubert M. Ogden. Cleveland and New York: Meridian Books—The World Publishing Co., 1960.

BuR.HST   Bultmann, Rudolf. *The History of the Synoptic Tradition.* Translated by John Marsh. New York: Harper & Row Publishers, 1963.

BuR.JCM   Bultmann, Rudolf. *Jesus Christ and Mythology.* New York: Charles Scribner's Sons, 1958.

BuR.JW   Bultmann, Rudolf. *Jesus and the Word.* Translated by Louise Pettibone Smith and Erminie Huntress Lantern. New York: Charles Scribner's Sons, 1958.

BuR.KM   Bultmann, Rudolf. "New Testament and Mythology." *Kerygma and Myth.* Edited by Hans-Werner Bartsch; translated by Reginald H. Fuller. New York: Harper & Row Publishers, 1961.

BuR.TNT   Bultmann, Rudolf. *Theology of the New Testament,* vol. 2. Translated by Kendrick Grobel. New York: Charles Scribner's Sons, 1951.

BuR.FC   Bultmann, Rudolf, and Kundsin, Karl. *Form Criticism.* Translated by F. C. Grant (Originally published by Willet, Clark, and Co., 1934.) New York: Harper and Brothers—Torchbook Edition, 1962.

BuL.DCR   Burkholder, Lawrence. In "A Dialogue on Christ's Resurrection." *Christianity Today* 12 (12 April 1958).

BuM.HAH   Burrows, Millar. "How Archaeology Helps the Student of the Bible." *Workers With Youth* (April 1948).

BuM.ML   Burrows, Millar. *More Light on the Dead Sea Scrolls.* New York: Viking, 1958.

BuM.WM   Burrows, Millar. *What Mean These Stones?* New York: Meridian Books, 1956.

           Cairns, David. A *Gospel Without Myth?* London: SCM Press Ltd., 1960.

CaEE.CT   Cairns, Earle E. *Christianity Through the Centuries.* Grand Rapids: Zondervan Publishing House, 1967.

CaEL.LC   Camus, E. L. *The Life of Christ,* vol. II. New York: Cathedral Library Assn., 1908.

CaDA.FS   Carson, D. A. *From Sabbath to Lord's Day.* Grand Rapids: Zondervan Publishing House, 1982.

CaDR.DSG   Cartlidge, David R., and Dungan, David L. *Documents for the Study of the Gospels.* Philadelphia: Fortress Press, 1980.

CaL.DJ   Cassels, Louis. "Debunkers of Jesus Still Trying." *Detroit News* (23 June 1973).

ChJ.R   Charlesworth, James H. "Research on the Historical Jesus Today: Jesus and the Pseudepigrapha, the Dead Sea Scrolls, the Nag Hammadi Codices, Josephus, and Archaeology." *Princeton Seminary Bulletin,* vol. VI, no. 2, pp. 98-116.

ChJM.L   Cheney, Johnston M. *The Life of Christ in Stereo.* Edited by Stanley A. Ellisen. Portland: Western Baptist Seminary Press, 1969.

CrW.CS   Craig, William L. "Contemporary Scholarship and the Historical Evidence for the Resurrection of Jesus Christ." *Truth* 1:89-95.

           Craig, William L. *The Historical Argument for the Resurrection of Jesus During the Deist Controversy.* Lewiston, NY: E. Mellen Press, 1985.

CrW.RO   Craig, William L. "The Resurrection of Jesus and the Origin of the Christian Way." Paper read at the "Jesus Christ: God and Man" conference, an international colloquium of scholars in Dallas, November 13–16, 1986.

           Craig, William L. *The Son Rises.* Chicago: Moody Press, 1981.

           Currie, George. *The Military Discipline of the Romans from the Founding of the City to the Close of the Republic.* An abstract of thesis published under auspices of Graduate Council of Indiana University, 1928.

DaG.JJ   Dalman, Gustaf. *Jesus—Jeshua.* Translated by Paul P. Levertoff (first published in 1929). New York: Ktav Publishing House, 1971.

DaW.IN   Davies, W. D. *Invitation to the New Testament.* London: Hodder & Stoughton, 1966.

           Davis, C. Truman. "The Crucifixion of Jesus." *Arizona Medicine* (March 1965), pp. 185-86.

DeA.LAE   Deissmann, Adolf. *Light From the Ancient East.* Fourth edition. Translated by R M. Strachen. New York: Doran, 1927.

DiM.FA   Dibelius, Martin. A *Fresh Approach to the New Testament and Early Christian Literature.* New York: Charles Scribner's Sons, 1936.

DiM.FTG   Dibelius, Martin. *From Tradition to Gospel.* Translated by Bertram Lee Woolf. New York: Charles Scribner's Sons, 1935.

DiM.GCC   Dibelius, Martin. *Gospel Criticism and Christology.* London: Ivor Nicholson and Watson, Ltd., 1935.

DiM. J   Dibelius, M. *Jesus.* Originally published in German in 1939. Reprint edition. London: SCM Press Ltd., 1963.

DoC.AP   Dodd, C. H. *The Apostolic Preaching and Its Developments.* London: Hodder & Stoughton, 1936. Reprint, Grand Rapids: Baker Book House, 1980.

DoC.FC   Dodd, C. H. *The Founder of Christianity.* London: The Macmillan Company, 1971.

DoC.FGN   Dodd, C. H. "The Framework of the Gospel Narrative." *Expository Times* 43 (June 1932).

           Dodd, C. H. *The Parables of the Kingdom.* Revised edition. New York: Charles Scribner's Sons, 1961.

DrS.F   Driver, S. R., and Neubauer, Adolf. *The Fifty-third Chapter of Isaiah According to the Jewish Interpreters*. New York: Ktav Publishing House, 1969. Reprint of Oxford, 1876-77 edition.

DuJ.E   Dunn, James D. G. *The Evidence for Jesus*. Philadelphia: The Westminster Press, 1986.

DuJ.HSG   Dunn, James D. G. "The Historicity of the Synoptic Gospels." A paper read at the "Jesus Christ: God and Man" conference, an international colloquium of scholars in Dallas, November 13–16, 1986.

DuA.DSS   Dupont-Sommer, A. *The Dead Sea Scrolls*. Oxford: Blackwell 1952.

DuW.SC   Durant, Will. *Caesar and Christ*. Volume 3 in *The Story of Civilization* series. New York: Simon & Schuster, 1944.

EaB.GBG   Easton, Burton Scott. *The Gospel Before the Gospels*. New York: Charles Scribner's Sons, 1928.

EdA.LTJ   Edersheim, Alfred. *The Life and Times of Jesus the Messiah*. Grand Rapids: William B. Eerdmans Publishing Co., 1971.

EdL.JVJ   Edgar, L. J. *A Jewish View of Jesus*. London: The Liberal Jewish Synagogue, 1940.

EiR.M   Eisler, R. *The Messiah Jesus and John the Baptist*. London, 1931.

    Ellwein, Edvard. "Rudolf Bultmann's Interpretation of the Kerygma." *Kerygma and History*. Edited by Carl E. Braaten and Roy A. Harrisville. New York: Abingdon Press, 1966.

EmJ.P   Emerton, J. A. "The Problem of Vernacular Hebrew in the First Century A.D. and the Language of Jesus." *Journal of Theological Studies* 24 (April 1973): 1-23.

EnH.JV   Enelow, H. G. A. *Jewish View of Jesus*. New York: Macmillan Publishing Co., 1920.

ErM.CT   Erickson, Millard J. *Christian Theology*. Grand Rapids: Baker Book House, 1983.

EvC.TR   Evans, C. F. "Tertullian's References to Sentius Saturninus and the Lukan Census." *Journal of Theological Studies* 24 (April 1973): 24-39.

FiF.FC   Filson, Floyd V. *Form Criticism*. Volume 1 of *Twentieth Century Encyclopedia of Religious Knowledge*. Lefferts A. Loetscher, ed. Grand Rapids: Baker Book House, 1955.

FiF.OG   Filson, Floyd V. *Origins of the Gospels*. New York: Abingdon Press, 1938.

FiJ.ANT   Finegan, Jack. *The Archaeology of the New Testament*. Princeton: Princeton University Press, 1969.

FiJ.BC   Finegan, Jack. *Handbook of Biblical Chronology*. Princeton: Princeton University Press, 1964.

    Finkel, Asher. *The Pharisees and the Teacher of Nazareth*. Leiden, Netherlands: Brill, 1964.

FiJA.MM   Fitzmyer, Joseph A. "Memory and Manuscript: The Origins and Transmission of the Gospel Tradition." *Theological Studies* 23 (September 1962).

FlJ.JAS   Fleming, Jim. Lecture on cassette tape and booklet entitled "Jesus Around the Sea." P.O. Box 71055, Jerusalem, Israel.

FlJ.JJ   Fleming, Jim. Lecture on cassette tape and booklet entitled "Jesus in Jerusalem." P.O. Box 71055, Jerusalem, Israel.

FlJ.LJ   Fleming, Jim. Lecture on cassette tape and booklet entitled "Survey of the Life of Jesus." P.O. Box 71055, Jerusalem, Israel.

FlD.NS   Flusser, David. "A New Sensitivity in Judaism and the Christian Message." *Harvard Theological Review* 61 (1968): 107-127.

FoG.TT   Foote, Gaston. *The Transformation of the Twelve*. Nashville: Abingdon Press, 1968.

FrR.E   France, R. T. *The Evidence for Jesus*. Downers Grove, IL: InterVarsity Press, 1986.

FrR.G   France, R. T. "The Gospels as Historical Sources for Jesus, the Founder of Christianity." *Truth* 1:81-87. *Free Inquiry* 5 (Buffalo, NY: Spring 1985): 23.

FrJP.A   Free, Joseph P. *Archaeology and Bible History*. Wheaton, IL: Scripture Press Publications, 1969.

FrJM.M   Freeman, James M. *Manners and Customs of the Bible*. Reprint edition. Plainfield: Logos International, 1972.

FuH.A   Furneaux, Henry. *The Annals of Tacitus*. Second edition. Revised by H. F. Pelham and C. D. Fisher. Oxford: Oxford University Press, 1907.

GaJ.JCM   Gartenhaus, Jacob. "The Jewish Conception of the Messiah." *Christianity Today* (March 13, 1970).

Geisler, Norman L. *Christian Apologetics*. Grand Rapids: Baker Book House, 1976.

GeN.IC   Geisler, Norman L. "The Importance of the Christological Issues." A paper read at the "Jesus Christ: God and Man" conference, an international colloquium of Christian scholars held in Dallas, November 13-16, 1986.

GeN.M   Geisler, Norman L. "Miracles and Modern Scientific Thought." *Truth* 1:67-73.

Geisler, Norman L. *Miracles and Modern Thought*. Grand Rapids: Zondervan Publishing House, 1982.

GeN.GIB   Geisler, Norman L., and Nix, William E. *A General Introduction to the Bible*. Chicago: Moody Press, 1986.

GeB.MM   Gerhardsson, Birger. *Memory and Manuscript*. Translated by Eric J. Sharpe. Copenhagen: Villadsen og Christensen, 1964.

GiE.D   Gibbon, Edward. *The Decline and Fall of the Roman Empire*. London, 1794. Reprint, New York: Peter Fenelon Collier & Son, 1900.

GlR.EP   Gleason, Robert W., ed. *The Essential Pascal*. Translated by G. F. Pullen. New York: Mentor-Omega Books, 1966.

GlN.RD   Glueck, Nelson. *Rivers in the Desert: A History of the Negev*. New York: Farrar, Straus and Cudahy, 1959.

GoM.JN   Goguel, Maurice. *Jesus the Nazarene: Myth or History?* Translated by Frederick Stephens. New York: D. Appleton and Co., 1926.

GoM.LJ   Goguel, Maurice. *The Life of Jesus*. New York: Macmillan Publishing Co., 1944.

GoMo.JJT   Goldstein, Morris. *Jesus in the Jewish Tradition*. New York: Macmillan Publishing Co., 1950.

GoL.UH50   Gottschalk, Louis R. *Understanding History*. New York: Alfred A. Knopf, 1950.

GoL.UH69   Gottschalk, Louis R. *Understanding History*. Second edition. New York: Alfred A. Knopf, 1969.

GraM.JHR   Grant, Michael. *Jesus: An Historian's Review of the Gospels*. New York: Charles Scribner's Sons, 1977.

GraR.HI   Grant, Robert. *Historical Introduction to the New Testament*. New York: Harper & Row Publishers, 1963.

GreM.EP   Green, Michael. Editor's Preface to *I Believe in the Resurrection of Jesus* by George Eldon Ladd. Grand Rapids: William B. Eerdmans Publishing Co., 1975.

GreM.MA   Green, Michael. *Man Alive!* Downers Grove, IL: InterVarsity Press, 1968.

GrS.ET   Greenleaf, Simon. *An Examination of the Testimony of the Four Evangelists by the Rules of Evidence Administered in the Courts of Justice*. New York: J. Cockroft & Co., 1874. Reprint edition. Grand Rapids: Baker Book House, 1965.

GrJ.I   Greenlee, J. Harold. *Introduction to New Testament Textual Criticism*. Grand Rapids: William B. Eerdmans Publishing Co., 1964.

Guignebert, Charles Alford. *Jesus*. New Hyde Park, NY: University Books, 1956.

GriJ.IS   Gribbin, John. *In Search of the Double Helix: Quantum Physics and Life*. New York: McGraw-Hill Book Co., 1986.

GuR.PR   Gundry, Robert R. "The Essentially Physical View of Jesus' Resurrection According to the New Testament." A paper read at the "Jesus Christ: God and Man" conference, Dallas, November 13-16, 1986.

GuS.C   Gundry, Stanley N. "A Critique of the Fundamental Assumption of Form Criticism, Part I." *Bibliotheca Sacra* 123 (January–March 1966).

GuD.NTI   Guthrie, Donald. *New Testament Introduction*. Third edition. Downers Grove, IL: InterVarsity Press, 1970.

HaN.AO   Haas, N. "Anthropological Observations on the Skeletal Remains from Giv'at ha-Mivtar." *Israel Exploration Journal* 20 (1970).

HaG.AE   Habermas, Gary R. *Ancient Evidence for the Life of Jesus.* Nashville: Thomas Nelson Publishers, 1984.

HaG.DJR   Habermas, Gary R., and Flew, Antony G. N. *Did Jesus Rise from the Dead?: The Resurrection Debate.* Edited by Terry L. Miethe. San Francisco: Harper & Row Publishers, 1987.

HaDA.R   Hagner, Donald A. *The Jewish Reclamation of Jesus.* Grand Rapids: Zondervan Publishing House, 1984.

HaE.ME   Haight, E. H. *More Essays on Greek Romances.* London: Longmans, Green and Co., 1945.

HaJ.AD   Haley, John W. *Examination of Alleged Discrepancies of the Bible.* Boston: Estes and Lauriat, 1874.

HaF.B   Hamilton, Floyd. *The Basis of Christian Faith.* Revised and enlarged edition. New York: Harper & Row Publishers, 1964.

HaR.IOT   Harrison, Ronald Kenneth. *Introduction to the Old Testament.* Grand Rapids: William B. Eerdmans Publishing Co., 1969.

HaA.J   Harvey, A. E. *Jesus and the Constraints of History.* Philadelphia: The Westminster Press, 1982.

HaDJ.RS   Hayles, David J. "The Roman Census and Jesus' Birth." *Buried History* 9 (December 1973): 113-32.

HaDJ.RSII   Hayles, David J. "The Roman Census and Jesus' Birth (Part II)." *Buried History* 10 (March 1974): 16-31.

HeC.LH   Hemer, C. J. "Luke the Historian." *Bulletin of the John Rylands University Library of Manchester* 60 (Autumn 1977): 28-51.

HeJ.UN   Hewitt, J. W. "The Use of Nails in the Crucifixion." *Harvard Theological Review* 25 (1932).

HoH.C   Hoehner, Harold W. *Chronological Aspects of the Life of Christ.* Grand Rapids: Zondervan Publishing House, 1977.

            Hoehner, Harold W. "Jesus, the Source or Product of Christianity?" Lecture at the University of California at San Diego in La Jolla, California, January 22, 1976.

HoG.W   Howard, George. "Was the Gospel of Matthew Originally Written in Hebrew?" *Bible Review* (Winter 1986): 15-25.

HuE.PF   Hudson, E. C. "The Principal Family of Pisidian Antioch." *Journal of Near Eastern Studies* 15 (1956).

HuD.IC   Hume, David. *An Inquiry Concerning Human Understanding.* Edited by Charles W. Hendel. Indianapolis: Bobbs-Merrill, 1956.

HuA.INT   Hunter, Archibald M. *Interpreting the New Testament: 1900–1950.* London: SCM Press Ltd., 1951.

HuA.WWJ   Hunter, Archibald M. *The Work and Words of Jesus.* Philadelphia: The Westminster Press, 1950.

            "A Jewish Bachelor." *Jerusalem Perspective* 1 (October 1987).

            Käsemann, Ernst. *Essays on New Testament Themes.* Naperville, IL: Alec R. Allenson, Inc., 1964; London: SCM Press Ltd., 1964.

KeC.COT   Keil, C. F., and Delitzsch, F. *Commentary on the Old Testament.* 10 volumes. Edinburgh: T. & T. Clark, 1866. Reprint edition. Grand Rapids: William B. Eerdmans Publishing Co., 1980.

KeD.WIB   Kennedy, D. James. *Why I Believe.* Waco: Word Books, 1980.

KeF.BA   Kenyon, Frederic. *The Bible and Archaeology.* New York: Harper & Row Publishers, 1940.

KeF.BMS   Kenyon, Frederic. *The Bible and Modern Scholarship.* London: J. Murray, 1948.

KeF.OB41   Kenyon, Frederic. *Our Bible and the Ancient Manuscripts.* New York: Harper & Brothers Publishers, 1941.

KeF.OB48   Kenyon, Frederic. *Our Bible and the Ancient Manuscripts.* New York: Harper & Brothers Publishers, 1948.

KiS.G   Kistemaker, Simon. *The Gospels in Current Study.* Grand Rapids: Baker Book House, 1972.

KiG.JH   Kittel, Gerhard. "The Jesus of History." *Mysterium Christi.* Edited by G. K. A. Bell and G. A. Deissmann. London: Longmans, Green, 1930.

Klausner, Joseph. *From Jesus to Paul.* New York: Macmillan Publishing Co., 1943.

Kl.JN   Klausner, Joseph. *Jesus of Nazareth.* New York: Menorah Publishing Co., 1925.

K1J.MI   Klausner, Joseph. *The Messianic Idea in Israel.* New York: Macmillan Publishing Co., 1955.

KuWG.INT   Kümmel, Werner Georg. *Introduction to the New Testament.* Revised edition. Translated by Howard Clark Lee. Nashville: Abingdon Press, 1875.

KuWG.NT   Kümmel, Werner George. *The New Testament: The History of the Investigation of Its Problems.* Translated by S. McLean Gilmour and Howard C. Kee. Nashville: Abingdon, 1972.

KuW.TR   Künneth, Walter. *The Theology of the Resurrection.* London: SCM Press Ltd., 1965.

LaGE.IBR   Ladd, George Eldon. *I Believe in the Resurrection of Jesus.* Grand Rapids: William B. Eerdmans Publishing Co., 1975. Editor's Preface by Michael Green.

Lake, Kirsopp. *The Historical Evidence for the Resurrection of Jesus Christ.* New York: G. P. Putnam's Sons, 1907.

LaG.IBE   Lamsa, George M. *Idioms in the Bible Explained and A Key to the Original Gospels.* San Francisco: Harper & Row Publishers, 1985.

LaW.CPAA   Lane, William L. "A Critique of Purportedly Authentic Agrapha." *Journal of the Evangelical Theological Society* 18 (Winter, 1975): 29-35.

LaW.GAM   Lane, William L. *The Gospel According to Mark.* Grand Rapids: William B. Eerdmans Publishing Co., 1974.

LaP.I   Lapide, Pinchas. "Insight From Qumran Into the Languages of Jesus." *Revue de Qumran.* No. 32, Tome 8, Fascicle 4 (December 1975): 483-501.

Lapide, Pinchas. *Israelis, Jews and Jesus.* Translated by P. Heinegg. Garden City, NY: Doubleday & Co., 1979.

LaP.NTT   Lapide, Pinchas. *New Testament Theology: The Proclamation of Jesus.* Translated by John Bowden. New York: Charles Scribner's Sons, 1971.

LaP.R   Lapide, Pinchas. *The Resurrection of Jesus: A Jewish Perspective.* Minneapolis: Augsburg Publishing House, 1983.

LaN.W   Lardner, Nathaniel. *The Works of Nathaniel Lardner.* Volume VI. London: William Ball, 1838.

LaWS.DSS   LaSor, William Sanford. *The Dead Sea Scrolls and The New Testament.* Grand Rapids: William B. Eerdmans Publishing Co., 1972.

LaK.HC   Latourette, Kenneth Scott. *A History of Christianity.* New York: Harper and Brothers Publishers, 1937.

LeL.CS   Legrande, L. "The Christmas Story in Luke 2:1-7." *Indian Theological Studies* 19 (December 1982): 289-317.

LeJ.HF   Leo, John. "A Holy Furor." *Time* (August 15, 1988).

LeC.CR   Lewis, C. S. *Christian Reflections.* Edited by Walter Hooper. Grand Rapids: William B. Eerdmans Publishing Co., 1974.

Lewis, C. S. *Fern-seed and Elephants.* London: Collins, 1975.

LeC.MC   Lewis, C. S. *Mere Christianity.* New York: Macmillan Publishing Co., 1943.

LeC.M   Lewis, C. S. *Miracles.* New York: Macmillan Publishing Co., 1960. Macmillan paperback edition, 1978.

LeC.SL   Lewis, C. S. *The Screwtape Letters.* New ed., London: Geoffrey Bles, The Centenary Press, 1961.

LiJ.AF   Lightfoot, J. B. *The Apostolic Fathers.* Grand Rapids: Baker Book House, 1956.

Lindeskog, G. *Die Jesusfrage im Neuzeitlichen Judentum.* Uppsala: Almqvist & Wiksells, 1938.

LiRL.HT   Lindsey, Robert L. *A Hebrew Translation of the Gospel of Mark.* Second edition. Jerusalem: Dugith Publishers, 1973.

LiR.MC   Lindsey, Robert. "On Jesus' Messianic Claims." *Through Their Eyes* 1 (November 1986).

LiP.KW   Little, Paul. *Know Why You Believe.* Wheaton, IL: Scripture Press Publications, 1971.

Loetscher, Lefferts A., ed. *Twentieth Century Encyclopedia of Religious Knowledge.* Grand Rapids: Baker Book House, 1955. Vol. 1: *Form Criticism,* by Floyd V. Filson.

Luther, Martin. *Luther's Works.* Edited by Franklin Sherman and Helmut T. Lehmann. Vol. 47: *The Christian in Society.* Philadelphia: Fortress Press, 1971.

Maccoby, Hyam. *The Mythmaker. Paul and the Invention of Christianity.* New York: Harper & Row Publishers, 1986.

MaH.RJ   Maccoby, Hyam. *Revolution in Judaea: Jesus and the Jewish Resistance.* London: Orbach and Chambers, 1973. Reprint edition. New York: Taplinger, 1981.

MaJG.OPR   Machen, J. Gresham. *The Origin of Paul's Religion.* New York: Macmillan Publishing Co., 1925.

MacJ.ET   Macquarrie, John. An *Existentialist Theology: A Comparison of Heidegger and Bultmann.* New York: Harper & Row Publishers, 1965.

Maier, Paul L. "The Empty Tomb as History." *Christianity Today* 19 (March 28, 1975): 5.

MaP.FE   Maier, Paul. *First Easter.* New York: Harper & Row Publishers, 1973.

MaT.QHJ   Manson, T. W. "The Quest of the Historical Jesus—Continues." *Studies in the Gospels and Epistles.* Edited by Matthew Black. Manchester: Manchester University Press, 1962.

MaT.SM   Manson, T. W. *The Servant-Messiah.* Cambridge, England: Cambridge University Press, 1953.

Manson, W. *Jesus the Messiah.* London, n.p., 1943.

MaIH.IB   Marshall, I. Howard. *I Believe in the Historical Jesus.* Grand Rapids: William B. Eerdmans Publishing Co., 1977.

MarJ.RG   Martin, James. *The Reliability of the Gospels.* London: Hodder & Stoughton, 1959.

MaJL.RM   Martyn, J. Louis. Review of *The Mythmaker,* by Hyam Maccoby. *New York Times Book Review* (20 July 1986), pp. 8-9.

McJ.A   McDowell, Josh, and Stewart, Don. *Answers to Tough Questions Skeptics Ask About the Christian Faith.* San Bernardino: Here's Life Publishers, 1980.

McJ.E   McDowell, Josh. *Evidence That Demands a Verdict.* San Bernardino: Here's Life Publishers, 1972.

McJ.ME   McDowell, Josh. *More Evidence That Demands a Verdict.* San Bernardino: Here's Life Publishers, 1975.

McJ.ME/81   McDowell, Josh. *More Evidence That Demands a Verdict.* Revised edition. San Bernardino: Here's Life Publishers, 1981.

McJ.MTC   McDowell, Josh. *More Than a Carpenter.* Wheaton, IL: Tyndale House Publishers, 1977.

McJ.RF   McDowell, Josh. *The Resurrection Factor.* San Bernardino: Here's Life Publishers, 1981.

McJ. D   McDowell, Josh, and Larson, Bart. *Jesus: A Biblical Defense of His Deity.* San Bernardino: Here's Life Publishers, 1983.

McJ.UO   McDowell, Josh, and Stewart, Don. *Understanding the Occult.* San Bernardino: Here's Life Publishers, 1982.

McL.FC   McGinley, Lawrence J. *Form Criticism of the Synoptic Healing Narratives.* Woodstock, MD: Woodstock College Press, 1944.

McE.WFC   McKnight, E. V. *What Is Form Criticism?* Philadelphia: Fortress Press, 1969.

McA.IS   McNeile, A H. *An Introduction to the Study of the New Testament.* London: Oxford University Press, 1953.

MeB.MR   Metzger, Bruce M. "Mystery Religions and Early Christianity." In his *Historical and Literary Studies.* Leiden, Netherlands: E. J. Brill, 1968.

MeB.MSM   Metzger, Bruce M. "Methodology in the Study of the Mystery Religions and Early Christianity." *Historical and Literary Studies: Pagan, Jewish, and Christian.* Grand Rapids: William B. Eerdmans Publishing Co., 1968.

MeB.TNT   Metzger, Bruce M. *The Text of the New Testament.* New York: Oxford University Press, 1968.

MeE.AREC   Meyers, Eric M., and Strange, James F. *Archaeology, the Rabbis and Early Christianity.* Nashville: Abingdon Press, 1981.

MiA.TBT   Millard, Alan. *Treasure From Bible Times.* Belleville, MI: Lion Publishing Corporation, 1985.

       Montefiore, C. G. "The Originality of Jesus." *Hibbert Journal* 28 (1929–30): 101.

MoC.WJT   Montefiore, C. G. "What a Jew Thinks About Jesus." *Hibbert Journal* 33 (1934–36).

MoJW.CTM   Montgomery, John W., ed. *Christianity for the Tough Minded.* Minneapolis: Bethany Fellowship, 1973.

MoJW.HC   Montgomery, John Warwick. *History and Christianity.* Downers Grove, IL: InterVarsity Press, 1971.

MoJW.WHG   Montgomery, John Warwick. *Where is History Going?* Minneapolis: Bethany Fellowship, 1967.

MoS.LM   Morais, Sabato. "A Letter by Maimonides to the Jews of South Arabia Entitled 'The Inspired Hope.'" *Jewish Quarterly Review* 26 (July 1934–April 1936).

MoJP.S   Moreland, J. P. *Scaling the Secular City.* Grand Rapids: Baker Book House, 1987.

MoL.SFG   Morris, Leon. *Studies in the Fourth Gospel.* Grand Rapids: William B. Eerdmans Publishing Co., 1969.

       Morison, Frank. *Who Moved the Stone?* London: Faber and Faber, 1930.

MoCF.IE   Moule, C. F. D. "The Intentions of the Evangelists." *New Testament Essays.* Edited by A.J. B. Higgins. Manchester at the Manchester University Press, 1959.

MoCF.PNT   Moule, C. F. D. *The Phenomenon of the New Testament.* London: SCM Press Ltd., 1967.

MuC.FH   Muller, Carl. *Fragmenta Historicum Graecorum* III.

MuF.BR   Muller, Frederick. "Bultmann's Relationship to Classical Philology." *The Theology of Rudolf Bultmann.* Edited by Charles W. Kegkry. London: SCM Press Ltd., 1966.

MuCu.W   Murphy, Cullen. "Who Do Men Say That I Am?" *Atlantic Monthly* (December 1986).

NaR.CF   Nash, Ronald. *Christian Faith and Historical Understanding.* Grand Rapids: Zondervan Publishing House, 1984.

NaR.CHW   Nash, Ronald. *Christianity and the Hellenistic World.* Grand Rapids: Zondervan Publishing House, 1984.

NeW.RB   Neil, William. *The Rediscovery of the Bible.* New York: Harper & Brothers, 1954.

NeS.INT   Neill, Stephen. *The Interpretation of the New Testament.* London: Oxford University Press, 1964.

       Newsweek (August 8, 1966), p. 51.

OrH.AI   Orlinsky, Harry. *Ancient Israel.* Ithaca: Cornell University Press, 1954.

PaW.DC   Pannenberg, Wolfhart. In "A Dialogue on Christ's Resurrection." *Christianity Today* 12 (April 1968).

PeN.RTJ   Perrin, Norman. *Rediscovering the Teaching of Jesus.* New York: Harper & Row Publishers, 1967.

PeN.WRC   Perrin, Norman. *What Is Relation Criticism?* Philadelphia: Fortress Press, 1969.

PhJ.RT   Phillips, J. B. *The Ring of Truth.* New York: Macmillan Publishing Co., 1967.

PiS.AVT   Pines, Shlomo. *An Arabic Version of the Testimonium Flavianum and Its Implications.* Jerusalem: Jerusalem Academic Press, 1971.

PiC.SF   Pinnock, Clark. *Set Forth Your Case.* New Jersey: The Craig Press, 1968.

PiC.TT   Pinnock, Clark. "The Tombstone That Trembled." *Christianity Today* 12 (April 1968): 8.

PrE.LY   Prophet, Elizabeth Clare. *The Lost Years of Jesus.* Livingston, MT: Summit University Press, 1984.

RaW.BRD15   Ramsay, W. M. *The Bearing of Recent Discovery on the Trustworthiness of the New Testament.* London: Hodder & Stoughton, 1915.

RaW.BRD53   Ramsay, W. M. *The Bearing of Recent Discovery on the Trustworthiness of the New Testament.* Reprint of London 1915 edition. Grand Rapids: Baker Book House, 1953.

RaW.SPT   Ramsay, W. M. *St. Paul the Traveller and the Roman Citizen.* Grand Rapids: Baker Book House, 1962.

RaW.WCB   Ramsay, W. M. *Was Christ Born at Bethlehem?* London: Hodder & Stoughton, 1898.

ReE.FC   Redlich, E. B. *Form Criticism.* Edinburgh: Thomas Nelson and Sons, Ltd., 1939.

ReB.RSG   Reicke, Bo. *The Roots of the Synoptic Gospels.* Philadelphia: Fortress Press, 1986.

RiG.TJ   Richards, G. C. "The Testimonium of Josephus." *Journal of Theological Studies* 42 (1941).

RiG.CN   Richards, G. C., and Shutt, R. J. H. "Critical Notes on Josephus' *Antiquities.*" *Classical Quarterly*
            31 (1937).

RiD.ETH   Richardson, Don. *Eternity in Their Hearts.* Ventura, CA: Regal Books, 1981.

            Ridderbos, Herman N. *Bultmann.* Translated by David H. Freeman. Grand Rapids: Baker Book
            House, 1960.

RiHN.POT   Ridderbos, Herman N. *Paul: An Outline of His Theology.* Grand Rapids: William B. Eerdmans
            Publishing Co., 1975.

RiH.GT   Riesenfeld, Harald. *The Gospel Tradition.* Philadelphia: Fortress Press, 1970.

RiH.GTB   Riesenfeld, Harald. *The Gospel Tradition and its Beginnings.* London: A. R. Mowbray & Co.
            Limited, 1961.

RiHA.TS   Rigg, Horace A., Jr. "Thallus: The Samaritan?" *Harvard Theological Review* 34 (1941).

RoJM.NHL   Robinson, James M, ed. *The Nag Hammadi Library.* New York: Harper & Row Publishers, 1981.

RoJA.RNT   Robinson, John A. T. *Redating the New Testament.* Philadelphia: The Westminster Press, and
            London: SCM Press Ltd., 1976.

SaS.TJE   Safrai, S., and Stern, M., ed. *The Jewish People in the First Century.* 2 volumes. Amsterdam: Van
            Corcum, Assen, 1976.

SaC.IR   Sanders, C. *Introduction to Research in English Literary History.* New York: Macmillan Publishing
            Co., 1952.

SaS.JU/56   Sandmel, Samuel. *A Jewish Understanding of the New Testament.* Cincinnati: Hebrew Union
            College Press, 1956.

            Sandmel, Samuel. *A Jewish Understanding of the New Testament.* Reprint. New York: Ktav
            Publishing House, 1974.

SaS.WJ65   Sandmel, Samuel. *We Jews and Jesus.* New York: Oxford University Press, 1965.

SaS.WJ73   Sandmel, Samuel. *We Jews and Jesus.* Reprint edition. New York: Oxford University Press, 1973.
            Saturday Review (December 3, 1966), p. 43.

ScP.HCC   Schaff, Philip. *History of the Christian Church.* New York: Charles Scribner's Sons, 1882.

ScH.TPP   Schonfield, Hugh. *The Passover Plot.* New York; Bantam Books, 1965.

ScE.HJP90   Schürer, Emil. *A History of the Jewish People in the Time of Jesus Christ.* Edinburgh: T. & T. Clark,
            1890.

ScE.HJP73   Schürer, Emil. *The History of the Jewish People in the Age of Jesus Christ* (175 BC–AD 135). Vol. 1.
            Edited and revised by Geza Vermes and Fergus Millar. Edinburgh: T. & T. Clark, 1973.

ScA.PI   Schweitzer, Albert. *Paul and His Interpreter.* London: n.p., 1912.

ScA.QHJ   Schweitzer, Albert. *The Quest of the Historical Jesus.* Translated from the first German edition,
            Von Reimarus zu Wrede, 1906. New York: Macmillan Publishing Co., 1961.

ScEF.KM   Scott, Ernest Findlay. *Kingdom and the Messiah.* Edinburgh: T. & T. Clark, 1911.

SeR.L   Selby, Ray. "The Language in Which Jesus Taught." *Theology* 86 (May 1983): 185-193.

ShT.TFC   Sheehan, Thomas. *The First Coming.* New York: Random House, 1986.

ShA.RS   Sherwin-White, A N. *Roman Society and Roman Law in the New Testament.* Grand Rapids: Baker
            Book House, 1963.

            Sider, Ronald. "A Case for Easter." *His* (April 1972), p. 29.

            Smalley, Stephen S. "Redaction Criticism." *New Testament Interpretation.* Grand Rapids:
            William B. Eerdmans Publishing Co., 1977, p. 181.

SmM.CA   Smith, Morton. *Clement of Alexandria and a Secret Gospel of Mark.* Cambridge, MA: Harvard
            University Press, 1973.

SmM.JTM   Smith, Morton. *Jesus the Magician.* New York: Harper & Row Publishers, 1978.

SmM.TSG   Smith, Morton. *The Secret Gospel.* New York: Harper & Row Publishers, 1973.

SmR.CD   Smith, Robert. "Caesar's Decree (Luke 2:1-2): Puzzle or Key?" *Currents in Theology and Mission* 7 (December 1980): 343-51.

     Smith, Wilbur M. *Therefore Stand: Christian Apologetics.* Grand Rapids: Baker Book House, 1965.

SpR.ANT   Spivey, Robert A., and Smith, D. Moody, Jr. *Anatomy of the New Testament* London: The Macmillan Company—Collier Macmillan Limited, 1969.

StE.JHS   Stauffer, Ethelbert. *Jesus and His Story.* Translated by Dorothea M. Barton. New York: Alfred A. Knopf, 1960.

StG.JH   Stein, Gordon. "The Jesus of History: A Reply to Josh McDowell." A circular published by The Free Thought Association, Culver City, CA, 1984.

StR.DS   Stein, Robert H. *Difficult Sayings in the Gospels.* Grand Rapids: Baker Book House, 1985.

StRA.ERT   Stewart, R. A. *The Earlier Rabbinic Tradition: And Its Importance for New Testament Background.* London: InterVarsity Fellowship, 1949.

     Strauss, David Frederick. *The Life of Jesus for the People.* Volume I. Second edition. London: William & Norgate, 1879.

StB.TFG   Streeter, B. H. *The Four Gospels, A Study of Origins.* London: The Macmillan Company, 1936.

StP.M   Stube, Paul. *Minim.* Rough draft. ©1987.

TaA.I   Tambasco, Anthony J. *In the Days of Jesus.* Ramsey, NJ: Paulist Press, 1983.

TaV.LMJ   Taylor, Vincent. *The Life and Ministry of Jesus.* London: n.p., 1954.

TaV.FGT   Taylor, Vincent. *The Formation of the Gospel Tradition.* Second edition. London: Macmillan and Co. Limited, 1935.

TaW.MGT   Taylor, W. S. "Memory and Gospel Tradition." *Theology Today* 15 (January 1959).

TeW.RIJ   Temple, W. *Readings in St. John's Gospel.* London: Macmillan and Company, Limited, 1939–40, 1945, p. 24.

TeM.HV   Tenney, Merrill C. "Historical Verities in the Gospel of Luke." *Bibliotheca Sacra* 135 (April-June 1978): 126-139.

     Tenney, Merrill C. "The Resurrection of Jesus Christ." *Prophecy in the Making.* Edited by Carl Henry. Carol Stream, IL: Creation House, 1971, p. 59.

ThH.JTM   Thackeray, Henry St. John. *Josephus the Man and the Historian.* New York: Hebrew Union College, 1929.

ThR.H   Thomas, Robert L., and Gundry, Stanley N. *A Harmony of the Gospels.* San Francisco: Harper & Row Publishers, 1978.

TrW.PP   Trotter, William Finlayson. *Pascal's Pensees.* New York: E. P. Dutton & Co., 1964.

     "TV Series Is Ridiculed." *The Universe* (6 April 1984).

     Tzaferis, V. "Jewish Tombs at and Near Giv'at ha-Mivtar, Jerusalem." *Israel Exploration Journal* 20 (1970): 30.

UnM.AOT   Unger, Merrill F. *Archaeology and the Old Testament.* Chicago: Moody Press, 1954.

VeM.MSG   Vermaseren, M. J. *Mithras: The Secret God.* London: Chatto and Windus, 1963.

VeM.DSS   Vermes, Geza. *The Dead Sea Scrolls in English.* Harmondsworth/Baltimore, MD: Penguin Books, 1968.

VeG.JWJ   Vermes, Geza. *Jesus and the World of Judaism.* London: SCM Press Ltd., 1983.

VeG.JTJ   Vermes, Geza. *Jesus the Jew:* A *Historian's Reading of the Gospels.* New York: Macmillan Publishing Co., 1973.

VoH.EE   von Campenhausen, Hans. "The Events of Easter and the Empty Tomb." *Tradition and Life in the Church.* Philadelphia: Fortress Press, 1968.

WaG.PB   Wagner, Günter. *Pauline Baptism and the Pagan Mysteries.* Edinburgh: Oliver and Boyd, 1967.

Wand, William. *Christianity: A Historical Religion?* Valley Forge: Judson Press, 1972.

WeJ.DE   Wellhausen, Julius. *Das Evangelium Lucae.* N.p., 1904.

WeG.DJE/75 Wells, G. A. *Did Jesus Exist?* London: Elek/Pemberton, 1975.

WeG.DJE86 Wells, G. A. *Did Jesus Exist?* Revised edition. London: Pemberton, 1986.

WeG.HE   Wells, G. A. *The Historical Evidence for Jesus.* Buffalo: Prometheus Books, 1982.

WeG.JEC   Wells, G. A. *The Jesus of the Early Christians.* London: Pemberton, 1971.

WeJW.EE   Wenham, John W. *Easter Enigma.* Grand Rapids: Zondervan Publishing House, 1984.

WeJW.GO   Wenham, John W. "Gospel Origins." *Trinity Journal* 7. 2 (1978).

We&H.TNT Westcott, Brooke Foss, and Hort, Fenton John Anthony. *The New Testament in the Original Greek.* New York: The Macmillan Company, 1946.

Whiston, William, trans. *The Works of Josephus.* Lynn, MA: Hendrickson Publishers, 1980.

WiA.NTI   Wikenhauser, Alfred. *New Testament Introduction.* Translated by Joseph Cunningham. Freiburg, West Germany: Herder and Herder, 1958.

WiI.JTE   Wilson, Ian. *Jesus: The Evidence.* San Francisco: Harper & Row Publishers, 1984.

WiM.W   Wilson, Marvin R. "Who Is Our Neighbor?" *Through Their Eyes* 1 (September 1986): 10-11.

WiP.J   Winter, Paul. "Excursus II—Josephus on Jesus and James." In Schürer, Emil, *The History of the Jewish People in the Time of Jesus Christ,* vol. I. Revised and edited by Geza Vermes and Fergus Millar. Edinburgh: T. & T. Clark, 1973.

WoH.MEC Workman, Herbert B. *The Martyrs of the Early Church.* London: Charles R. Kelly, 1913.

WrM.BAC   Wrenn, Michael J. "The Biblical Account of Christmas—A True Story." *The Wanderer* (December 22, 1983).

YaE.EMH   Yamauchi, Edwin M. "Easter—Myth, Hallucination, or History? Part One." *Christianity Today* 4 (March 15, 1974).

YaE.PCG   Yamauchi, Edwin M. *Pre-Christian Gnosticism.* Second edition, Grand Rapids: Baker Book House, 1983.

YaE.SSS   Yamauchi, Edwin M. "Stones, Scripts, Scholars." *Christianity Today* 13 (February 14, 1969).

ANCIENT SOURCES:

The Apocrypha. Translated by Edgar J. Goodspeed. New York: Random House, 1959.

BeH.FU   Bell, H. L., and Skeat, T. C., eds. *Fragments of an Unknown Gospel and Other Early Christian Papyri.* Published by Trustees of the British Museum, 1935.

Cicero, Marcus Tullius. 28 volumes in the Loeb Classical Library. London: William Heinemann; Cambridge, MA: Harvard University Press, 1972–.

Clement. *Corinthians.*

Diodorus Siculus. 12 volumes in the Loeb Classical Library. London: William Heinemann, 1933—.

Diogenes Laertius. *Lives of Eminent Philosophers.* The Loeb Classical Library. London: William Heinemann, 1959.

Eusebius. "The Epistle of the Church in Smyrna." *Trials and Crucifixion of Christ.* Edited by A. P. Stout. Cincinnati: Standard Publishing, 1886.

Eusebius. *Demonstration of the Gospel.*

Eusebius. *The History of the Church.* Translated by G. A Williamson. Minneapolis: Augsburg Publishing House, 1965.

FuH.A   Furneaux, Henry. *The Annals of Tacitus.* Second edition. Revised by H. F. Pelham and C. D. Fisher. Oxford: Oxford University Press, 1907.

J.A/L   Josephus. *Antiquities,* vol. IX, Loeb edition. Translated by Louis H. Feldman. Cambridge, MA: Harvard University Press, 1965.

Josephus. *The Works of Josephus*. Translated by William Whiston. Lynn, MA: Hendrickson Publishers, 1980.

LiJ.AF   Lightfoot, J. B. *The Apostolic Fathers*. Grand Rapids: Baker Book House, 1956.

Lucian. *The Death of Peregrine*. In *The Works of Lucian of Samosata*, 4 vols. Translated by H. W. Fowler and F. G. Fowler. Oxford: The Clarendon Press, 1949.

Pausanius. *Description of Greece*. Loeb Classical Library. London: William Heinemann, 1931.

Philo. 17 volumes in the Loeb Classical Library. London: William Heinemann, 1929.

Plinius Secundus. *Letters and panegyricus*. 2 volumes in the Loeb Classical Library. Cambridge, MA: Harvard University Press, 1969.

Pliny. *Natural Histories*. 10 volumes in the Loeb Classical Library. Cambridge, MA: Harvard University Press, 1967.

Plutarch. *Lives*. 11 volumes in the Loeb Classical Library. Cambridge, MA: Harvard University Press, 1948.

Prudentius. 2 volumes in the Loeb Classical Library. London: William Heinemann, 1961–62.

RoA.ANF   Roberts, Alexander, and Donaldson, James, eds. *The Ante-Nicene Fathers*. Revised by A. Cleveland Coxe, 1885. American reprint of Edinburgh edition. Grand Rapids: William B. Eerdmans Publishing Co., 1973.

Suetonius. *The Twelve Caesars*. Translated by Robert Graves. Revised by Michael Grant. New York: Viking Penguin, Inc., 1979.

Tacitus. *The Annals of Imperial Rome*. Revised and translated by Michael Grant. New York: Viking Penguin, Inc., 1971.

Tacitus. 4 volumes in the Loeb Classical Library. London: William Heinemann, 1931–.

WaB.AT   Walker, Bessie. *The Annals of Tacitus*. Manchester: Manchester University Press, 1960.

RABBINIC SOURCES:

Babylonian Talmud. Edited by Isidore Epstein. London: The Soncino Press, 1948.

The Mishnah. Herbert, Danby, ed. Oxford: Oxford University Press, 1933.

The Talmud of the Land of Israel (Jerusalem Talmud). Edited by Jacob Neusner. Chicago: The University of Chicago Press, 1982–1988.

The Tosefta. Translated by Jacob Neusner. New York: Ktav Publishing House, 1979–1981.

REFERENCE WORKS:

Encyclopedia Britannica. 16th edition.

Encyclopedia International. 1972.

Encyclopedia Judaica. Edited by C. Roth. 1971.

AcP.HBD   *Harper's Bible Dictionary*. Paul J. Achtemeier, ed. San Francisco: Harper & Row Publishers, 1985.

The International Standard Bible Encyclopedia, 1979 edition.

The Jewish Encyclopedia. Volume 8. New York: Funk and Wagnalls Co., 1906.

RoJM.NHL   *The Nag Hammadi Library*. Edited by James M. Robinson. New York: Harper & Row Publishers, 1981.

New American Standard Bible. The Lockman Foundation, 1977.

DoJ.IDCC   *The New International Dictionary of the Christian Church*. J. D. Douglas, ed. Revised edition. Grand Rapids: Zondervan Publishing House, 1974.

TeM.ZPE   *The Zondervan Pictorial Encyclopedia of the Bible*. 5 volumes. Merrill C. Tenney, General Editor. Grand Rapids: Zondervan Publishing House, 1975.

INDEX

Note: The listings below were selected on the basis of usefulness to the reader. Some names, such as Jesus, James and John, occur so often that an index listing would not have been helpful. In such cases, a careful examination of the table of contents may be more helpful in locating the desired information.

NUMERALS

LXX (the Septuagint) 217, 218

A

a priori 127, 137, 141, 250

accretion myth 169

Acts of Pilate 22, 81, 82

Adam 293

Adonis 167, 176

adultery 44, 66, 78, 93, 314

Aenon 219

Aetheria (Egeria) 208

African 83, 314

Africanus 33, 34, 323, 324

agrapha 5, 18, 87, 89-91, 93-95,
   97-101, 326, 327, 340

agraphon 93, 94

Akiba, Rabbi 55, 59-61, 63, 64, 157, 280

Albinus 36

Alexander 24, 50, 73, 100, 160, 170, 206, 328

Alexandria 16, 23, 39, 71, 73, 86,
   96, 97, 146, 156, 190, 217

amen 226

Amoraic 54, 56, 57, 59, 60, 63, 66

Ananias (Ananus) 36, 115, 206, 324

Andrew 49, 64, 77, 113, 158, 224

Ani hu 294

Antioch 76, 86, 92, 193, 195, 227, 265

Antipas 192, 195

anti-Semitic 239, 246, 247, 330

antisupernatural 113, 138, 148

Antoninus Pius 22, 74, 80, 174

apocrypha 5, 18, 87, 89, 91, 93,
   95, 97, 99, 101, 326

Apollo 169

Apollonius (-os) 179, 254, 255, 318

apologist(s) 22, 39, 40, 74, 80, 83

Aquila 49, 50, 217

Aquila and Priscilla 49, 50

Arabic 42

Aramaic 78, 107, 125, 148, 152, 156, 157, 165,
   166, 205, 210, 224-227, 232, 266, 271

Arbel 27

archaeological 105, 153, 196, 203-205,

207, 210, 212-214, 219-221

archaeologist(s) 14, 94, 105, 106, 112, 148, 192, 193, 201, 203, 205, 209, 212, 214, 215, 220, 221, 226, 236

archaeology 6, 18, 112, 198, 203, 204, 207, 209, 212, 220, 221, 268, 337

Archelaus 192, 193

archives 22

Aristides 74, 80, 326

Aristion 77

Aristotle 108, 194, 327, 329

Ark (of the covenant) 14

Armageddon 190

Armenian 80, 183

Artemis 195

artistic 30

ascetic 34, 71, 91

Asclepius (or Asklepios) 167, 176, 186

Asia 43, 45, 48, 83, 100, 106, 112, 117, 194, 201, 211

atheist(s) 69, 78

Athens 51, 73, 80, 169, 170, 195, 254

Attis 167, 174, 176, 177

attorney 272

Augustus 22, 191, 192, 194

autographs 122, 216

B

Balaam 53, 59, 60, 279

baptism(al) 35, 36, 133, 134, 155, 167, 174, 175, 181, 182, 187, 228, 236

baraitha (baraita) 56, 58, 60, 62-65, 247, 325

baraithoth 54, 56

Barnabas 74, 79, 115, 164, 180

Bartholomew 70, 114, 225

Beatty, Chester 105

Ben Stada 53, 58, 59

Bethany 220, 300, 342

Bethlehem 191, 192, 204, 289, 293

Bethphage 198, 285

Bethsaida 153, 197, 234

bias 16, 18, 25, 45, 48, 99, 113, 138, 181, 201, 215, 246, 305, 306

biased 18, 201, 215, 246

biographer 135

biographical 132, 134-136, 139, 218

biographies 135

Bithynia 43, 45

bizarre 15, 17, 312, 314

boat 209, 210

Bodmer Papyri 105

Buddhism 173

C

Caesar 24, 30, 33, 34, 78, 83, 108, 109, 127, 186, 191-193, 214, 234, 239

Caesarea 23, 140, 196, 197, 205, 206, 234

Caesarea Philippi 140, 196, 197, 234

Caiaphas 246, 247, 286, 294, 310

calamities 40

Cana 16, 184, 186, 197, 219, 254, 259, 318

canon 88, 89, 146, 187, 193, 217, 289, 326

canonical 17, 87, 89-101, 311

Capernaum 27, 197, 207-209, 238, 244

Caracalla 73, 254, 255

carpenter 105, 133, 190

Carthage 88

catacombs 73, 144

Celsus 34, 61, 63, 66, 72, 170, 261, 324-326, 328, 330

censors 56

censorship 56, 57, 245

census(es) 22, 190-195

Chanina ben Dosa (*see* Hanina ben Dosa)

children 7, 15, 26, 60, 72, 96, 147, 169, 204, 214, 219, 224, 229, 232, 245, 256, 295, 296

Chorazin 197, 210

Chrestus 49, 50, 325

Christendom 15, 100, 314

Christmas 182, 328

Christos 37, 38

Christus 46, 47, 49, 50

chronological(-ly) 35, 109, 126, 134, 135, 138, 152, 159, 160, 209, 323, 324

chronology 40, 123, 169, 175, 191, 218, 235, 270, 331

church fathers 18, 33, 42, 61, 94, 149

Cicero 24, 30, 195, 323, 329

Cichlidae 198

cistern 107, 147, 256

classical 23, 36, 38, 107, 108, 112, 143, 194

classics 12, 36, 43, 46, 108

classification according to form 126, 127

Claudius 22, 49, 213, 214, 325

Clement of Alexandria 16, 39, 71, 73, 86, 96, 97, 146, 156

Clement of Rome 71, 74-77, 86

Colosseum 69, 76

confessors 5, 69, 72, 74, 325

Conon 207

Constantine 206

contradict(-s, -ory, -ing, -ed) 6, 16, 60, 96, 112, 132, 147, 154, 204, 250, 306, 317, 324, 331

contradiction(s) 6, 109, 118, 126, 153, 156, 190, 194, 199-201, 204, 228, 233, 272, 273, 311, 317, 329, 331

controversialists 74

Corinth 49, 163, 265

correspondent 21

creative community 123, 130-134, 140, 149

creed(-s, -al) 164, 165, 195, 266, 267

Criobolium 177, 181

Cybele 172-174, 177

Cybelene 172

Cyrenius 81

D

Daniel 38, 274, 287-289

Daunian bear 171

Dead Sea 196, 198, 215, 216, 238

Dead Sea Scrolls 6, 204, 210, 214-221, 235, 237, 299, 308

Decapolis 197, 199-201, 234, 241

Demeter 168

devil 17, 256

Didache 74, 79, 132

Diodorus 170, 328

Diogenes 169, 328

Diognetus 74

Dionysian 172

Dionysos (-sus) 167, 172, 186, 254

Dioscuri 167

dissimilarity 137

docetic 92, 98, 99

documentary hypothesis 123

dogs 46, 94, 224, 234, 245

Domitian 75

dunamis 250

duumvirs 195

E

earthquake 34

Easter 131, 183, 269, 272, 275, 311

echod 298

eclipse 33, 34

Egeria (Aetheria) 208

Egypt 23, 25, 58, 83, 176, 190, 192, 219, 234, 252, 258, 286, 318

Egyptian(s) 58, 167, 176, 192, 260

Einstein 253

eisegesis 15, 313

elephant(s) 129

Eleusinian 168, 177

Eliezer 58-60, 64-66, 261

Elijah 241, 244, 256

Elisha 38, 189, 244

emperor(s) 22, 23, 35, 43-45, 47, 48, 69, 74, 80, 178, 194, 213, 214, 254, 257, 300

espousal 253

Essene(s) 11, 219, 235-238, 241, 242

ethical 74, 85, 142

ethics 66, 141, 172

Ethiopia(-n, -ns) 183-185, 313

etiological myth 168, 169

Eusebius 38, 39, 42, 49, 69, 71, 75, 77, 78, 80, 82, 84, 111, 324-328

exaggeration 18, 149, 181, 232, 233

execute 279, 289

executed 25, 43, 72, 195

execution(-s, -ers) 21, 22, 36, 39, 45, 73, 128, 168, 213, 324

extracanonical 87, 89

eyewitness(es) 31, 73, 75, 85, 86, 88, 109-111, 114, 121, 125, 127, 132, 135, 136, 141, 151, 154-156, 158-160, 170, 176, 177, 186, 196, 227, 255, 256, 267, 283, 317

Ezra 54, 55, 280, 325

F

fathers 18, 33, 34, 42, 61, 71, 74, 79, 82, 94, 149, 297, 331

Felix 58

fertility 17, 71, 169, 173, 188, 215, 333

Festus 28, 36, 110

fickle(-ness) 116, 180

fiction(-al) 14, 16, 18, 139, 169, 178, 186, 255, 314, 318

fig 198, 259

First World War 140

form classification 128-130

form criticism 13, 14, 16, 18, 107, 122-131, 134, 137, 140, 141, 145, 307, 323

Formgeschichte 123, 143

fundamentalists 307

G

Gadara 197, 200, 329

Galilean 35, 49, 206, 209, 210, 238, 241-243, 246, 256, 294, 300

Galilee 23, 27, 28, 109, 111, 179, 189, 192, 193, 196-200, 206, 209, 214, 219, 235, 238, 241, 243, 244, 270, 275, 280, 300, 310

galli 173

Gamala 27, 197

Gamaliel 239, 256, 300, 330

Gaulanitis 241

Gaulonite 27

Gedeo 183-185

gemara 54, 56

Gennesaret 153, 197, 278

geographical(-ly) 6, 109, 134, 138, 189, 196, 199, 200, 201, 219, 220, 234, 241

geography 6, 18, 112, 189, 190, 193, 196-199, 314, 328

Gerasa 200

Gnostic(-s, -ism) 12, 90-92, 95, 97-99, 101, 127, 171, 218, 219

Gnosticizing 99

godspell 146

golden rule 229

governor 22, 25, 27, 39, 41-43, 45, 72, 74, 76, 109, 191, 193, 194, 205, 213

goyim 243-245, 283

Greek gnosticism 218

guru 11

H

Hades 168, 196, 283

Hadrian 5, 24, 48, 49, 74, 80

haggadah 55

halakhah 55

hallucinating 310

hallucinogenic 12, 17, 312

Hanina (Chanina) ben Dosa 242, 243, 256, 257, 271

Hasid 241-243

Hasidim 241-243, 256, 257

healing 26, 63, 64, 76, 153, 197, 200, 244, 257-260, 280

Hebraic 125, 166, 223, 245, 285, 296

Hegesippus 82, 92, 324

Helena 206, 207

Hellenistic(-ally) 125, 143, 168, 170, 172, 173, 176, 179, 212, 218, 219, 254, 257, 258, 261, 268, 269, 276, 296, 308, 318

Herakles 167, 170, 186

heresies 74, 90, 326, 327

heretical 53, 88, 89, 93, 97

Hermes 180

Herod 26, 27, 35, 36, 71, 77, 109, 153, 190-192, 194, 195, 198, 204, 205, 210, 248, 316

Herodium 198

Herodotus 108, 263

Hierapolis 77, 78, 111

Hillel 55, 228-230, 239, 309

Hippo 88

Hippolytus 86

Hippus 197, 200

historical criticism 122, 123

Holy Blood, Holy Grail 15, 16, 98, 99, 245, 313

Homanadensian(s) 193

Honi 242, 243, 256

hosanna 296

humanist 17, 215, 307, 311

humanitarian 17

Hume, David 138, 250-254

humour 11, 28

hymns 61, 164, 165

hyperbole 231, 232

hypnosis 11, 16, 259-261, 310

hypnotic 259-261, 310

hypnotism 259, 260

hypnotist 259, 310

hypothesis (-theses) 15-17, 67, 97, 98, 106, 123, 126, 143, 177, 187

I

Iamblichos 328

Ignatius 71, 74, 76, 77, 86, 326

illegitimate 14, 61, 63, 66

illusion 16, 93, 116, 153, 179, 300

Immanuel 231, 296

imperial legate 194

impudent 60, 61

India(-ns) 15, 131, 298, 314

Iranian 273

Irenaeus 71, 73, 74, 77, 78, 82, 83, 86, 112, 138, 146, 148, 326, 327

Irian Jaya 183

Isis 40, 69, 176

Italy 49, 82, 144

J

Jamnia 55, 217

Jerome 75, 83, 326

Jesus: The Evidence 16, 96, 98, 191, 199, 215, 259, 308, 310, 327

Jezreel 190

John the Baptist 33, 35, 36, 71, 190, 193, 219, 235, 243, 285, 314, 323

Jordan 97, 196, 197, 212, 220, 244

Joseph of Arimathea 267, 317

Josephus 5, 24, 27-29, 34-43, 57, 58, 65, 70, 71, 91, 115, 190-193, 202, 205, 206, 210, 236, 241, 242, 246, 256,

258, 314, 315, 323-326, 329, 330

Judah, Rabbi 55, 157

Judea (Judaea) 21, 22, 28, 39, 46, 50, 57, 58, 81, 109, 191, 192, 197, 205, 214, 241, 246, 278, 280, 300

Julias 197

Julius Caesar 24, 30

Justin Martyr 22, 39, 74, 80, 81, 86, 183, 323, 325, 326, 328

Justus of Tiberias 25

Juvenal 24

K

Kathros 247

knee(s) 213, 300, 301

Kokhba (Kochbah) 55, 64, 280

Kore 168

Kosiba (Kosebah) 55, 280

L

lamb(s) 174, 175, 181, 235, 246, 291

"Last Temptation of Christ" 314

Latin(-isms) 46, 55, 71, 135, 146, 152, 177, 186, 195, 205, 211, 213, 255

Lazarus 31, 96, 97, 250, 260, 274, 313

Lebanon 200

legend(-s, -ary) 6, 13, 18, 24, 30, 47, 61, 67, 82, 91, 99, 100, 105, 106, 123-125, 128, 129, 135, 136, 166, 170, 183, 185, 187, 188, 212, 267-271, 276, 314, 316

Leonides 83

levirate marriage 233

liberal(-s, -ism) 13, 16, 17, 106, 161, 169, 220, 221, 306

literary criticism 122, 123, 125, 143, 144, 152, 169, 308

Lord's supper 163, 172, 181-183

lower criticism 122, 144

Lucian 5, 50, 263, 325

Lyons 78, 112, 148

Lysanias 109, 195

Lystra 180, 296

M

Maccabean 179, 241, 242

Maccabees 24, 57, 273

Macedonian 23, 205

Magano 183-185

Magdalene 12, 15, 16, 59, 268-270, 272

magic 16, 62, 187, 195, 255, 261, 318

magical 252

magician 11, 16, 26, 101, 157, 254, 256, 317, 318

Malta 195, 196

Marcus Aurelius 74, 82

marriage 15, 164, 232, 233, 299, 313

martyr(s) 5, 22, 39, 69, 70, 72-75, 78, 82,
84-86, 113-115, 131, 201, 207, 273, 325

martyrdom(s) 69-71, 73, 75,
76, 78, 86, 148, 167

martyred 73, 83

Massoretic (Masoretic) 215, 216, 218, 299

Megiddo 190

Meir, Rabbi 55, 158, 225

memorize(-d) 55, 83, 107, 125,
157, 228, 233, 307

messiahs 38, 279, 282

messianic 6, 13, 25, 27, 37, 117, 118, 205,
238, 243, 258, 262, 277-281, 283,
286-289, 291, 293, 294, 307, 315

messianic expectations 6, 27, 277,
278, 280, 281, 286, 289, 307

Midrash 55, 61, 271, 325

mikvah 94, 206

millstones 209

minim 64, 65

minuth 64, 65

miracle(s) 6, 13, 14, 16, 18, 22, 25, 38, 61, 62,
67, 70, 73, 80, 110, 111, 127, 128, 130, 138,
143, 161, 165, 167, 179, 190, 198, 242, 243,
245, 249-263, 269, 301, 306, 313, 318, 330

miraculous 18, 66, 117, 165, 167, 169,
170, 179, 249-253, 255, 257, 262

Mishnah (Mishna) 54-56, 59, 107, 147, 148,
158, 225, 226, 228, 229, 245, 246, 328, 330

Mithraism 177, 182, 183

Mithra/Mithras 176, 182, 183, 188

Moses 81, 88, 158, 210, 290, 291, 297, 332

Mount Hermon 196, 197

Mount of Olives 58, 198, 199, 226

MT (Masoretic Text) 216-218

multitude(s) 25, 26, 36, 44, 58, 73, 140,
180, 197, 208, 240, 243, 280, 307, 324

mushroom 12, 16, 17, 215, 312

mustard 27, 91, 198, 199

mystery religions 6, 168, 172-175, 177-
182, 185, 187, 188, 260, 269, 273

mystical 85, 97, 173, 314

mythical 6, 168, 170, 174, 176,
178, 185, 189, 308

mythological 127, 167, 171, 177-
179, 182, 187, 268, 276, 317

myths 18, 105, 106, 123, 128, 129, 136, 166,
171, 179, 183, 185-187, 269, 273, 316

N

Naaman 244

Nag Hammadi 95, 99

Nain 189, 190

Napoleon 18, 113

Nazarene 62, 110, 213, 214, 262, 275

Nazareth 11, 13, 15, 21, 25, 27, 56, 58, 65, 67,
74, 131, 133, 190, 192, 197, 202, 206, 207,
213, 214, 223, 226, 234, 243, 256, 265, 287

Nero 24, 38, 45, 46, 50, 70, 116, 148, 183, 325

Neronian 73, 112

Newtonian 253

Nicaea 82, 277

Nicholson 282

noncanonical 87, 95, 100

O

obscurity 12, 26, 280

ochloi 25, 26

Onkelos 60

oral tradition(s) 14, 55, 82, 106, 107, 124-126, 136, 138, 142-144, 147-151, 153, 156-158, 162, 166, 225, 256

oral transmission 123, 145, 147

Origen 34, 37, 39, 40, 42, 63, 64, 66, 71-75, 83, 86, 92, 99, 116, 138, 170, 218, 324-326, 328, 330

orthodox 17, 39, 82, 89, 100, 101, 197, 199, 206, 234, 242, 244, 314

Osiris 167, 176

Oxyrhynchus 94, 99

P

pagans 28, 183

paleographical 25

palm 205, 285, 286

Pandera (-tera, -teri, -thera, -tira, -tiri) 58, 59, 63-65

paper civilization 147

Papias 74, 77, 78, 84, 86, 93, 94, 111, 138, 148, 326

papyri 92, 99, 105, 108

parables 106, 123, 127, 128, 133, 158, 230, 231, 238, 239, 241, 297

paschal 33, 246

Passover 61, 62, 67, 172, 175, 182, 234, 235, 246, 285, 313

Pausanias 254

pedagogical 227

pedagogy 183

pericopes 123, 126, 138, 140

Phaedrus 23

Pharisee(s) 17, 28, 29, 55, 66, 67, 128, 134, 153, 178, 180, 199, 210, 225, 233, 237, 239-242, 246, 258, 273-275, 279, 282, 286, 287, 295, 309

Philip 49, 70, 77, 78, 98, 109, 113, 158, 161, 190, 224, 297

Philippi 140, 195-197, 234

Philo 23, 331

Philopon 34

philosopher(s) 12, 16, 50, 67, 81, 116, 167, 169, 170, 172, 178, 255, 328

philosophical 24, 138, 250, 253, 255, 308

philosophy 12, 16, 23, 31, 74, 131, 133, 138, 144, 168, 201, 218, 255, 269, 293, 308

Philostratus 254, 255

Phlegon 5, 33, 34

Phrygia 77, 167

phylacteries 210

Pilate 5, 21-23, 38-43, 47, 48, 62, 76, 77, 81, 82, 90, 98, 109, 118, 131, 177, 205, 224, 247, 248, 287, 309, 316

Pisidian 193, 194

Plato 51, 81, 169, 170

platonist 81

platypus 251

Pliny 5, 24, 43, 45, 48, 49, 69, 325

Plutarch 176, 328

Plutus 168

poetic(-s, -a) 108, 129, 166, 327, 329

poetical 107, 125, 225

poetry 107, 165, 327, 329

Poland 56

Polycarp 71, 74, 76-79, 82, 86, 112, 148, 326

Pompey 24, 278, 316

pool(s) 96, 208, 210, 219

praetors 195

prefect 21, 193, 205

probability 12, 158, 159, 215, 250

proconsul(s) 45, 48, 78, 194

procurator(s) 46, 47, 57, 58, 64, 81, 214

prophet(-s, -ic) 15, 16, 36, 38, 42, 50, 58, 60, 70, 79, 81, 82, 88, 127, 128, 133, 157, 158, 190, 223, 231, 235, 238, 241-243, 256-258, 261, 262, 271, 279, 282, 290, 292, 295, 299-301, 309, 314, 332

Prudentius 174, 175, 328

pseudepigrapha(-l) 5, 18, 87, 89, 95, 100, 101

pseudonymous 88

psychological 85, 118, 239

Ptolemy 186, 217

Publius 195

Pythagoras 51, 170, 171, 328

Pythagorean 81, 254, 255

Q

Q (document) 123, 128, 146, 148, 150-154, 228

Quadratus 74, 80, 86

Quirinius 6, 190-195, 329

Qumran 24, 25, 208, 210, 215, 218, 219, 235, 236, 237, 279

R

rationalism 13, 14

redaction criticism 5, 122, 123, 140-142, 306, 327

religio illicita 75

remember(-ed, -ing) 23, 25, 71, 75, 76, 78, 93, 129, 130, 132, 148, 154, 155-158, 170, 179, 196, 210, 232-236, 241, 242, 247, 285, 294

revolution(s) 214

revolutionary 18, 212, 275, 316

Rome 21-24, 28, 40, 43, 45, 46, 48-50, 61, 69, 71, 73-77, 79, 81-83, 86, 112, 148, 156, 170, 182, 205, 212-214, 226, 227, 254, 278, 280, 285, 287, 309, 325, 326

Rousseau 186

Rufus 160

rumor 45, 46, 48, 251

Rylands Papyri 219

S

Sabbath 67, 94, 134, 237, 240, 241, 243, 272, 274, 289, 295, 301

Sadducees 29, 36, 233, 241, 273, 275, 287, 309, 332

Samaritan 81, 186, 218, 234, 244, 245, 286, 332

Sanhedrin 29, 36, 55, 59, 62, 229, 247, 258, 261, 267, 268, 287, 294, 310, 317, 324, 325, 328, 330

Satan(ic) 183, 226, 256, 261, 284, 296

semeion 250

scourged 81

scourging 118, 168, 247

Scythopolis 197

Sea of Galilee 27, 196-200, 209, 270, 280, 310

seat of Moses 210

Second World War 140

secrecy 97, 171

secret 12, 13, 17, 61, 63, 87, 96-98,

125, 170, 171, 315, 317

sect(s) 13, 27, 36, 46, 57, 89, 132, 219, 236, 275

secular 5, 17, 18, 21, 26-28, 33, 47, 50, 96, 112, 139, 182, 215, 225, 249, 275, 307, 311, 323

sedarim 55

seed 27, 72, 76, 91, 129, 168, 198, 199

seminars 17

Semitic 6, 16, 129, 143, 152, 166, 223-227, 231, 232, 234, 239, 246, 247, 268, 312, 314, 330

senate 83, 194, 195

senators 23, 72

Seneca 24

Sepphoris 65, 197, 234

Septuagint (LXX) 217, 224, 299

servant(s) 78, 109, 115, 159, 232, 242, 244, 247, 248, 259, 290-292, 316, 323

Severus 73, 83, 254

Shechem 80

Sibylline 46, 278

Sicarii 278

Sidon 63, 199, 200, 219, 234

signs 12, 61, 110, 250, 254, 257, 258, 261, 262, 272, 280

Simon 92, 98, 106, 113, 116, 124, 160, 163, 206, 239, 241, 262, 266, 280

Simon of Cyrene 160

Sitz im Leben 14, 123, 130, 141, 142, 155, 156

skeptic(s) 17, 48, 88, 112, 161, 162, 172, 201, 250, 280

skeptical 12, 30, 31, 134, 161, 179, 220, 273

skepticism 12, 13, 17, 67, 113, 121, 124, 130, 138, 143, 144, 167, 189, 220

Smyrna 78, 82, 112, 148, 326

Socrates 50, 51

Sol Invictus 182

Solomon 38, 278, 291, 293, 331

Son of God 6, 16, 18, 77, 80, 113, 178, 277, 284, 285, 292-294, 317, 331

Son of Man 6, 93, 134, 277, 282, 286, 287-289, 292, 294, 295, 301, 332

sorcery 58, 62, 64, 67, 261

source criticism 122, 123

Spain 24

Stoic 50, 81

stone waterpots 209

strange (-ly, -rs, -st) 25, 28, 41, 116, 129, 184, 186, 188, 189, 207, 220, 228, 233, 237, 254

Suetonius 5, 28, 49, 50, 280, 325, 331

suffer (-s, -d, -ing, -ings) 14, 34, 56, 64, 70, 72, 73, 75-77, 79, 84, 85, 92, 96, 97, 116-119, 131, 180, 270, 284, 286, 290, 291, 292

suppression 18

sycamore 184, 185, 211, 212, 226

synoptic 25, 111, 124, 130, 132, 133, 135, 143, 146, 148, 153-156, 220, 228, 231, 233, 240, 246, 282, 310, 311, 323, 327

Syria 28, 57, 82, 91, 190-194, 197, 214

Syriac 80, 325

Syrian 50, 156, 167, 170, 195, 225, 226, 244, 265

Syrophoenician 153, 224, 245

T

Tacitus 5, 24, 28, 45-48, 50, 73, 280, 325, 331

Talmud(s, ic, ist) 54, 56-58, 60, 61, 63-66, 147, 157, 158, 190, 206, 210, 233, 246, 258, 261, 285, 291, 325, 328-330

Tammuz 167

Tannaitic 54, 56, 57, 59, 60, 65, 66

Targum(s) 157, 271

Tatian 156

Taurobolium 174, 175, 177, 178, 181

Teacher of Righteousness 235, 237, 238

tear vases 233

television (see also TV) 15, 29, 98, 121, 310

temple(s) 40, 44-46, 55, 57, 61, 69, 175, 180, 190, 195, 199, 206, 209-211, 216, 219, 226, 228, 233-235, 241, 245, 248, 254, 255, 257, 280, 289, 294, 295, 315

Tertullian 22, 39, 47, 49, 61, 71-75, 83, 86, 116, 138, 323, 325, 326

Testimonium (Flavianum) 35, 37-42, 261, 324, 342-343

tetramorphic gospel 146

tetrarch(ies) 77, 109, 192, 195

textual criticism 108, 122, 216, 218

Thaddaeus 113

Thallus 5, 33, 34

Theophilus 109, 149, 159, 161

Thomas (the disciple) 70, 77, 91, 113, 114, 255, 270, 300

Gospel of Thomas 90, 95, 98, 99, 311

Thucydides 108

Tiberias 23, 25, 197

Tiberius 22, 23, 33, 34, 46, 47, 63, 83, 109, 193, 323

Titus 40, 60, 75, 162

toledoth (*tol'doth*) 61

Torah 157, 231, 241, 245, 296, 309

Tosefta 54, 56, 64, 65, 229, 245, 325, 330

Trajan 24, 43-45

transmission 105, 107, 123-125, 132, 143, 145, 147, 157, 163, 240

transmit(-ting) 144, 157, 355

transmitted 4, 124, 132, 152, 153, 221, 256, 257

tribe(s) 38, 41, 183-185, 192, 206, 215, 292, 307

TV (*see also* television) 16, 98, 311, 327, 332

Tyana 179, 254, 318

Tyre 199, 234

UV

Valentinus 91

Varus 194

Vespasian 35, 40, 45, 331

Virgil 205

virgin(s) 17, 18, 63, 66, 72, 77, 80, 95, 125, 169, 170, 249

W

wedding 16, 186, 254, 259, 313

wife 15, 49, 168, 176, 226, 232, 254, 257, 298, 313

wine 172, 228, 236, 254, 259, 318

witness(-es, -ed, -ing) 15, 30, 45, 50, 70, 72, 93, 100, 109-116, 123, 133, 136, 139, 149, 154-156, 159, 160, 171, 185, 199, 220, 253, 258,
261, 262, 266-268, 272, 283, 291, 294, 311

women 25, 26, 45, 46, 48, 50, 55, 58, 59, 72, 74, 98, 116, 133, 172, 201, 209, 236, 251, 268-270, 272, 276, 281, 300, 301

World War I (see First World War) 13, 123

World War II (see Second World War) 223

XY

yachid 298

Yeshu(-a) 61-63, 65, 67

Yohanan 55, 63, 213, 241, 242, 285

Z

Zealot(s) 11, 13, 27, 101, 197, 201, 225, 238, 239, 278, 315-317, 330

Zebulun 206, 207, 273

Zeus 170, 172, 180

RESOURCES FROM JOSH AND SEAN MCDOWELL

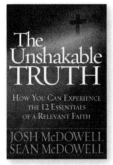

THE UNSHAKABLE TRUTH™
How You Can Experience the 12 Essentials of a Relevant Faith

As a Christian, you may feel unsure about what you believe and why. Maybe you wonder if your faith is even meaningful and credible.

Unpacking 12 biblical truths that define the core of Christian belief and Christianity's reason for existence, this comprehensive yet easy-to-understand handbook helps you discover

- the foundational truths about God, his Word, sin, Christ, the Trinity, the church, and six more that form the bedrock of Christian faith

- how you can live out these truths in relationship with God and others

- ways to pass each truth on to your family and the world around you

Biblically grounded, spiritually challenging, and full of practical examples and real-life stories, *The Unshakable Truth* is a resource applicable to every aspect of everyday life.

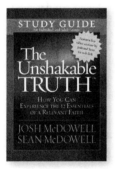

THE UNSHAKABLE TRUTH™ STUDY GUIDE
This study guide offers you—or you and your group—a *relational experience* to discover...

- 12 foundational truths of Christianity—in sessions about God, his Word, the Trinity, Christ's atonement, his resurrection, his return, the church, and five more

- "Truth Encounter" exercises to actually help you live out these key truths

- "TruthTalk" assignments on ways to share the essentials of the faith with your family and others

Through twelve 15-minute Web-link videos, Josh and Sean McDowell draw on their own father-son legacy of faith to help you feel adequate to impart what you believe with confidence. *Includes instructions for group leaders.*

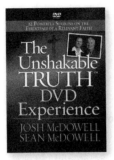

THE UNSHAKABLE TRUTH™ DVD EXPERIENCE
12 Powerful Sessions on the Essentials of a Relevant Faith

What do I believe, and why do I believe it? How is it relevant to my life? How do I live it out?

If you're asking yourself questions like these, you're not alone. In 12 quick, easy-to-grasp video sessions based on their book *The Unshakable Truth*, Josh and Sean McDowell give a solid introduction to the foundations of the faith.

Josh and Sean outline 12 key truths with clear explanations, compelling discussions, and provocative "on-the-street" interviews. And uniquely, they explain these truths *relationally*, showing you how living them out changes you and affects family and friends—everyone you encounter. *Helpful leader's directions included.*

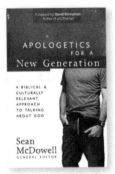

APOLOGETICS FOR A NEW GENERATION
A Biblical and Culturally Relevant Approach to Talking About God
Sean McDowell

This generation's faith is constantly under attack from the secular media, skeptical teachers, and unbelieving peers. You may wonder, *How can I help?*

Working with young adults every day, Sean McDowell understands their situation and shares your concern. His first-rate team of contributors shows how you can help members of the new generation plant their feet firmly on the truth. Find out how you can walk them through the process of...

- formulating a biblical worldview and applying scriptural principles to everyday issues
- articulating their questions and addressing their doubts in a safe environment
- becoming confident in their faith and effective in their witness

MORE HARVEST HOUSE RESOURCES TO HELP YOU UNDERSTAND AND PASS ON YOUR FAITH

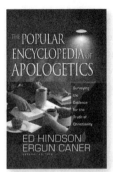

THE POPULAR ENCYCLOPEDIA OF APOLOGETICS
Surveying the Evidence for the Truth of Christianity
Ed Hindson and Ergun Caner

"An indispensable reference work on apologetics for this generation... This is not a textbook—it is a lifeline!"
JOSH MCDOWELL
International apologist and author

With more than 175 articles and 55 expert contributors (including Christian converts from some of the belief systems discussed within), *The Popular Encyclopedia of Apologetics* provides the most current essentials you need to know about a wide variety of apologetic concerns, including....

- critical issues related to God, Christ, the Spirit, and the Bible
- scientific and historical controversies (including creationism and biblical inerrancy)
- ethical matters (including abortion, stem cell research, and homosexuality)
- a Christian response to major world religions and cults
- a Christian response to major worldviews and secular philosophies

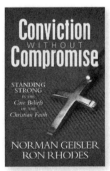

CONVICTION WITHOUT COMPROMISE
Standing Strong in the Core Beliefs of the Christian Faith
Norman Geisler and Ron Rhodes

Is it possible for Christians to know unity even when they disagree? Is it ever all right for Christians to set aside doctrinal convictions for the sake of unity? What is the difference between an essential teaching and a nonessential teaching?

From the earliest days of the church, Christians have struggled with questions related to unity and the handling of doctrinal differences. In this book you'll find clear guidance from Scripture about the doctrines on which it's essential for Christians to agree, and the doctrines on which believers can graciously agree to disagree.

This landmark resource will equip you to take an uncompromising stand on the essentials of the Faith while promoting love and unity among true believers.

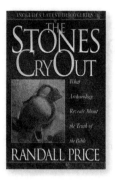

THE STONES CRY OUT

How Archaeology Reveals the Truth of the Bible
Randall Price

Discover what recent archaeological finds have to tell us about Israel's journey to the Promised Land, the Dead Sea Scrolls, the time of and people with Jesus, and much more. Archaeologist and Middle East expert Dr. Randall Price surveys exciting finds and interviews leading archaeologists in Bible lands. *The Stones Cry Out* will give you new appreciation for the accuracy and applicability of the Scriptures!

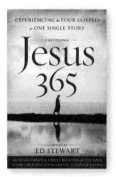

JESUS 365

Experiencing the Four Gospels as One Single Story
Ed Stewart

*A new edition of the Scripture text
from the famous* Life of Christ in Stereo *by Johnston Cheney*

This vivid chronological walk through the events of Jesus' time on earth weaves together the four Gospels into a single, flowing narrative. The 365 compact readings confront you with the total impact of Christ's life and message, heightened by

- up-to-date, natural language that brings the story alive
- the presence of everything recorded by the Gospel authors, with nothing added or omitted
- sidebars, maps, and notes providing cultural and historical insights

Take a fresh look at Jesus—deepen your insight into what He came to say and do, and what it means to you.

"A very fine way…to understand more clearly the life of Christ."
Josh McDowell

To learn more about other Harvest House books
or to read sample chapters, log on to our website:

www.harvesthousepublishers.com

HARVEST HOUSE PUBLISHERS
EUGENE, OREGON